CAMP GROUNDS

CAMP GROUNDS

STYLE AND HOMOSEXUALITY

EDITED BY

David Bergman

University of Massachusets Press

AMHERST

Copyright © 1993 by
The University of Massachusetts Press
All rights reserved
Printed in the United States of America
LC 93-8818
ISBN 0-87023-877-9 (cloth); 878-7 (pbk.)
Designed by Jack Harrison
Set in Adobe Minion by Keystone Typesetting, Inc.
Printed and bound by Thomson-Shore, Inc.
Library of Congress Cataloging-in-Publication Data
Camp grounds : style and homosexuality / edited by David Bergman.
p. cm.
Includes bibliographical references.
ISBN 0-87023-877-9 (alk. paper) — ISBN 0-87023-878-7
(pbk. : alk. paper)
1. Homosexuality and literature.
2. Gays' writings—History and criticism.
3. Life style. I. Bergman, David, 1950– .
PN56.H57C36   1994
809'.93353—dc20   93–8818
CIP

British Library Cataloguing in Publication data are available.

In Memory of Karl Keller

"Do you think the friendship of me would be unalloy'd satisfaction?"
—WALT WHITMAN

Contents

Acknowledgments

I thank Mark Cheshire for his invaluable editorial assistance.

The following chapters of this book have appeared previously and are reprinted with permission:

Jack Babuscio, "Camp and the Gay Sensibility," in Richard Dyer, ed., *Gays and Films* (British Film Institute, 1977). Reprinted by kind permission of Richard Dunn.

David Bergman, "Strategic Camp: The Art of Gay Rhetoric," in his *Gaiety Transfigured: Gay Self-Representation in American Literature* (University of Wisconsin Press, 1991). Copyright 1991 by the University of Wisconsin Press.

Karl Keller, "Walt Whitman Camping," *Walt Whitman Review* 26 (1981). Copyright 1981 by Wayne State University Press. Reprinted by permission of Wayne State University Press.

Scott Long, "The Loneliness of Camp" first appeared as "Useful Laughter: Camp and Seriousness," *Southwest Review* 74 (Winter 1989).

Esther Newton, "Role Models," in her *Mother Camp: The Female Impersonator in America* (University of Chicago Press, 1972). Copyright 1972, 1979 by Esther Newton.

Pamela Robertson, "The Kinda Comedy that Imitates Me," *Cinema Journal*, Winter 1993. Copyright Board of Trustees of the University of Illinois. Reprinted by permission of the University of Illinois Press.

David Roman, " 'It's My Party and I'll Die If I Want To!' Gay Men, AIDS, and the Circulation of Camp in U.S. Theater," *Theater Journal* 44, no. 3 (October 1992).

Andrew Ross, "Uses of Camp," *Yale Journal of Criticism* 2, no. 2 (1988). Copyright 1988 by Yale University.

CAMP GROUNDS

Introduction

DAVID BERGMAN

In 1979, Karl Keller, a distinguished critic of American literature, and I conceived of a collection of essays on camp. We believed that the topic was an important one for understanding gay literature and culture and a subject it would be fun to write about. Karl's persuasive powers as well as his physical energy were enormous, and he convinced a number of scholars to write for the volume. But despite many letters to publishers, only one, Urizen Press, showed any interest. Urizen was a small, avant-garde house, known for its editions of George Bataille and studies on such topics as excrement. Karl visited its offices and reported, "They want to do for us what they did for shit." But, alas, in the final editorial analysis, camp did not hold, at least in their eyes, the same allure. They dropped the book. Karl wrote one essay, "Walt Whitman Camping" (included here), and then we turned our attention to other projects. A few years later he died, an early fatality of AIDS.

The idea, however, would not go away, and Karl's death made realizing the project a sentimental obligation. I bided my time, and then, in 1989, I tried once more to interest a publisher. This time the reception was very different. Almost immediately, sympathetic editors at the University of Massachusetts Press took on the project. And that was not all. An energetic editor from another press half-jokingly tried to lure me away when the work was nearly completed. One of the more interesting aspects of this book, and the issue I would like to address at the outset, is accounting for this change in reception: Why in the interval of merely a dozen years did the idea of a collection of essays on camp go from being a notion that aroused no interest to one that seemed to have takers at every turn?

3

One reason for resistance to a discussion of camp was the problem of defining it. "To talk about Camp," Susan Sontag wrote, "is . . . to betray it."[1] Charles Ludlam, the master of camp theater, wrote, "I don't think camp can be defined."[2] Christopher Isherwood's novel *The World in the Evening* contains perhaps the earliest discussion of the subject. To Stephen, the bisexual protagonist of the novel, Charles, a gay doctor and advocate of Quaker Camp, "admit[s] it's terribly hard to define. You have to meditate on it and feel it intuitively, like Laotse's *Tao*." Yet Charles insists, "Once you've done that, you'll find yourself wanting to use the word whenever you discuss aesthetics or philosophy or almost anything. I never can understand how critics managed to do without it."[3]

Through Charles, Isherwood divides camp into two categories: Low and High Camp. Low Camp is "a swishy little boy with peroxided hair, dressed in a picture hat and a feather boa, pretending to be Marlene Dietrich." Isherwood is uninterested in Low Camp, and his rejection indicates not a little of his uneasiness with effeminacy and vulgarity. Isherwood's concerns are with High Camp: "High Camp is the whole emotional basis of the ballet, for example, and of course of baroque art. You see, true High Camp always has an underlying seriousness. You can't camp about something you don't take seriously. You're not making fun *of* it; you're making fun *out* of it. You're expressing what's basically serious to you in terms of fun and artifice and elegance."[4]

Bruce Rodgers spends two densely packed, highly contradictory pages discussing camp in his dictionary of gay slang. Camp, he tells us, pokes "a jocular finger at one's own frustrations and guffaws at the struggles of other pathetics, homosexuals or famous, influential people." But then he tells us, "A cripple is not camp unless he has a mordant sense of humor."[5] Susan Sontag is a bit more helpful. She claims that camp "is a certain form of aestheticism," which elevates objects "not in terms of Beauty, but in terms of degree of artifice, of stylization."[6] Scott Long tells us that "camp is a conscious response to a culture in which kitsch is ubiquitous. Camp is essentially an *attitude toward* kitsch." But such generalizations have been as problematic as they have been helpful, and most of the authors in the book have supposed that readers will recognize camp when they see it without its being defined. Indeed Ludlam insists that the normal strategy of listing campy things such as Tiffany lamps, narrative ballets, and spaghetti westerns is a wholly mistaken enterprise. Such lists, according to Ludlam, "[nail camp] to the wall and [make] it very literal. . . . The value of camp, the ability to perceive things in this unique way, is that it turns values upside down."[7]

Still I would like to point out the areas where there is some agreement. First, everyone agrees that camp is a style (whether of objects or of the way objects are perceived is debated) that favors "exaggeration," "artifice," and "extremity." Second, camp exists in tension with popular culture, commercial culture, or consumerist culture. Third, the person who can recognize camp, who sees things as campy, or who can camp is a person outside the cultural mainstream. Fourth, camp is affiliated with homosexual culture, or at least with a self-conscious eroticism that throws into question the naturalization of desire. I should note that *all* of Isherwood's examples of camp—Flaubert, Rembrandt, El Greco, and Dostoevski—were basically heterosexual. Isherwood's omission of gay artists of camp may be taken—as should so much of *The World in the Evening*—as a very dry example of High Camp.

Yet each of these points of general agreement raises highly contested issues: whether camp inheres in objects or in the subject perceiving them; whether camp is opposed to mass culture or is a way of making it acceptable; whether camping is elitist or egalitarian behavior, a privileged position or a means of coping with powerlessness; whether it's a celebration of eroticism or a way of emptying sexuality of desire.

The problems of defining camp and how it works have only grown deeper in the decades since *The World in the Evening*. Yet camp is hardly the only concept that scholars find difficult to define: *nature, romanticism, the renaissance* have proved equally slippery terms. So it was not the issue of locating camp's definition alone that caused it to be an unwelcome topic in the late seventies and an attractive one in the late eighties. The reasons for the change in attitude, I believe, must be found elsewhere.

One reason, no doubt, is the change in the academy toward works of cultural criticism in general and of gay literature in particular. In the late seventies, few presses were willing to commit their resources to such questionable enterprises, and camp was questionable in several respects: gay literature had not achieved even the measure of academic respectability it enjoys today; books on gay cultural questions had produced no track record for sales; and the discipline (not to mention courses) in which such works would be important was still in its infancy. With no discernible readers, no reliable sales, and no attractive cache—as the equation of camp with excrement made clear—a book on homosexual style was not the sort of thing to which publishers, always a careful lot, were willing to commit their meager resources.

By the early nineties, all this had changed: conferences on gay and lesbian studies circulate among the Ivy League campuses, attracting thousands of scholars; Eve Kosofsky Sedgwick, Douglas Crimp, Jonathan Dollimore, and Judith Butler are academic stars; and courses on gay and lesbian subjects have become, if not commonplaces, at least unsurprising additions to the curricula of many campuses. In the marketplace of ideas, lesbian and gay studies has established itself, perhaps not yet as a trusted firm, but surely as one of the liveliest and most fashionable boutiques.

Such changes alone would have been enough, I suppose, to alter the prospects of *Camp Grounds*, but I think there were more interesting changes going on in gay studies itself. In 1978, at just about the time Karl Keller and I were circulating our proposal, Edmund White wrote in the ground-breaking manual *The Joy of Gay Sex* that camping was a "form of gay humor that seems to be dying out. . . . It may well have been the by-product of oppression, secrecy and self-hatred, and now that gays are more self-accepting and somewhat less condemned by straight society they may have less of a need to camp."[8] In "The Political Vocabulary of Homosexuality," an essay White wrote for the influential volume *The State of the Language,* White develops this notion at greater length:

> In the past a regular feature of gay male speech was the production of such sentences as: "Oh, *her!* She'd do anything to catch a husband. . . ." in which the "she" is Bob or Jim. This routine gender substitution is rapidly dying out, and many gay men under twenty-five fail to practice it or even to understand it. This linguistic game has been attacked for two reasons: first, because it supposedly perpetuates female role playing among some gay men; and second, because it is regarded in some quarters as hostile to women. Since one man generally calls another "she" in an (at least mildly) insulting context, the inference is that the underlying attitude must be sexist: to be a woman is to be inferior.
>
> Following the same line, a large segment of the lesbian and gay male population frowns on drag queens, who are seen as mocking women, all the more so because they get themselves up in the most *retardataire* female guises (show girls, prostitutes, sex kittens, Hollywood starlets).[9]

As Marty Roth argues in his essay, such pronoun substitutions are an essential part of the grammar of gay language and an important part of camp. From the very beginning transvestism and drag were the epitome of Low Camp. Indeed, if the word *camp* is drawn from the French *camper,* to pose, to strike an attitude, then the drag performance is the essential act of the camp.[10]

Low Camp as exemplified by the drag queen has always played a strange and ambiguous role both in the homosexual perception of homosexuality and in the heterosexual perception of homosexuality. As I discuss in my chapter, "Strategic Camp," among the first reports in English of a homosexual subculture is the anonymous *Secret History of the London Clubs,* a chapter of which is devoted to the Mollies Club, in which half the members are cross-dressed and carry on in the campiest manner. The narrator's response to this behavior is amused disdain. No "real" man will allow himself to express fear of another man dressed in women's clothing. For most heterosexuals, the drag artist is the least threatening and most visible part of gay subculture, and consequently the first element of gay social practice that straight people are willing to confront, probably because they can feel superior to it. It is not surprising then that Esther Newton's study of drag queens, *Mother Camp,* would be among the first academic books outside of psychology to deal with aspects of gay life. The subject could titillate without threatening the delicate sensibilities of academics. Of course, it is and remains a first-class work, and its central chapter on camp is reprinted here. But because the transvestite aspects of camp fit into heterosexual stereotypes of gay behavior, many gay activists and thinkers rejected camp and transvestism as politically retrograde.

Yet, as White points out, not all feminists, even in what "queer" theorists regard as the dark days of gay liberation, were hostile to the political implications of camp. White found that "at its best camp is a rebellious, dada and anarchic force in gay life."[11] Kate Millet in *Sexual Politics* wrote:

> as she minces along a street in the Village, the storm of outrage an insouciant queen in drag may call down is due to the fact that she is both masculine and feminine at once—or male, but feminine. She has made gender identity more than frighteningly easy to lose, she has questioned its reality at a time when it has attained the status of a moral absolute and a social imperative. She has defied it and actually suggested its negation. She has dared obloquy, and in doing so has challenged more than the taboo on homosexuality, she has uncovered what the source of this contempt implies—the fact that sex role is sex rank.[12]

But it was not merely intellectuals and theoreticians who argued for the political importance of camp as a subversive strategy; certain gay activists also saw the radical possibilities of their performance. Writing in 1974 in *Gay Sunshine,* a journal that Matias Viegener associates with " 'assimilationist' gays," Christopher Lonc describes "Genderfuck and Its Delights" in terms that parallel Kate Millet: "It is my choice to not be a man, and it is my choice to be beautiful. I am not a female impersonator; I don't want to mock women. I want to criticize and to poke fun at the roles of women and of men too. I want to try and show how not-normal I can be. I want to ridicule and destroy the whole cosmology of restrictive sex roles and sexual identification."[13] In short, at the time that Karl Keller and I first began to arrange for a book on camp, when many gays and feminists were attacking the subject, such voices as Kate Millet, Christopher Lonc, and Edmund White were even then arguing that camp could have a powerful, radical role to play in cultural politics.

Camp also suffered among intellectuals from its early successes. Susan Sontag's "Notes on Camp" not only attempts to be the last word, it also almost became the last one on the subject. Even Sontag wished to bury the subject, as her comments in subsequent articles made clear. In "The *Salmagundi* Interview" she informs us that she decided "to write 'Notes on Camp' instead of 'Notes on Death'" because she's "dawdled in the cultural graveyard, enjoying what camp taste could effect in the way of ironic resurrection." In the end, however, she found that "Camp's extremely sentimental relation to beauty is no help to women."[14] Marcie Frank's essay in this volume shows deeper and less flip reasons for Sontag's rejection of camp.

Sontag's approach proved to be a dead end for other thinkers. One reason Sontag's approach proved so unproductive is that she was never genuinely interested in camp in itself, but only in how she might expropriate camp for her own cultural purposes, to create, as she says in "Against Interpretation," "an erotics of art." Her insistence on emptying camp of content derived from her belief that "the idea of content is today mainly a hindrance, a nuisance, a subtle or not so subtle philistinism."[15] When camp could not be so easily emptied, it was tossed away as yet one more "hindrance" or "nuisance."

Her hauteur is reflected in the way she stigmatizes camp, not as an expression of homosexuality, but as a creation of snobbery. She writes in "Notes on Camp":

> The history of Camp taste is part of the history of snob taste. . . . who is the bearer of this taste? Answer: an improvised self-elected class, mainly homosexuals, who constitute themselves as aristocrats of taste. . . . Homosexuals have pinned their integration into society on promoting the aesthetic sense. Camp is a solvent of morality. It neutralizes moral indignation, sponsors playfulness.[16]

I suppose it does little to point out the inconsistencies in even this short passage: Why would aristocratic snobs wish to be integrated in the democratic mass? In what sense could promoting the aesthetic ever integrate one into society? Is the interior decorator to become Everyman? But given Sontag's analysis, one can easily see why camp would become politically suspect for the post-Stonewall gay activists. In claiming their civil rights—something quite different from social integration—activists relied on the moral indignation of those gays who were excluded. Activists did not wish to neutralize moral outrage. Nor did those trying to win gay civil rights wish to cloak themselves as "aristocrats of taste." The Gay Liberation Front as well as the Gay Activists Alliance presented homosexuals as an oppressed minority needing housing and employment protection, as indeed they were. The drag queens who began the Stonewall riots did not promote themselves as aristocrats; they were often homeless, usually lower-class men who had seen police sweeps systematically remove what little protection they enjoyed.

Although in 1964, five years before the Stonewall Riots when "Notes on

Camp" was first published, Sontag might understandably believe "homosexuals have pinned their integration into society on promoting the aesthetic sense," we now can see how such a comment made her analysis a dead end. First, she assumes that gays want "integration," and second, that camp was a strategy for such integration. While it is true that the Mattachine Society and other homophile groups sought what might be called "integration," these groups were *not* bastions of camp. In fact, they maintained the same high moral tone that Sontag attributes to Jewish groups. Moreover, by ascribing a political end to camp, Sontag contradicts her earlier assertion that "it goes without saying that the Camp sensibility is disengaged, depoliticized, or at least apolitical." But perhaps whether camp is political or not is unimportant since, for Sontag, it is inscribed by failure. Camp is "failed seriousness," organized by "a disparity between intention and result," something "good *because* it's awful."[17]

For Sontag, camp's ultimate effect is a kind of amelioration, a form of consolation for the man of taste who would otherwise be missing satisfying objects of appreciation and contemplation. As she says, camp "makes the man of good taste cheerful when before he ran the risk of being chronically frustrated. It is good for the digestion."[18] Given the bromidic function Sontag allows for camp, its appeal, unsurprisingly, was short lived.

I originally hoped to include "Notes on Camp" in this volume as an important document in the history of the discourse on camp. At first, I was disturbed when Ms. Sontag refused absolutely to allow her essay to be reprinted. Now, I see its absence as positive. The current discussion has left it far behind, and some of the essays in the volume do not feel the obligation to make even a nod in its direction because they owe nothing to the work.

However, the tensions in Sontag's essay are repeated in the history of essays on camp. Writers will argue either for the disruptive potential of camp or for its ability to be coopted by and integrated with oppressive forces. Perhaps no two writers stand more opposed than Andrew Ross and Scott Long. Long's essay is filled with the dark and difficult insights that camp can provide the postmodern spectator. Ross is disturbed by how easily camp can grease the grinding gears of late capitalism's consumerist machinery.

It took AIDS and poststructuralist theory to make camp intellectually and politically respectable again, even as those who turn to camp reject the very notion of intellectual and political respectability. As Carole-Anne Tyler has tartly noted: "Not so long ago camp languished, theorized as a shameful sign of an unrecognized self-hating, and even woman-hating, homosexual by gay, feminist and lesbian critics alike. Now camp has been rehabilitated with a vengeance: not only feminist, but even macho masculinity is read as camp and, therefore radical."[19] In part because the intellectual and political climate of the nineties looks favorably upon the camp, academic publishers have now reversed their attitude toward *Camp Grounds*. Perhaps in twenty years (or even a dozen), this book will be regarded as an example of the intellectual and political fashions at the end of the twentieth century, quaint and benighted academicizing typical of its age. I don't wish to reject the timeliness of the book. I see it, to use the present jargon, as a useful "intervention in the academic discourse." But I do wish to point out that camp's roots are deeper and, for me at least, the questions about camp are ones that need to be asked repeatedly: How does one speak to a double audience? How does one dramatize one's sexual role and in so doing simultaneously make it apparent and call it into question? How can one deal with oppression without duplicating the very terms of the oppressor? How can the oppressed speak? How does one make room for difference in a system that no longer merely marginalizes minorities, but now, because of its drive for totalization, recolonizes those who would move to the margins? In short, camp raises the issues of any minority culture.

Yet it should be quite clear that I am uncomfortable striking the conventional pose of an editor introducing readers to a collection. Typically, the editor is at pains to defend the selection against critics. But these essays on camp don't need to be defended, so much as defended against. For the very nature of the critical exercise is to fix the subject, stabilize it, and somehow arrest its fall into the abyss of infinite ironic regress, and that is why no one in this volume has adopted a sustained campy tone while addressing the subject of camp. Kevin Kopelson's essay directly addresses this uneasiness. But it is the very sincerity of the critical enterprise that defeats all our attempts to do the subject justice. Several of these articles break typical academic decorum by cracking jokes or employing obviously overelaborate syntax. Patricia Juliana Smith, Pamela Robertson, Matias Viegener as well as Kevin Kopelson have tried to rise to the level of camp. Scott Long even invites us to imagine him "wearing a gold lamé cocktail dress, black pumps with three-inch stiletto heels, a raven wing, and a beaded cloche." These essayists follow Susan Sontag who numbered her paragraphs as though her text were some German philosophic tract. Yet even she never achieved the proper level of campiness necessary to launch a successful alternative mode that would be consistent with her subject. Camp has its revenge on those who would make it a respectable subject of academic discourse. I read Kevin Kopelson's nervous and seemingly frivolous essay as an example of the anxiety that camp (as well as gay studies) has on those who would comment about it, an essay that enacts the very skittery superfluousness that is its subject. Sometimes I see myself in a horror picture shot by John Waters. I play an outraged parent who discovers his favorite son in drag. As I scrub the mascara and foundation from his face, my own face gets splattered with makeup. When I get to the last layer of foundation, the boy suddenly and mysteriously vaporizes. The camera turns for a reaction shot and reveals the truth—I have become Divine. In fact, as I think about this scenario, I wonder if it hasn't already been shot, for isn't this the essence of Jean Cocteau's camp classic *Orpheus?*

The person who has done the most to revise the academic standing of camp and to suggest its politically subversive potential is Judith Butler, whose writing has a bewitching way of fusing Hegel and Peter Pan. Jonathan Dollimore has done a fine job of showing Butler's indebtedness to earlier thinkers,[20] and it strikes me that Butler's success is derived at least in part from celebrating camp in a language as leadenly academic and as far from the site of camp as she could find. It is the "high seriousness" with which she invests camp's frivolity that has made her espousal so welcome in a profession that has yet to shed its Arnoldian manner.

In a passage that in a very short time has become one of the touchstones of gay and lesbian theory, Butler argues:

> The replication of heterosexual constructs in non-heterosexual frames brings into relief the utterly constructed status of the so-called heterosexual original. Thus gay is to straight *not* as copy is to original, but, rather, as copy is to copy. The parodic repetition of "the original," . . . reveals the original to be nothing other than a parody of the *idea* of the natural and the original. Even if heterosexist constructs circulate as the available sites of power/discourse from which to do gender at all, the question remains: What possibilities of recirculation exist? Which possibilities of doing gender repeat and displace through hyperbole, dissonance, internal confusion, and proliferation the very constructs by which they are mobilized?[21]

For Butler, as for Christopher Lonc, Edmund White, and Kate Millet—who are to a great extent the children of Oscar Wilde—the hyperbolic, parodic, anarchic, redundant style of camp is the very way to bring heterosexist attitudes of "originality," "naturalism," and "normality" to their knees. For Butler nothing succeeds in subverting the straight like excess. She postulates some Ricardo-like law of the cultural imagination: recognition grows arithmetically, while signifiers can grow geometrically. Push up the supply side, and the gender system will collapse by its own weight. Or as she puts it at the end of *Gender Trouble:*

> The critical task for feminism is not to establish a point of view outside of constructed identities; that conceit is the construction of an epistemological

model that would disavow its own cultural location and, hence, promote itself as a global subject, a position that deploys precisely the imperialist strategies that feminism ought to criticize. The critical task is, rather, to locate strategies of subversive repetition enabled by those constructions, to affirm the local possibilities of intervention through participating in precisely those practices of repetition that constitute identity and, therefore, present the immanent possibility of contesting them.[22]

There is an enormous appeal to a politics of camp, drag, and other "strategies of subversive repetition": it is free from the tedium of organizing, assembling, or lobbying. It is enormously labor unintensive. After all, how much time does it take a man to find the right pair of come-fuck-me-pumps to wear with his three-piece suit? And the lesbian femme has always already wanted to dress up as Donna Reed, hasn't she? What better political strategy could one find than the one that certifies one's own camp fantasies of rebellion and humor? Didn't we see in the eighties the effectiveness of those brigades of punk women in mohawks in bringing into question Margaret Thatcher's bouffant and her Victorian notions of gender role?

Drawing attention to the artifice of the gender system through exaggeration, parody, and juxtaposition appeals to lesbian, feminist, and gay academicians who are overwhelmingly white and by definition (if not by income) middle class and are insulated from the violence of homophobia, but it hardly seems to me to be the Archimedean lever or rock that will move the gender system off its path. Only the rarified world of academe could imagine such a feather stopping such an elephant—even shot right up the trunk, such a weapon would hardly create more than a sneeze. As Carole-Anne Tyler argues, it is because camp is embedded in the gender system that it appeals to "a white and bourgeois imaginary" and has at least potentially "oppressive effects."[23] The relative security in which gay and lesbian academics live—so often in educated, sophisticated, collegiate ghettos—perhaps has isolated them from the world of violence and abuse that still attend many gays and lesbians. I write this preface after one of my students, a straight woman, was severely beaten for defending me to a male student, who has subsequently issued death threats to the student and me. Part of the description of the assailant was that he wore an earring. Clearly the crossgender meaning of earring wearing was lost on him. Whatever educative potential camp has is dwarfed by the resistance and violence of a dedicated minority.

Butler also minimizes, I believe, the ways camp's effectiveness is limited by class. Camp with its "hyperbole, dissonance, internal confusion, and proliferation" can be mobilized only within a very privileged setting. Sontag is quite correct when she argues, "Camp taste is by its nature possible only in affluent societies, in societies or circles capable of experiencing the psychopathology of affluence."[24] The playful excess of camp can resonate only against the already fluttering strains of extensive superfluousness.

Kevin Kopelson's analysis of transgressive sexual behavior in W. S. Gilbert's *Patience* points to the failure that performative gender can have as a political act. It is by acting the aesthete that some of the dragoons meet heterosexual success. Playing Wilde does not open their eyes to the gender system that informs their prejudices. Nor has gay pornography or academic optics necessarily opened up the range of behavior. If anything, Kopelson shows how the anxiety of performance can make gender rules more rigid, more in need of policing, more difficult to transgress. Similarly, David Román shows how camp in contemporary gay theater is used as an anxious way to avoid—and therefore to mark—the subject of AIDS by presenting nostalgic images of a pre-AIDS gay life.

I think the essays in the book show that camp—as well as other related stylistic strategies—are useful in a number of ways and at a number of points in the cultural political battles around gender, but they also point out its limitations. In a pre-Stonewall world, camp functioned as an argot that provided an oppressed group some measure of coherence, solidarity, and humor, and it allowed gay men and women to talk to one another within the hearing range of heterosexuals who might be hostile to them. Gregory Woods shows how camp in Proust allows Proust to participate in transgressive behavior the novel argues against and to subvert the ostensible moral message. Marty Roth's analysis of *The Bad and the Beautiful* shows the double conversation that camp allows, a conversation carried on in silence beneath the movie's glossy surface.

The various silences that Roth identifies are essential to camp because they are so obvious, so pregnant, so ostentatiously policed. In *The Mystery of Irma Vep*, Ludlam plays a similar theme. As in *Rebecca*, Ludlam does not allow us to hear about Irma. The silence is underscored by rising organ chords. Sontag tells us that "camp sees everything in quotation marks."[25] Roth speaks not about silence, but about "silence."

In pre-Stonewall days camp provided on occasion a way to parry the homophobic attacks. During the sixties, Don Holliday wrote a series of soft pornographic novels including *The Man from C.A.M.P.* C.A.M.P. is "an international, underground organization dedicated to the advancement and protection of homosexuals," and its star agent Jackie Holmes—no doubt named for the porn star John Holmes—always gets his man, one way or the other.[26] C.A.M.P. field agents are controlled by a top secret central office named High Camp. Jackie's home and office are reached through a false wall at the back of a public toilet, which is under perpetual but inept surveillance by the Los Angeles vice squad. Like James Bond who is always struggling with CHAOS, Jackie is on twenty-four-hour alert against the agents of B.U.T.C.H. For Don Holliday and his readers of the mid-sixties, camp would save them any time of the day or night.

In *Brideshead Revisited,* twenty Oxford students threaten Anthony Blanche with total immersion in a fountain. He hears them chanting his name while reading *Antic Hay* and answers them in a manner that I suppose is a forerunner of psychoanalytic deconstructive criticism:

> "Dear sweet clodhoppers, if you knew anything of sexual psychology you would know that nothing could give me keener pleasure than to be manhandled by you meaty boys. It would be an ecstasy of the very naughtiest kind. So if any of you wish to be my partner in joy come and seize me. If on the other hand, you wish to satisfy some obscure and less easily classified libido and see me bathe, come with me quietly, dear louts, to the fountain."[27]

This is a highly effective use of camp to ward off physical abuse in a homophobic society, an early use of what I think of as "The Liberace Effect," that is, to be so exaggerated an example of what you in fact are that people think you couldn't possibly be it. But such effects work not by dismantling the gender system but by trading on its blindness. The Liberace Effect, by the way, is hardly foolproof strategy: Oscar Wilde's deployment of it in his trials failed miserably. Patricia Juliana Smith's account of the rock singer Dusty Springfield shows how camp provided some cultural space for Springfield to insulate herself from heterosexism and to communicate with her lesbian audience, but it did not provide enough space.

In the immediate post-Stonewall era, camp's effectiveness was clearly equivocal. Andrew Ross has written about the conservative side of camp, and I would argue that its tendency to dissolve identity—a potential that William Lane Clark discusses at length—made it inimical to those trying to forge a gay and lesbian political movement based on sexual identity. Yet as I have pointed out, camp was an important marker around which a gay identity politics could coalesce. Jack Babuscio's, Esther Newton's, and Karl Keller's essays all stem from a desire to forge an identity politics. In the immediate post-Stonewall years, no gay rights parade was complete without a bevy of drag queens blowing kisses to the crowd. The Castro clone might have appeared to be the emblem of an anticamp faction in gay life, but I never met a clone who did not admire Divine.

Now that the gay and lesbian political movement is off the ground and has already established a variety of institutional anchors, those in the theoretical vanguard are anticipating a time when the appeal of identity politics will no longer be needed to create political action, and a truly antihumanist, anti-identity, postenlightened, postmodern politics can take place, a time in Judith Butler's phrase when we can "do gender" right. Camp, masquerade, and genderfuck may once again be useful political tools—but they will never be ends in themselves, for if all gender is merely style, then no style can ever be compelling in itself. At best camp can be a strategy to win room, freedom for different ways of conducting one's life; at worst it can give the illusion of freedom when in fact it only repeats in a different key the old prescriptions. I cannot separate the value of camp from the locality or the historical stage in which it is deployed. To afford it too much power will in the end disappoint those who will use it as a strategy, but to afford it no power is to neglect an important force that has allowed some to survive and others to prevail.

Thus to discuss camp alone is to do a disservice to its provisional, destabilizing, transitional outrageousness. To appreciate camp fully, we must explore what camp can give way to, how it can lay the foundations for what Robert K. Martin calls *écriture gaie*. Not that camp will disappear as a useful strategy, but it will be accompanied by other styles by which sexuality may be inscribed and transcribed, other performative modes.

Consequently *Camp Grounds: Style and Homosexuality* is divided into three sections. The first section is general studies about camp. For the most part these are older essays, reprinted here from other sources. The second section relates camp and other sexual encoded styles to a number of specific works and figures: AIDS drama, Dusty Springfield, Ronald Firbank, Marcel Proust, Walt Whitman, and gayzines, among others. These are a mixture of old and new essays. This last section follows the general trend of recent queer criticism and looks at issues of stylistics and sexuality in general. These essays have all been written for this book. In the last section, camp is rarely mentioned, if at all, but it becomes the backdrop against which the entire play of homosexual stylistics is performed, in which gays and lesbians "do gender," for no style is so highly charged by sexual politics, no manner so clearly a sexual political act as is camp. For the foreseeable future it will be the stylistic mode against which all other sexual styles will resonate or oppose themselves.

Notes

1. Susan Sontag, "Notes on Camp" in *Against Interpretation and Other Essays* (New York: Dell, 1966), 277.

2. Charles Ludlam, "Camp," in *Ridiculous Theatre—Scourge of Folly: The Essays and Opinions of Charles Ludlam,* ed. Steven Samuels (New York: Theatre Communications Group, 1992), 227.

3. Christopher Isherwood, *The World in the Evening* (New York: Avon, 1956), 106.

4. Ibid.

5. Bruce Rodgers, *Gay Talk: A (Sometimes Outrageous) Dictionary of Gay Slang* (New York: Paragon Books, 1972), 40.

6. Sontag, "Notes on Camp," 279.

7. Ludlam, "Camp," 226.

8. Edmund White, "Camping," in *The Joy of Gay Sex*, by Charles Silverstein and Edmund White (New York: Crown, 1977), 36.

9. Edmund White, "The Political Vocabulary of Homosexuality," in *The State of the Language*, ed. Leonard Michaels and Christopher Ricks (Berkeley: University of California Press, 1980), 240.

10. Rodgers suggests other origins for the term in *Gay Talk*, 40.

11. White, "Camping," 36.

12. Quoted by White in "Political Vocabulary," 240.

13. Christopher Lonc, "Genderfuck and Its Delights," in *Gay Roots: Twenty Years of Gay Sunshine*, ed. Winston Leyland (San Francisco: Gay Sunshine Press, 1992), 225.

14. Susan Sontag, "The *Salmagundi* Interview," in *The Susan Sontag Reader* (New York: Farrar, Straus and Giroux, 1982), 339.

15. Sontag, "Against Interpretation," in *Against Interpretation and Other Essays*, 15.

16. Sontag, "Notes on Camp," 291–92.

17. Ibid., 279, 289, 288, 293 (Sontag's italics).

18. Ibid., 293.

19. Carole-Anne Tyler, "Boys Will Be Girls: The Politics of Gay Drag," in *Inside/Out: Lesbian Theories, Gay Theories*, ed. Diane Fuss (New York: Routledge, 1991), 33.

20. Jonathan Dollimore, *Sexual Dissidence: Augustine to Wilde, Freud to Foucault* (Oxford: Clarendon Press, 1991), 319–20.

21. Judith Butler, *Gender Trouble: Feminism and the Subversion of Identity* (New York: Routledge, 1990), 31.

22. Ibid., 147.

23. Tyler, "Boys Will Be Girls," 58.

24. Sontag, "Notes on Camp," 291.

25. Ibid., 281.

26. Don Holliday, *Color Him Gay* (San Diego: Corinth Publications, 1966), 18.

27. Evelyn Waugh, *Brideshead Revisited* (New York: Harcourt Brace, 1973), 50.

GENERAL CAMP

Camp and the Gay Sensibility

JACK BABUSCIO

What I aim to do in this essay is to consider some of the ways in which individual films, stars, and directors reflect a gay sensibility. In the course of this exploration, I hope to accomplish the following aims: to provide a more precise definition of what is, at present, a most confused area of response that goes under the vague label of *camp;* to ascertain the relationship of camp and gayness; to consider some of the social patterns and mechanisms that make for the gay sensibility; to relate these considerations to cinema with the purpose of stimulating discussion of a hitherto neglected aspect of film; to promote solidarity and a greater sense of identification among gays; to remind readers that what we see in cinema is neither truth nor reality, but fabrications: individual, subjective perceptions of the world and its inhabitants; and, finally, to argue that there is far more fun in art and art in fun than many of us will even now allow.

The Gay Sensibility

I define the gay sensibility as a creative energy reflecting a consciousness that is different from the mainstream; a heightened awareness of certain human complications of feeling that spring from the fact of social oppression; in short, a perception of the world which is colored, shaped, directed, and defined by the fact of one's gayness. Such a perception of the world varies with time and place according to the nature of the specific set of circumstances in which, historically, we have found ourselves. Present-day society defines people as falling into distinct types. Such a method of labeling ensures that individual types become polarized. A complement of attributes thought to be "natural" and "normal" for members of these categories is assigned. Hence, heterosexuality = normal, natural, healthy behavior; homosexuality = abnormal, unnatural, sick behavior. Out of this process of polarization there develops a twin set of perspectives and general understandings about what the world is like and how to deal with it. For gays, one such response is camp.

Camp

The term *camp* describes those elements in a person, situation, or activity that express, or are created by, a gay sensibility. Camp is never a thing or person per se, but, rather, a relationship between activities, individuals, situations, *and* gayness. People who have camp, e.g., screen "personalities" such as Tallulah Bankhead or Edward Everett Horton, or who are in some way responsible for camp—Busby Berkeley or Josef von Sternberg—need not be gay. The link with gayness is established when the camp aspect of an individual or thing is identified as such by a gay sensibility. This is not to say that all gays respond in equal measure to camp, or, even, that an absolute consensus could easily be reached within our community about what to include or emphasize. Yet though camp resides largely in the eye of the beholder, there remains an underlying unity of perspective among gays that gives to someone or something its characteristic camp flavor. Four features are basic to camp: irony, aestheticism, theatricality, and humor.

Camp/Irony

Irony is the subject matter of camp, and refers here to any highly incongruous contrast between an individual or thing and its context or association. The most common of incongruous contrasts is that of masculine/feminine. Some of the best examples of this can be found in the screen personalities of stars whose attraction, as camp, owes much to their androgynous qualities, e.g., Greta Garbo in all her films, but particularly *Queen Christina* (1933), where she masquerades as a man; Mick Jagger in *Performance,* where the pop star's persona is achieved through radical neutering via the elision of masculine/feminine "signs"; the Andy Warhol stars Holly Woodlawn, Candy Darling, and Jackie Curtis in films such as *Flesh* and *Women in Revolt* (1972).

Another incongruous contrast is that of youth/(old) age: the Gloria Swanson–William Holden relationship in *Sunset Boulevard* (1950), or that of Bud Cort–Ruth Gordon in *Harold and Maude* (1971); as well as the Bette Davis characters Fanny Trellis and Jane Hudson in *Mr. Skeffington* (1944) and *Whatever Happened to Baby Jane?* (1962): aging, egocentric women obsessed with the romantic illusions of youth and unable to reconcile themselves to the reality of old age.

Other, less frequently employed contrasts are the sacred/profane (*The Picture of Dorian Gray* [1945]), spirit/flesh (*Summer and Smoke* [1961]), *The Roman Spring of Mrs. Stone* [1961]), and high/low status, as in dozens of rags-to-riches musicals (*The Countess of Monte Cristo* [1934]) and melodramas (*Ruby Gentry* [1952]).

At the core of this perception of incongruity is the idea of gayness as a moral deviation. Two men or two women in love are generally regarded by society as incongruous—out of keeping with the "normal," "natural," "healthy" order of things. In sum, it is thought to be morally wrong.

Camp/Aestheticism

The aesthetic element is also basic to camp. Irony, if it is to be effective, must be shaped. The art of camp therefore relies largely upon arrangement, timing, and tone. Similarly, the ironic events and situations which life itself presents will be more or less effective depending on how well the precision, balance, and economy of a thing are maintained. Camp is aesthetic in three interrelated ways: as a view of art; as a view of life; and as a practical tendency in things or persons: "It is through Art, and through Art only, that we can shield ourselves from the sordid perils of actual existence."[1]

Wilde's epigram points to a crucial aspect of camp aestheticism: its opposition to puritan morality. Camp is subversive of commonly received standards. As Susan Sontag has said, there is something profoundly "propagandistic" about it: "homosexuals have pinned their integration into society on promoting the aesthetic sense. Camp is a solvent of morality. It neutralizes moral indignation."[2]

Consistently followed as a comprehensive attitude, aestheticism inevitably leads to an ingrown selfishness in life, and to triviality in art. As a means to personal liberation through the exploration of experience, camp is an assertion of one's self-integrity—a temporary means of accommodation with society in which art becomes, at one and the same time, an intense mode of individualism and a form of spirited protest. And while camp advocates the dissolution of hard and inflexible moral rules, it pleads, too, for a morality of sympathy. Its viewpoint suggests detachment from conventional standards. Here again, as R. V. Johnson has pointed out, there is an aspect of aestheticism which diverges from "a puritan ethic of rigid 'thou shalt nots,'" preferring, instead, to regard people and ideas with due consideration to circumstances and individual temperament.[3]

A good example of this is found in Jack Hazan's quasi-documentary portrait of artist David Hockney, *A Bigger Splash*. Here the director manages to convey the wry, distancing nature of his subject's visual humor as an integral part of a gay sensibility that is defiantly different from the mainstream. Because Hockney responds to his gay "stigma" by challenging social and aesthetic conventions in life and art, Hazan's concern is to show the various ways in which his subject's private life affects his art—or how art records personal experience and determines our future. Thus, the film relates to the artist's work in much the same way as the paintings do to life. The presence of the unseen beneath the surface is no less important than what one actually sees.

This double aspect in which things can be taken is further emphasized by the semi-documentary nature of Hazan's film. Hockney and his friends appear as themselves, so that the relationships portrayed are much the same as in reality. But the reality is also rehearsed: Hazan occasionally suggests themes for his "characters" to act out, and the line separating being and role-playing becomes blurred. This convention appears to suit Hockney, whose deceptive innocence and disorientating self-created face (platinum blonde hair, owl-rimmed spectacles) exhibit a special feeling for performance and a flair for the theatrical. And though the film remains, in the final analysis, a subjective record of *one* gay life in which the conjunction of fantasy and experience make common cause, it does effectively isolate the strong strain of protest that resides in the gay sensibility. By wit, a well-organized evasiveness, and a preference for the artificial, Hockney manages a breakthrough into creativity.

This detached attitude does not necessarily indicate an inability to feel or perceive the seriousness of life. In Hockney's case, it is a means of defiance: a refusal to be overwhelmed by unfavorable odds. When the world is a rejecting place, the need grows correspondingly strong to project one's being—to explore the limits to which one's personality might attain—as a way of shielding the inner self from those on the outside who are too insensitive to understand. It is also a method whereby one can multiply personalities, play various parts, assume a variety of roles—both for fun as well as out of real need.

In film, the aesthetic element in camp further implies a movement away from contemporary concerns into realms of exotic or subjective fantasies; the depiction of states of mind that are (in terms of commonly accepted taboos and standards) suspect; an emphasis on sensuous surfaces, textures, imagery, and the evocation of mood as stylistic devices—not simply because they are appropriate to the plot, but as fascinating in themselves. Such tendencies as these are consonant with the spirit of aestheticism in camp, and also go some way toward explaining the charm which particular film genres have for a certain section of our community.

The horror genre, in particular, is susceptible to a camp interpretation. Not all horror films are camp, of course; only those which make the most of stylish conventions for expressing instant feeling, thrills, sharply defined personality, outrageous and "unacceptable" sentiments, and so on. In addition, the psychological issues stated or implied, along with the sources of horror, must relate to some significant aspect of our situation and experience; e.g., the inner drives which threaten an individual's well-being and way of life (Tourneur's *The Cat People* [1942], Mamoulian's *Dr. Jekyll and Mr. Hyde* [1941]), coping with pressures to conform and adapt (Siegel's *Invasion of the Body Snatchers* [1956]), the masking of "abnormality" behind a façade of "normality" (Robson's *The Seventh Victim* [1943], Ulmer's *The Black Cat* [1943]), personal rebellion against enforced restrictions (Burrowe's *Incense for the Damned* [1970]).

As a practical tendency in things or persons, camp emphasizes style as a means of self-projection, a conveyor of meaning, and an expression of emotional tone. Style is a form of consciousness; it is never "natural," always acquired. Camp is also urban; it is, in part, a reaction to the anonymity, boredom, and socializing tendencies of technological society. Camp aims to transform the ordinary into something more spectacular. In terms of style, it signifies performance rather than existence. Clothes and décor, for example, can be a means of asserting one's identity, as well as a form of justification in a society which denies one's essential validity.[4] Just as the dandy of the nineteenth century sought in material visibility (as Auden has said of Baudelaire) "a way out of the corrupt nature into which he, like everyone else, is born,"[5] so many of our community find in the decorative arts and the cultivation of exquisite taste a means of making something positive from a discredited social identity. Hence, the *soigné* furniture and furnishings of the flat designed for Franz in Fassbinder's *Fox and His Friends,* or the carefully cluttered modishness of Michael's apartment in William Friedkin's film adaptation of Mart Crowley's *The Boys in the Band.**

By such means as these one aims to become what one wills, to exercise some control over one's environment. But the emphasis on style goes further. Camp

---

*A distinction must be drawn here between kitsch and camp. The latter implies fervent involvement—an ability to strongly identify with what is perceived as camp. Not so the former, which refers to the artistically shallow or vulgar, and is marked by sensationalism, sentimentalism, and slickness. With regard to décor, kitsch can be seen in George Schlatter's *Norman . . . Is That You?* where the furniture, curtains, chandeliers, paintings, ornaments, etc., provided by set decorator Fred R. Price function principally as things to be mocked.

is often exaggerated. When the stress on style is "outrageous" or "to much," it results in incongruities: the emphasis shifts from what a thing or a person *is* to what it *looks* like; from *what* is being done to *how* it is being done.

This stress on stylization can also explain why the musical comedy, with its high budgets and big stars, its open indulgence in sentiment, and its emphasis on atmosphere, mood, nostalgia, and the fantastic, is, along with horror, a film genre that is saturated with camp. This can best be seen in the boldly imaginative production numbers of Busby Berkeley, whose work reveals a penchant for total extravagance, voyeurism, and sexual symbolism that is particularly blatant in "The Lady in the Tutti-Frutti Hat" sequence of *The Girls He Left Behind* [1943] (also called *The Gang's All Here*), with its acres of female flesh, outrageously phallic dancing bananas, and Carmen Miranda at her most aggressively self-assertive.

Camp/Theatricality

The third element of camp is theatricality. To appreciate camp in things or persons is to perceive the notion of life-as-theater, being versus role-playing, reality and appearance. If "role" is defined as the appropriate behavior associated with a given position in society, then gays do not conform to socially expected ways of behaving as men and women. Camp, by focusing on the outward appearances of role, implies that roles, and, in particular, sex roles, are superficial—a matter of style. Indeed, life itself is role and theater, appearance, and impersonation.

Theatricality relates to the gay situation primarily in respect to roles. Gays do not conform to sex-role expectations: we do not show appropriate interest in the opposite sex as a possible source of sexual satisfaction. We are therefore seen as something less than "real" men and women. This is the essence of gay stigma, our so-called failing. Gayness is seen as a sort of collective denial of the moral and social order of things. Our very lifestyle indicates a rejection of that most cherished cultural assumption which says that masculinity (including sexual dominance over women) is "natural" and appropriate for men, and femininity (including sexual submissiveness toward men) is "natural" and appropriate for women. The stigma of gayness is unique insofar as it is not immediately apparent either to ourselves or to others. Upon discovery of our gayness, however, we are confronted with the possibility of avoiding the negative sanctions attached to our supposed failing by concealing information (i.e., signs which other people take for gay) from the rest of the world. This crucial fact of our existence is called *passing for straight*, a phenomenon generally defined in the metaphor of theater, that is, playing a role: pretending to be something that one is not; or, to shift the motive somewhat, to camouflage our gayness by withholding facts about ourselves which might lead others to the correct conclusion about our sexual orientation.[6]

The art of passing is an acting art: to pass is to be "on stage," to impersonate heterosexual citizenry, to pretend to be a "real" (i.e., straight) man or woman. Such a practice of passing (which can be occasional, continuous, in the past or present) means, in effect, that one must be always on one's guard lest one be seen to "deviate" from those culturally standardized canons of taste, behavior, speech, and so forth, that are generally associated with the male and female roles as defined by the society in which we live. Because masculinity and femininity are perceived in exclusively heterosexual terms, our social stereotype (and often, self-image) is that of one who rejects his or her masculinity or femininity. Those unwilling to accept their socially defined roles are appropriately stigmatized. Proving one's "manhood" or being a "lady" is thus closely linked to the rejection of gay characteristics. In women, repression is often internalized; in men, it may be externalized in aggressive behavior.

The experience of passing is often productive of a gay sensibility. It can, and often does, lead to a heightened awareness and appreciation for disguise, impersonation, the projection of personality, and the distinctions to be made between instinctive and theatrical behavior. The experience of passing would appear to explain the enthusiasm of so many in our community for certain stars whose performances are highly charged with exaggerated (usually sexual) role-playing. Some of these seem (or are made to seem) fairly "knowing," if not self-parodying, in their roles: Jayne Mansfield holding two full milk bottles to her breasts in *The Girl Can't Help It* (1957); Bette Davis in *Beyond the Forest* (1949); Anita Ekberg in *La dolce vita;* Mae West in all her films; Cesar Romero as the Cisco Kid and in *The Good Fairy* (1935). Others are apparently more "innocent" or "sincere": Jane Russell in *The Outlaw* (1943); Raquel Welch; Mamie van Doren; Jennifer Jones in *Duel in the Sun* (1947); Johnny Weismuller as Tarzan and Jungle Jim; Ramon Novarro, particularly in *Ben Hur* (1927) and *The Student Prince* (*in Old Heidelberg*) (1928).

The time factor is also crucial to one's appreciation of camp theatricality. A good deal of the screen acting which only recently appeared quite "natural" will, in the goodness of time, doubtless become camp for its high degree of stylization (that is, if it is not already camp). Examples: the "method" acting of Rod Steiger and early Brando; so, too, the charming, "dated" styles of George Arliss, Luise Rainer, or Miriam Hopkins. Similarly, a number of personalities from the silent cinema, once revered for their sexual allure, now seem, in the seventies, fairly fantastic: Theda Bara and Pola Negri. Men, as David Thomson has observed, have always had an insecure hold on the camera,[7] so that male sex appeal, for example, in the case of Rudolph Valentino, vanished much more quickly than did the sway exerted by women. Finding such stars camp is not to mock them, however. It is more a way of poking fun at the whole cosmology of restrictive sex roles and sexual identifications which our society uses to oppress its women and repress its men—including those on screen. This is not to say that those who appreciate the camp in such stars must, ipso facto, be politically "aware"; often, they are not. The response is mainly instinctive; there is something of the shock of recognition in it—the idea of seeing on screen the absurdity of those roles that each of us is urged to play with such a deadly seriousness.

Thus, camp as a response to performance springs from the gay sensibility's preference for the *intensities* of character, as opposed to its content: what the character conveys tends to be less important than *how* or *why* it is conveyed. Camp is individualistic; as such, it relishes the uniqueness and the force with which personality is imbued. This theatricalization of experience derives both from the passing experience (wherein, paradoxically, we learn the value of the self while at the same time rejecting it) and from a heightened sensitivity to aspects of a performance which others are likely to regard as routine or uncalculated.[8] It is this awareness of the double aspect of a performance that goes a long way to explain why gays form a disproportionately large and enthusiastic part of the audience of such stars as, most notably, Judy Garland.

In part, at least, Garland's popularity owes much to the fact that she is always, and most intensely, herself. Allied to this is the fact that many of us seem able to equate our own strongly felt sense of oppression (past or present) with the suffering/loneliness/misfortunes of the star both on and off the screen. Something in the star's personality allows for an empathy that colors one's whole response to the performer and the performance. As Vicki Lester in Cukor's *A Star is Born* (1954), but, especially, as the concert singer in Ronald Neame's *I Could Go on Singing* (1962), Garland took on roles so disconcertingly close to her real-life situation and personality that the autobiographical connections actually appeared to take their toll on her physical appearance from one scene to the next. Such performances as these solidified the impression, already formed in the minds of her most ardent admirers, of an integrity arising directly out of her great personal misfortunes.

Camp/Humor

The fourth characteristic of camp is its humor. This results from an identification of a strong incongruity between an object, person, or situation and its context. The comic element is inherent in the formal properties of irony. There is a basic contradiction or incongruity, coupled with a real or pretended inno-cence. But in order for an incongruous contrast to be ironic it must, in addi-tion to being comic, affect one as "painful"—though not so painful as to neutralize the humor. It is sufficient that sympathy is aroused for the person, thing, or idea that constitutes the target of an incongruous contrast. To be affected in this way, one's feelings need to clash. It follows, then, that—as A. R. Thompson has argued in his study of irony: "contrasts which conform exactly to the objective definitions of irony are not ironical at all when they do not arouse . . . conflicting feelings."[9]

Humor constitutes the strategy of camp: a means of dealing with a hostile environment and, in the process, of defining a positive identity. This humor takes several forms. Chief of these is bitter-wit, which expresses an underlying hostility and fear. Society says to gays (and to all stigmatized groups) that we are members of the wider community; we are subject to the same laws as "normals"; we must pay our taxes, and so on; we are, in short, "just like everybody else." On the other hand, we are not received into society on equal terms; indeed, we are told that we are unacceptably "different" in ways that are absolutely fundamental to our sense of self and social identity. In other words, the message conveyed to us by society is highly contradictory: we are just like everyone else, and yet . . . we are not. It is this basic contradiction, this joke, that has traditionally been our destiny.

Not surprisingly, this contradiction has produced, in many, an identity-ambivalence that has found expression in our talk, our behavior, our artistic efforts; in fact, our whole perception of the world and of our place in it. Like other oppressed groups, gays have developed skills out of much the same need to concentrate on strategy when the rules are stacked against us. Those of us who are sufficiently sensitive to criticism of ourselves may develop a commen-surate ability to isolate, dissect, and bring into vivid focus the destructiveness and hypocrisy of others. It is thus that in much of our humor lies a strain of irony that is strongly flavored with hostility for society, as well as for ourselves. As Erving Goffman has said: "Given that the stigmatised individual in our society acquires identity standards which he applies to himself in spite of failing to conform to them, it is inevitable that he will feel some ambivalence about his own self."[10]

This tendency to see ourselves as others do is to some extent changing, and will continue to change as we come to define ourselves in terms that do not assume heterosexuality as the norm. In the past, however, and, to a lesser extent, in the present, our response to this split between heterosexual stan-dards and self-demands has been a bitter-wit that is deeply imbued with self-hate and self-derogation. This can best be illustrated in films such as *Staircase,*

Boys in the Band, and *The Killing of Sister George,* all of which are perhaps far too maudlin to be called camp, but whose characters do reflect, in exaggerated form, much of that bitter-wit that goes by the name of camp.

For example, in *Staircase,* directed by Stanley Donen, the humor is saturated with the sadness of those perceived as doomed to live their lives with "unsuitable" emotions in a world where such feelings are tacitly recognized but officially condemned. Thus, throughout the film, the dialogue comments on the central couple's awful-funny confrontation with the "normal" world outside; it is riddled with the self-hatred and low self-esteem of those who have successfully internalized straight society's opinion of us. Self-pity and an aching sense of loss are the prevailing themes: "You've been a father," Charlie hisses at Harry, "a privilege denied thousands of us!" Such dialogue, geared for a "superior" laugh, is squarely based on the tacit acceptance of the hegemony of heterosexual institutions. As for Donen's own patronizing view of these proceedings, this finds its most appropriate metaphor in the maudlin tones of Ray Charles pleading in song on the soundtrack over the flickering images of gay angst to "Forgive them for they know not what they do." Finally, the very conventions of the commercial cinema provide their own language of lament via the presence of such big-name, belligerently straight-associated types as Rex Harrison (Charlie) and Richard Burton (Harry).

Camp can thus be a means of undercutting rage by its derision of concentrated bitterness. Its vision of the world is comic. Laughter, rather than tears, is its chosen means of dealing with the painfully incongruous situation of gays in society. Yet it is also true that camp is something of a protopolitical phenomenon. It assumes gayness to be a category that defines the self, and it steadfastly refuses to repudiate our long heritage of gay ghetto life. Any appreciation of camp, therefore, expresses an empathy with typical gay experiences, even when this takes the form of finding beauty in the seemingly bizarre and outrageous, or discovering the worthiness in a thing or person that is supposedly without value. Finally, camp can be subversive—a means of illustrating those cultural ambiguities and contradictions that oppress us all, gay and straight, and, in particular, women.

Yet because camp combines fun and earnestness, it runs the risk of being considered not serious at all. Usually overlooked by critics of the gay sensibility is camp's strategy of irony. Camp, through its introduction of style, aestheticism, humor, and theatricality, allows us to witness "serious" issues with temporary detachment, so that only later, after the event, are we struck by the emotional and moral implications of what we have almost passively absorbed. The "serious" is, in fact, crucial to camp. Though camp mocks the solemnities of our culture, it never totally discards the seriousness of a thing or individual.

As a character in a Christopher Isherwood novel says: "You can't camp about something you don't take seriously; you're not making fun *of* it; you're making fun *out* of it. You're expressing what's basically serious to you in terms of fun and artifice and elegance."[11]

Camp and the Serious: Fassbinder's Bitter Tears

As a way of illustrating camp in service of the serious, consider Rainer Werner Fassbinder's *The Bitter Tears of Petra von Kant.* Here, as in almost all of this director's work, the problem of how to make radical social commentary without alienating audiences is resolved by distancing the action—finding a common denominator to anchor the message. In *Bitter Tears* the mannerist stylization which dominates the mise en scène, the grand gestures, comic routines, and the melodramatic tendencies of the plot, constitute the strategy whereby Fassbinder aims to both distance and engage his audience. As Thomas Elsaesser has pointed out in "A Cinema of Vicious Circles," Fassbinder's search for an "unprovocative realism" has led the director to discover for the German cinema "the importance of being artificial" as a strategy for forcing an audience to question its assumptions about society and its inhabitants.[12]

This artificiality is the camp aspect of *Bitter Tears.* A highly theatricalized world devoid of the very passions that constitute its subject is provided by the director's formalized, almost Racinian dialogue; his elaborate, carefully calculated compositions locked into theatrical tableaux; the anachronistic costumes and masklike makeup that reflect the psychological situation of the characters; the comic pop/classical music references—the incongruous juxtaposition of Verdi, the Platters, and the Walker Brothers; the stylized performances and ritualized division of the film into five acts, each heralded by the heroine's change of dress and wig; the expressive lighting effects that emphasize a world of masters and servants, predators and victims; and, generally, the formalized editing style which makes the most of the film's single set—a studio apartment that is dominated by a huge brass bed, a wall-sized mural-with-male-nude that bears ironic witness to the action below, and a scattered group of bald-pated mannequins whose poses are continuously rearranged as commentary on their human counterparts.

Each scene is so organized as to heighten the irony of Petra von Kant's (Margit Carstensen) inability to reconcile theory (a loving relationship must be free, honest, and nonpossessive) and practice. This failure is particularly apparent in Petra's sadomasochistic relationship with the omnipresent Marlene (Irm Hermann), a silent witness to her mistress's jealous possession of the sensual young model Karen (Hanna Schygulla), who ultimately rejects her benefactress in favor of her (Karen's) former husband. When, in the bitterly ironic final scene, an outrageous mixture of comedy and cruelty, the chastened Petra reverses roles and offers "freedom and joy" to Marlene in return for companionship, the chalk-faced "slave" dispassionately packs her bags and makes a hasty exit, pausing only to drop "The Great Pretender" on the gramophone by way of vocal reply.

It is the very artificiality of Fassbinder's *Bitter Tears* that serves to support the characters and their emotions. The camp aspect of the work emerges in the use of calculated melodrama and flamboyant visual surfaces to accentuate the film's complex of interrelated themes: the interdependence of sex and power, love and suffering, pleasure and pain; the lover's demand for exclusive possession, which springs from vanity; the basic instability of love in the absence of a lover's sense of positive self-identity; the value of pose as an escape and protective shield; the inevitability of inequities within relationships so long as love, ego, or insights are distributed in unequal proportions. Such themes as these carry a special resonance for the gay sensibility. As outsiders, we are forced to create our own norms; to impose our *selves* upon a world which refuses to confront the arbitrariness of cultural conventions that insist on sexual loyalty, permanence, and exclusive possession. Fassbinder's film, by paying close attention to the ironic functions of style, aims to detach us, temporarily, from the serious content of the images—but which, later, encourages a more reflective analysis.

Further studies of the gay sensibility in relation to cinema will need to take account of the interaction of camp and genres, *auteur* theory, images of women, and so on. What follows are two brief, tentative case studies concerning camp and the gay sensibility in relation to the work of a single director (Josef von Sternberg) and in various films based on the drama and fiction of Tennessee Williams.

Sternberg as Camp

To explain the relation of Sternberg to camp it is necessary to return, briefly, to the phenomenon of passing for straight. This strategy of survival in a hostile world has sensitized us to disguises, impersonations, the significance of surfaces, the need to project personality, the intensities of character, and so on. Sternberg's films—in particular, the Dietrich films from *Morocco* (1930) to *The Devil Is a Woman* (1935)—are all camp insofar as they relate to those adjustment mechanisms of the gay sensibility. But they are also camp in that they reflect the director's ironic attitude toward his subject matter—a judgment that says, in effect, that the content is of interest only insofar as it remains susceptible to transformation by means of stylization. What counts in one's view of Sternberg's films as a camp, then, is the perception of an underlying emotional autobiography—a disguise of self and obsessions by means of the artificial. One does not need to see these disguises in a strictly literal way. It is enough to sense the irony in the tensions that arise from Sternberg's anguish and cynicism, and his predilection for the most outrageous sexual symbolism as a means of objectifying personal fantasies.

Those who view camp either as a trivialization of taste or as a cultural conspiracy will frown on any labeling of Sternberg as camp. Indeed, several of this director's staunchest admirers have already attempted to "rescue" him from ridicule and replace his reputation in a suitably dignified light.[13] For such critics neither the total experience nor the attitudes and emotional philosophy of the sensibility that produces camp are to be taken seriously. The validity of the camp statement, along with its cultural origins and associations, are regarded as of scant significance. Totally ignored is the fact that camp takes a radically different approach to the serious, one which relies heavily on aesthetic rather than moral considerations. Thus, to find camp in Sternberg is not to surrender to the joys of "over-decorated 'aesthetic' nothings."[14] It is, rather, to appreciate the wit by which Sternberg renders his insights artificial; to sense something of an "affaire" between Dietrich and her director; to perceive the deep significance of appearances—a sumptuous surface that serves not as an empty and meaningless background, but as the very subject of the films: a visual context for Sternberg's fantasies.

Sternberg's style is the inevitable result of his need to impose himself upon his material; to control all the elements with which creative work concerns itself. Self-revelation is best accomplished when viewers are left undistracted by the story line. The more hackneyed the material, the better the opportunities for self-projection. There is no place for spontaneity in such a scheme, as one needs always to be in total control of the information conveyed by camera, sets, actors, and so on. Thus, the director demanded complete domination over every aspect of his films. His pictures were "acts of arrogance." Not only did the act of creation derive from him, but he, Sternberg, was also the object created: "Marlene is not Marlene," he insisted, "she is me."[15]

Claire Johnston has said of *Morocco* that

in order for a man to remain at the centre of the universe in a text which focuses on the image, the *auteur* is forced to repress the idea of woman as a social and sexual being (her Otherness) and to deny the opposition man/woman altogether. The woman as sign, then, becomes the pseudo-centre of the filmic discourse.

The incongruous contrast posed by the sign is "male/non-male," which the director established by disguising Dietrich in men's clothing.[16] This is a masquerade that connects with the theme of sexual ambivalence, of central concern to the gay sensibility, and recurrent in Sternberg's work. Dietrich, then, functions principally as a primary motif. It is she, woman, who becomes the focus of Sternberg's symbolism, psychology, and sense of humor. As Amy Joly in *Morocco;* X-27, prostitute and spy, in *Dishonoured* (1931); Shanghai Lily, prostitute, in *Shanghai Express* (1932); Helen Faraday, nightclub entertainer and archetypal mother in *Blonde Venus* (1932); Sophia Frederica, later Catherine II, in *The Scarlet Empress* (1934); and Concha Perez in *The Devil Is a Woman* (1935), Dietrich as woman becomes a manifestation of Sternberg's fantasies. The man takes over; the woman recedes into myth and the details of the décor. The image that emerges is man-made. But it is also an integral part of the larger camp structure. Hence, the danger to which camp enthusiasts expose themselves is as inevitable as it is irreducible, i.e., the danger of surrendering to the corroboration of Sternberg's fantasies as each, in turn, is thrown back on us by the male-manufactured image of the star who illuminates the screen.

The Gay Sensibility in the Films of Tennessee Williams

In the films based on the work of Tennessee Williams (I shall refer to these as "Williams's films" since, even when the plays and fiction are adapted for the screen by someone other than the author, they retain the spirit of the original) the image of women is again of central concern in any consideration of camp and the gay sensibility.[17] The point I wish to take up here is one that various critics have used to denigrate both Williams's films and the gay sensibility; namely, that the typical heroine of these films is a "drag queen."[18]

This interpretation is nowhere more relentlessly pursued than in Molly Haskell's *From Reverence to Rape: The Treatment of Women in the Movies.* Haskell perceives Williams's women as products of the writer's own "baroquely transvestised homosexual fantasies." By no stretch of the imagination, she argues, can they conceivably be seen as "real" women. Hence, Vivien Leigh's Blanche DuBois and Karen Stone in *A Streetcar Named Desire* (1951) and *The Roman Spring of Mrs. Stone* (1961); Geraldine Page's Alexandra Del Lago (the Princess Kosmonopolis) and Alma Winemiller in *Sweet Bird of Youth* (1962) and *Summer and Smoke* (1958); Joanne Woodward's Carole Cutrere in *The Fugitive Kind* (1958); Ava Gardner's Maxine Faulk and Deborah Kerr's Hannah Jelkes in *The Night of the Iguana* (1964); Elizabeth Taylor's Flora (Sissy) Goforth in *Boom!* (1968), and on and on. All these characters, Haskell argues, are "hermaphrodites" who flow from out of "the palpable fear and self-pity, guts and bravura of the aging homosexual." What happens here, the argument further goes, is that the gay author, seething with repressed desires, dons his female mask (Blanche, Karen, etc.) and hungrily heads, in print as on screen, for a host of fantasy males of his own creation: Stanley Kowalski/ Marlon Brando, Paolo/Warren Beatty, Chance Wayne/Paul Newman. The "cultured homosexual" (Williams) is thus seen as being compelled, "often masochistically and against his taste," to love brutes and beachboys, natives and gigolos, primitives and peasants—as well as all the other unavailable prototypes of uninhibited sensuality.[19]

There is some truth in all this, of course. Williams has "used" women to his own advantage. His initial passing strategy for coping with the fact of his gayness was productive of deep anxiety which led to a certain conservatism in his work: a desire to protect himself against the prying eyes of others; an unwillingness to parade his feelings as a gay man in public. Thus, in films based on such early work as *A Streetcar Named Desire, Summer and Smoke,* and *The Roman Spring of Mrs. Stone,* Williams's crypto-gayness found relief in the form of female guise: Blanche, Alma, Karen. These characters do express their creator's own "unacceptable" emotions as a gay man. They all do declare the nature of Williams's own fantasy life at the time of their creation. In them the artist has found a means of dealing with the tensions that plagued and defined him—tensions that reside in such dualities as flesh/spirit, promiscuity/pride, youth/(old) age.

Yet it is also true that such a strategy of survival in a hostile world constitutes an imaginative act of which any artist is capable. Most male artists, whatever their sexual orientation, assume the habit of it as a necessary qualification in dealing with female emotions. What one needs to be concerned about is not the *fact* of an artist's fantasies; but, rather, the way in which these fantasies are *shaped* so that they speak to and for other people.

Still, there remains the threat from certain critical quarters to reduce the whole of such problems of interpretation to generalities about the limitations of the gay artist. The central assumption of such criticism is that gays, generally, can know little of life as lived by those who take their place in the "real" world of straight, rather than gay, relationships. This point is most succinctly expressed by Adelaide Comerford, who, writing in *Films in Review,* claims that when Williams is not dealing with "sex degenerates or other psychopaths" his "ignorance of life is boringly patent."[20]

This notion that the work of gay artists cannot be taken seriously because it deals with facts of feeling unknown to straights does have a certain awful logic to it.[21] People insufficiently sensitive to those aspects of our situation which give to an artist's work a measure of dignity surely cannot be expected to be open to the understandings that spring from our unique encounters with self and society. Those who malign or reject the existence of a gay sensibility will all too often overlook the fact that the feelings and creative productions of artists, gay or straight, are the sum total of their experiences—education, relationships, repressions, fortunes, and misfortunes—which have entered into their inner lives. To dismiss the creative efforts that spring from such influences on the ground that the artist is gay serves no useful purpose whatsoever. Certainly it is true enough that gays *do* develop a unique perception of the world, just as do all members of minority groups which have been treated, in essential respects, as marginal to society. And since sexuality can be divorced from no aspect of the inner workings of the human personality, it cannot be divorced from creativity. What one wants to know is this: Given the nature of our unique situation, what special insights does the gay artist have to offer?

In defining the gay sensibility it is important to remember that gays are members of a minority group, and that minorities have always constituted some sort of threat to the majority. Thus, gays have been regarded with fear, suspicion, and, even, hatred. The knowledge of these attitudes has developed in us what I have referred to above as a unique set of perspectives and understandings about what the world is like and how best we can deal with it. It is true that gay artists may at times protect themselves from the social pressures imposed upon them by our cultural contradictions and social prejudices. Hence, it may be that fantasies of revenge are sometimes transformed into art as a way of allowing vicarious play to erotic wishes renounced in the interests of social acceptance; resentments are expressed over treatment received; appeals for sympathy are made through the demonstration of damage wrought by continued injustice and oppression; psychic wounds are recorded so that art becomes, as Williams has said of his own work, "An escape from a world of reality in which I felt acutely uncomfortable";[22] female masks are donned; charades enacted; false identities assumed.

But are not such forms of expression—"deceptions"—in fact everywhere the rule? In Freud's formulation of the creative impulse, the artist is originally one who turns away from reality out of a refusal to come to terms with the demand for his or her renunciation of instinctual satisfactions, and who then, in fantasy life, allows full play to erotic and ambitious wishes.[23] Creativity is thus an inevitable outcome of repressed impulses or relationships. As such it constitutes a defiance against "unlived life."[24] True, the insights offered by so many of the female characters in Williams's films are the product of a gay sensibility. But then the gay artist is one who is graced with a double vision—a vision which belongs to all members of oppressed groups. Those on the outside better understand the activities of the insider than vice versa. As Benjamin

DeMott has pointed out in his essay, "But He's a Homosexual . . . ," the gay artist often speaks more frankly than the straight on such matters as the tedium of marriage, the horrors of family life, the lover's exploitation of personality, and the slow erosion of character in promiscuity.[25]

If we are not too rigid about drawing the line between thought and fantasy, but, rather, conceive of creative endeavor as encompassing a great range of covert mental processes, then it should be possible to view more sympathetically Williams's female creations as important both to the conservation and change of this artist's own sense of identity, as well as for what they reveal of an aspect of love that is neither gay nor straight, but, simply, human. These are facts of feeling which gays, who have early in life recognized irony in the incompatible demands of gayness and society, cannot easily avoid. Yet these are facts which can scarcely be understood by those oblivious to the peculiarities, past or present, of our situation in the general culture.

To say this is not to suggest that *only* gays can be objective about heterosexual institutions and arrangements. It is, rather, a way of saying that gays, because of the demands constantly made upon us to justify our existence, have never been able to simply accept, passively, the cultural assumptions that nongays may well take for granted.[26] The insights provided by, for example, the Deborah Kerr and Ava Gardner characters in *The Night of the Iguana,* are not those of "drag queens," as has been suggested. Rather, they spring from a gay sensibility that is not so completely identified with its "masculine" persona roles that it cannot give expression to its "feminine" component. It is also one that refuses to lapse into unthinking acceptance of what others have insisted is appropriate behavior for two people in love. When the Deborah Kerr character (Hannah Jelkes) speaks of her acceptance of the "impermanence" of relationships, Shannon (Richard Burton) chides her, offering up the metaphor of birds who build their nests "on the very highest level." To this Hannah quickly replies: "I'm not a bird, Mr. Shannon, I'm a human being. And when a member of that fantastic species builds a nest in the heart of another, the question of permanence isn't the first or even the last thing that's considered." Echoing these sentiments precisely, the Ava Gardner character (Maxine Faulk) tells Burton that sooner or later we all reach a point where it is important to "settle for something that works for us in our lives—even if it isn't on the highest kind of level." This is the message advocated time and again by the Williams female, and it is very much an insight of the gay sensibility.

Conclusion

Camp and the gay sensibility have rarely, if ever, been explored in relation to cinema.[27] On the rare occasions when it has (outside of gay periodicals) analyses have tended to draw upon stereotypes of gayness with which we are all, by now, familiar. The term *camp* has been widely misused to signify the trivial, superficial, and "queer." The original meaning and complex associations of the term, some of which I have attempted to outline in this essay, are ignored. Thus, just as it has always been a sign of worthiness to speak out on behalf of any oppressed minority group *other* than gays, so, it seems, there exists a corresponding reluctance on the part of people who take the cinema seriously (either out of contempt, or of seeming suspect, or whatever) to perceive in camp a means of heightening their appreciation of any particular performance, film, or director.

Camp, as a product of the gay sensibility, has existed, right up to the present moment in time, on the same sociocultural level as the subculture from which it has issued. In other words, camp, its sources and associations, have remained secret in their most fundamental aspects, just as the actual life of gays in our culture has remained secret to the overwhelming majority of nongays. Many critics have, of course, appropriated the term *camp,* but without any understanding of its significance within the gay community. The subcultural attitudes, catalysts, and needs that have gone to produce camp as a creative expression of gay feelings are never considered. Yet camp is, in its essence, the expression of these feelings.

The real trouble with the usual speculations on what the critics have thought to term *camp* (aside from the fact that most of it is not) is that they never illuminate the gay sensibility, but, rather, go far to reinforce those very standards of judgment and aesthetic excellence which are often antithetical to it. It is thus that critics conclude, by implication, that camp has emerged from out of no intelligent body of sociocultural analysis.

To say this is not, however, to plead for the application of any narrow sociological analysis. Rather, it is a way of saying that the worth of camp can simply not be understood in critical terms unless some attention is first given to the attitudes that go to produce it—attitudes that spring from our social situation and that are crucial to the development of a gay sensibility.

Notes

1. Oscar Wilde, *The Decay of Lying* (London: Osgood, McIlvane & Co., 1891).
2. Susan Sontag, *Against Interpretation, and Other Essays* (New York: Delta, 1967). This point and a number of other insights provided by Sontag in her seminal essay, "Notes on Camp," have been most helpful to me in formulating my own ideas on the subject.

3. This point is developed by R. V. Johnson in *Aestheticism* (London: Methuen, 1969).

4. Esther Newton has explored the relationship of costume to female impersonators in "The 'Drag Queen': A Study in Urban Anthropology" (Ph.D. diss., University of Chicago, 1968). I am much indebted to Newton for her insights on the style and humor systems of "Drag Queens."

5. W. H. Auden in his "Introduction" to *The Intimate Journals of Charles Pierre Baudelaire*, trans. Christopher Isherwood (London: Methuen, 1949).

6. I have developed these ideas at greater length in "Passing for Straight: The Politics of the Closet," *Gay News*, no. 62 (January 1974).

7. David Thomson, *A Biographical Dictionary of the Cinema* (London: Secker & Warburg, 1975).

8. Erving Goffman discusses the "passing" strategy in relation to stigmatized groups in *Stigma: The Management of Spoiled Identity* (Englewood Cliffs, N.J.: Prentice-Hall, 1963).

9. A. R. Thompson, *The Dry Mock: A Study of Irony in Drama* (Berkeley: University of California Press, 1948).

10. Goffman, *Stigma*.

11. Christopher Isherwood, *The World in the Evening* (London: Methuen, 1954).

12. Thomas Elsaesser, "A Cinema of Vicious Circles," in *Fassbinder*, ed. Tony Rayns (London: BFI, 1976).

13. See, for example, Robin Wood, *Personal Views: Exploration in Film* (London: Gordon Fraser, 1976); and Andrew Sarris, in *The Films of Josef von Sternberg* (New York: Museum of Modern Art/Doubleday, 1966), and "Summer Camp," *Village Voice*, 21 July 1975.

14. Wood, *Personal Views*.

15. Quoted in Herman Weinberg, *Josef von Sternberg: A Critical Study* (London: E. P. Dutton, 1967).

16. Claire Johnston, "Women's Cinema as Counter-Cinema" in *Notes on Women's Cinema* (London: SEFT, 1973).

17. The *Memoirs* of Tennessee Williams (London: W. H. Allen, 1976) have also been useful to me here for the light they throw on the ways in which the author's gayness has affected his creative output.

18. The instances of critics labeling a Williams heroine "drag queen" are too numerous to cite. However, the most extended development of this particular line of interpretation can be found in Molly Haskell, *From Reverence to Rape: The Treatment of Women in the Movies* (New York: Holt, Rinehart & Winston, 1973) and Elaine Rothschild in *Films in Review*, August/September 1964, where the reviewer speaks of Williams's "mal-formed females" and "anti-female" imagination; see also Marjorie Rosen, *Popcorn Venus: Women, Movies, and the American Dream* (New York: Avon, 1974); Foster Hirsch, "Tennessee Williams," in *Cinema* (USA) 8, no. 1 (Spring 1973); *The Guardian*, 27 October 1976; *Interview*, April 1973.

19. Haskell, *From Reverence to Rape*.

20. Adelaide Comerford, *Films in Review*, December 1962.

21. Peter J. Dyer refers to the "difficulty" of taking the film *Summer and Smoke* "at all seriously," other than as "a case-book study in arrested development" (in *Monthly Film Bulletin* 29, no. 339); similarly, Molly Haskell in *From Reverence to Rape* writes: "Williams's women can be amusing company if we aren't asked to take them too seriously" (251).

22. Tennessee Williams in *New York Times*, 8 March 1959.

23. Sigmund Freud, "The Relation of the Poet to Daydreaming," *Collected Papers*, vol. 4 (New York: Basic Books, 1959).

24. See, in this regard, Antonia Wenkart, "Creativity and Freedom," *American Journal of Psychoanalysis* 23, no. 2 (1963).

25. Benjamin DeMott, *Supergrow: Essays and Reports on Imagination in America* (London: E. P. Dutton, 1970).

26. This so-called communion of touch in relationships is further developed in Babuscio's *We Speak for Ourselves* (London: SPCK, 1976).

27. The notable exception is *Gay News,* a fortnightly newspaper published in London.

Role Models

ESTHER NEWTON

The Actress

Female impersonators, particularly the stage impersonators, identify strongly with professional performers. Their special, but not exclusive, idols are female entertainers. Street impersonators usually try to model themselves on movie stars rather than on stage actresses and nightclub performers. Stage impersonators are quite conversant with the language of the theaters and nightclubs, while the street impersonators are not. In Kansas City, the stage impersonators frequently talked with avid interest about stage and nightclub "personalities." The street impersonators could not join in these discussions for lack of knowledge.

Stage impersonators very often told me that they considered themselves to be nightclub performers or to be in the nightclub business, "just like other [straight] performers."

When impersonators criticized each other's on- or off-stage conduct as "unprofessional," this was a direct appeal to norms of show business. Certain show business phrases such as "break a leg" (for good luck) were used routinely, and I was admonished not to whistle backstage. The following response of a stage impersonator shows this emphasis, in answer to my question, "What's the difference between professionals and street fairies?" This impersonator was a "headliner" (had top billing) at a club in New York:

> Well (laughs), simply saying . . . well, I can leave that up to you. You have seen the show. You see the difference between *me* and some of these other people (his voice makes it sound as if this point is utterly self-evident) who are working in this left field of show business, and I'm quite sure that you see a *distinct* differ-

ence. I am more conscious of being a performer, and I think generally speaking, most, or a lot, of other people who are appearing in the same show are just doing it, not as a lark—we won't say that it's a lark—but they're doing it because it's something they can drop in and out of. They have fun, they laugh, have drinks, and play around, and just have a good time. But to *me*, now, playing around and having a good time is [*sic.*] important to me also; but primarily my interest from the time I arrive at the club till the end of the evening—I am there as a performer, as an entertainer, and this to me is the most important thing. And I dare say that if needs be, I probably could do it, and be just as good an entertainer . . . I don't know if I would be any more successful if I were working in men's clothes than I am working as a woman. But comparing myself to some of the people that I would consider real professional entertainers—people who are genuinely interested in the show as a show, and not just as I say, a street fairy, who wants to put on a dress and a pair of high heels to be seen and show off in public.

The stage impersonators are interested in "billings" and publicity, in lighting and makeup and stage effects, in "timing" and "stage presence." The quality by which they measure performers and performances is "talent." Their models in these matters are established performers, both in their performances and in their off-stage lives, insofar as the impersonators are familiar with the latter. The practice of doing "impressions" is, of course, a very direct expression of this role modeling.

From this perspective, female impersonators are simply nightclub performers who happen to use impersonation as a medium. Many stage impersonators are drab in appearance (and sometimes in manner) off stage. These men often say that drag is simply a medium or mask that allows them to perform. The mask is borrowed from female performers, the ethos of performance from show business norms in general.

The stated aspiration of almost all stage impersonators is to "go legit," that is, to play in movies, television, and on stage or in respectable nightclubs, either in drag *or* (some say) in men's clothes. Failing this, they would like to see the whole profession "upgraded," made more legitimate and professional (and to this end they would like to see all street impersonators barred from working, for they claim that the street performers downgrade the profession). T. C. Jones is universally accorded highest status among impersonators because he has appeared on Broadway (*New Faces of 1956*) and on television (Alfred Hitchcock) and plays only high-status nightclubs.

The Drag Queen

Professionally, impersonators place themselves as a group at the bottom of the show business world. But socially, their self-image can be represented (without the moral implications) in its simplest form as three concentric circles. The impersonators, or drag queens, are the inner circle. Surrounding them are the queens, ordinary gay men. The straights are the outer circle. In this way, impersonators are "a society within a society within a society," as one impersonator told me.

A few impersonators deny publicly that they are gay. These impersonators are married, and some have children. Of course, being married and having children constitute no barrier to participation in the homosexual subculture. But whatever may be the actual case with these few, the impersonators I knew universally described such public statements as "cover." One impersonator's statement was particularly revealing. He said that "in practice" perhaps some impersonators were straight, but "in theory" they could not be. "How can a man perform in female attire and not have something wrong with him?" he asked.

The role of the female impersonator is directly related to both the drag queen and camp roles in the homosexual subculture. In gay life, the two roles are strongly associated. In homosexual terminology, a drag queen is a homosexual male who often, or habitually, dresses in female attire. (A drag butch is a lesbian who often, or habitually, dresses in male attire.) Drag and camp are the most representative and widely used symbols of homosexuality in the English-speaking world. This is true even though many homosexuals would never wear drag or go to a drag party and even though most homosexuals who do wear drag do so only in special contexts, such as private parties and Halloween balls.[1] At the middle-class level, it is common to give "costume" parties at which those who want to wear drag can do so, and the others can wear a costume appropriate to their gender.

The principle opposition around which the gay world revolves is masculine-feminine. There are a number of ways of presenting this opposition through one's own person, where it becomes also an opposition of "inside" = "outside" or "underneath" = "outside." Ultimately, all drag symbolism opposes the "inner" or "real" self (subjective self) to the "outer" self (social self). For the great majority of homosexuals, the social self is often a calculated respectability and the subjective or real self is stigmatized. The "inner" = "outer" opposition is almost parallel to "back" = "front." In fact, the social self is usually described as "front" and social relationships (especially with women) designed to support the veracity of the "front" are called "cover." The "front" = "back" opposition also has a direct tie-in with the body: "front" = "face"; "back" = "ass."

There are two different levels on which the oppositions can be played out. One is *within* the sartorial system[2] itself, that is, wearing feminine clothing "underneath" and masculine clothing "outside." (This method seems to be used more by heterosexual transvestites.) It symbolizes that the visible, social, masculine clothing is a costume, which in turn symbolizes that the entire sex-role behavior is a role—an act. Conversely, stage impersonators sometimes wear jockey shorts underneath full stage drag, symbolizing that the feminine clothing is a costume.

A second "internal" method is to mix sex-role referents *within* the visible sartorial system. This generally involves some "outside" item from the feminine sartorial system such as earrings, lipstick, high-heeled shoes, a necklace, worn *with* masculine clothing. This kind of opposition is used very frequently in informal camping by homosexuals. The feminine item stands out so glaringly by incongruity that it "undermines" the masculine system and proclaims that the inner identification is feminine.[3] When this method is used on stage, it is called "working with (feminine) pieces." The performer generally works in a tuxedo or business suit and a woman's large hat and earrings.

The second level poses an opposition between a one sex-role sartorial system and the "self," whose identity has to be indicated in some other way. Thus when impersonators are performing, the oppositional play is between "appearance," which is female, and "reality," or "essence," which is male. One way to do this is to show that the appearance is an illusion; for instance, a standard impersonation maneuver is to pull out one "breast" and show it to the audience. A more drastic step is taking off the wig. Strippers actually routinize the progression from "outside" to "inside" visually, by starting in a full stripping costume and ending by taking off the bra and showing the audience the flat chest. Another method is to demonstrate "maleness" verbally or vocally by suddenly dropping the vocal level or by some direct reference. One impersonator routinely tells the audience: "Have a ball. I have two." (But genitals must *never* be seen.) Another tells unruly members of the audience that he will "put on my men's clothes and beat you up."

Impersonators play on the opposition to varying extents, but most experienced stage impersonators have a characteristic method of doing it. Generally speaking, the desire and ability to break the illusion of femininity is the mark of an experienced impersonator who has freed himself from other impersonators as the immediate reference group and is working fully to the audience. Even so, some stage impersonators admitted that it is difficult to break the unity of the feminine sartorial system. For instance, they said that it is difficult, subjectively, to speak in a deep tone of voice while on stage and especially while wearing a wig. The "breasts" especially seem to symbolize the entire feminine sartorial system and role. This is shown not only by the very common device of removing them in order to break the illusion, but in the command, "tits up!" meaning, "get into the role," or "get into feminine character."

The tension between the masculine-feminine and inside-outside oppositions pervades the homosexual subculture at all class and status levels. In a sense the different class and status levels consist of different ways of balancing these oppositions. Low-status homosexuals (both male and female) characteristically insist on very strong dichotomization between masculine-feminine so that people must play out one principle or the other exclusively. Low-status queens are expected to be very nellie, always, and low-status butch men are so "masculine" that they very often consider themselves straight.[4] (Although the queens say in private that "today's butch is tomorrow's sister.") Nevertheless, in the most nellie queens the opposition is still implicitly there, since to participate in the male homosexual subculture as a peer, one must be male inside (physiologically).

Recently, this principle has begun to be challenged by hormone use and by the sex-changing operation. The use of these techniques as a final resolution of the masculine-feminine opposition is hotly discussed in the homosexual subculture. A very significant proportion of the impersonators, and especially the street impersonators, have used or are using hormone shots or plastic inserts to create artificial breasts and change the shape of their bodies. This development is strongly deplored by the stage impersonators who say that the whole point of female impersonation depends on maleness. They further say that these "hormone queens" are placing themselves out of the homosexual subculture, since, by definition, a homosexual man wants to sleep with other *men* (i.e., no gay man would want to sleep with these "hormone queens").

In carrying the transformation even further, to "become a woman" is approved by the stage impersonators, with the provision that the "sex changes" should get out of gay life altogether and go straight. The "sex changes" do not always comply, however. One quite successful impersonator in Chicago had the operation but continued to perform in a straight club with other impersonators. Some impersonators in Chicago told me that this person was now considered "out of gay life" by the homosexuals and could not perform in a gay club. I also heard a persistent rumor that "she" now liked to sleep with lesbians!

It should be readily apparent why drag is such an effective symbol of both the outside-inside and masculine-feminine oppositions. There are relatively few ascribed roles in American culture and sex role is one of them; sex role radiates a complex and ubiquitous system of typing achieved roles. Obvious examples are in the kinship system (wife, mother, etc.) but sex typing also extends far out into the occupational-role system (airline stewardess, waitress, policeman, etc.). The effect of the drag system is to wrench the sex roles loose from that which supposedly determines them, that is, genital sex. Gay people know that sex-typed behavior can be achieved, contrary to what is popularly believed. They know that the possession of one type of genital equipment by no means guarantees the "naturally appropriate" behavior.

Thus drag in the homosexual subculture symbolizes two somewhat conflicting statements concerning the sex-role system. The first statement symbolized by drag is that the sex-role system really is natural: therefore homosexuals are unnatural (typical responses: "I am physically abnormal"; "I can't help it, I was born with the wrong hormone balance"; "I am really a woman who was born with the wrong equipment"; "I am psychologically sick").

The second symbolic statement of drag questions the "naturalness" of the sex-role system in toto; if sex-role behavior can be achieved by the "wrong" sex, it logically follows that it is in reality also achieved, not inherited, by the "right" sex. Anthropologists say that sex-role behavior is learned. The gay world, via drag, says that sex-role behavior is an appearance; it is "outside." It can be manipulated at will.

Drag symbolizes both these assertions in a very complex way. At the simplest level, drag signifies that the person wearing it is a homosexual, that he is a male who is behaving in a specifically inappropriate way, that he is a male who places himself as a woman in relation to other men. In this sense it signifies stigma. At the most complex, it is a double inversion that says "appearance is an illusion." Drag says, "my 'outside' appearance is feminine, but my essence 'inside' [the body] is masculine." At the same time it symbolizes the opposite inversion: "my appearance 'outside' [my body, my gender] is masculine but my essence 'inside' [myself] is feminine."

In the context of the homosexual subculture, all professional female impersonators are "drag queens." Drag is always worn for performance in any case; the female impersonator has simply professionalized this subcultural role. Among themselves and in conversation with other homosexuals, female impersonators usually call themselves and are called drag queens. In the same way, their performances are referred to by themselves and others as drag shows.

But when the varied meanings of drag are taken into consideration, it should be obvious why the drag queen is an ambivalent figure in the gay world. The drag queen symbolizes all that homosexuals say they fear the most in themselves, all that they say they feel guilty about; he symbolizes, in fact, *the* stigma. In this way, the term *drag queen* is comparable to *nigger*. And like that word, it may be all right in an ingroup context but not in an outgroup one. Those who do not want to think of themselves or be identified as drag queens under any circumstances attempt to disassociate themselves from "drag" completely. These homosexuals deplore drag shows and profess total lack of interest in them. Their attitude toward drag queens is one of condemnation combined with the expression of vast social distance between themselves and the drag queen.

Other homosexuals enjoy being queens among themselves, but do not want to be stigmatized by the heterosexual culture. These homosexuals admire drag and drag queens in homosexual contexts, but deplore female impersonators and street fairies for "giving us a bad name" or "projecting the wrong image" to the heterosexual culture. The drag queen is definitely a marked man in the subculture.

Homosexuality consists of sex-role deviation made up of two related but distinct parts: "wrong" sexual object choices and "wrong" sex-role presentation of self.[5] The first deviation is shared by all homosexuals, but it can be hidden best. The second deviation logically (in this culture) corresponds with the first, which it symbolizes. But it cannot be hidden, and it actually compounds the stigma.

Thus, insofar as female impersonators are professional drag queens, they are evaluated positively by gay people to the extent that they have perfected a subcultural skill and to the extent that gay people are willing to oppose the heterosexual culture directly (in much the same way that Negroes now call themselves blacks). On the other hand, they are despised because they symbolize and embody the stigma. At present, the balance is far on the negative side, although this varies by context and by the position of the observer (relative to the stigma). This explains the impersonators' negative identification with the term *drag queen* when it is used by outsiders. (In the same way, they at first used masculine pronouns of address and reference toward each other in my presence, but reverted to feminine pronouns when I became more or less integrated into the system.)

The Camp

While all female impersonators are drag queens in the gay world, by no means are all of them "camps." Both the drag queen and the camp are expressive performing roles, and both specialize in transformation. But the drag queen is concerned with masculine-feminine transformation, while the camp is concerned with what might be called a philosophy of transformations and incongruity. Certainly the two roles are intimately related, since to be a feminine man is by definition incongruous. But strictly speaking, the drag queen simply expresses the incongruity while the camp actually uses it to achieve a higher synthesis. To the extent that a drag queen does this, he is called "campy." The drag queen role is emotionally charged and connotes low status for most homosexuals because it bears the visible stigmata of homosexuality; camps, however, are found at all status levels in the homosexual subculture and are very often the center of primary group organization.[6]

The camp is the central role figure in the subcultural ideology of camp. The camp ethos or style plays a role analogous to "soul" in the Negro subculture.[7] Like soul, camp is a "strategy for a situation."[8] The special perspective of the female impersonators is a case of a broader homosexual ethos. This is the perspective of moral deviance and, consequently, of a "spoiled identity," in Goffman's terms.[9] Like the Negro problem, the homosexual problem centers on self-hatred and the lack of self-esteem.[10] But if "the soul ideology ministers to the needs for identity,"[11] the camp ideology ministers to the needs for dealing with an identity that is well defined but loaded with contempt. As one impersonator who was also a well-known camp told me, "No one is more miserable about homosexuality than the homosexual."

Camp is not a thing. Most broadly it signifies a *relationship between* things, people, and activities or qualities, and homosexuality. In this sense, "camp taste," for instance, is synonymous with homosexual taste. Informants stressed that even between individuals there is very little agreement on what is camp because camp is in the eye of the beholder, that is, different homosexuals like different things, and because of the spontaneity and individuality of camp, camp taste is always changing. This has the advantage, recognized by some informants, that a clear division can always be maintained between homosexual and "straight" taste.

An informant said Susan Sontag was wrong about camp's being a cult,[12] and the moment it becomes a public cult, you watch the queens stop it. Because if it becomes the squares, it doesn't belong to them any more. And what will be "camp art," no queen will own. It's like taking off the work clothes and putting on the home clothes. When the queen is coming home, she wants to come home to a campy apartment that's hers—it's very queer—because all day long she's been very straight. So when it all of a sudden becomes very straight—to come home to an apartment that any square could have—she's not going to have it any more.[13]

While camp is in the eye of the homosexual beholder, it is assumed that there is an underlying unity of perspective among homosexuals that gives any particular campy thing its special flavor. It is possible to discern strong themes in any particular campy thing or event. The three that seemed most recurrent and characteristic to me were *incongruity, theatricality,* and *humor.* All three are intimately related to the homosexual situation and strategy. Incongruity is the subject matter of camp, theatricality its style, and humor its strategy.

Camp usually depends on the perception or creation of *incongruous juxta-*

positions. Either way, the homosexual "creates" the camp, by pointing out the incongruity or by devising it. For instance, one informant said that the campiest thing he had seen recently was a midwestern football player in high drag at a Halloween ball. He pointed out that the football player was seriously trying to be a lady, and so his intent was not camp, but that the *effect* to the observer was campy. (The informant went on to say that it would have been even campier if the football player had been picked up by the police and had his picture published in the paper the next day.) This is an example of unintentional camp, in that the campy person or thing does not perceive the incongruity.

Created camp also depends on transformations and juxtapositions, but here the effect is intentional. The most concrete examples can be seen in the apartments of campy queens, for instance, in the idea of growing plants in the toilet tank. One queen said that *TV Guide* had described a little Mexican horse statue as campy. He said there was nothing campy about this at all, but if you put a nude cut-out of Bette Davis on it, it would be campy. Masculine-feminine juxtapositions are, of course, the most characteristic kind of camp, but any very incongruous contrast can be campy. For instance, juxtapositions of high and low status, youth and old age, profane and sacred functions or symbols, cheap and expensive articles are frequently used for camp purposes. Objects or people are often said to be campy, but the camp inheres not in the person or thing itself but in the tension between that person or thing and the context or association. For instance, I was told by impersonators that a homosexual clothes designer made himself a beautiful Halloween ball gown. After the ball he sold it to a wealthy society lady. It was said that when he wore it, it was very campy, but when she wore it, it was just an expensive gown, unless she had run around her ball saying she was really not herself but her faggot dress designer.

The nexus of this perception by incongruity lies in the basic homosexual experience, that is, squarely on the moral deviation. One informant said, "Camp is based on homosexual thought. It is all based on the idea of two men or two women in bed. It's incongruous and it's funny." If moral deviation is the locus of the perception of incongruity, it is more specifically role deviation and role manipulation that are at the core of the second property of camp, *theatricality.*

Camp is theatrical in three interlocking ways. First of all, camp is style. Importance tends to shift from what a thing *is* to how it *looks,* from *what* is done to *how* it is done. It has been remarked that homosexuals excel in the decorative arts. The kind of incongruities that are campy are very often created by adornment or stylization of a well-defined thing or symbol. But the emphasis on style goes further than this in that camp is also exaggerated, consciously "stagey," specifically theatrical. This is especially true of *the* camp, who is definitely a performer.

The second aspect of theatricality in camp is its dramatic form. Camp, like drag, always involves a performer or performers and an audience. This is its structure. It is only stretching the point a little to say that even in unintentional camp, this interaction is maintained. In the case of the football player, his behavior was transformed by his audience into a performance. In many cases of unintentional camp, the camp performs to his audience by commenting on the behavior or appearance of "the scene," which is then described as "campy." In intentional camp, the structure of performer and audience is almost always clearly defined.

Third, camp is suffused with the perception of "being as playing a role" and "life as theatre."[14] It is at this point that drag and camp merge and augment each other. I was led to an appreciation of this while reading Parker Tyler's appraisal of Greta Garbo. Garbo is generally regarded in the homosexual community as "high camp." Tyler stated that " 'Drag acts,' I believe, are not confined to the declassed sexes. Garbo 'got in drag' whenever she took some heavy glamour part, whenever she melted in or out of a man's arms, whenever she simply let that heavenly-flexed neck . . . bear the weight of her thrown-back head." He concludes, "How resplendent seems the art of acting! It is all *impersonation,* whether the sex underneath is true or not."[15]

We have to take the long way around to get at the real relationship between Garbo and camp. The homosexual is stigmatized, but his stigma can be hidden. In Goffman's terminology, information about his stigma can be managed. Therefore, of crucial importance to homosexuals themselves and to non-homosexuals is whether the stigma is displayed so that one is immediately recognizable or is hidden so that he can pass to the world at large as a respectable citizen. The covert half (conceptually, not necessarily numerically) of the homosexual community is engaged in "impersonating" respectable citizenry, at least some of the time. What is being impersonated?

The stigma essentially lies in being less than a man and in doing something that is unnatural (wrong) for a man to do. Surrounding this essence is a halo effect: violation of culturally standardized canons of taste, behavior, speech, and so on, rigorously associated (prescribed) with the male role (e.g., fanciful or decorative clothing styles, "effeminate" speech and manner, expressed disinterest in women as sexual objects, expressed interest in men as sexual objects, unseemly concern with personal appearance, etc.). The covert homosexual must therefore do two things: first, he must conceal the fact that he sleeps with men. But concealing this *fact* is far less difficult than his second problem, which is controlling the *halo effect* or signals that would announce that he sleeps with men. The covert homosexual must in fact impersonate a *man*, that is, he must *appear* to the "straight" world to be fulfilling (or not violating) all the requisites of the male role as defined by the "straight" world.

The immediate relationship between Tyler's point about Garbo and camp/drag is this: if Garbo playing women is drag, then homosexuals "passing" are playing men; they are in drag. This is the larger implication of drag/camp. In fact, gay people often use the word "drag" in this broader sense, even to include role-playing which most people simply take for granted: role-playing in school, at the office, at parties, and so on. In fact, all of life is role and theater—appearance.

But granted that all acting is impersonation, what moved Tyler to designate Garbo's acting specifically as "drag"? Drag means, first of all, role-playing. The way in which it defines role-playing contains its implicit attitude. The word "drag" attaches specifically to the outward, visible appurtenances of a role. In the type case, sex role, drag primarily refers to the wearing apparel and accessories that designate a human being as male or female, when it is worn by the opposite sex. By focusing on the outward appearance of role, drag implies that sex role and, by extension, role in general is something superficial, which can be manipulated, put on and off again at will. The drag concept implies *distance* between the actor and the role or "act." But drag also means "costume." This theatrical referent is the key to the attitude toward role-playing embodied in drag as camp. Role-playing is *play;* it is an act or show. The necessity to play at life, living role after superficial role, should not be the cause of bitterness or despair. Most of the sex role and other impersonations that male homosexuals do are done with ease, grace, and especially humor. The actor should throw himself into it; he should put on a good show; he should view the whole experience as fun, as a camp.[16]

The double stance toward role, putting on a good show while indicating distance (showing that it is a show) is the heart of drag as camp. Garbo's acting was thought to be "drag" because it was considered markedly androgynous, and because she played (even overplayed) the role of femme fatale with style. No man (in her movies) and very few audiences (judging by her success) could resist her allure. And yet most of the men she seduced were her victims because she was only playing at love—only acting. This is made quite explicit in the film *Mata Hari*, in which Garbo the spy seduces men to get information from them.

The third quality of camp is its *humor.* Camp is for fun; the aim of camp is to make an audience laugh. In fact, it is a *system* of humor. Camp humor is a system of laughing at one's incongruous position instead of crying.[17] That is, the humor does not cover up, it transforms. I saw the reverse transformation—from laughter to pathos—often enough, and it is axiomatic among the impersonators that when the camp cannot laugh, he dissolves into a maudlin bundle of self-pity.

One of the most confounding aspects of my interaction with the impersonators was their tendency to laugh at situations that to me were horrifying or tragic. I was amazed, for instance, when one impersonator described to me as "very campy" the scene in *Whatever Happened to Baby Jane* in which Bette Davis served Joan Crawford a rat, or the scene in which Bette Davis makes her "comeback" in the parlor with the piano player.

Of course, not all impersonators and not all homosexuals are campy. *The camp is a homosexual wit and clown*; his campy productions and performances are a continuous creative strategy for dealing with the homosexual situation, and, in the process, defining a positive homosexual identity. As one performer summed it up for me, "Homosexuality is a way of life that is against all ways of life, including nature's. And no one is more aware of it than the homosexual. The camp accepts his role as a homosexual and flaunts his homosexuality. He makes the other homosexuals laugh; he makes life a little brighter for them. And he builds a bridge to the straight people by getting them to laugh with him." The same man described the role of the camp more concretely in an interview:

> Well, "to camp" actually means "to sit in front of a group of people" . . . not on-stage, but you *can* camp on-stage . . . I think that I do that when I talk to the audience. I think I'm camping with 'em. But a "camp" herself is a queen who sits and starts entertaining a group of people at a bar around her. They all start listening to what she's got to say. And she says campy things. Oh, somebody smarts off at her and she gives 'em a very flip answer. A camp is a flip person who has declared emotional freedom. She is going to say to the world, "I'm queer." Although she may not do this all the time, but most of the time a camp queen will. She'll walk down the street and she'll see you and say, "Hi, Mary, how are you?" right in the busiest part of town . . . she'll actually camp, right there. And she'll swish down the street. And she may be in a business suit; she doesn't have to be dressed outlandishly. Even at work the people figure that she's a camp. They don't know what to *call* her, but they hire her 'cause she's a good kid, keeps the office laughing, doesn't bother anybody, and everyone'll say, "Oh, running around with Georgie's more fun! He's just more fun!" The squares are saying this. And the other ones [homosexuals] are saying, "Oh, you've got to know George, she's a camp." Because the whole time she's light-hearted. Very seldom is camp sad. Camp has got to be flip. A camp queen's got to think faster than other queens. *This* makes her camp. She's got to have an answer to anything that's put to her. . . .[18]

Now *homosexuality* is *not* camp. But you take a camp, and she turns around and she makes homosexuality funny, but not ludicrous: funny but not ridiculous . . . this is a great, great art. This is a fine thing. . . . Now when it suddenly became the word . . . became like . . . it's like the word "Mary." Everybody's "Mary." "Hi, Mary. How are you, Mary." And like "girl." You may be talking to one of the butchest queens in the world, but you still say, "Oh, girl." And sometimes they say, "Well, don't call me 'she' and don't call me 'girl.' I don't feel like a girl. I'm a *man*. I just like to go to bed with you *girls*. I don't want to go to bed with another man." And you say, "Oh, girl, get you. Now she's turned butch." And so you camp about it. It's sort of laughing at yourself instead of crying. And a good camp will make you laugh along with her, to where you suddenly feel . . . you don't feel like she's made fun of you. She's sort of made light of a bad situation.

The camp queen makes no bones about it; to him the gay world is the "sisterhood." By accepting his homosexuality and flaunting it, the camp undercuts all homosexuals who won't accept the stigmatized identity. Only by fully embracing the stigma itself can one neutralize the sting and make it laughable.[19] Not all references to the stigma are campy, however. Only if it is pointed out as a joke is it camp, although there is no requirement that the jokes be gentle or friendly. A lot of camping is extremely hostile; it is almost always sarcastic. But its intent is humorous as well. Campy queens are very often said to be "bitches" just as camp humor is said to be "bitchy."[20] The campy queen who can "read" (put down) all challengers and cut everyone down to size is admired. Humor is the campy queen's weapon. A camp queen in good form can come out on top (by group consensus) against all the competition.

Female impersonators who use drag in a comic way or are themselves comics are considered camps by gay people. (Serious glamour drag is considered campy by many homosexuals, but it is unintentional camp. Those who see glamour drag as a serious business do not consider it to be campy. Those who think it is ludicrous for drag queens to take themselves seriously see the whole business as a campy incongruity.) Since the camp role is a positive one, many impersonators take pride in being camps, at least on stage.[21] Since the camp role depends to such a large extent on verbal agility, it reinforces the superiority of the live performers over record performers, who, even if they are comic, must depend wholly on visual effects.

Notes

1. In two Broadway plays (since made into movies) dealing with English homosexuals, *The Killing of Sister George* (lesbians) and *Staircase* (male homosexuals), drag played a prominent role. In *George*, an entire scene shows George and her lover dressed in tuxedos and top hats on their

way to a drag party. In *Staircase,* the entire plot turns on the fact that one of the characters has been arrested for "going in drag" to the local pub. Throughout the second act, this character wears a black shawl over his shoulders. This item of clothing is symbolic of full drag. This same character is a camp and, in my opinion, George was a very rare bird, a lesbian camp. Both plays, at any rate, abounded in camp humor. *The Boys in the Band,* another recent play and movie, doesn't feature drag as prominently but has two camp roles and much camp humor.

2. This concept was developed and suggested to me by Julian Pitt-Rivers.

3. Even one feminine item ruins the integrity of the masculine system; the male loses his caste honor. The superordinate role in a hierarchy is more fragile than the subordinate. Manhood must be achieved, and once achieved, guarded and protected.

4. The middle-class idea tends to be that any man who has had sexual relations with men is queer. The lower classes strip down to "essentials," and the man who is "dominant" can be normal (masculine). Lower-class men give themselves a bit more leeway before they consider themselves to be gay.

5. It becomes clear that the core of the stigma is in "wrong" sexual object choice when it is considered that there is little stigma in simply being effeminate, or even in wearing feminine apparel in some contexts, as long as the male is known to be heterosexual, that is, known to sleep with women or, rather, not to sleep with men. But when I say that sleeping with men is the core of the stigma, or that feminine behavior logically corresponds with this, I do not mean it in any causal sense. In fact, I have an impression that some homosexual men sleep with men *because* it strengthens their identification with the feminine role, rather than the other way around. This makes a lot of sense developmentally, if one assumes, as I do, that children learn sex-role identity before they learn any strictly sexual object choices. In other words, I think that children learn they are boys or girls before they are made to understand that boys *only* love girls and vice versa.

6. The role of the "pretty boy" is also a very positive one, and in some ways the camp is an alternative for those who are not pretty. However, the pretty boy is subject to the depredations of aging, which in the subculture is thought to set in at thirty (at the latest). Because the camp depends on inventiveness and wit rather than on physical beauty, he is ageless.

7. Charles Keil, *Urban Blues* (Chicago: University of Chicago Press, 1966), 164–90.

8. This phrase is used by Kenneth Burke in reference to poetry and is used by Keil in a sociological sense.

9. Erving Goffman, *Stigma* (Englewood Cliffs, N.J.: Prentice-Hall, 1963).

10. I would say that the main problem today is heterosexuals, just as the main problem for blacks is whites.

11. Keil, *Urban Blues,* 165.

12. I don't want to pass over the implication here that female impersonators keep up with Susan Sontag. Generally, they don't. I had given an informant Susan Sontag's "Notes on 'Camp' " (*Partisan Review* [Fall, 1964]: 515–30) to see what he would say. He was college educated and perfectly able to get through it. He was enraged (justifiably, I felt) that she had almost edited homosexuals out of camp.

13. Informants said that many ideas had been taken over by straights through the mass media, but that the moment this happened the idea would no longer be campy. For instance, one man said that a queen he knew had gotten the idea of growing plants in the water tank of the toilet. But the idea is no longer campy because it is being advertised through such mass media as *Family Circle* magazine.

How to defend *any* symbols or values from the absorbing powers of the mass media? Jules Henry, I believe, was one of the first to point to the power of advertising to subvert traditional values by appropriating them for commercial purposes (*Culture against Man*, New York: Random House, 1963). But subcultural symbols and values lose their integrity in the same way. Although Sontag's New York avant-garde had already appropriated camp from homosexuals, they did so in the effort to create their own aristocracy or integrity of taste as against the mass culture.

14. Sontag, "Notes on 'Camp,'" 529.

15. Parker Tyler, "The Garbo Image," in *The Films of Greta Garbo*, ed. Michael Conway, Dion McGregor, and Mark Ricci (New York: Citadel Press, n.d.), 9–31. Citations from 12, 28.

16. It is clear to me now how camp undercuts rage and therefore rebellion by ridiculing serious and concentrated bitterness.

17. It would be worthwhile to compare camp humor with the humor systems of other oppressed people (Eastern European Jewish, Negro, etc.).

18. Speed and spontaneity are of the essence. For example, at a dinner party, someone said, "Oh, we forgot to say grace." One woman folded her hands without missing a beat and intoned, "Thank God everyone at this table is gay."

19. It's important to stress again that camp is a pre- or protopolitical phenomenon. The anticamp in this system is the person who wants to dissociate from the stigma to be like the oppressors. The camp says, "I am not like the oppressors." But in so doing he agrees with the oppressors' definition of who he is. The new radicals deny the stigma in a different way, by saying that the oppressors are illegitimate. This step is only foreshadowed in camp. It is also interesting that the lesbian wing of the radical homosexuals have come to women's meetings holding signs saying: "We are the women your parents warned you against."

20. The "bitch," as I see it, is a woman who *accepts* her inferior status, but refuses to do so gracefully or without fighting back. Women and homosexual men are oppressed by straight men, and it is no accident that both are beginning to move beyond bitchiness toward refusal of inferior status.

21. Many impersonators told me that they got tired of being camps for their friends, lovers, and acquaintances. They often felt they were asked to gay parties simply to entertain and camp it up, and said they did not feel like camping off stage, or didn't feel competent when out of drag. This broadens out into the social problem of all clowns and entertainers, or, even further, to anyone with a talent. He will often wonder if he is loved for himself.

Uses of Camp

ANDREW ROSS

"It's beige! *My* color!"

—Elsie De Wolfe, on
facing the Parthenon for the first time

Take four iconic moments from the sixties:

1961: *Whatever Happened to Baby Jane?* the first "women's picture," as Bette Davis pointed out, for over ten years, bringing together, for the first time, the aging, uncrowned royalty of classic Hollywood—Davis and Joan Crawford. "Baby Jane" Hudson, ex-child-star, now grotesquely made-up (at Davis's own inspirational insistence) like a pantomime Ugly Sister, serves up steamed rat to her wheelchair-bound sister Blanche, a big star in the thirties, until her career was tragically cut short by a car accident. Blanche spins in terror in her wheelchair, shot from above; Jane laughs from the belly up, her face twitching with glee. Their House of Usheresque present refracts the Babylonish history of Hollywood stardom, while it creates a new horror film genre for the new decade.

1964: A different Baby Jane, in a New York photographer's studio in the year of the British Invasion—Baby Jane Holzer, in Tom Wolfe's "Girl of the Year," cavorting at her twenty-fourth birthday party which doubled as a publicity stunt for her star guests, the Rolling Stones. Back from the London "Pop" summer of 1963, sporting the Chelsea Look, and talking Cockney ("Anything beats being a Park Avenue housewife"), Holzer, for Wolfe, for *Vogue,* and for Andy Warhol, is the living symptom of the new, pluralistic, "classless" melting pot culture, where socialites—though not the Social Register type—enthusiastically took up the styles and subcultural idioms of arriviste "raw-vital proles" (the party's theme was Mods vs. Rockers), albeit by way of the exotic British importation of "East End vitality" ("they're all from the working class, you know").

1969: The evening of the funeral of Judy Garland (a long-time gay icon), members of the New York City Vice Squad come under fire, from beer cans, bottles, coins, and cobblestones, as they try to arrest some of the regulars at the Stonewall Inn in Christopher Street. The mood of the protesters, many of them street queens in full drag, had changed from that of reveling in the spectacle of the arrest, even posing for it, to one of anger and rage, as one of the detainees, a lesbian, struggled to resist her arrest. Within minutes, the police were besieged within the burning bar. Some of those present heard the chant "Gay Power," while others only saw a more defiant than usual show of posing; it wasn't clear whether this confrontation was "the Hairpin Drop Heard around the World" or the "Boston Tea-Party" of a political movement.

Later in 1969: A different scene of violence at the Altamont free festival, the dark sequel to Woodstock, and the Stones again, Jagger up front, berobed and mascara'd, swishing, mincing, and strutting before a huge audience barely in check, while on every side of the stage are posted Hell's Angels, confrontation dressers all—the sometime darlings of hardliners who saw in them a critique of the counterculture's "male impotence." Here employed as "soft" police, they stare, bluntly and disdainfully, at the narcissistic Jagger, some of them openly mocking his turns and gyres, while the offstage violence escalates, to end soon in the death of eighteen-year-old Meredith Hunter, caught on film in *Gimme Shelter,* the Stones's blatant attempt at self-vindication, in which Jagger poses the rhetorical question: "Why does something always happen when we start to play that song?"—"Sympathy for the Devil."

There are many common sixties themes that could link these moments together. And for those who like to tell the "story" of the sixties, such moments would probably mark significant points in the stock narrative of rise and fall, of hope and disillusion, which has become the dominant or favored media version of that decade's events. The purpose they serve here is to illustrate particular aspects of the history of *camp,* that category of cultural taste, which, more than anything else, shaped, defined, and negotiated the way in which intellectuals of the sixties tried to "pass" as newly enlightened subscribers to the Pop aesthetic in the attractive, throwaway world of immediacy created by the mass culture industries. On the importance to the sixties of this category of taste, George Melly, the English jazz musician and Pop intellectual, was adamant: camp was "central to almost every difficult transitional moment in the evolution of pop culture. . . . [it] helped pop make a forced march around good taste."[1]

But if there is a story to tell about the transitional function of camp as an *operation of taste,* then it will be a story of unequal and uneven development. It will demonstrate the different uses and meanings camp generated for different groups, subcultures and elites in the sixties. The exercise of camp taste raised different issues, for example, for gay people *before* and *after* 1969; for gay males and lesbians; for women, lesbian and straight, before and after the various movements for sexual liberation; for straight men, before and after the call to androgyny had been fully sounded; for traditional intellectuals (obliged now, in spite of their prejudices, to go "slumming") and organic intellectuals (whose loyalty to the Pop ethic of instant gratification and expendability left little space for political philosophy or discriminations of resistance); for disadvantaged working-class subcultures (whose relation to Pop culture was a glamorous, and seldom inadequate, semiotic of their aspirations and dreams of social mobility and leisure) and the middle-class counterculture (whose wholesale withdrawal from the everyday commodity world thrived upon a heady, premodernist fantasy of self-sufficiency).

While it would be wrong to see camp as the privileged expression of any of these groups, even the traditional pre-Stonewall, gay male culture for which the most legitimate claim can be made, there are certain common conditions which must be stressed. Just as the new presence of the masses in the social and cultural purview of the postwar State had required a shift in the balance of *containment* of popular democracy, so too, the reorganization of the capital bases of the cultural industries, the new media technology and the new modes of distribution that accompanied that shift necessarily changed the aesthetic face of categories of taste. New markets—youth and swinging "Playboy" males in the fifties (to be followed by women in the sixties and gays in the seventies)—had produced massive changes in the patterns of consumption. These changes, in turn, produced the affluence and the material social conditions out of which the newly constructed, interlocking subcultures of the fifties emerged in the sixties as visible phenomena in the writing of Wolfe and Pop intellectuals. The changes in cultural technologies had quite specific effects, which I shall discuss, in turn, with respect to the four iconic moments with which I began.

What triggers the narrative action and the new sadistic-jealous mood of "Baby Jane" Hudson is the showing of one of Blanche's old movies on television. The most recent version of the myth of Old Hollywood was in decline, the star-system had foundered, and the whole corporate economy of the studio system had been challenged, outpaced, and largely outdated by the television industry. The late fifties and early sixties saw the recirculation of classic Hollywood films on television, giving rise to the first wave of revivalist nostalgia, and to the cult of Hollywoodiana—with all of those necrophilic trappings that embellish its decadent fascination with the links between glamour and death.² No longer was this a taste reserved for members of film societies and clubs or for avant-garde filmmakers like the celebrated Jack Smith, who had studied every frame of certain thirties films and whose cult of Maria Montez, one of the most cherished of the pantheon of camp screen goddesses, was to irradiate important sectors of the early "Underground" film scene.

True to Hollywood logic, of course, the stylized morbidity of this cult had long since become an institution—a horror film subgenre—in its own right. In Billy Wilder's *Sunset Boulevard* (1950), Hollywood had produced its baroque funeral elegy for silent film. Joe Gillis (William Holden), the young, down-on-his-luck scriptwriter and heel, recognizes the hallmark of movie history in the faded glamour of Norma Desmond (Gloria Swanson): "You used to be in silent pictures. You used to be big." Desmond shoots back: "I *am* big. It's the pictures that got small." In a sense Desmond is correct (in spite of Gillis's painfully crass and "authoritative" voiceover, Norma is almost always correct). But her outrageous self-conceits and her tirades against "words," "writing," and "dialogue" can only produce their truly camp effect in a film, like Wilder's, that relies so heavily upon words and dialogue, and in which the new Hollywood—the "smallness" of today's pictures—is represented by the no-nonsense, professional earnestness of Betty Schaefer (Nancy Olson), a scriptreader who finds "social interest" themes to develop in the scripts of the noirish gigolo Gillis.

The cult meaning of Norma Desmond's *grande damerie* is generated out of a contemporary predicament, which is suggested here by the incongruous juxtaposition of the present with the trauma of the passing of silent film. By 1950, the studio star-system, already in trouble with television, is entering its last phase—the Monroe phase. The anxiety of that moment is ironically figured in another film of the same year, Joseph Mankiewicz's *All about Eve,* in which a young Monroe plays the role of a talentless ingénue in hot pursuit of a career in one of the vacuums created by the retirement of a great Broadway actress (played by Bette Davis), while the traditional hierarchy of prestige between Broadway and Hollywood is broadened to include a third, and much despised, term—television (as the theater critic in the film, Addison De Witt, affirms: "That's all television is, my dear, nothing *but* auditions"). As Hollywood is passing out of its "bourgeois" moment, the origins of that moment are invoked in the spectacle of Norma Desmond, a residual survivor of the pre-bourgeois age of screen gods and goddesses, whose crumbling aristocracy now serves as a displaced symptom of the current, further decline (or increased democratization) of the film medium. It is the historical incongruity of this displacement that creates the world of tragic-ironic meanings that camp exploits.

Over a decade later, a similar collision of meanings ensures the success of the macabre tragicomedy of *Whatever Happened to Baby Jane?* The conclusion of this film is more incongruous yet. Where Norma Desmond noirishly basks, at the ending of *Sunset Boulevard,* in the garish light of camera flashes, and in the knowledgeable attention of a crowd of reporters and voyeurist hangers-on, Jane Hudson strikes up her blithe child-star routine in the beach heat of a California sun, surrounded by an oblivious group of teenagers.

The camp effect, then, is created not simply by a change in the mode of cultural production (and the contradictions attendant on that change), but rather when the products (stars, in this case) of a much earlier mode of production, which has lost its power to produce and dominate cultural meanings, become available, in the present, for redefinition according to contemporary codes of taste.

A similar relation to disempowered modes of production can be seen in the importance of the so-called British invasion to the Pop version of camp. For here was the first evidence of a foreign culture making sense of the American popular culture which had been widely exported abroad since the war. For Britons, the importation of American popular culture, even as it was officially despised, contained, and controlled, brought with it guaranteed immunity to those traditional "European" judgments of elitist taste to which it was structurally oblivious.[3] By the early sixties, the "success" of this wave of American exports among British tastemakers was such that they were able to set the final seal of approval on the formation and acceptance of Pop taste in the United States itself. Thus, the British version of Pop (always an *imaginary* relation to a foreign culture—James Hadley Chase, for example, invented the America of his many best-selling novels, after one short visit to Florida as a tourist)[4] was somehow needed to legitimize American pop culture for Americans in accord with the higher canons of European taste to which they were still, in some way, obliged to defer.

The "camp" moment in this complex process, however, is the ironic recognition of the eclipsed capacity of real British power to play the imperialist game of dominating foreign taste. That is why the British flag, for Mods and other subcultures, and Victoriana, for the later Sergeant Pepper culture, became camp objects; precisely because of their historical association with a power that was now spent. The Stars and Stripes, and Americana, by contrast, could only be kitsch, because its serious intentions were still the historical support of a culture that holds real imperialist power in defining the shape of foreign cultures. It makes sense, then, to find, in "Girl of the Year" that the "supermarvellous" Baby Jane Holzer plays her part opposite a group of Cockney primitives, or Teen Savages, among whom Jagger is described as almost not human, "with his wet giblet lips," speaking a deformed language, a slurred, incomprehensible "Bull Negro" when he is not mumbling a forcibly inarticulate native Cockney. At the very moment when the balance of a transatlantic taste is being redefined, it is only fitting that Wolfe invoke terms and images from the historical discourse of colonial subjugation. (Elsewhere he describes the natives of his "discovered" Californian subcultures as "Easter Islanders."[5]—Who are they and how did they achieve this level of civilization?)

But what was the meaning of this newly proclaimed "classless" culture? The purist Pop intellectual like Warhol simply proclaimed that everyone (and everything) was equal: "It was fun to see the Museum of Modern Art people next to the teeny-boppers next to the amphetamine queens next to the fashion editors."[6] Others, like Wolfe, made righteous claims about the new cultural power of the disenfranchised—"now high style comes from low places . . . the poor boys . . . teenagers, bohos, camp culturati . . . have won by default"—and went on to emphasize the pioneering risks they themselves were taking to champion those who had neither "stature nor grandeur": the "petty bureaucrats, Mafiosi, line soldiers in Vietnam, pimps, hustlers, doormen, socialites, shyster lawyers, surfers, bikers, hippies and other accursed Youth, evangelists, athletes. . . ."[7] While for intellectuals like Susan Sontag, with more traditional knee-jerk avant-garde tastes, it meant a passport from the top down (but not necessarily from the bottom up) to all corners of a cultural garden of earthly delights: "From the vantage point of this new sensibility, the beauty of a machine or of the solution to a mathematical problem, of a painting by Jasper Johns, of a film by Jean-Luc Godard, and of the personalities and music of the Beatles is of equal access."[8]

Each of these responses pays tribute in its own way to the official national ideology of liberal pluralism; a heterogeneous set of culturally diverse groups with "special interests," ranged together in harmonious coexistence. The noncommittal, "documentary" stance of many Pop intellectuals, while it was an important break with the morally charged paternalism of their forebears, did little to expose what the liberal pluralist model had excluded—all of the signs of conflict generated by the uneven development of the "affluent society," and the antagonism of huge numbers of oppressed people excluded by or marginalized within the new pluralist conjuncture. In fact, Wolfe's use of the term "subculture" as a "statusphere" appealed to a simple, functionalist description of an autonomous group seeking its share of the pie. There was no consideration of the conflicts and contradictions that result from the antagonistic relation of any single subculture to a parent culture, or from its relation to other subcultures, or from multiple membership in different groups and subcultures.[9]

That the existence of a pluralistic range of subcultures does not spell harmony, and that even a counterhegemonic bloc of oppositional subcultures will be riven with internal contradictions proved to be one of the "lessons" of the sixties. Hence the mock-heroic anger and frustration of Wolfe at the turn of events in the later sixties, when a law-and-order, or "control," society was hurriedly being put in place to contain the antiwar movement. Appearing in a symposium at Princeton with Paul Krassner, Günter Grass, Allen Ginsberg, and Gregory Markopoulos, he is blithely offended by their talk of police repression, "the knock on the door" and other strategies of coercion. "What are you talking about?" he said. "We're in the middle of a Happiness Explosion."[10]

The deficiencies of the liberal pluralist model can be seen more clearly in the examples of Altamont and Stonewall, where subcultures within the evolved "counterculture" are at odds with each other. The Pop slogans of immediate gratification, hedonism, accessibility had informed a grammar of achievement and mobility for working-class cultures. For the middle-class counterculture, they had also come to generate a vocabulary of dissent and antiauthoritarianism, wielded against the guardians of a system struggling to resolve, through consumerism, its long crisis of overproduction. As a result, the discourses of hedonism began to outstrip the limits of the controlled structures of consumer society, and soon a wholesale ideology of disaffiliation from the institutions of Establishment culture was in place, complete with its own alternative structures (in the areas of family, education, labor, media, taste, lifestyle, and morality), founded upon utopian premises. Loosely incorporating the dominant white student faction of the New Left (itself divided between sectarian political elements and, increasingly, along gender lines), this countercultural bloc was obliged, largely by the pressure of the media's definition of its aims, to recognize its alternative culture heroes (its own organic intellectuals) as leaders *even as* it proclaimed its self-reliance (that is, reliance on grass-roots community organizations), and thus its opposition to vanguardist leadership.[11]

One example of this contradiction was the running battle, from the mid-sixties on, with the youth-oriented entertainment industries who sought to absorb, assimilate, and exploit countercultural values for profit, and whose management of this process increasingly demanded the celebrification of rock stars as culture hero-leaders. The free music festival became a privileged symbol of this struggle, a test of the capacity to mobilize the alternative networks in support of a vast noncommercial celebration of the "liberated" sector of the population. At Altamont, planned as little more than an end-of-tour publicity stunt for the Rolling Stones, the violence, associated with the "retarded" masculinity of the Hell's Angels, and the "bad vibes," associated with exploitative drug trafficking, came to be seen as symptomatic of the contradictions of the counterculture. In fact, it is important to see that the Angels, recruited as alternative "police," represented a different, working-class, ethic of *delin-*

quency, which, unlike the counterculture, had never sought to devolve itself entirely from the parent culture, and which retained its suspicion and resentment of the libertarian privileges of student and other middle-class cultures. Although they found it offensive to be cast as "police," and were right in thinking they were being patronized (no properly countercultural group would play this role), they were in fact more likely to be found marching against the students (as happened in Berkeley) and with the real riot police, with whom they shared a common, if uneasy, class constituency.[12]

At Stonewall, where a traditionally persecuted minority group fought back and made history, but not under conditions of its own making, a more clearcut picture of the new "control" society emerges. The immediate local problem at stake in the Stonewall "riots" was as much Mafia control of gay bars as routine acts of police repression.[13] Thus, the commercial control of a gay subculture that existed hitherto as a network of codes of concealment was *already* an issue in the founding moment of the overtly *identified* subculture that was soon to emerge under the aegis of Gay Pride, Gay Power, and the Gay Liberation Front (GLF). Formed explicitly on the model of the civil-rights movement for blacks, the gay liberation movement was committed to going beyond the reformist aims—polite integration—of the liberal homophile politics that had been urged since the early fifties by the Mattachine Society and the Daughters of Bilitis.[14] Inheriting the irreverent but militant style of the New Left, and following the example of community organizing fostered in the South by the Student Nonviolent Coordinating Committee (SNCC), gay leaders contended that the liberation movement could not simply be a question of gay businessmen taking control of the bars, stores, and clubs; alternative institutions had to be created. The success of the lesbian community in creating such a network of institutions (along with its crucial participation in the women's movement) has been seen as the most positive legacy of this movement. For gay males— one of the prime target, higher-income, cachet groups that were ripe for new consumer marketing in the seventies—the gains have been less certain. Today, gay intellectuals who were active in the GLF or the Gay Activists Alliance view with ambivalence the commercial development of the gay scene and the complicity of gay communities in the creation of that scene.[15] Today's gay male is the "new model intellectual" of consumer capitalism, at the forefront of the business of shaping and defining taste, choice, and style for mainstream markets. So too, the sexual freedoms won by the liberation movements are often inseparable from the commodification of sex, on the one hand, and the use of categories of sexuality to socially control and quarantine groups identified by sexual orientation, on the other.

It is in this dialectic between sexual *liberation* and corporate-State *regulation* that we can locate the problems faced by gay cultural politics, today, in a control society reinforced by its capacity to define the "threat" of AIDS on its own terms. How does a subculture make sense of this dialectic? This is where the question of "camp," which is often posed as an embarrassment to post-Stonewall gay culture ("the Stepin Fetchit of the leather bars"),[16] becomes political all over again, not only because of its articulate engagement with the (commodity) world of popular taste, but also because camp contains an explicit commentary on feats of *survival* in a world dominated by the taste and interests of those whom it serves.

Camp Oblige

In her seminal "Notes on Camp" (1964), Susan Sontag raises the question of survival in a quite specific way: "Camp is the answer to the problem; how to be a dandy in an age of mass culture."[17] Her formula—one among many memorable aperçus to be found in her essay—suggests that what is under attack in an age of mass culture is precisely the power of taste-making intellectuals to patrol the higher canons of taste, and that the significance of the "new sensibility" of camp in the sixties is that it presents a means of salvaging that privilege.

The pseudoaristocratic patrilineage of camp can hardly be overstated. Consider the etymological provenance of the three most questionable categories of American cultural taste: schlock, kitsch, and camp. None is of Anglo origin, although it is clear, from their cultural derivation, where they belong on the scale of prestige: *Schlock,* from Yiddish (literally, "damaged goods" at a cheap price), *Kitsch,* from German, petty bourgeois, and *Camp,* more obscurely from the French *se camper,* with a long history of upper-class English usage. While schlock is truly unpretentious—nice things in nice taste—and is designed primarily to fill a space in people's lives and environments, kitsch has serious pretensions to artistic taste, and, in fact, contains a range of references to high or legitimate culture which it apes in order to flatter its owner-reader-consumer. Its seriousness about art, and its aesthetic chutzpah is associated with the class aspirations and upward mobility of a middlebrow audience, deemed "insufficient" in cultural capital to merit access to legitimate culture.[18]

Of course, kitsch is no more a fixed category than schlock or camp. These categories are constantly shifting, their contents are constantly changing; what is promoted one year may be relegated again the next. What is important is their persistently subordinate relation to the dominant culture, by which they are defined as examples of "failed taste." Neither can they be regarded as categories defined with equal objectivity but which signify different value, since schlock and kitsch are more often seen as categories of objects, while camp tends to refer to a subjective process: Camp, as Thomas Hess put it, "exists in the smirk of the beholder."[19] If certain objects and texts tend to be associated with camp more readily than others, they are often described as "campy," suggesting a self-consciousness about their lack of pretension which would otherwise, and more accurately, be attributed to the sophisticated beholder. Not surprisingly, Sontag downgrades this self-consciousness, reserving her purist praise for the category of *naive* camp, presumably because, with the latter, it is the critic and not the producer who takes full cultural credit for discerning the camp "value" of a text.

It is clear, at any rate, that the division between kitsch and camp partially reflects a division between manual and mental labor, or, in camp's own terminology, between ignorati and cognoscenti. The producer or consumer of kitsch either is unaware of the extent to which his or her intentions or pretensions are alienated in the kitsch text, or else is made to feel painfully aware of this alienation in some way. Camp, on the other hand, involves a celebration, on the part of cognoscenti, of the alienation, distance, and incongruity reflected in the very process by which it locates hitherto unexpected value in a popular or obscure text. Camp would thus be reserved for those with a high degree of cultural capital. It belongs to those who have the accredited confidence to be able to devote their idiosyncratic attention to the practice of cultural slumming in places where others would feel less comfortable.

Just as it is absurd to speak of a lasting canon or pantheon of camp texts, objects, and figures (though such exclusive lists do exist, temporarily, for certain groups who "use" camp), universal definitions of camp are rarely useful. In Philip Core's encyclopedia of camp, for example, camp is defined as "the lie that tells the truth" or as "the heroism of people not called upon to be heroes," while Christopher Isherwood finds that camp is a matter of "expressing what's basically serious to you in terms of fun and artifice and elegance."[20] This is why Sontag chose to write her essay about this "fugitive sensibility" in the form of notes or jottings, although her decision to do so has as much to do with her unpolitical conviction that there are "almost, but not quite, ineffable" causes which give rise to a "logic of taste," as it has to do with her expressed anxiety about writing something ridiculous—"a very inferior piece of camp," as she puts it. More useful is Mark Booth's expanded and exhaustive account of Sontag's "pocket history of camp" (her note no. 14—embracing rococo, mannerism, *les précieux*, Yellow Book aestheticism, art nouveau), a history that is polemically governed by his thesis that "to be camp is to present oneself as being committed to the marginal with a commitment greater than the marginal merits." The advantage of this formulation is that it clearly defines camp *in relation to the exercise of cultural power*. Booth argues, for example, that camp, far from being a "fugitive sensibility," belongs to the history of the "self-presentation" of arriviste groups. Because of their marginality, because they lack inherited cultural capital, and thus the accredited power to fully legitimize dominant tastes, these groups parody their subordinate or uncertain social status in "a self-mocking abdication of any pretensions to power."[21]

Unlike the traditional intellectual, whose function is to legitimize the cultural power of a ruling group, or the organic intellectual, who promotes the interests of a rising class, the marginal (or camp) intellectual expresses his impotence as the dominated fraction of a ruling bloc in order to remain there (i.e., as a nonthreatening presence) while he distances himself from the conventional morality and taste of the growing middle class. The nineteenth-century camp intellectual may well be a parody or negation of dominant bourgeois forms: anti-industry, pro-idleness; antifamily, probachelorhood; antirespectability, proscandal; antimasculine, profeminine; antisport, profrivolity; antidecor, proexhibitionism; antiprogress, prodecadence; antiwealth, profame. But his aristocratic affectations are a sign of his *disqualification,* or remoteness from power, because they comfortably symbolize, to the bourgeois, the deceased power of the aristocrat, while they are equally removed from the threatening, embryonic power of the masses.

Hitherto associated with the high-culture milieu of the theater, camp intellectuals become an institution in the twentieth century, within the popular entertainment industries, reviving their role there as the representative or stand-in for a class that is no longer in a position to exercise its power to define official culture. So too, they maintain their parodic critique of the properly educated and responsibly situated intellectual who speaks with the requisite tone of moral authority and seriousness as the conscience and consciousness of society as a whole (i.e., as the promoter of ruling interests).

Thus it is ironic that Sontag chooses to link her account of the (largely homosexual) influence of camp taste with the intellectual successes of Jewish moral seriousness, as the two "pioneering forces of modern sensibility" (note no. 51). More than any other publication, her essay (and the book in which it appeared, *Against Interpretation*), signaled the challenge to, if not the demise of, the tradition of Jewish moral seriousness that had governed the cultural crusading of the cold-war liberal. Not that Sontag herself is willing to jettison entirely the prerogative of the liberal's act of judgment; in fact, she is careful to record her ambivalence about camp—"a deep sympathy modified by revulsion." Nonetheless, the importance of her own critical intervention in the mid-sixties was in the service of pleasure and erotics, and against judgment, seriousness, interpretation; against, in short, the hermeneutics of depth with which established intellectuals—the New Critics and the New York Intellectuals alike—had dictated literary taste since the war.

Camp, in the form in which it came to be received and practiced in the sixties, symbolized an important break with the style and legitimacy of the old liberal intellectual. I shall now examine two important contexts of this break: first, Pop, and its reorientation of attitudes toward mass culture; and second, the question of sexual liberation, the redefinition of masculinity, and the concomitant rise of the gay movements.

Pop Camp

In England in the fifties, the fledgling studies of Pop by members of the International Group at the Institute of Contemporary Art had come directly out of the postwar mass culture debates. Against the cold-war "consensus" thesis about manipulation, standardization, and lobotomization, Reyner Banham and others argued that the consumers of mass culture were experts, trained to a high degree of connoisseurship in matters of consumer choice and consumer use; for them, there was no such thing as an "unsophisticated consumer."[22] Lawrence Alloway wrote passionately against the received wisdom that mass culture produced a passive, undifferentiated audience of dupes:

> We speak for convenience about a mass audience but it is a fiction. The audience today is numerically dense but highly diversified. Just as the wholesale use of subception techniques in advertising is blocked by the different perception capacities of the members of any audience, so the mass media cannot reduce everybody to one drugged faceless consumer. Fear of the Amorphous Audience is fed by the word "mass." In fact, audiences are specialized by age, sex, hobby, occupation, mobility, contacts, etc. Although the interests of different audiences may not be rankable in the curriculum of the traditional educationist, they nevertheless reflect and influence the diversification which goes with increased industrialization.[23]

In the drab cultural climate of Britain in the fifties, popular culture and mass media were much more than a functional and necessary guide to modern living; they were, in Alloway's eloquent phrase, "a treasury of orientation, a manual of one's occupancy of the twentieth century." To the paternalist Establishment culture, they represented the specter of "Americanization." To the working-class consumer, they brought a taste of glamour, affluence, immediate gratification, and the dream of a pleasure-filled environment to transcend the workaday drudgery of their circumstances. To middle-class aficionados,

American popular culture was a Cockaigne of the perverse intellect, a fantasy of taste turned upside down with which to avenge themselves against the tweedy sponsors of European tradition. The very idea of Richard Hamilton's painting "Hommage à Chrysler Corp," for example, exudes the bittersweet flavor of camp—a highly wrought conceit of the European as a fake American.

While the American experience of commercial, popular culture was, of course, much more *lived* and direct, we should not fall into the trap of assuming that it was less mediated or less fantasmatic. The uses made of comic strips, science fiction, "Detroit" auto styling, Westerns, rock 'n' roll, and neon advertising by different social groups cannot be read as if they were spontaneous responses to real social conditions. On the contrary, they represent an *imaginary relation* to these conditions, and one which is refracted through the powerful lens of the so-called Great American Dream—a pathologically seductive infusion of affluence, ordinariness, and achieved utopian pleasure. The American as a dream American.

Pop's commitment to the new and everyday, to quantity and to the throwaway was a direct affront to those who governed the boundaries of official taste. Nothing could be more execrable to a tradition of taste held together by the precepts of "universality," "timelessness," and "uniqueness" than a culture of obsolescence: that is, designed not to endure. Camp, however, offered a negotiated way by which this most democratic of cultures could be partially "recognized" by intellectuals. In fact, Pop camp, as Melly argues, is a contradiction in terms, because camp is the "in" taste of a minority elite.[24] Pop, on the other hand, was supposed to declare that everyday cultural currency had value, and that everything had more or less equal value. Culture was to be described and enjoyed, not prescribed like a dose of medicine by those with the cultural capital to decide "what's good for you."

In fact, Pop could no more shut out history than the sublime Coke bottle could escape its future as an empty but *returnable* commodity item. For the immediacy and self-sufficiency of the consumption of the Pop experience *already contains the knowledge that it will soon be outdated*—spent, obsolescent, or out of fashion. A throwaway culture, even a disposable culture, moreover, is not one which simply disappears once its meaning has been consumed; whether it figures as waste, to be recycled, or as detritus, to lie in wait until it is tastefully redeemed twenty years hence, it contains messages about the historical *production* of the material and cultural conditions of taste.

This knowledge about history is the precise moment when camp takes over, because camp is a rediscovery of history's waste. Camp irreverently retrieves not only that which had been excluded from the serious high-cultural "tradition," but also the more unsalvageable material that has been picked over and found wanting by purveyors of the "antique." For the camp liberator, as with the high modernist, history's waste matter becomes all too available as a "rag-bag," but irradiated, this time around, with glamour, and not drenched with tawdriness by the mock-heroism of Waste Land irony. But, in "liberating" the past in this way, it also bolsters the economy whereby objects and discourses of disdain are transformed into collector's items. Camp, in this respect is more than just a remembrance of things past, it is the *re-creation of surplus value from forgotten forms of labor.*

By the late sixties, this parasitical practice had become a survivalist way of life for the counterculture, whose patronage of flea markets was a parody of the hand-me-down working-class culture of the rummage sale. The flea-market ethos, like most countercultural values, paid its respects to a notion of prelapsarian authenticity. In an age of plastic, authentic value could only be found in the "real" textures of the past, along with traces of the "real" labor that once went into fashioning clothes and objects. By sporting a whole, exotic range of preindustrial, peasant-identified, or non-Western styles, the students and other denizens of the counterculture were confronting the guardians (and the workaday citizens) of commodity culture with the symbols of a spent historical mode of production, or else one what was "Asiatic," or "underdeveloped." By doing so, they signaled their complete disaffiliation from the semiotic codes of contemporary cultural power. In donning gypsy and denim, however, they were also patronizing the current aspirations of those social groups for whom such clothes called up a long history of poverty, social exclusion, and oppression. And in their maverick Orientalism, they romanticized other cultures by plundering their stereotypes. By contrast, the confrontation dressing of the later punk subculture was staged in the readily accessible, contemporary milieu of consumer culture, and was loosely organized around the tactic of reappropriating and redefining the current meanings of its objects and discourses, rather than invoking historical signifiers already saturated with the unequal opportunities accorded to class, race, sex, and nationhood.

The earlier phase of Pop camp arose directly out of the theatrical encounter of a culture of *immediacy* with the experience of history's amnesia. In reviving a period style, or elements of a period style that were hopelessly, and thus "safely," dated, camp acted as a kind of *memento mori*, a reminder of Pop's own future oblivion which, as I have argued, Pop cannot help but advertise. For the Pop intellectual, camp was also a defense against the threat of being stripped of the traditional panoply of tastemaking powers which Pop's egalitarian mandate poses. Camp was an antidote to Pop's contagion of obsolescence. It is no surprise, then, to find that Sontag had been contemplating an essay on death and morbidity before she decided to write "Notes on Camp."[25] The switch, in her mind from thinking about "mortuary sculpture, architecture, inscriptions and other such wistful lore" to the sociability of camp wit was, perhaps, triggered by a quite understandable flight from the realms of chilled seriousness to the warmer climate of theatrical humor. It is symptomatic, however, of the necrophilic economy that underpins the camp sensibility, not only in its resurrection of deceased cultural forms, but also in the way in which it serves an ambivalent notice of mortality to the contemporary intellect.

When Sontag associates the camp sensibility with the principle of "the equivalence of all objects" (note no. 47), she is making claims for its "democratic esprit." What Sontag means, however, is that camp declares that anything, given the right circumstances, could, in principle, be redeemed by camp. Everything thereby becomes fair game for the camp cognoscenti to pursue and celebrate *at will*. This is a different thing altogether from the "democratic" proposition of Pop philosophy, which simply *complies* with, rather than exploits, the principle of general equivalence. Sontag no doubt acknowledges this difference when she characterizes Pop as "more flat and more dry" ("ultimately nihilistic") than camp, and when she describes camp, by contrast, as "tender," "passionate," and nurtured "on the love that has gone into certain objects and personal styles" (notes 55–56). While Pop tries to disavow the traces of production behind its objects of attention, and concentrates on surface immediacy, camp cultivates an attitude toward the *participation* of the producers, past and present. In effect, the Pop intellectual is the new technocratic recruit, committed to accepting the realm of creative consumerism as the new site of cultural power. Camp, by contrast, celebrates the survival of the avant-garde intellectual, who patronizes and liberates by mobilizing attention to labor as the productivist site of cultural power.

A striking example of what I mean is the inexorable process by which *bad taste*—Sontag's formulation of "the ultimate Camp statement; it's good because it's awful"—has come to be accepted as a semilegitimate expression of its own, and consequently, as a commercial market unto itself. There is no question that camp's patronage of bad taste, which thrives today in the work of John Waters and on the cult "bad film" circuit, was as much an assault on the established canons of taste as Pop's eroticization of the everyday had been. This, however, was by no means a clean break with the logic of cultural capital, for it must also be seen from the point of view of those whom it indirectly patronized, those lower-middle-class groups who, historically, have had to bear the stigma of "failed taste." The objet retrouvé of camp's bad taste could hardly shake off its barbaric associations with the social victimization of its original audience. In fact, this process of camp rehabilitation, which cannot avoid the exploitation of these barbaric associations, lies at the root, today, of that vast and lucrative sector of the culture industry devoted to the production of "exploitation" fare. Camp apologists will say that the initial aim of "bad taste" was to ridicule the institutional solemnity with which social groups were linked to hierarchical cultural categories. There is a thin line, however, between the political appeal of this directed satire and the more unsavory caricature of social taste with which it runs parallel and with which it infrequently joins forces in the fully commercialized forms of bad taste. The fun and pleasure created by camp is often only enjoyed at the expense of others, and this is largely because camp's excess of pleasure, finally, has very little to do with the (un)controlled hedonism of a consumer; it is the work of a producer of taste, and "taste" is only possible through exclusion *and* depreciation.

If we want to look beyond specialized taste, however, then it is in the realm of performance rock, pop, and rock 'n' roll that camp's penchant for the deviant has crossed over the threshold of restricted consumption into the mass milieux of homes, schools, colleges, clubs, and workplaces all over the country. But the outrageousness of performance rock has, among other things, always been something of a family affair—the object of what teenagers (and record-company producers) imagine is every good parent's worst fantasy. It is almost impossible, then, to talk about the history of that ever-shifting pageant of eroticized spectacle, from Elvis's gyrating hips to Annie Lennox's gender-blurred sangfroid, without first giving an account of how sexual difference was articulated, from the late fifties onward, in ways that redefined the social categories of masculinity and femininity, inside and outside the family.

Prisoners of Sex?

Female and male impersonation, representations of androgyny, and other images of gender-blurring have all played an important historical role in cinema's creation of our stockpile of social memories. For most spectators, whose voyeuristic captivity (as captors *and* prisoners) of the cinema image is an eroticized response to a psychic scenario on the screen, the suggestive incidence of cross-dressing among those memories is readily explicable. It has proved much more difficult, however, to provide a systematic account of how "masculine" and "feminine" positions of spectatorship are assumed as part of the process of reading and responding to these ambiguous images.

Molly Haskell has argued that the overwhelming disparity of images of female to male impersonation in films can be explained by the fact that, historically, male impersonation is a source of power and aggrandizement for women, while the theatrical adoption of female characteristics by men is a process of belittlement. Male impersonation is serious and erotic, while female impersonation is simply comical.[26] In a book about cross-dressing in Hollywood cinema, Rebecca Bell-Metereau argues that Haskell's serious/comical distinction no longer applies, by pointing to the change in attitudes toward female impersonation that have occurred in the last two decades—with its range of "legitimate" and sometimes popular, female impersonators of "women of power." So too, in the pre–1960 examples, "tragic" or "comic" readings of a film's treatment of cross-dressing are not simply the result of gender alignment. More important is whether the male or female imitation is "willingly performed and sympathetically accepted by the social group within the film."[27]

Just as the reading of these images is inflected by the complex interplay between spectacle and narrative, or between transgressive display and social judgment, there is no guarantee that what is *encoded* in these film scenarios will be *decoded* in the same way by different social groups with different sexual orientations. This is nowhere more obvious than in the highly developed gay subculture that evolved around a fascination with classical Hollywood film and, in particular, with film stars like Judy Garland, Bette Davis, Mae West, Greta Garbo, Marlene Dietrich, Joan Crawford, and performers like Barbra Streisand, Diana Ross, and Bette Midler. Denied the conventional "masculine" and "feminine" positions of spectatorship, and excluded by conventional representations of male-as-hero or narrative agent, and female-as-image or object of the spectacle, the gay male and lesbian subcultures express their lived spectatorship largely through imaginary or displaced relations to the images and discourses of a straight, "parent" culture.

Unlike Pop or countercultural camp, the gay camp canon of film stars has very little to do with transformations of taste. In its pre-Stonewall heyday (before "gay" was self-affirming), it was part of a survivalist culture that found, in certain fantasmatic elements of film culture, a way of imaginatively expressing its common conquest of everyday oppression. As with persecuted or economically subordinate groups, the fantasy possibilities of life on the screen allowed the utopian privilege of imagining a better world. In the gay camp subculture, glamorous images culled from straight Hollywoodiana were appropriated and *used* to make sense of the everyday experience of alienation and exclusion in a world socially polarized by sexual labels. Here, a tailored fantasy—which, by definition, never "fits" the real—is worn in order to suggest an imaginary control over circumstances.

Gay male identification with the power and prestige of the female star was, first and foremost, an identification with women as *emotional* subjects in a film world in which men "acted" and women "felt."[28] In this respect, camp reasserted, for gay males, the "right to ornamentation and emotion, that West-

ern and particularly Anglo-Saxon society has defined as feminine preoccupations."[29] Since these are qualities rarely emphasized by the legitimate representations of masculine sexuality, there are few male culture heroes in the camp
pantheon; gay-identified actors like Montgomery Clift and Tab Hunter are an
exception, but for obvious reasons, while the emotional sensitivity of Brando
and Dean was more of a focus of interest for women in a pre- or protofeminist
conjuncture.

The identificatory envy of the female film star's own "power" is not, of
course, without its contradictions, since that power is not unconditionally
granted, and since its exercise in the service of some transgression of male-
defined behavior is usually directly met with punishment and chastisement. As
Michael Bronski argues, however, the mere idea that sexuality brings with it a
degree of power, "albeit limited and precarious, can be exhilarating" for the
gay male who "knows that his sexuality will get him in trouble."[30] But what can
the relation of this everyday triumph of the will to the commodity-controlled
spectacle of a major star's "sexuality" tell us about the power exercised by the
institution of sexuality itself? This is the question gay politics has come to ask
of camp.

In answering that question, it is important always to bear in mind that the
traditional gay camp sensibility was an *imaginary* expression of a relation to
real conditions, both past and present—an ideology, if you like—just as it still
functions today, in the "liberated" gay and straight world, as a kind of imaginary challenge to the new *symbolic* conditions of gay identity. Whether as a
pre-Stonewall, utopian, survivalist fantasy, or as a post-Stonewall return of the
repressed, camp transforms, destabilizes, and subverts the existing balance of
acceptance of sexual identity and sexual roles. It never proposes a *direct* relation between the conditions it speaks to—everyday life in the present—and the
discourse it speaks with—usually a bricolage of features pilfered from conditions of the past.

This knowledge might help us to answer the charge of misogyny that is
often brought to bear upon camp representations of "feminine" characteristics.[31] It could be argued that the camp idolization of female film starts contributes to a radical desexualization of the female body. In the context of a
social spectacle where the female has little visible existence outside of her being
posed as the embodiment of the sexual, any reading that defetishizes the erotic
scenario of woman-as-spectacle is a progressive one. In the classic camp pantheon, film stars are celebrated for reasons other than their successful dra-
matization of erotic otherness. Here, camp joins forces with feminist ap-
praisals of the "independent" women of Hollywood—West, Davis, Crawford,
and Garbo—who fought for their own roles, either against the studios them-

selves, or in the highly mannered ways in which they acted out, acted around, or acted against the grain of the sexually circumscribed stereotypes they were contracted to dramatize.

In a 1975 interview, Sontag has suggested that the diffusion of camp taste in the earlier part of the sixties ought to be credited "with a considerable if inadvertent role in the upsurge of feminist consciousness in the late 1960s." In particular, she claims that the fascination with the "corny flamboyance of femaleness" in certain actresses helped to "undermine the credibility of certain stereotyped femininities—by exaggerating them, by putting them between quotation marks."[32] In acknowledging this, Sontag was clearly withdrawing from one of her controversial positions in "Notes on Camp"—that camp was essentially "apolitical," and that it was essentially an "aesthetic" (especially pertinent to the times) of "failed seriousness." While gay intellectuals have long challenged this view,[33] its flaws became increasingly visible as a full-blown sexual politics began to explore and criticize existing definitions of femininity and masculinity. Much of the ensuing debate has focused on questions camp had already highlighted, about the relation between "artifice" and "nature" in the construction of sexuality and gender identity. In fact, camp was a highly developed way of talking about what nonessentialist feminism has come to call sexual difference.

To nonessentialist feminism and to the gay camp tradition, the importance of particular film stars lies in their various challenges to the assumed "naturalness" of gender roles. Each star presents a different way, at different historical times, of living with the "masquerade" of femininity.[34] Each demonstrates how to *perform* a particular representation of womanliness. And the effect of these performances is to demonstrate, in turn, why there is no "authentic" femininity, why there are only representations of femininity, socially redefined from moment to moment. So too, the "masculine" woman, as opposed to the androgyne, represents to men what is unreal about masculinity, while actors whose masculinity is overdone and dated (Victor Mature is the classic camp example, not least, I think, because of the symmetry of his names) invoke the dialectic between (past) imprisonment and (present) liberation that helped to inspire the sexual politics of the late sixties.

The politics of camp assumes that there is no easy escape from these definitions, and in this respect, it is opposed to the search for alternative, utopian, or essentialist identities that lay behind many of the countercultural and sexual liberation movements. Because of its zeal for artifice, theatricality, spectacle, and parody, camp has often been seen as prepolitical, even reactionary. In its commitment to the mimicry of existing cultural forms, and its refusal to advocate wholesale breaks with these same forms, the politics of camp fell out of step and even into disrepute (as a kind of blackface) with the dominant ethos of the women's and gay liberation movements. Nonetheless, its survival, and its crossover presence in straight, masculine culture, has been directly responsible for the most radical changes in the constantly shifting, or hegemonic, definition of masculinity in the last two decades.

As makeup and dressing-up became a common feature of the flamboyant counterculture, "drag," hitherto the professional conscience of camp, took on the generalized meaning, for straight culture, of all forms of everyday role-playing.[35] Countercultural liberation for men was one moment in the two decades of "permissiveness" (the right-wing definition) that began with the swinging *Playboy* ethic of the mid-fifties and ended with the stirrings of the neoconservative backlash in the mid-seventies. Barbara Ehrenreich has argued that the fifties "male revolt" against the suburban bondage of breadwinning, announced by the consumerist *Playboy* lifestyle, also delivered men from suspicions of homosexuality that had hitherto been attached to those who shunned marriage.[36] So too, the "ethnicization" of homosexuality, which gay liberation had brought about in the seventies by advocating the policy of "coming out," meant that straight men could pursue their exploration of androgyny without the fear of their heterosexuality being questioned. The new macho man was gay. The radical "moment" of bisexuality was lost.

The privileges of androgyny, however, were not available for women until well into the seventies, and only *after* gender-bending had run its spectacular, public course through a succession of musical youth heroes: David Bowie (the first and the best, although Jagger and Lou Reed of the Velvet Underground had been pioneers), Alice Cooper, the New York Dolls, Elton John, Iggy Pop, Marc Bolan, and other dandies of glam rock. It was not until punk ushered in a newer and more "offensive" kind of oppositional drag that women fully participated in the confrontational strategies of iconoclastic posing and transgressing: Patti Smith, trash-princess; Siouxsie Sue, Wendy O. Williams, and the ebullient Poly Styrene.

To look for today's most socially threatening expressions of camp and drag, we must go to the outrageously spectacular heroes of the youth heavy metal (Cock Rock) scene, a subculture that is also supposed to harbor and perpetuate the most retarded features of traditional working-class masculinity. In heavy-rock culture today, the most "masculine" images are spliced with miles of manicured long hair, risqué costumes, elaborate makeup, and a whole range of fetishistic body accessories, while it is the cleancut, close-cropped, fifties-style Euro crooners who are seen as lacking masculine legitimacy. It is ironic, then, to consider that when, in 1984, the affable and nonthreatening Boy George received a Grammy Award on network television, he told his audience:

"Thank you, America, you've got style and taste, and you know a good drag queen when you see one." Behind this ambiguous compliment, there was a long history of smug European attitudes toward American puritanism. But what does Boy George's comment mean in the age of Motley Crue, Twisted Sister, Kiss, Ratt, and Bon Jovi, whose use of drag is synonymous with a certain kind of American masculinity? There are more than just class differences at stake here, although it is important to recognize that heavy metal is as much a critique of middle-class masculinity as it is an affirmation of working-class sexism. It is also a question of international relations. The violence associated with heavy-metal "drag" speaks, in its own way, to the legitimate power of American masculinity in the world today. By contrast, the jolly decorum of Boy George transmits the cheerful European features of a masculinity in the twilight of its power. One is emboldened and threatening, the other is genial and peaceloving.

Postscript: Warhol's Bottom Line

I have suggested that camp can be seen as a *cultural economy* at work from the time of the early sixties. It challenged, and, in some cases, helped to overturn legitimate definitions of taste and sexuality. But we must also remember to what extent this cultural economy was tied to the capitalist logic of development that governed the mass culture industries. Nowhere is this more obsessively demonstrated than in the following remarks of Warhol, tongue-in-cheek certainly, but religiously devoted nonetheless to the "idea" of his philosophy of work:

> I always like to work on leftovers, doing the leftover things. Things that were discarded and that everybody knew were no good, I always thought had a great potential to be funny. It was like recycling work. I always thought there was a lot of humor in leftovers. . . . I'm not saying that popular taste is bad so that what's left over is probably bad, but if you can take it and make it good or at least interesting, then you're not wasting as much as you would otherwise. You're recycling work and you're recycling people, and you're running your business as a byproduct of other businesses. Of *other directly competitive* businesses, as a matter of fact. So that's a very economical operating procedure. It's also the funniest operating procedure because, as I said, leftovers are inherently funny.[37]

Warhol here reveals what he knows about camp's re-creation of surplus value; the low risks involved, the overheads accounted for, and the profit margins expected. This at least was one artist's way of talking about the massive reorganization of cultural taste that took place in the course of the sixties. It was a way of talking that offended some intellectuals because it suggested, even if Warhol never seemed to mean what he said, that its attention to "economy" was more than just a metaphor for the critique of capitalism that, in their eyes, all art must surely deliver. On the contrary, it suggested that art had something more directly to do with conditions of production and consumption than it had to do with the aesthete's idea of a windless realm of "taste."

As for what Warhol calls the "inherent funniness" of leftovers, that is the other side of camp—the creamy wit, the wicked fantasies, and the *gaieté de coeur.* All that was, and still is, priceless.

Notes

Readers should be aware that a longer version of this chapter appears in Ross's *No Respect.*

1. George Melly, *Revolt into Style: The Pop Arts in Britain* (London: Allen Lane, 1970), 160–61.

2. No one has pursued more assiduously the task of exposing the seedy and tragic side of Hollywood's own celebration of this cult than Kenneth Anger, in his *Hollywood Babylon* (New York: Bell, 1975) and *Hollywood Babylon II* (London: Arrow Books, 1986).

3. For accounts of the postwar British experience and reception of American popular culture, see Dick Hebdige, "Towards a Cartography of Taste: 1936–1962," in *Popular Culture: Past and Present,* ed. Bernard Waites, Tony Bennett, and Graham Martin (London: Croom Helm and Open University, 1982), 194–218, and "In Poor Taste: Notes on Pop" in *Block* 8 (1983): 54–68; Melly, *Revolt into Style;* Jeff Nuttall, *Bomb Culture* (London: Paladin, 1970); and Iain Chambers, *Popular Culture: The Metropolitan Experience* (London & Methuen, 1986).

4. Cited by Chambers, *Popular Culture,* 40.

5. Tom Wolfe, *The Kandy-Kolored Tangerine-Flake Streamline Baby* (New York: Farrar, Straus and Giroux, 1965), 86.

6. Andy Warhol and Pat Hackett, *Popism: The Warhol 60s* (New York: Harper and Row, 1970), 162.

7. Tom Wolfe, *The New Journalism,* an essay with an anthology, ed. Tom Wolfe and E. W. Johnson (New York: Harper and Row, 1973), 38.

8. Susan Sontag, *Against Interpretation* (New York: Farrar, Straus and Giroux, 1966), 304.

The use of the term "subculture" in the context of delinquent youth groups dates from Albert Cohen's *Delinquent Boys* (Glencoe, Ill.: Free Press, 1955). The most developed version of this tradition is in the work produced at the Birmingham Center for Contemporary Cultural Studies. The classic exposition can be found in Stuart Hall and Tony Jefferson, eds., *Resistance through Rituals: Youth Subcultures in Postwar Britain* (London: Hutchinson, 1975).

10. Tom Wolfe, *The Pump-House Gang* (Farrar, Straus and Giroux, 1968), 14.

11. Todd Gitlin examines at length the contradictions of a student movement that was pledged to democratically redefine "leadership" but that was forced to produce celebrities in order to gain access to the press. *The Whole World Is Watching: Mass Media in the Making and Unmaking of the New Left* (Berkeley: University of California Press, 1980).

12. For an analysis of the biker subculture, see the British study by Paul Willis, *Profane Culture* (London: Routledge & Kegan Paul, 1978). Also see Hunter S. Thompson's exercise in participatory journalism, *Hell's Angels: A Strange and Terrible Saga* (New York: Random House, 1966).

13. Toby Marotta, *The Politics of Homosexuality* (Boston: Houghton Mifflin, 1981), especially 70–99.

14. The best history of this period is John D'Emilio's *Sexual Politics, Sexual Communities: The Making of a Homosexual Minority in the United States 1940–1970* (Chicago: University of Chicago Press, 1983). Also, see Jonathan Katz, ed., *Gay American History: Lesbians and Gay Men in the U.S.A.* (New York: Thomas Crowell, 1976).

15. Dennis Altman, *The Homosexualization of America* (Boston: Beacon Press, 1982), and his "What Changed in the Seventies?" in *Homosexuality: Power and Politics*, ed. Gay Left Collective (London: Allison and Busby, 1980), 52–63; Michael Bronski, *Culture Clash: The Making of Gay Sensibility* (Boston: South End Press, 1984); Jeffrey Weeks, *Sexuality and Its Discontents: Meanings, Myths, and Modern Sexualities* (London: Routledge & Kegan Paul, 1985).

16. The phrase is Melly's, in his preface to Philip Core, *Camp: The Lie that Tells the Truth* (New York: Delilah, 1984).

17. Sontag, "Notes on Camp," in *Against Interpretation*, 288.

18. Curtis F. Brown, *Star-Spangled Kitsch* (New York: Universe Books, 1975); Jacques Sternberg, *Kitsch* (New York: St. Martin's Press, 1972).

19. Thomas Hess, "J'Accuse Marcel Duchamp," *Art News* 63, no. 10 (1965): 53.

20. See Core, *Camp*, and Christopher Isherwood, *The World in the Evening* (London: Methuen, 1954).

21. Mark Booth, *Camp* (New York: Quartet, 1983), 18, 29.

22. Reyner Banham, "Who Is This 'Pop'?" in *Design by Choice*, ed. Penny Sparke (New York: Rizzoli, 1981), 94–96.

23. Lawrence Alloway, "The Long Front of Culture," in *Pop Art Redefined*, ed. Suzi Gablik and John Russell (New York: Praeger, 1969), 42.

24. Melly, *Revolt into Style*, 174.

25. Susan Sontag, "The *Salmagundi* Interview," with Robert Boyars and Maxine Bernstein, in *A Susan Sontag Reader* (New York: Farrar, Straus and Giroux, 1982), 338–39.

26. Molly Haskell, *From Reverence to Rape* (New York: Holt, Rinehart and Winston, 1973), 61.

27. Rebecca Bell-Metereau, *Hollywood Androgyny* (New York: Columbia University Press, 1985), 117ff.

28. Bronski, *Culture Clash*, 95. While a case for the lesbian relation to camp has been made, it is the gay male "possession" of that culture which has been stressed most often. See, however, Caroline Sheldon, "Lesbians and Film: Some Thoughts," in *Gays and Film*, ed. Richard Dyer (London: British Film Institute, 1977), 5–26; Christine Riddiough, "Culture and Politics," in *Pink Triangles: Radical Perspectives on Gay Liberation*, ed. Pam Mitchell (Boston: Alyson, 1980), 14–34, especially 21–22. It has often been pointed out, however, that the subaltern position of lesbians in traditional gay culture enabled them to construct a more successful autonomous "liberation" culture than did gay males.

29. Altman, *Homosexualization*, 154.

30. Bronski, *Culture Clash*, 96. Also see Richard Dyer's study of Judy Garland in *Heavenly Bodies: Film Stars and Society* (New York: St. Martin's Press, 1986).

31. Garland, Davis, and the other queens of Hollywood are one thing. Maria Montez, Tallulah Bankhead, Carmen Miranda, and Eartha Kitt are another. If they are also figures celebrated by gay camp, then it is not for their thespian talents or for their stylized parodies of femininity. On the contrary, the widespread cultivation of these exploited actresses (*Myron*'s cult of Montez, in Gore Vidal's novel, is representative) is inevitably tinged with ridicule, derision, even misogyny. Their moments in the camp limelight cannot fail to conceal a "failed seriousness" that is more often

pathetic and risible than it is witty or parodic. So too, it is difficult to finally justify those Warhol films like *Lupe,* which depicts Lupe Velez's death by drowning in the toilet bowl after taking a Seconal overdose, or *Ecstasy and Me,* about the shoplifting tribulations of Hedy Lamarr. Michael Bronski asks the relevant questions of this cult practice: "It would be absurd to want to pretend that any of these women had a great talent, but what does it mean for a large group of gay men to like a female performer expressly because of the fact that she is terrible?" "Judy Garland and Others: Notes on Idolization and Derision," in *Lavender Culture,* ed. Karla Jay and Allen Young (New York: Harcourt Brace Jovanovich, 1978), 210.

32. Sontag, "*Salmagundi* Interview," 338–39.

33. Jack Babuscio, "Camp and the Gay Sensibility," in Dyer, *Gays and Film,* 40–58; and Bronski, *Culture Clash,* 42–46, 92–144.

34. In the psychoanalytic tradition, the classic essay (1929) on the "masquerade" of femininity is Joan Riviere's "Womanliness as Masquerade," reprinted in *Formations of Fantasy,* ed. Victor Burgin, James Donald, and Cora Kaplan (London: Methuen, 1986), and accompanied by an incisive commentary by Stephen Heath, "Joan Riviere and the Masquerade," which sets out the choices for feminist film theory in the light of Riviere's arguments. See also Mary Ann Doane, "Film and the Masquerade: Theorizing the Female Spectator," *Screen* 23, nos. 3–4 (1982).

35. On the history of drag, see Kris Kirk and Ed Heath's fascinating oral history, *Men in Frocks* (London: Gay Men's Press, 1984); Peter Ackroyd, *Dressing Up: Transvestism and Drag* (New York: Simon and Schuster, 1979); Esther Newton, *Mother Camp: Female Impersonators in America* (Chicago: University of Chicago Press, 1972).

36. Barbara Ehrenreich, *The Hearts of Men: American Dreams and the Flight from Commitment* (Garden City, N.Y.: Doubleday, 1983). Ehrenreich concludes, in fact, that the antifeminist backlash of the late seventies was an attack, not on feminism itself, but on the "male revolt" that had threatened to dispense with the breadwinner ethic altogether, and deprive married women of the privilege of living off their husband's incomes.

37. Andy Warhol, *The Philosophy of Andy Warhol (From A to B and Back Again)* (New York: Harcourt Brace Jovanovich, 1975), 93.

The Loneliness of Camp

SCOTT LONG

This essay is a defense of camp as a moral activity. It is predicated in part on the idea that terms such as *moral* are more and more being vitiated and stripped of meaning in our society. Hence to use this term here, as though I am somehow privileged to speak it or invest it with force, may seem a contradiction in terms.

I cannot easily resolve this. There will inevitably be times when my rhetoric will seem too high, my language too inflated, to treat justly the calculated triviality that is my subject. I risk sententiousness, I court self-parody, at every turn. Camp is, of course, based on just this sort of disparity between high seriousness and the absurd. I could thus, were I bolder, turn the disjunction I speak of into an exhibition of camp sensibility itself, a display of its freedom; but to write campily about camp lies, I fear, beyond my powers. With the reader's cooperation, however, the problem can in part be solved. Imagine this essay delivered as an address by a small, mustachioed man wearing a gold lamé cocktail dress, black pumps with three-inch stiletto heels, a raven wig, and a beaded cloche with peacock feathers. Now we can proceed.

Camp is, of course, associated with male homosexuals, and the nature of their oppression is essential to its nature. In the film *Before Stonewall*, Dean Rusk, then secretary of state, is shown at a news conference in 1965. He says to the assembled reporters with a smile, "I understand this building is being picketed by a group of . . . homosexuals." Laughter.

There is no homosexual who has not heard that laughter.

The purest form of oppression practiced against the homosexual deprives him of the minimal power even to threaten. It subjects him to an imperial mistranslation. His existence is tragic; everywhere it is perceived as funny. He is like a politician in a foreign country, at the mercy of a perverse interpreter: he cannot understand why, no matter what he says, his incomprehensible audience guffaws.

The ingenuity of the device is to rob its victim of a voice. Met by laughter, he cannot react as he would if met by fear or rage: any serious response can be defused by another laugh. His tragedy becomes trivial. He responds by adopting a sensibility which, in its most common form, takes the trivial absolutely seriously. In camp, he defuses by parody the devices of oppression.

Another variety of camp imitates the oppressive mechanism only to expose it by forcing it to its extremes: the tragedy grows so grotesquely great that only madness can persist in the attempt to domesticate it. Here tragic events are contained within formal constructs that strive vainly to normalize or deny them. The "body in the closet" form of comedy-of-manners is the best example I can offer: a monstrous fact, often putrefying slowly, lurks somewhere in the country house, and the reader's knowledge of it makes ludicrous the veneer of tea-table conversation carried on upstairs. Compton-Burnett manages this with expertise.

To take a blue feather boa, or a *crime passionelle* in which a matron mutilates her gardener with pinking shears, as an absolutely serious thing, to devote to it all available energies of appreciation and understanding, is an act of mockery and defiance against the configurations of power that control the labels and signs of absurdity, that define as dismissible certain attitudes or products or lives. Camp assaults a society that presumes it knows what is serious and what is not. It strives not to imitate this authority in distorted form but to expose it explicitly as inadequate. Hence it does not merely invert the opposition between the trivial and the serious: it posits a stance, detached, calm, and free, from which the opposition as a whole and its attendant terms can be perceived and judged.

The process of camp might be called dialectical. It asserts an opposition between the absurd and the serious. Then it gestures toward a point—a moment of consciousness, a shock, a synthesis—from which that opposition can be seen as absurd in turn, based on a higher and more encompassing sense of absurdity, since it includes far more in its sway: it separates the beholder in a vertiginous moment from a whole encrusted body of cultural dictates and values. Camp does not consist merely in a disproportion between form and content, but also in the creation of an attitude by which the whole relationship of form and content within a cultural setting can be seen with new eyes.

This point exists in the *spectator.* All the energies in the camp object are directed toward bringing about such a moment in the consciousness that views it. More than almost any other aesthetic, camp thus turns continually outward. The camp moment is incomplete, it is not camp, without the satisfactory response from its audience.

The difference between what Susan Sontag calls "naïve" and "deliberate" camp, of course, is in the intent of the intelligence that produced it. The camp object can be created deliberately, by an artist anxious to violate boundaries between the serious and the absurd; or it can be produced unawares, like a blind man's distorted drawing, by those for whom the boundaries are genuinely blurred. Laura in Ronald Firbank's *The Flower beneath the Foot* prays, "Lord, help me always to be decorative and to do right": Firbank delights in the conjunction. Nancy Reagan no doubt prays the same thing, but without a sense of humor.

Precisely because camp commits its ultimate act of creation so completely to the spectator, it makes no real difference whether it is deliberate or naïve. Indeed—intentionality being notoriously obscure in such matters—it is often impossible to tell. The spectator *creates* camp by observing from a camp attitude, one that questions the serious and the absurd. Camp is found in the final movement of the dialectic, in the observer.

One must emphasize: camp plays with notions of seriousness and absurdity not to deny them but to redefine them. It is dialectical, not deconstructive, so to speak. Its tendency is not toward an infinite oscillation of meanings in an evaluative vacuum, but toward a new and ultimately stabler sense of what the serious and nonserious are. Its particular endeavor is to fix the nature of the absurd: the society that laughs at the wrong things has gone wrong. To perceive the absurd is to realize that two conjoined ideas do not belong together. Behind camp is the expectation that, once the absurd is properly recognized, a sense of the serious will follow.

It is no coincidence that the first acts of homosexual liberation were undertaken by drag queens.

To claim cultural importance for the act of asserting the absurd threatens a sense of priorities. What I wish to argue, though, is precisely the overriding significance of understanding absurdity. It is perhaps the principal responsibility of the just man today.

A man moves into a house between an airport and a construction site. Battered by noise, he begins to lose his hearing. His friends tell him he should leave, that he is being foolish, but he brushes aside their warnings. They have to shout louder and louder to make him hear. Finally, of course, he goes deaf. His friends grieve for his deafness. But they still shout at him, even though he cannot hear a word. "You blockhead," they scream when they visit, "you idiot, you fool," while he sits there smiling, benignly impervious to sound. They do it as a release of tension and as a private joke among themselves. They do it because they enjoy it.

This is an allegory of the position of camp in our culture. It may seem a doubtful position from which to mount a defense. But the man is deaf, after all, and *il faut s'amuser*. What else are the friends to do?

It is a commonplace that language has lost nuance in our time, has been somehow sapped of the full forces by which it once apprehended the world. It no longer seizes objects, but gropes for them blindly and bluntly—like Shakespeare's Lavinia, her hands cut off, scrawling with bleeding stumps in the sand. The defenders of the dialect of the tribe trace from this weakness a myriad of subsidiary effects in the realms of thought and feeling: the disease of language is presumed to infect the whole man. The subject has become a cliché of sorts. One notes with interest how much dead language is spoken and written about the death of language. The illness expropriates the remedy.

Yet the problem is really one of perception. We have ceased adequately to *see* objects; we accuse our language of furnishing their disguises. I can only outline here the history of this loss.

> A multitude of causes, unknown to former times, are now acting with a combined force to blunt the discriminating powers of the mind, and, unfitting it for all voluntary exertion, to reduce it to a state of almost savage torpor. The most effective of these causes are the great national events that are daily taking place and the increasing accumulation of men in cities, where the uniformity of their occupations produces a craving for extraordinary incident, which the rapid communication of intelligence hourly gratifies.

That is Wordsworth. In the late eighteenth century there began an extraordinary and exponential multiplication of the objects available for contemplation. The things that could be known increased; so, more significantly, did the means of recording and transmitting them, until the circulation of facts embarked on an incessant acceleration to ever more incredible speeds.

> The doubts of day-time and the doubts of night-time, the curious whether and how, whether that which appears so is so, or is it all flashes and specks?
> Men and women crowding fast in the streets,
> if they are not flashes and specks what
> are they?

Whitman's "flashes and specks" too have their place in a rudimentary history of perception. Urban culture, "the increasing accumulation of men in cities," entailed a kind of sensory overload; the ubiquity of anonymous faces obliterated the features of the individual. Poe's "man of the crowd" and Baudelaire's *flâneur* are characteristic figures, seeking out traces of unique existence amid the simultaneous, stultifying multifariousness and monotony of the street. They find their reward in small epiphanies, things perceived with rare intensity through some accident of insight, rather than let run indifferently through the hardened brain. *Pendant que des mortels la multitude vile / sous le fouet de Plasir,* these epicures of detail discover beauty in a wounded swan, dabbing its chafed beak in the dust of a cobbled lane.

> Others will teach us how to dare,
> And against fear our breast to steel;
> Others will strengthen us to bear;
> But who, ah! who, will make us feel?

The remarkable *utility* of Wordsworth to the nineteenth century, as Arnold (and, still more immediately, Mill) understood, lay in his capacity to rouse a reduced receptivity to original perception, by powerful emotional stimulation. Nature was valuable to him—still more so to his readers—precisely because of its unfamiliarity to urbanized, jaded man. He urged the excitement of a return to a forgotten, almost fantastic country, a dream of exile overcome.

Others found different recourses, seeking finer discriminations and intenser gradations of pleasure in an aristocratic retreat from the banal diversions of the multitude. Their assumption, adumbrated even as early as Shelley, was that Nature too had been debased, an exhausted treasure. They announced their own tropism toward the so-called—and undefined—unnatural, anticipating the revival of the senses in unprecedented realms. *A Rebours.*

All these were responses to a disease. The great illness of our age, brought about by the increasing accessibility and acceleration of facts, is the replacement of *knowledge* by *information.*

To amass knowledge requires an active effort of understanding. Information asks only a passive acceptance on the part of the receiver. The seeker of knowledge struggles to perceive each new and old tenet—each fact comprehended—in its particularity, and perpetually evaluates and discriminates between them. Information is absorbed indiscriminately, at times almost unconsciously as an advertisement: it arrives in an unceasing stream, too busily and quickly for the receiver to make distinctions. The holder of knowledge imposes limitations, as part of the rules of the pursuit to which he has committed himself. His knowledge ideally rejects contradictions, resents the confusion of levels, ruminates, and chooses. Information is the creature of profusion. Any body of facts can be reduced to its monotony, if the receiver is too exhausted to select among them. It is a cornucopia of wax fruits, a satiety without content. It smothers senses tired of resisting. Information is the life of the waking dream.

I can offer a few examples of the relation to reality that an information culture imposes. An undergraduate, in a term paper, speaks of David Copperfield's "lifestyle." In network coverage of a Democratic convention, a speech by Cesar Chavez is interrupted for a Gallo wine commercial. In a network miniseries on the Holocaust, Himmler is shown complaining about the stench from the gas chambers; moments later, the show breaks for a commercial for air freshener. A traveling salesman and evangelical Christian anticipates Heaven: "I'll play golf. I'll do wonderful things throughout the galaxies of time that will please God." An undergraduate begins a term paper on Simone Weil with a quotation from Shirley Maclaine.

All these indicate a basic failure to discriminate between kinds of fact. Some—particularly the inanities of television—simply show an ignorance of irony. Others, conflating God with golf or true mysticism with self-help clichés, reflect a moral insensitivity to value. In each case the confusion is caused by a deep inability to understand the objects involved. The ideas juxtaposed have plainly not been contemplated but merely consumed, treated as indistinguishable units of unexamined information.

Increasingly we think as it were in a kind of Russian, without definite or indefinite articles. Perception is infected with a hopeless vagueness; thoughts accumulate by virtue of our gathering inability to tell them apart. We are losing the skill to seek the unique form of any object we encounter, and that is the true sense of taking something seriously. We rarely interrogate anything to find its story.

The *form* of an object, in the sense in which I use the term, is the accumulation of traces its history has left on its present state. To find it is not unlike counting the rings of a tree.

An anecdote recorded of Goethe. "The old poet suddenly got out of the carriage to examine a stone, and I heard him say: 'Well, well! how did *you* get here?'—a question, which he repeated. . . ."

Knowledge deals in forms; information, in superficies and images. The ultimate unit of information is the image.

Brecht observed that a photograph of the Krupp works reveals nothing about its function. Our speech has become rather like those sterile photographs, a play of images. People use words to refer to abstract and frozen qualities, not to actual processes taking place in history, in time. Just as few who drive a car or commit their lives to an airplane could explain how the machines they trust actually run, so few who soar on winged words think of them as having a real and palpable application in the life of man or of the world. No one takes an idea apart to see how it works.

What I am really talking about is the importance of process, a matter of— and within—time. Our present language has subtly canceled that suggestion from its repertory; we freeze everything, relentlessly we reify the world. Growth and change themselves become frozen in our minds. The same paralysis infects my own voice. Can you hear its vacuous chill encroaching? Even as I form the word *process,* it is like expelling a stone.

Like everything else, words should have a *value,* which is different from meaning; it is the speaker in them, waiting to be found. I have friends with whom I talk as though words had a *price.*

Price and meaning are both representations, imposed on the object from without by various economies of capital or language. Both fix the object in a demonstrative stasis, displaying it divorced from the marks of its development in time. Value is not strictly a representation but the articulation of an essence, not an imposition but a revelation from within of the true form of the object. As with any natural thing, one must partake a little of the mystical to understand it.

The value of the world would be what is called the Name of God.

Value is form discovered. It is form revealed to the understanding of an Other, placed in the context of other values, other things known. The ideal location of value is in dialogue.

A relationship of dialogue need not be governed by the exchange of price or even of meaning. Driven as we are to affix price to everything, we no longer fully understand the primitive relation of the *gift* and its full import. That relationship formerly had its own rules, its own grammar, its own totemic force—all now lost in ephemera, in wrapping-paper and ribbons, cards and thank-you notes, the trappings of consumption masquerading as generosity. Yet it is the only material form of human intercourse which suggests that there can be such a thing as an economy of value.

In an information culture, attention to value disappears in the relentless activity of circulation. Nothing stays still long enough for understanding. The only relation to perceived facts such a culture can accommodate is one not of comprehension but of consumption.

Defining this empire of consumption is *desire.* It is the only exertion of spirit that can be permitted on the part of the essentially passive receiver. All other emotions or modes of reacting to the world are gradually crowded aside by its omnipresence and power.

The marks of this are everywhere around us. Desire becomes the metaphor and paradigm for every sort of human experience: readers feel "narrative desire," revolutionaries feel "political desire," a musician's engagement with his instrument or a priest's with the Host are read as rechannelings or sublimations of a single vast and pullulating impulse. We understand this impulse—no longer anonymous, we flatter ourselves, but now at last properly defined—as sexual, a central ground of being echoed or imitated at distorting distances by all the other activities of life. One should say, really, not that desire is a metaphor for other forms of being, but that all these secondary experiences are taken as metaphors for the central truth of desire. They derive their being wholly from it. Everything we see is eroticized: almost the whole weight of our culture pushes the world around us into a gyrating burlesque. No action, no emotion can continue to exist save as a version of desire.

With the universal valorization of pure desire comes an increasing reluctance to tolerate those subsidiary modes of existence that merely parody it. When all other human experience is regarded as an anthology of metaphors for sexual satisfaction, a pressure grows to dismiss these inadequate substitutes and spend as much time as possible with the real thing. A debased Platonic urgency invests the task of penetrating through earthly deformations to the true ideal. One can imagine a state of society in which sex would replace conversation; I have known some who, finding in carnal intercourse an adequate image of the transcendent banality they called heaven, seemed on the verge of bringing this about.

Desire—whether in its sexual form or in its metaphorical avatars that infect all surrounding discourse—is notoriously indifferent to the self of its object, that is, to value. It operates on the levels of price or of meaning, of imposed representations: the erotic urge can, in fact, enact an elaborate theater of such representations upon the body of its object (think of the staginess of sadomasochism, think of any fantasy or fetish). But the human being on which these fantasies are projected degenerates easily into an interchangeable part. Such stories as desire creates for itself are a circulation of images. The identity of the object that underlies them, and is the field on which they play, is irrelevant to its appetites.

Pornography points to an essential fact: that desire lives by the proliferation of images.

It grows harder and harder to affirm value. The words we use to do so used to be a bridge between the realms of feeling and action. *Good* and *evil* referred then in dual directions, to sentiments and deeds. Now they are either unsupported by precise feelings on the one hand, or unconsummated by actions on the other. For some, such words refer to neither. In this final corruption, they cease altogether to be stimulants to choice and judgment, become merely edible ideas. Evil things are things we do not want to consume; good things are things we do. People do not want a world without evil. They want a world in which evil can be turned off.

To speak affirmatively is to risk being confused with those who have expropriated affirmative language and debased it. At present, before we affirm a thing, we must first rediscover it. It is no longer adequate to say "yes" to our lives. What we need instead is as often as possible to say, "aha!"

For many no sense of context is left. They perceive the world as uniform, since they perceive too much of it to tell its aspects apart. Both genocide and the removal of bathroom smells can be leveled to the same unemotive monotony: entertainment. In this, what is called kitsch reveals itself as the characteristic product of our age. Certainly it is the most common. It is wholly mass-produced, made in effect by machines not minds. Hence it has no sense of context at all. Manufactured in a vacuum, it thinks nothing of urging toothpaste as the solution to a national crisis.

Kitsch is kitsch because it does not recognize contradictions in value: toothpaste and national crises should exist on different orders of being. Minds with an awareness of surroundings can still destroy it, by recognizing its attendant improprieties—by bringing to bear upon it the power of context, to reveal the incompatible value of the objects involved. Innocent of the world around it, kitsch is art without an immune system. It is created without a sense of context: context then takes its just revenge, and destroys it.

Camp is a conscious response to a culture in which kitsch is ubiquitous. Camp is essentially an *attitude toward* kitsch.

So we return to the subject of camp. The disparities that define and destroy kitsch are elevated, in the camp object, to the level of a principle. The camp object proclaims how bizarre it is. It flaunts its grotesqueness, defies us to desire it. It reminds us that differences in value do exist; it displays, with the relish of a Breughel, the enormous carnival of their distortion.

Only our attitude toward the object distinguishes the camp creation from kitsch. It is in this sense, of course, that the camp attitude can create the camp object. One "reads" the kitsch object as a terrible accident, its tastelessness the product of ignorance or confusion. One "reads" the camp object, wherever it came from, *as though* it were deliberate (hence laughable): taking its contradictions to heart, as it were. Nearly any camp object can be read as kitsch, if we assume that its maker did not know what he was doing. (If we imagine Mae West really believed herself an irresistible beauty queen. . . .) Likewise, nearly any kitsch object can be read as camp, if we take its tastelessness as deliberate. (Camp sees a Busby Berkeley extravaganza as an immense mockery of film and musical clichés, not for its naïve acceptance of them.) This is not to say that the camp attitude must really believe grotesqueness to have been planned. It indulges in the luxury of speculation. Its frequent perspective is a form of "What if it *were* for real. . . ."

Sontag notes that the "naïve" camp object is purer than its intentional counterparts. This is precisely because, in this case, the camp reading of it is a conscious *misreading*. The reading itself becomes absurd; the camp attitude can then in turn become, to the right observer of it, a kind of camp object.

Much of Hitchcock—*Vertigo, Marnie,* for examples—can be taken either "straight" or as camp. The straight interpretation does not reduce the work to kitsch: it does, however, in specific ways reduce its value. A camp appreciation offers more complexities to the eye.

A straight interpretation of *Marnie* or *Vertigo* seeks catharsis: the satisfactory resolution of the films' conflicts in a frame that allows both emotional involvement and intellectual acceptance on the viewer's part. It wants no distance. Yet it runs afoul of the fact that the narrative content of the films clearly romanticizes men's manipulation of women, a process in which even the films' technique seems to participate (think with what loving brutality Hitchcock shows that Kim Novak is *ugly* without a strong man to dress her and pay for her facials). The straight approach, if practiced by an intelligent and enlightened mind, cannot accept the evident complicity of the films' formal perfection in a reactionary project. Its recognition of the aesthetic worth of the works is shadowed by the sense of their damaging divisions. Demanding an ethical equivalence between meaning and form, it is unable to see in the works any basis for a unified response. In the end, it finds them flawed.

The camp interpretation enjoys its distance: by definition it refuses to identify with the films except in mocking fashion. It searches not for unity but for disparities. The images most redolent of idealized patriarchal domination are precisely the ones it is likely to remember as "great," in a sense colored by multiple ironies: Tippi Hedren raped romantically by her shadowy, strong husband; James Stewart's mad and instant infatuation with Madeline, all gloss and grace and pure victim-surface; Kansas-born Kim Novak forced to suffer for her whorelike sins by striding in her aristocratic alter ego's high heels. It focuses on these because, at one level or another, it sees the impossible ironies they contain. It zeroes in on moments when the films devote the most energy to stylizing or beautifying unassimilable realities of power or pain. And its response to these moments is always distanced, "knowing." It acknowledges tension. It senses the disparity between event and treatment, and it laughs.

That laughter is both purifying and enabling. I assert paradoxically that the camp interpretation is in the end more politically meaningful than the straight one.

The straight reading formalizes the films: it demands that their content mutely reflect the exigencies of form. It cannot accept the form of the films as beautiful without devouring, digesting, the content, taking it to heart and stomach whole. *Marnie* and *Vertigo* thus confront it with a dilemma. It must either embrace the films' content—male domination—while blunting the edges with comforting ideological constructs ("romance," "the power of love"): this is certainly what most sentimentalists do. Or it must reject the film. Rejecting an art work, given the commodity-function imposed on art in modern society, means simply to refuse to *see* it, to put it out of mind. Rejection says, "This is not good: if its content were as beautiful as its technique, if they participated together in a unified descent through my mind and gullet to my gut, I would hold the work in my memory as a valuable thing, but they do not, and to that extent my memory will not treasure it." But this also entails rejecting, as useless on all levels, the depiction of patriarchal manipulation that the films contain.

In a society that emphasizes only the pleasure any artifact can offer in consumption, aesthetic objects are stripped of the right to speak to the productive lives of men. They are treated as entertainment to be consumed, and the principal demand placed on them is for a cathartic unity of effect: smoothness, simplicity, and clarity of line, the architectonics of the suppository. A work reflecting contradictions in the belief-structure of society is not doing its job, not offering the appropriate escape from the ubiquitous antinomies of reality. Few viewers will care to think their way seriously from its internal disjunctions to their predicates to be found in society, because that contravenes the escapist purpose of "aesthetic enjoyment." Instead, they will dismiss the representation of contradictions altogether from their minds.

The critic, the viewers' tribune, is thus spared the tender task of asking about the implications of that portrayal; he simply discards them along with the rest. In particular, in the case of Hitchcock's films, he need no longer analyze the peculiar seductive appeal that male manipulativeness can hold—a cultural phenomenon, a call to fantasy, which the films both portray (think of Stewart's cold blue gaze, fixed on Madeline the victim) and exemplify by their sentimental popularity. The straight interpretation too often accepts, we might say, only representations it can take on the level of simple desire. It is a curious critical response in that it dreams of an ideal work to which it can submit in uncritical and complete self-cancellation, in an ecstasy of surface and an abnegation of thought. There are such products; Hitchcock's are not among them. The straight approach resists the effort of irony in extracting value from a work: when it does in fact descend to accept ironies, it insists that the work furnish them up readily and explicitly, as part of the unity of its effect. It will not exert itself to discover them. It takes its representations straight, or not at all.

Camp escapes this dilemma. It is a particular form of the analytic—which we no longer recognize as an analytic—of laughter. It presents as absurd the romance the films weave around male domination. Grasping the disparity between the content of the experience and the associations imposed on it, it is convulsed by the attempts to contain the fact of power in the frame of idealized love. It still sees the films as successful, in that it can still enjoy them: but that enjoyment is contingent on the camp observer extracting from them what I would venture to call a message. The unity the observer finds is not the formal unity bourgeois criticism seeks (a camp aesthetic necessarily mocks formalism, does not respect the separation between the art object and the "real" world of content and contradiction): it is a different unity, dialectical in that it emerges from a conflict of values. It consists in that message, which is the discovery of something ridiculous. And the message is not divorced from political application. It criticizes the fantasies a culture has draped around the operation of power. It distances audiences attentive to it from that pervasive deception. The few who apprehend this message may seem to the uninitiated eye aesthetes or trivializers. They are not: their very "aestheticism" is the visible representation of a productive distance. In appreciating *Vertigo* campily, the least of them is engaged—even if covertly or inarticulately—in separating himself from a matrix of lies.

Absurdity is based on recognizable discriminations in value, which make it impossible reasonably to conjoin certain ideas. To recognize the absurd is to be reminded of those essential distinctions. A healthy culture has a structure: absurdity is its vindication.

In an age when the capacity for discrimination is rapidly eroding, a cultivated absurdity is one of the few benign methods by which the numb may be shocked back into realizing that distinctions exist. Brecht argued, against the aesthetic traditionalism of Lukács, that the process of reification could not be reversed by a blind retreat into modes of expression now coarsened, hardened into insensitivity, dead. Such recourses would only confirm and reinforce the process. It could only be undone by applying shocks to alienate the observer from his protective buffer of *idées reçues*. Camp with its distancing laughter is one such of productive alienation.

But can one really shock Bouvard and Pécuchet?

The question is important. I compared camp earlier to a vain shout in the ear of a deaf man. Yet I am tempted to offer a more optimistic account, that it can somehow shock even the deaf—those no longer accustomed to winnowing the images and information they absorb—into an awareness of difference and a closer attention. I find seductive the idea that its capacity to surprise can itself disseminate renewed alertness.

Perhaps it can. This seems a messianic delusion, though. Where so many powerful forces combine to obliterate the capacity for particular perception, a marginal sensibility can in the end do little. Camp may only occupy something like a terrorist's status, conducting intermittent raids on the authoritative centers of ignorance and indifference, but marking only minor victories on a giant backdrop of defeat.

Yet even if this is so, its uses remain important. It can serve as a code, a rudimentary language uniting a small company of the alienated or excluded or alone. For those who appreciate it, it can signal something shared. Reading of Auden in America, reading of him shouting "Hideola!" at small towns from a train, one feels for a giddy second part of a peculiar company: the grateful, widely separated band of those who have felt the same thing, and just now found the word for it. It is wonderful, you cannot know how wonderful it is, after long silence at last to have the word.

Camp—even at its most pessimistically conceived—still asseverates a kind of hope: it is a system of signs by which those who understand certain ironies will recognize each other and endure. It is a private language for some who intuit that public language has gone wrong. Through it, they can still adumbrate a truth or two amid the slavering and palavering. In it, a particular form of sensitivity to particulars may be preserved.

That is my darkest vision. One still holds another hope, that, even if only occasionally and incrementally, it may still speak outside its bounds: that here and there it may stimulate in some observer an unaccustomed or unburdened impression, a momentary shock that appears to be pure novelty but actually is the recognition of old practices entailing evaluation and choice.

If so, it is the camp figure who will give rise to the shock, the man who *represents* camp: who, striking a camp attitude, becomes himself a camp object. In his very comedy he takes on the burden of society's contradictions. He makes himself an "inhuman figure" in order to say, as Benjamin imagines the great Karl Kraus saying: "Nature would produce such a creature if she wished to create something befitting the world as your kind have fashioned it, something worthy of it."

Style, when successful, is sincere about something, no less than the most imperious earnestness; only it conceals rather than proclaims its object. Style is the expression of a deflected sincerity.

In the course of this essay I have spoken of the increasing corruption of our common public discourse, so that as a vehicle for the expression of subtle ideas it has faded to near senility. But I have said very little about the status of private discourse, the intimate speech of people far from the microphone, the light. I feel this as a flaw.

Yet I cannot speak of private discourse here. I have no choice: I do not know how. Everywhere the pressure of public discourse seems to me to invade the private, the hermetic, the unknown. Who thinks himself very far from the microphone any more? Who imagines himself out of the glare? I feel that pressure of the known constantly; the banalities of public voices invade my own speech, for they batter my senses every day. There are no secrets anymore: or rather every secret at once becomes a mask, worn to arouse the prurient interests of others rather than to guard some genuine center of shadow and self. There are no shadows left, save as concessions to the effect of contrast. Even concealment becomes an act of theater in the great entertainment factory of our lives. I speak as though for an audience, even with my closest friends. And why should I do otherwise? For an audience is there; it glimmers in the lamp over a late-night conversation, it whistles in the kettle on the stove; a humanity made anonymous, made faceless, can materialize anywhere, so tenuous and ethereal is its once-vivid substance; everywhere around me, in the wave-clogged air, I can feel rather than hear the voice of the mass, a vibration without meaning, and of course I respond. Of course I respond.

This essay has been, after its fashion, a drag show. I stand before you in high heels and cocktail dress, in wig and beaded cloche with peacock feathers. It is customary at the end of such a performance to pull off one's wig, while the audience gasps and at best applauds. It is an old tradition and the climactic moment of camp: to expose the calibration of contradictions for what it is, an immense artifice; to reveal explicitly the shock under the style.

It is customary but I cannot. I have no private self to show. All I can manage is a response to the ubiquity of public voices, public selves; it seems years, now, somehow, since I have even had a conversation. How can I reveal what I would not recognize myself? Things will have to stand as they are. I grow hoarse, my voice dies down, I close. Ladies and gentlemen, I am sorry: but the wig stays on.

Strategic Camp: The Art of Gay Rhetoric

DAVID BERGMAN

"**N**otes on Camp," Susan Sontag's groundbreaking essay, was meant to be only the first attempt to define a species of expression. Its numbered paragraphs were themselves a spoof of the canonical and definitive texts "camp" was set against. Sontag subordinated camp to her larger concern, the creation of "an erotics of art" (14), and if she emptied camp of content, she did so to heighten the significance of its style. Here was a mode, Sontag argued, that asked nothing but to give pleasure to each moment. Sontag linked camp to the homosexual subculture, but she did not indicate how the "erotics" of such a literature was related to the sexuality of its creators and audience. In the polymorphous perversity of Sontag's ideal readers, such concerns of gender would, I assume, have been shed like their clothing: when you get into bed with a campy book, it should not matter what sex you have on.

Yet, camp has not developed in such a utopian setting nor for such ideal readers. Indeed, camp probably would never have evolved in such a liberated or permissive atmosphere as Sontag postulates. Camp is an outgrowth of the particular historical and cultural environment in which gay artists and readers have had to function, and it has served as a means of giving gay people a larger space in which to move, loosened from the restraints of the dominant society. As Jack Babuscio has commented: "As a means to personal liberation through the exploration of experience, camp is an assertion of one's integrity—a temporary means of accommodation with society in which art becomes, at one and the same time, an intense mode of individualism and a form of spirited protest" (42).

Some critics, such as Andrew Ross, have confined camp to the twentieth century, and particularly to the 1950s and years after. Robert F. Kiernan argues that though "one can speak of a tradition of camping in the English novel . . . such a tradition is largely happenstantial . . . [and does] not constitute a tradition in the sense of designating an essential line of development" (148). I am uncertain of what Kiernan means by an "essential line of development," but I do think that certain gay writers have learned to camp from their friends and from what they have read and that such a line may be thought of as a tradition. The campiness that runs from Firbank to Compton-Burnett to Jane Bowles through to Alfred Chester does not seem to me to be purely as "accidental and . . . peripheral" as Kiernan claims (148).

In fact, the earliest records of a gay subculture in Euro-American society depict rather elaborate camp ceremonies. In 1709, the author of *The London Spy* investigated The Mollies Club, "a particular Gang of Wretches . . . degenerated from all Masculine Deportment or Manly exercises that they fancy themselves women." There he witnessed "a jointed Baby they had provided, which wooden Offspring was to be afterwards Christened, whilst one in a High Crowned Hat, I am old Beldam's Pinner, representing a Country Midwife, & another dizen'd up in a Huswife's Coif for a Nurse & all the rest of an impertinent *Decorum* of a Christening" (28). Although the author scorns this "unbecoming mirth," he does not seem particularly shocked by it and prefers to let the Reforming Society handle these "preternatural polotions." In fact, by allowing the voice of the old Beldam's Pinner to erupt into his text, he shows how willing he is to join in the festivities. He saves his most savage attacks in his *Secret History of the London Clubs* for the Quacks' Club. "Of all the Plagues with which our Land is cursed," he argues, "The Frauds of Physic seem to be the worst" (31). He believes that camp is clearly better than quackery and less dangerous to the body politic. Nor would the Mollies have tried to disabuse him of the thought since their survival depended on such tolerance; conviction on even lesser charges than sodomy meant, if not hanging, time in the pillory which many prisoners also did not survive.

The molly houses were only one eighteenth-century institution that gave opportunity for the emerging gay subculture to express its campy self. Terry Castle has written how the masquerade—the first public one held in 1717 by John James Heidegger at the Haymarket Theatre—became a venue for "cutting across historic lines of rank and privilege" (159) and presented oppressed groups, such as the lower classes, women, and sodomites, "unprecedented liberties" (168).

Camp is the extreme expression of what Thomas E. Yingling has described as the general problem of homosexual style. According to Yingling, merely because they were male, "gay men have historically had access" to the system of "culturally determined codes" and the means of literary production, but because these authors were gay, the codes "denied validity to their existence" (25). Consequently, "gay writers . . . have found literature less a matter of self-expression and more a matter of coding: from Byron through John Ashbery, the consistent locus of parody in gay texts suggests a self-consciousness about what texts may or may not do" (25). Camp is the mode in which coding is most self-consciously played with and where the apparent emptying of self-expression is most conspicuous. Of course, by making these "culturally determined codes" self-conscious and conspicuous, gay writers destabilize them and open them to analysis and criticism. Thus the avoidance of "self-expression" becomes paradoxically a powerful expression of gay selfhood. One might say that camp is the poststructuralist mode *par excellence.*

Oscar Wilde clarified how the foregrounding of style is a strategic move in a much larger battle with the forces of society.

> Art begins with abstract decoration, with purely imaginative and decorative work dealing with what is unreal and nonexistent. This is the first stage. Then Life becomes fascinated with this new wonder, and asks to be admitted into this charmed circle. Art takes Life as part of her rough material, recreates it and refashions it in fresh forms, is absolutely indifferent to fact, invents, imagines, dreams, and keeps between herself and reality the impenetrable barrier of beautiful style, of decorative and ideal, treatment. The third stage is when Life gets the upper hand and drives Art out of the wilderness. This is true decadence, and it is from this that we are now suffering. (*Artist as Critic,* 301)

Style, for Wilde, is not an end in itself, but a protective device which the imaginative, decorative, and—in his particular cultural genealogy—primitive world of art used to keep itself from being appropriated, corrupted, and destroyed by social controls and conformity. Unlike the Mollies, Wilde views style (and his own campy style in particular) as the buffer between the private erotic world and the public civil world. To those on the side of Life, Art consists only of its style. To those on the side of Art, style is the chameleon skin used to preserve the imaginative freedom against Life. One cannot speak about camp without evoking metaphors of inside and outside, flatness and depth, and such metaphors underscore the homosexual world from which camp arises. In her study of female impersonators completed a year after Sontag's essay, Esther Newton claims that "the gay world revolves" around images of masculinity and femininity which become the opposition between inside and out. "Ultimately," she writes, camp "opposes 'inner' or 'real' self (subjective self) to the 'outer' self (social self)" (100). Babuscio places "incongruity" at "the core" of camp in the way it challenges the very notions of deviance and normality (41). Yet if camp constantly plays with notions of inside and outside, masculine and feminine, it does not locate the truth at these polarities. Instead, as I argue later, camp constantly questions the dualisms of the dominant society. Wilde, for example, is satisfied with neither the face nor the mask as symbols of selfhood; he demands an unending production of identities.

To those looking in on camp, its style seems flat and extreme; consequently, the heterosexual readers' response to overtly gay literature is always problematical, especially when that literature is particularly campy. Usually the problem has been masked by denial of the homosexual or campy component (as in the case of Whitman), hostility, or avoidance. Several years ago Adam West, the star of the television version of *Batman,* provided *Gay Community News* with its "Quote of the Week" in his angry denial that the series was camp. "I detest the word," he is reported to have said. "I don't even know the definition. If you spoof and satirize something, if you make it bigger than life, if you make fun of it—I don't think that's camp. Camp to me, means *La Cage aux Folles,* if anything. If you're flouncing around as a cross-dresser, that says camp" (25 June 1988, 2). Rarely have straight critics—especially straight male critics—acknowledged that their difficulties with a work are related to issues of gender. At a conference I heard Charles Molesworth, Charles Altieri, and Cary Nelson complain that they could not locate the tone of several passages in James Merrill's poetry. At first, none of these ostensibly heterosexual readers was willing to admit his inability to recognize camp and shifted the blame for the "indeterminacy" of tone onto Merrill.

One of the few exceptions, an early one at that, is M. L. Rosenthal, who is willing to recognize—at least in the case of Robert Duncan—that his difficulties derive from gender differences. While Rosenthal's position is almost comically stuffy and heterosexist, he is also refreshingly honest. While praising Duncan in *The New Poets* as "probably the figure with the richest natural genius among the Black Mountain poets," he nevertheless concludes that Duncan's "art is to some degree self-defeating" because "in a number of poems an acceptance of homosexual love is taken for granted; that is, it assumed that everyone will share the poem's felt meanings" (183). Rosenthal implicitly assumes that only male heterosexual expressions of love can be shared by everyone. Rosenthal exposes his prejudice by choosing "A Sequence of Poems for H.D.'s Birthday" as his illustration of Duncan's "self-defeating" tendencies:

> The young Japanese son was in love with a servant boy.
> To be in love! Dont you remember how the whole world is governd
> by a fact that embraces
>   everything that happens?

(183)

Rosenthal comments:

> I will not say that such a passage is an imposition on the heterosexual reader. It is only one instance among many in our modern literature of the freedom of sexual expression; one can find cognate passages in writers otherwise as unlike Duncan and each other as Ginsberg and Paul Goodman. But the shift from the literal statement of the first line to the girlish outcry and sentimental philosophizing of the ensuing lines is emptily facile. At best it will induce a certain depression in most of us at the exploitation of what is anyway a romantic cliche in such a context. (183)

Although Rosenthal situates the poem within the broader trend of sexual expression in modern literature, the poem contains nothing sexually explicit and is as chaste and, in its way, as old-fashioned as Spenser's January eclogue, which also speaks of youthful love and homosexual desire. Compared to the works of Lowell, Sexton, or Berryman, Duncan's poetry is hardly an example of modern sexual license.

Duncan takes the opportunity in his preface to *Caesar's Gate* to rebut Rosenthal's argument. Duncan comments that he intended this "pathetic exclamation . . . not as some affect of the writer's indisposition in need of expression, but as the content of the poem itself" (i). Duncan had all along intended "the pitch of the outcry" to be "questionable" (ii). In short, the very excessiveness in style cues the reader to the passage's camp, a cue Rosenthal failed to respond to appropriately. Duncan also could have noted that Rosenthal improperly analyzed the poem's audience. Duncan rightly assumed that as a birthday present for H.D. and for the enjoyment of her friends, the poem would have had readers who, in Rosenthal's words, shared "an acceptance of homosexual love" and "the poet's felt meanings." To be sure, Duncan never limits himself to a gay readership, and rejects a gay separatist position, yet he is not obliged artistically to write for readers hostile to homosexual love. In his essay "The Homosexual in Society," Duncan specifically rejects "the cultivation of a secret language, the *camp*, a tone and a vocabulary" when it is "loaded with contempt for the human" (320). He does not thereby commit himself, however, to write for a public that will not imagine the possibility of one man's love for another. Rosenthal expects all poets to write for heterosexual readers and is unwilling to make adjustments to homosexual writers. He does not like finding himself in the awkward position of being on the outside looking in, yet such uneasiness is the best evidence of the unconscious political dimensions of camp and its effectiveness.

Rosenthal's uneasiness with Duncan's sexual assumptions is telling in another respect: as a Jew, Rosenthal might have criticized Ezra Pound's anti-

Semitic assumptions on the same grounds. But Rosenthal, who wrote an early and useful book on Pound, either ignores his exclusion from the gentile readership assumed by Pound or accepts it as part of the price Jews must pay to be readers of English literature. Duncan, in fact, draws the connection between the Jewish and the homosexual reader and writer when in "The Homosexual in Society" he explains: "In drawing rooms and in little magazines I celebrated the cult [of homosexuality] with a sense of sanctuary such as a Medieval Jew must have found in the ghetto" (322). The differences between the Jewish reader of Christian texts and the heterosexual reader of gay texts are that the Jewish reader is a minority and has centuries of practice reading hostile texts, but only in the twentieth century, and especially since the Second World War, have heterosexual readers had the chance to read overtly homosexual literature explicitly addressed to gay people.

Before the Second World War, gay writers went to extreme lengths to control their audience and avoid explicitly identifying themselves or their readers as homosexual. They did so, of course, to avoid blackmail, social stigma, and imprisonment. The police that D. A. Miller finds ubiquitous in Victorian novels also enforced more private communications (xii). Although not particularly good readers, they were persistent ones, searching for sexual texts they could interpret. In one of the many passages of *The Importance of Being Earnest* in which Wilde prefigures his own trial, we learn that the text of a cigarette case may be used in evidence (256–58). In fact, the authorities favor homosexual texts written inadvertently: the revealing gesture, the details of dreams, as well as the excremental scrawl of hotel sheets, the last of which Wilde saw used against him (Ellmann, 460). Though the prosecutor could not fathom the paradoxes of Wilde's "Phrases and Philosophies for the Use of the Very Young," he could read the writing on the bedroom linens.

Yet even where sodomy laws were overlooked or repealed, gay men had difficulty addressing each other directly as homosexuals. Though France had under Napoleon abolished laws against adult sodomy, Gide published the first two dialogues of *Corydon* in 1911 in an unsigned, private edition of twelve copies. In 1920, when he expanded the edition to twenty-four copies and added two more dialogues and the preface, he continued to publish the work privately and anonymously (Howard, "Note," xv). Similarly, John Addington Symonds composed *A Problem of Greek Ethics* in 1873, but not until 1883—a decade later—did he print it privately, and then in an edition of only ten copies. He took such care in limiting to whom he lent and gave copies that in 1892—nine years after the printing—he could give Edward Carpenter one. Despite such careful control, Symonds did not feel comfortable alluding to his own case and on the title page insists that his "inquiry into the phenomenon of sexual inversion" be "addressed especially to medical psychiatrists and jurists." In 1891, when Symonds printed *A Problem of Modern Ethics,* the edition of fifty copies still was addressed to doctors and judges.

Such precautions would seem protection enough for his readers, but apparently they did not reassure one famous admirer of Symonds's ideas: Henry James, who had acquired his copy through Edmund Gosse. During Oscar Wilde's trial for sodomy, James returned "the fond outpourings of poor J. A. S." in registered envelopes, noting: "These are days in which one's modesty is, in every direction, much exposed, and one should be thankful for every veil that one can hastily snatch up or that a friendly hand precipitately muffles one withal" (Edel, 4:12). This picture of James as a demure Salome cloaking his seductive dance in as many veils as he could possibly gather suggests not only what James feared the book's discovery might reveal, but also the vulnerability at the time of any man with homosexual feelings. James had enormous sympathies for Symonds. On hearing of Symonds's death he wrote Gosse: "somehow I too can't help feeling the news as a pang—and with a personal emotion. It always seemed as if I *might* know him—and of few men whom I didn't know has the image so much come home to me. Poor much-living, much-doing, passionately out-giving man!" (Edel, 3:409).

James wrote several letters to Symonds, but only one has survived. Attempting to communicate what cannot be safely said, it is a study in the need for and employment of camp: "I did send you the *Century* more than a year ago with my paper on Venice," he reminds Symonds.

> I sent it to you because it was a constructive way of expressing the good will I felt for you in consequence of what you had written about the land of Italy—and of intimating to you, somewhat dumbly, that I am an attentive and sympathetic reader. I nourish for the said Italy an unspeakably tender passion, and your pages always seemed to say to me that you were one of the small number of people who love it as much as I do—in addition to your knowing it immeasurably better, I want to recognize this (to your knowledge); for it seemed to me that the victims of a common passion should exchange a look. (Edel, 3:29–30)

I think one would be wrong to see in the circuity of the passage only the typical Jamesian evasiveness, for the sentence is a flirtation of quite a literal sort. James wants Symonds to recognize that he is more than "an attentive and sympathetic reader" of his histories, and that he, like Symonds, is "one of the small number of people" that share an "unspeakably tender passion," a passion that can be signaled by the style of text or in passing by the exchange of a look in the street. James is, to use a dated gay expression, "dropping his beads," defined by

Bruce Rodgers as "leav[ing] broad hints about one's homosexuality," a singularly important disclosure between gay men (69).

Symonds seems to have brought out the camp in James in letters he exchanged with Gosse and Morton Fullerton which Leon Edel characterizes as "coy." On receipt of *A Problem of Modern Ethics,* James wrote Gosse:

> J. A. S. is truly, I gather, a candid and consistant creature, and the exhibition is infinitely remarkable. It's on the whole, a queer place to plant the standard of duty, but he does it with extraordinary gallantry. If he has, or gathers, a band of emulous, we may look for capital sport. But I don't wonder that some of his friends and relations are haunted with a vague malaise. I think one ought to wish him more *humour*—it is really *the* saving salt. But the great reformers never have it—and he is the Gladstone of the affair. That perhaps is a reason the more for conveying him back to you one of these days. (Edel, 3:398)

The passage has all the elements of classic camping: (1) both the author and the reader wear disguises—the disguise of heterosexuality; (2) the masquerade enforces an intimacy even as it distances the participants in the masquerade; (3) it is maintained with a buoyant humor (lacking in Symonds), the "camp" laugh; (4) the entire affair is conducted in an elaborate style which while seemingly superficial, reveals to the initiated an unspoken subtext.

Camp shares many of the qualities of a now academically far more respectable condition, what Mikhail Bakhtin has dubbed, "the carnivalesque." Indeed in the English translation by Helene Iswolsky, one of the most common words to describe the "carnivalesque" is "gay": "The entire world is seen in its droll aspect, in its gay relativity. . . . it is gay, triumphant, and at the same time mocking and deriding" (11–12). To be sure, Iswolsky and Bakhtin mean "gay" in its more traditional sense of "lively," "carefree," "light-hearted." But since the carnivalesque enjoys punning especially in sexually provocative ways, and since the homosexual subculture has carried in its celebration of Mardi Gras and Halloween the very traditions of the carnivalesque, the two meanings blend in a form Bakhtin virtually licences.

The connection between camp and the carnivalesque is further suggested by Peter Stallybrass and Allon White who in their study of *The Politics and Poetics of Transgression* argue that the carnivalesque is best applied to works "where the political difference between the dominant and subordinate culture is particularly charged" (11). Although they use neocolonial and Soviet Yiddish literature as two examples, certainly camp gay literature would fall under this rubric quite as easily, for it, too, asks for "licenced release" (13) and develops an "inverted hierarchy" (2). Even more telling a comparison may be found in the "*grammatica jocosa*," an essential part of carnivalesque literature. According to Stallybrass and White, the *grammatica jocosa* is a style in which "grammatical order is transgressed to reveal erotic and obscene or merely materially, satisfying counter-meaning" (10). So, too, is camp a network of puns, innuendoes, and allusions arrayed with bawdy abandon.

But before I explore further the connection between camp and the carnivalesque, I should point out that they are not synonymous. The carnivalesque is always visible, an open provocation of the dominant culture; while camp frequently separates gay culture from straight culture. Bakhtin also places stress on the literally reproductive aspects of the carnivalesque: "one of the fundamental tendencies of the grotesque image of the body is to show two bodies in one. . . . From one body a new body always emerges in some form or other" (26). Camp, however, often depicts reproduction as one of the aspects of heterosexual society that must be inverted, as in the "sacred parody" of christening performed by the Mollies. Finally, Bakhtin regards the folk grotesque as "a festival of spring, of sunrise, of morning," and while camp does not entirely reject these periods, it does not celebrate "the natural" with the abandon that the "carnivalesque" embraces it. It is in its critique of "the natural" that the camp grotesque may be said to offer a more radical posture of opposition than the carnivalesque. For if the folk grotesque pits the social against the natural, camp pits both nature and society against art. Camp, while nostalgic for the medieval festival, is self-consciously very modern in its questioning of categories. For example, Alfred Chester's *The Exquisite Corpse* plays repeatedly with the artifice of fatherhood:

> Mary Poorpoor was only a child herself when her son was conceived. She was unmarried and alone in the world. She was homeless, hungry and skinny. She had no idea who the father could be, but it came to pass that she hoped more and more it was the kindly fat social worker who befriended her a few months after she became pregnant. The social worker was named Emily. . . . a stately-looking sober yet playful woman with large breasts under either or both of which she was given to hiding one-dollar bills. (38)

The passage inverts and subverts one category after another. Mary's hope that Emily is the father shifts the word *conceived* from its biological to its aesthetic meaning. Chester's subtle introduction of the faintly biblical locution "it came to pass" further transforms this magical pregnancy into an immaculate conception. Moreover Emily's social work becomes the sexual exploitation of the poor. To this set of ironies is added one more: according to Ira Cohen, Mary Poorpoor is based on Susan Sontag, "to whom Alfred gave the secret of Camp" (364).

Another fine example of camp's self-conscious questioning of the categories embraced by the carnivalesque is Joel Peter Witkins's 1981 photograph, "Androgyny Breastfeeding a Fetus" (Weiermair, 174). In it a man with a sizable penis holds to his enlarged breast a doll whose waxy surface reflects the texture of the breast at which it nurses. The very title of the photograph mocks the maternity it might appear to celebrate, for fetuses do not breastfeed, just as this androgyne has no organ through which to deliver a baby. The photograph goes further than the mock christening in the Mollies Club to question the very categories of the natural.

Despite these serious differences, camp and the carnivalesque occupy many of the same cultural positions. For example, Bakhtin argues that the carnivalesque has three basic forms: the ritual spectacle, comic verbal composition, and various forms of abuse such as curses and oaths. Camp takes such equivalent forms as the drag show, the queeny repartee, and the gay put-down. Like the carnivalesque, it merges the sublimely grand with the earthily ridiculous. The Sisters of Perpetual Indulgence, the name of a San Francisco political awareness group, expresses the carnivalesque contempt for religious sanctimoniousness even as it asserts its own moral agenda.

Yet camp shows its greatest similarity to the carnivalesque, even as it questions the dualisms that structure the carnivalesque, in its depictions of the body. Bakhtin distinguishes two styles of depictions of the body, the classical and the grotesque:

> The Renaissance saw the body in quite a different light than the Middle Ages, in a different aspect of life, and a different relation to the exterior nonbodily world. As conceived by the canons, the body was first of all a strictly completed, finished product. Furthermore, it was isolated, alone, fenced off from all other bodies. All signs of its unfinished character, of its growth and proliferation were eliminated. . . . The ever unfinished nature of the body was hidden. . . . The age represented was as far removed from the mother's womb as from the grave, the age most distant from either threshold of individual life. The accent was placed on the completed, self-sufficient individuality of the given body. Corporeal acts were shown only when the borderlines dividing the body from the outside world were sharply defined. . . . Such were the fundamental tendencies of the classic canons. (29)

Commenting on this distinction, Stallybrass and White have written: "The classical statue has no openings or orifices whereas grotesque costume and masks emphasize the gaping mouth, the protuberant belly and buttocks, the feet and the genitals. In this way the grotesque body stands in opposition to the bourgeois individualist conception of the body, which finds its image and legitimization in the classical" (21–22). Camp plays with the categories of the classical and the grotesque particularly in drag shows and gay photography. By representing both the classical and the grotesque body as artifice, camp questions the "naturalness" which both claim as their own.

The drag queen is, I suppose, more closely associated with the grotesque than with the classical. The heavily glossed lips, rather than smoothing away the flesh, act to emphasize the gaping mouth. The rouge and facial powder draw our attention to the beard stubble below. We are reminded only too often that this is a man dressed up, and because the drag artist often imitates a famous woman—Marilyn Monroe, Bette Davis, Liza Minelli—we compare this representation with the larger, classical representation we know from film or television. By alluding to the classical—and camp is highly allusive—drag forces the classical to participate in the grotesque. Moreover, as Esther Newton has pointed out, the drag queen's "genitals must *never* be seen" (101) just as the classical nude had genitals stylized or concealed. The drag queen stands apart, nostalgic for a classicism it cannot lay claim to. In this sense, the drag queen does function as Andrew Ross's utterly humorless analysis suggests he does, by assuming "aristocratic affectations [as] a sign of his *disqualification,* or remoteness from power, because they comfortably symbolize, to the bourgeois, the deceased power of the aristocrat, while they are equally removed from the threatening, embryonic power of the masses" (11, Ross's italics). The drag artist is classical, a failed classicism, just as one of the cliches of Gothicism is the classical temple in ruins. The drag is the remains of classicism as is the overdeveloped weight lifter he often poses beside and against.

Heterosexuals accept the drag queen more readily than any other part of the homosexual world or any other aspect of the camp style, as witnessed by the popularity of *La Cage aux Folles* or *Torch Song Trilogy.* Consequently, drag has lost a good deal of its immediate transgressive power. Quentin Crisp, who aroused hostility in the Britain of the 1940s and 1950s, had become by his own admission an "old homosexual institution" in the late 1960s. Yet the seemingly ineffectual should not be mistaken for the truly powerless. The limpidity that Ross sees as one of the defects of camp disguises a cutting edge. By projecting an image of powerlessness, Crisp exercised his considerable powers to avoid attack, successfully defending himself against charges of homosexual solicitation by arguing that looking as he did, no one would possibly engage him in broad daylight. The argument seemed powerful enough to win release from the magistrate. Crisp's case is not unique. In 1819 Jane Pirie and Marianne Woods, two mistresses of a girls' boarding school, won libel damages against Dame Helen Cumming Gordon when the House of Lords decided that middle-class women had no sexual desires and "that the crime here alleged has no existence" (Faderman, 147–49). The guise of absolute powerlessness provided at least some protection to generations of lesbian women.

Drag camp has not lost all power to transgress and disturb the categories of bourgeois society. Jim Hubbard's film, *Homosexual Desire in Minnesota,* for example, started a near riot before a gay audience when it was first shown, in part because it segues between gay rights marches and drag queen performances. Among Hubbard's points is that gay political activity originated in drag performance: the Stonewall riots of 1969—the three nights of confrontations between the gay citizens of New York and the city's police, usually regarded as the beginning of the gay liberation movement—were touched off, not by homophile organizations, but by boys in drag drowning their sorrow over the death of Judy Garland, who had been buried that day. The controversies over Robert Mapplethorpe's retrospective, *The Perfect Moment,* are perhaps the most potent of recent examples of camp's power to offend.

Mapplethorpe is a good example of how an artist can modify camp so that it retains its power to offend its audiences. His technically immaculate prints with their silvery, luminous lighting made his viewers distinctly uneasy by presenting images that challenged their very conceptions of themselves, which as Stallybrass and White have noted are: "continuously defined and redefined . . . through the exclusion of what [is] marked out as 'low'—as dirty, repulsive, noisy, contaminating" (191). I have in mind two self-portraits that Mapplethorpe executed in 1980. In the first, he is naked from the waist up, so that from the outset the viewer is aware of his boyish chest. His long hair is swept back. His face is carefully made-up in the tasteful way teen magazines instruct their readers. The result is not the Janus-like head of a drag queen with the male features protruding through the obvious artifice of cosmetics, but something far more disturbing—a very womanly if somewhat stressed man. The companion photograph shows him in a leather jacket, a dark shirt, his hair in a pompadour that descends down his forehead, and a cigarette dangling from his lips. But the effect is not a mock-biker. The hair is not greased; the face far from menacing. Since both photographs are shot in soft focus, the nude seems silky; while the portrait in leather appears vulnerable and delicate. Mapplethorpe has thrown into question the naturalness of the androgyne and savageness of the biker by gaily inverting our expectations of inversion. In yet another photograph, a double portrait of Brian Ridley and Lyle Heeter (1979), Mapplethorpe captures an S-M couple. The older man stands in leather holding chains that are connected to a younger man who is seated, his hands and feet manacled, his neck collared and chained as well. But what keeps this portrait from becoming a Diane Arbus study in the pathological is the young man's face—it is as quiet, calm, and self-possessed as the boy's next door. His slightly rumpled hair gives him a boyishness that goes along with his tired eyes. These are not monsters born from the sleep of reason, but humans who do not fit the mold.

Mapplethorpe is most disturbing not because he sets up the simpleminded demonology that has proved so popular with heavy-metal bands—a self-conscious immorality—but because the glossy surface of his fashion photographs of the latest vinyl suits for masochists into water sports provides no easy resting place for his ironies. As Kiernan points out, the ideal camper possesses a "shameless love of all that is exaggerated" and an "amoral mode of laughter" (16).

Through the studied avoidance of the usual gargoyles, Mapplethorpe retains the carnivalesque atmosphere in *Certain People* that a less subtle and more conventional artist would reduce to the pathological. Gilbert and George, for example, turn their gallery of working-class boys into the predictable chorus of fallen angels which reflect heterosexual stereotypes of homosexuals. Mapplethorpe approaches each subject as a separate aesthetic and erotic object, freed from all but formalistic concerns. The only category that embraces these subtly unclassifiable portraits is the aesthetic. As Sontag noted in her preface to the collection, Mapplethorpe

> is not looking for the decisive moment. His photographs do not claim to be revelatory. He is not in a predatory relation to his subject. He is not voyeuristic. He is not trying to catch anyone off-guard. The rules of the game of photography, as Mapplethorpe plays it, are that the subject must cooperate—must be lit. Mapplethorpe wants to photograph everything, that is, everything that can be made to pose.

All of Mapplethorpe's people are poseurs: gothic and classic alike.

Mapplethorpe is heir to a long line of gay photography that has played with the aesthetic tensions between the classic and gothic. At the turn of the century Frederick Rolfe, better known as Baron Corvo, Fred Holland Day, Wilhelm von Pluschow, John Gambril Nicholson, Vincenzo Galdi, and perhaps most famous, Wilhelm von Gloeden recorded beautiful young men in the nude or nearly so. Often they posed the models in classical positions, as a young Bacchus, or as Pan playing on his pipe, or else in the presence of classical statuary. The result never quite managed, however, to achieve the right Hellenic sweetness and light—and even they seemed to feel some humor in the situation. Roland Barthes, writing about von Gloeden, has accurately put his finger on the camp effect of these fin de siècle photographs:

> The Baron's photographs are of a *ruthless* kind. And the sublime legend enters in collision (one has to use this word to understand our astonishment and perhaps our great joy) with the realism of the photography; for what is a photograph thus conceived non[e] other than an image where *all is seen;* a collection of details without hierarchy, without 'order' (the great classic principle). These

little greek gods (already contradicted by their darkness) have dirty peasants' hands, badly cured fingernails, worn out and dirty feet; their foreskins are swollen and well in evidence, no longer stylized, that is, pointed and smaller; they are uncircumcised, this is all one sees. (21)

Barthes concludes that these photographs—indeed the very medium von Gloeden used—was a "carnaval [sic] of contradictions" (21). In these portraits we see at once why photography, rather than painting or drawing, has been the best medium for the erotics of camp, for by pitting classic and grotesque versions of the body together and rendering them both as mere poses it was able to create a "carnaval of contradictions" beyond even Bakhtin's inverted hierarchy. This tradition of mixing classical and grotesque images continued unbroken through the works of Cocteau, George Platt-Lynes, and Cecil Beaton, so that when Mapplethorpe shot his now famous portraits of black men in severely classical poses, he alluded to what was already an on-going "carnaval of contradictions." Thus, as we adjust our eyes to the dark 1981 picture of Ajitto in fetal position, we come to note below the X formed by his arms and legs the enormous silhouette of his genitals. In the double portrait of Ken Moody and Robert Sherman (1984), the faces have become so severely and chastely sculptural, shorn of any hair at all, that he has blended grotesque and classical images of the body into an entirely camp category of the mannequin. This confusion is heightened by Mapplethorpe's practice of photographing actual classical sculpture as though it were human. Perhaps the epitome of Mapplethorpe's playful confusion between Gothic and classic, human and sculpture, natural and artificial is in his "Man in Polyester Suit" (1980) in which the enormous black penis hanging out of the pants seems constructed from the same materials as the suit which failed to contain it. Although the human, real, and natural has erupted from the synthetic, man-made, and unnatural, those categories seem inverted or meaningless. In such pictures Mapplethorpe has replaced the diadic structure of the carnivalesque with the triadic oscillations of camp.

Some may object that much of what I have identified as camp is not funny, and camp, they would argue, is essentially silly. But the humor of camp, while it may be full-throated, can also leave a lump. As Andrew Holleran says of Charles Ludlam's Theatre of the Ridiculous performances, "He played both tragedy and Farce and refused to tell us which was which. He died onstage of tuberculosis, or heartache, and left us not knowing whether to laugh or to cry, suspended somewhere (with parted lips) between the two; so when he raised his gloved hand to his lips, as Camille, and coughed those three coughs—just three—the audience both howled and stopped laughing altogether" (*Zero*, 97).

Richard Howard describes the impulse behind Mapplethorpe's witty flower pictures—which identify the buds not with female genitalia as is usually the case, but with the phallus—as part of "Mapplethorpe's task . . . to restore the gravity which has leaked out of what is unspeakable" ("Mapplethorpe," 155). The word "restore" implies that the "unspeakable" has been trivialized. Camp, then, is not trivial, but a reaction to trivialization. Its sacred parodies are a strategy to reinvoke a divinity that has fled; it seeks entrance to the Dionysian mysteries through its bawdy revelries.

Camp finds itself today at a crisis. Many of the social conditions for which camp was an adequate, even successful, response no longer obtain, at last with the same urgency. Most gay people no longer feel the terrible need to hide homosexual communication for fear of blackmail or criminal prosecution. Indeed, gay men now prefer to assert their political strength by making themselves visible. Again, camp's appearance of powerlessness, which gay men and women affected to make themselves less threatening to the heterosexual majority and avoid retaliation, is a strategy that the AIDS crisis and organizations such as ACT UP have found to be counterproductive.

But the crisis in camp goes further than the change in political climate. Andrew Ross's "Uses of Camp" presents a rather critical view of the style. For Ross, camp is co-opted by bourgeois values insofar as it has tried to appeal to the broad spectrum of the American public or to the lower classes. It pays tribute, he claims, "to the official national ideology of liberal pluralism" in its very attempt to short circuit established categories (6). I think Ross underestimates the provocative nature of such camp works as John Waters's *Pink Flamingos,* in which the transvestite Divine eats a dog turd to prove once and for all that she *is* the filthiest woman in the world. Ross also points out that camp's commitment to the marginal dooms it forever to a certain elitism and insignificance, its very process of challenging the categories of bourgeois seriousness already foreshadowing its failure to dislodge those categories. Ross's argument against camp duplicates the argument raised against the carnivalesque: Can such "licenced release"—as Stallybrass and White call it—really alter the dominant culture, or does it merely serve as a safety value that, in fact, helps the dominant continue? Can there ever be an opposition to the codes of the dominant culture that is not committed to its own marginality? The only answer is that cultural codes do alter, and it is impossible to say whether they have changed only through their own internal evolution or through a dialectical operation that involves opposing values. What is clear is that an elite, however marginal, is not insignificant and that camp has had its rippling effect throughout the culture.

Ross does not, it seems to me, appreciate fully that a style can be destabilizing without being overtly oppositional. Gay people have recognized that they can achieve their rights not by becoming the majority, but by finessing the entire issue of power. Or to put it another way, were gay culture to develop a discourse of power in parity to the dominant society's discourse, it would only end up reproducing the machismo which has oppressed it. The aggressive passivity of camp has been among its most potent tools in giving gay people a voice that we ourselves could hear and then use to speak to others.

At a recent Gay Pride Day celebration in Baltimore, a drag queen in an elaborate lamé gown pried himself into a dunking booth to raise money for a special AIDS ward at Johns Hopkins Hospital. Having straightened his tiara on top of his puffed-up tresses, he barked at the gathering crowd, "Which of you brutes is going to make my mascara run?" It was a scene that typified not only the aggressive passivity of camp, but quite literally the carnivalesque world Bakhtin so much admired. It broke down the categories of brutality and cultivation and mocked the very notions of opposition it so gaily employed. It testified to the fact that camp is far from dead and celebrated the life of a community beset by the morbid.

In many ways, it strikes me that camp is the voice of survival and continuity in a community that needs to be reminded that it possesses both. It has come to serve those purposes before AIDS, and it will probably do so again. Camp appears in the most unlikely places. Allen Ginsberg is not a poet usually associated with camp, yet *Howl* is a supremely campy poem, and as time has gone on, Ginsberg has recited it with greater and greater emphasis on its comically carnivalesque tone. And in Ginsberg's "A Supermarket in California," a poem wistful and joyous, comic and sad by turns, the powers of camp to bind wounds and unsettle expectation, to destabilize even as it seems most accommodating are clearly in evidence:

> I saw you, Walt Whitman, childless, lonely old grubber,
> poking among the meats in the refrigerator and eyeing the
> grocery boys.
> I heard you asking questions of each: Who killed the
> pork chops? What price bananas? Are you my Angel?
> I wandered in and out of the brilliant stacks of cans
> following you, and followed in my imagination by the store
> detective.
> We strode down the open corridors together in our
> solitary fancy tasting artichokes, possessing every frozen
> delicacy, and never passing the cashier.

> (136)

D. A. Miller might find in the reference to the store detective a clear sign of the importation of normative justice into gay society. The detective reminds us of the codes this poem so gaily transgresses, for Ginsberg and Whitman float through the store without passing the cashier. Camp does not do away with the dominant society, but rather finds a way to live within it. It also knows that its salvation is not found in that dominant society. Camp may ask the grocery boy "Are you my Angel?" but the question is all but rhetorical. He is not. And though Ginsberg shares the supermarket—symbol of petit bourgeois society— with "whole families shopping at night! Aisles full of husbands! Wives in the avocados, babies in the tomatoes!" his words are saved for Whitman and García Lorca "down by the watermelons."

Works Cited

Babuscio, Jack. "Camp and the Gay Sensibility." In *Gays and Film,* edited by Richard Dyer, 40–57. Revised edition. New York: Zoetrope, 1984.

Bakhtin, Mikhail. *Rabelais and His World.* Translated by Helene Iswolsky. Cambridge: MIT Press, 1968.

Barthes, Roland. *Wilhelm Von Gloeden.* Naples: Amelio Editore, 1978.

Chester, Alfred. *The Exquisite Corpse.* New York: Carroll and Graf, 1986.

Cohen, Ira. "Our Ancestor Alfred Chester." In *Head of a Sad Angel: Stories 1953–1966,* by Alfred Chester, 364–65. Santa Rosa, Calif.: Black Sparrow, 1990.

Duncan, Robert. "The Homosexual in Society." In *Young Robert Duncan: Portrait of the Poet as Homosexual in Society,* edited by Ekbert Fass, 319–22. Santa Barbara, Calif.: Black Sparrow, 1983.

———. Preface to *Caesar's Gate: Poems 1949–50.* N.p.: Sand Dollar, 1972.

Edel, Leon, ed. *Henry James Letters.* Vols. 3 and 4. Cambridge: Harvard University Press, 1984.

Ellmann, Richard. *Oscar Wilde.* New York: Knopf, 1988.

Faderman, Lillian. *Surpassing the Love of Men: Romantic Friendship and Love Between Women from the Renaissance to the Present.* New York: William Morrow, 1981.

Ginsberg, Allen. *Howl and Other Poems.* San Francisco: City Lights, 1956.

Holleran, Andrew. *Ground Zero.* New York: New American Library, 1989.

Howard, Richard. "The Mapplethorpe Effect." In *Robert Mapplethorpe,* by Richard Marshall, 152–59. New York: Whitney Museum, 1988.

———. "Translator's Note." In *Corydon,* by Andre Gide, vii–xvii. London: Gay Men's Press, 1985.

Kiernan, Robert F. *Frivolity Unbounded: Six Masters of the Camp Novel.* New York: Continuum, 1990.

Miller, D. A. *The Novel and the Police.* Berkeley: University of California Press, 1988.

Newton, Esther. *Mother Camp: Female Impersonators in America.* Chicago: University of Chicago Press, 1979.

Rodgers, Bruce. *Gay Talk: A (Sometimes Outrageous) Dictionary of Gay Slang.* New York: Paragon, 1972.

Rosenthal, M. L. *The New Poets.* New York: Oxford University Press, 1967.

Ross, Andrew. "Uses of Camp." *Yale Journal of Criticism* 2, no. 2 (1988): 1–24.

Sontag, Susan. *Against Interpretation and Other Essays.* New York: Farrar, Straus and Giroux, 1966.

———. "Certain Mapplethorpes." In *Certain People: A Book of Portraits,* by Robert Mapplethorpe. N.p.: Twelvetrees Press, 1985.

Stallybrass, Peter, and Allon White. *The Politics and Poetics of Transgression.* Ithaca: Cornell University Press, 1986.

Weiermair, Peter. *The Hidden Image: Photographs of the Male Nude in the Nineteenth and Twentieth Centuries.* Cambridge: MIT Press, 1988.

Wilde, Oscar. *The Artist as Critic: The Critical Writings of Oscar Wilde,* edited by Richard Ellmann. New York: Random House, 1968.

———. *The Importance of Being Earnest.* In *Plays,* 247–315. Harmondsworth: Penguin, 1971.

Yingling, Thomas E. *Hart Crane and the Homosexual Text: New Thresholds, New Anatomies.* Chicago: University of Chicago Press, 1990.

APPLIED CAMP

Walt Whitman Camping

KARL KELLER

'**I** . . . am stucco'd with quadrapeds and birds all over.'[1]

The humor of a line like that from "Song of Myself," is difficult to explain. At first glance, the persona of the poem appears to have been thoroughly bedunged or has turned into a Dada-ist piece of mock-sculpture. Such outrageousness in Whitman can be dismissed as ludicrous extravagance until one recognizes the aesthetic sensibility from which it comes.

There has been considerable difficulty in naming and describing Whitman's humor. Frontier humor, by all odds the largest tradition of humor in American letters, is one category into which his is quite often put but in which he sits very uncomfortably; breadth and sweep of telling has too often been confused with tall-tale-ing. Social satire is another category into which his humor has often been put but only with an equal confusion: as egalitarian, he often identifies himself sympathetically with that which he pokes fun at, and the edge of the humor is therefore blunted. Verbal irony is a third category in which Whitman is often made to do service, even if awkwardly so; but his paradoxes ('I discover myself on the verge of a usual mistake'; 'Do I contradict myself?/Very well then I contradict myself'; etc; 88) are so easily resolvable within his Compensationism that the irony is dissolved; he *means* the contradictions.

And in addition, in locating Whitman's humor, it will not do to point to the self-parodying he fell into in his later work, when he was perhaps overenamored of his own success with poetic style and prophetic roles. Nor will it do to point to Whitman's gaffes as representing his humor—such as when, in outlining his sexual politics, he speaks of "Plunging his seminal muscle [that is, his phallus] into [America's] merits and demerits" (344), or when, in one of his "Calamus" poems, he speaks of homosexual companions with their "robust love" as a "new city of Friends" (with a Capital 'F'; that is, Quakers; 133). These are the slips of poetic enthusiasm.

Rather, I would like to suggest an additional way of understanding Whitman's humor, one which takes both the sensibility of the poet and his forms of language into consideration, and one which will assist us in realizing more fully the tone with which he addresses his material and with which we might read the resulting verse. "Camp" seems to me to come closest to naming accurately the urbane, flamboyant theatricality and the richly varied gestures and postures of Whitman's humorous lines. Whitman-as-a-camp can be a serious and refreshing way of reading the poetry.

Of course, a camp reading of Whitman has always been possible. This was evident in a number of the literary parodies of his style from the 1870s on. But such is usually more a description of a critic's attitude toward the poetry than it is a description of qualities in the poetry itself. That is one's own campiness, not Whitman's. And of course, Whitman also does service in camp situations—as in the use of an imprint of his face on recent gay lib T-shirts with the lines (playing with Whitman's own terms) "SO MANY COMRADES, SO LITTLE TIME" and "I SING THE BAWDY ELECTORATE."That, again, is a campy use of Whitman and not necessarily anything he intended himself. But to read Whitman's humor seriously as camp, as I would like to argue, is to discover something new about his attitudes, personality, and abilities.

Camp—to rehearse the definition of the term as a critical/analytical tool—means exaggeration of personality mannerisms, a theatricality in posture and gesture, the turning of temperament and manner into a style, a flamboyance of expression, an extravagance in content and form, the stylization of the fantastic, passionate, and naive, the outlandish and outrageous formalized as a style of speaking or writing, a theatrical manner in playing with ideas and language, excess itself as a playful manner.

In literature, camp appears in the form of the epiphanal tease, the theatricalization of a narrator, character, or point of view, the use of extreme mannerisms as personality gestures, the invention of awkward intensities in syntax or metaphor, the mock-play with inflated conventions of narration and characterization, extravagance of style as a disguise for the writer, the tone of voice that is "too much" and therefore entertaining in its flamboyant playfulness. Literary camp is anti-ironic, for it intends its excesses. It is antisatiric, for it mocks its own enjoyment of its own excesses. It celebrates the voice for its erratic range, its arbitrary intensities, its *italics*—and therein lies a literary representation of the heroism of the anarchic, autonomous personality.

Susan Sontag, who co-opted the term *camp* for a short while, barely noticed the existence of camp in literature; nothing at all of American poetry appears in what she calls her "canon of Camp." That is because her understanding of the concepts comes largely from fin de siècle art and wit or from opera and mannered Hollywood acting. She has little or no sense of camp as joy-from-the-fringe-of-society, no sense of rejuvenation-of-art-forms-as-criticism-of-contemporary-aesthetics, no sense of camp as politically-artful-defense-and-assertion, no sense of camp as extravagant-play-for-serious-ends.[2]

It might be possible to connect Whitman with a tradition of camp in American literature if it weren't for the probability that he created it anew himself for his own works, that in fact it grew quite naturally out of his own personality and his own aesthetics. We have literary camp in the baroque prose of Cotton Mather's *Magnalia Christi Americana,* in what Mather called his "massy way of writing . . . stuck with as many jewels as the gown of a Russian ambassador." We probably have camp in Poe's theatrical, paragothic horror— cheap phantasmagoria as cosmic thrills. We may even have camp in the encyclopedic pedantry of the cetology sections of *Moby-Dick.* We have camp when Emily Dickinson plays little girl before God and vamp to the Creation; as she put it, she was "the only Kangaroo among the Beauty." And we have camp in the theatrical syntax of Henry James's prolix, oblique sentences; this is what Ms. Sontag calls "the quality of excruciation."[3]

But Whitman is a camp out of an aesthetic all his own: the individual personality, as a voice, allowing itself full range and, as a role, allowing itself instant character, therefore emerging in the form of a quirky extravagance, an assertive, self-mocking tease, a playfulness with epiphanal states that are half-serious because therapeutically high and half-comical because deliberately overblown. The poet is *performing.*

Those who have bemoaned the contradiction between Whitman's claim that his poetry, especially "Song of Myself," revealed his personality well and the paucity of autobiographical detail in the poems have only failed to look, I feel, at the workings of Whitman's voice—that is, the gestures and roles that his tones of voice create. Whitman's style is kinetic if anything, and one must look for the voices and roles he plays with as indicators of a person revealing himself, recognizing that a writer like Whitman is less interested in flashing his entire person at us than he is in showing the range of *possibilities* of his personality.

It is time we recognized that the persona that the "Chanter of Personality" slips into is often a camp one. We see this in the flamboyant gestures, the exaggerated tone, the operatic voice, the inflated role-playing, the dilation of language—all of these in order to achieve what he called his "ecstatic songs."

I know now why the earth is gross, tantalizing, wicked, it is for my sake,
I take you specially to be mine, you terrible, rude forms. (354)

Camp humor is one of the factors separating Whitman's early, dry newspaper verse from the mature works of 1854 and 1855 and afterwards, and one factor missing as his poetry fell off after 1865. It will be possible to give only a few examples here. We have an early instance of Whitman's campiness in "Starting from Paumanok" when, as he proclaims his sexual-political programme for America, he strikes a theatrical pose and with affected earnestness exclaims seductively/heroically:

I will sing the song of companionship . . .
I will therefore let flame from me the burning fires that were threatening to consume
     me . . .
I will give them complete abandonment,
I will write the evangel-poem of comrades and of love,
For who but I should understand love with its sorrows and joy?
And who but I should be the poet of comrades? . . .
(I may have to be persuaded many times before I consent to give myself
     really to you, but what of that?
Must not Nature be persuaded many times?) (19; 26)

The transcendentalist-coy voice here is one of stylized flamboyance, idealized artifice, mock-seriousness. The come-on proposes itself seriously but also with joy in the extravagant anarchism. The poet-prophet is a pimp! In the camp voice here, the real (that is, Whitman's own personal desires for bonding) and the ideal (that is, his hopes for a mass-promiscuous America) come together. The artifice of the theatrical pose and the theatrical voice makes this possible. Whitman poses for us as butch goddess of anarchic abandon.

One can find a similar campy flamboyance and serious teasing in lines of "Children of Adam" and "Calamus":

One hour to madness and joy! O furious! O confine me not! . . .
O to drink the mystic deliria deeper than any other man! . . .
O to be yielded to you whoever you are, and you to be yielded to me
     in defiance of the world! . . .
I am he that aches with amorous love (105–6; 109)

Who can imagine any of these get-ups without laughing at Whitman? Even when the intention is serious, the means are hilarious. He can be absolved of the charge of ludicrousness in such intense lines, however, if one appreciates them as literary camp. Such humor here rides on conventions of the sublime; but it is critical of them, mocks them, has fun with them, using them for one's own effect. The affected emphasis, exaggerations, and pretense throws the persona into high animation. Whitman's own personality thereby emerges above the conventions.

"Song of Myself" has the best examples of Whitman's ability to slip into and out of a camp kind of humor. This occurs most naturally for him when he reaches the epiphanal point of a section and needs an extravagant, flamboyant, theatrical voice for expressing his delight in the height (often sexual) at which he finds himself:

> Smile O voluptuous cool-breath'd earth! . . .
> Smile, for your lover comes . . .
> I believe you refuse to go back without feeling of me,
> We must have a turn together, I undress, hurry me out of sight of the land,
> Cushion me soft, rock me in billowy drowse,
> Dash me with amorous wet, I can repay you. (49)

Here, the sly, teasing campiness is ecstatic and seductive; at one and the same time, it is earthy and transcendent; it is most certainly a theatricalized piece of come-on. The playful pantheism is pitched high, though it is an awkward intensity, for the flamboyant facetiousness is also a serious hope led on by his passion. This particular description of Whitman in the "billowy drowse" is sexual bodysurfing raised lovingly and seriously to the level of the sexual-outrageous. When the Self is thus merged with the ridiculous-sublime, we have poetic camp of a high order.

In "Song of Myself," when Whitman reaches the point of self-aggrandizing affectation, we often get camp humor like the following:

> I dote on myself, there is that lot of me and all so luscious,
> Each moment and whatever happens thrills me with joy . . . (54)

The tone in such lines is a little precious, a little exhibitionistic, a little theatrically over-done. In such lines, Whitman poses as for a brief, flashy role, half-way meaning what he says (that he is desirable) and halfway *not* meaning it (that he desires himself). The verbal gestures are flamboyant and funny. He camps for us.

There is similar campy extravagance in "Song of Myself" when Whitman plays promiscuously with the landscape around him and needs to be sure that his close identification with abundance has a tone of flamboyant enjoyment about it:

> What is commonest, cheapest, nearest, easiest, is Me,
> Me going in for my chances, spending for vast returns,
> Adorning myself to bestow myself on the first that will take me . . . (41)

The aggrandized generosity of self here is a theatrical pose—aloof, flip, a little grand, a little loose. He charades in teasing verbal attire. The Over-Soul is a whore!

This extravagant posing and gesturing amid nature (as if it itself were some vast, spiritual androgyne in elaborate drag and Whitman is imitating it) is seen in a number of additional lines, in which the ludicrous is so apt as to create a kind of comic grotesquery:

> I . . . am stucco'd with quadrapeds and birds all over . . . (59)

> The scent of these arm-pits [is an] aroma finer than prayer . . . (53)

> I have instant conductors all over me whether I pass or stop . . . (57)

> By my life-lumps! becoming already a creator,
> Putting myself here and now to the ambush'd womb of the shadows. (76)

There is an underlying seriousness with such extravagant posturing. Whitman camps on such occasions *because* he takes his enjoyments seriously; he is not making fun of the things he talks about but making fun out of them. In other words, camp humor is a way Whitman has of verbally intensifying his enjoyment of the world around him. He expresses what is basically serious to him in terms of play and artifice.

There are two extremely funny ways in which Whitman becomes campy in the poetry of the 1850s. And even though they are slight gestures, they became hallmarks of his style throughout his mature writing years. These are gestures which I think are not easily explainable apart from an understanding of camp humor.

The first is Whitman's affectation of throwing in a French (or sometimes an Italian or Spanish) word. This, it seems to me, is a piece of artifice, even an outlandish contrivance, to make a line a little bit more theatrical. The exotic term lifts the context campily. Listen to the affected italics in such lines as the following:

> I, habitan of the Alleghanies . . .
>   Exalté, rapt, ecstatic,
> The visible but their womb of birth . . .
> Me imperturbe, standing at ease in Nature . . .
> I with my leaves and songs, trustful, admirant . . .
> See . . . Countless masses debouch upon them . . .
> Melange mine own, the unseen and the seen . . .
> No dainty dolce affettuoso I . . .

Now list to my morning's romanza . . .
Always our old feuillage!
Always Florida's green peninsula . . .
[She] was not so desperate at the battues of death . . .
And I guess some chansonniers there will understand . . .
I will yet sing a song for you ma femme. (4, 7, 11, 12, 16, 21, 26, 166, 171, 236)

The motive in such lines as these is no doubt affected emphasis, or perhaps verbal animation. In any event, the result is emphasis made incredible by being outlandishly unnecessary. The mannerism is a campy tic, but it serves the purpose of intensifying, if theatrically, Whitman's enjoyment of his subject. One's personality is thereby projected on to things.

The other camp mannerism that became a hallmark of Whitman's style is his macho pose—that is, a line or two thrown in to assure us that a "rough" (a term Whitman occasionally liked to use for himself) is speaking:

Stout as a horse, affectionate, haughty, electrical,
I and this mystery here we stand . . . (31)

Who goes there? hankering, gross, mystical, nude;
How is it I extract strength from the beef I eat? . . . (47)

I am Walt Whitman, liberal and lusty as Nature . . . (387)

I too am not a bit tamed, I too am untranslatable,
I sound my barbaric yawp over the roofs of the world. (89)

This mannered posing is outlandishly contrived. The affected emphasis on verbal machismo, if only in passing in a poem, is not sufficiently hardboiled to create a thorough characterization, but nonetheless it makes a voice Whitman liked to slip into for theatrical effect.

I feel that such examples show the range of camp humor in "Song of Myself" and other poems up to 1865. In each case, where one is tempted to charge careless diffusion of Self or mere egotism or other flaws of conception and self-conception, the poet's camp humor can be seen as a way of asserting one's own personality playfully. The campiness, while being mocking and mockable, artificial and artful, is a genuinely original humor. It animates his poses and roles well. It shows him *enjoying* his serious ideas. Whitman is—if one accepts his campy humor as it grew naturally out of his own sensibility— one of American literature's best examples of *homo ludens:* he is the poet at play. Does it go too far to suggest that Walt Whitman is the Mae West of American literature?

Notes

1. Walt Whitman, *Leaves of Grass,* Comprehensive Reader's Edition, ed. Harold W. Blodgett and Sculley Bradley (New York: New York University Press, 1965), 59. Further citations to this edition will be given within the text.

2. Susan Sontag, "Notes on 'Camp,'" *Against Interpretation and Other Essays* (New York: Farrar, Straus and Giroux, 1966), 275–92.

3. Ibid., 287.

High Culture and High Camp:

THE CASE OF MARCEL PROUST

GREGORY WOODS

When Philip Core includes Marcel Proust in his pantheon of camp figures, he does so on the grounds that Proust's novel *A la recherche du temps perdu* is an "immense survey of French society from the 1880s through the early 1920s," offering "a unique example of camp on an epic scale" (153). Trading on a similarly narrow version of camp, Mark Booth makes a similar point: "Marcel Proust wrote some delightfully camp Comedy of Manners, but unfortunately he kept on spoiling it by drifting into a dreary Pateresque neo-platonism" and thereby "becoming too introspective to be considered properly camp" (70).

Proust's novel does contain and represent gossip; but it is not at all *like* gossip. It is far too long-winded for that; far too "serious," in an aesthetic sense. The connoisseur of tittle-tattle must, inevitably, be disappointed by it, even if it does frequently offer real pearls of scandal, such as the flagellation of the baron de Charlus in its final volume. Gérard Genette recognizes this aspect of Proust's fiction when he examines its frequent use of the "principle of deferred or postponed significance" and of subsequent revelations—a technique common in popular fiction. As Genette expresses it, in a wonderful put-down, "There is something of 'it was Milady' in the *Recherche*" (57).

Those who are most appreciative of this dimension of the book are, perhaps, also most likely to buy such books as Borrel, Senderens, and Naudin's *Dining with Proust*, which lavishly re-creates the novel's most significant culinary experiences, or to attend such occasions as a concert of "The Music of Marcel Proust," held in St John's, Smith Square, London, to mark the seventieth anniversary of the author's death. The most elementary kinds of literary camp are thus expected to overstep the bounds of artistic form, thence to reemerge in a space of readerly inquisitiveness where they may spring to life as elegant tittle-tattle. The outcome is a situation in which those who have read the *Recherche*—those who have *endured*—see themselves as an embattled social elite, making up for what they lack in aristocratic credentials with a display of aesthetic appreciation.

This kind of response to a book is also the one most likely to dwell on the author's life. When the line between art and life becomes blurred—as it always will wherever camp codes and values operate—all aspects of the literary experience become available to gossip. Indeed, more than many authors, Proust gives plenty of scope for prurient speculation. My favorite version of his life, although brief, contains a number of ingredients likely to delight the camp sensibility: "Proust always loved to peddle gossip, was indecisive and procrastinating in practical affairs, received strange friends at night, took sudden short secret trips about which little is known, and led an irresponsible, self-centered life. After his mother's death he became entangled with strange characters, some of whom he kept virtual prisoners in his apartment" (Brée 88). If only this were all the biography we needed.

Proust had both the prying curiosity of an addicted gossip and the secretive discretion of the sexually perverse. For all his reputation as a high-minded aesthete, remote and sickly in his cork-lined boudoir, he was nevertheless wholly committed to social and sexual life. What he may have lacked in direct physical involvement, he made up for in a restless imagination: as with all rumormongers, observed reality lapsed into fiction.

However, the concentration, by connoisseurs of camp, on Proust's novel's status as a grand act of gossip gives a somewhat reductive view of the extent to which camp operates within its structure. In any case, the social-survey approach to Proust was soundly denounced by Walter Benjamin, as long ago as 1929, when he complained of hack critics in Germany who wrote about the *Recherche* as if it were merely "a literary supplement to the *Almanach de Gotha*" (208). Of course, the *Recherche* is camp insofar as it pays homage to such works of highbrow gossip as Saint-Simon's memoirs and Mme de Sevigné's letters, and to the scandalous aspect of such realist fiction as Balzac's *Comédie humaine*. The book is, indeed, as Roland Barthes called it, "among other things, a tremendous intrigue, a farce network" (138). Many of its effects depend on pleasures one can associate with those afforded by gossip.

Looking forward to his own Marxist version of the classless utopia, Fredric Jameson sees the Proustian social world as an anticipation, albeit in caricature, of such a society; and he continues: "In this sense it is perhaps not too much to say that *gossip*—that meeting place of conversation and art, that profoundly fertile vice of both Saint-Simon and Proust (and indeed of Balzac as well, in a very different social milieu)—may itself stand as a kind of distorted figure of that passion for the human in its smallest details which will be ours in the transfigured society and the transfigured world" (154). Here, Jameson has a political agenda with which, for the purposes of the present essay, I am not concerned; nor am I convinced by it. I quote him here as another major cultural critic whose readings of the *Recherche* center on the idea of the joys of gossip.

However, when we read the book itself in hope of a frisson of camp recognition, what comes between our social curiosity and the titbits on which it thrives is the character of Marcel, the narrator. He is both conduit and obstruction to the flow of information. He is a gossip, but not a good one. Much of the time he is more interested in himself than in the social panorama which his position has promised; and even so, as we shall see, he is not entirely open about himself. Furthermore, he thinks of himself, accurately, as having a profound mind. He is not content to act, merely, as a kind of gossip columnist to the salons; he needs, also, to philosophize. Since we are told that camp aestheticism operates only at a shallow level, we do not really expect to see Marcel's profound *Recherche* appearing on any canonical list of camp texts.

But apart from its status as an act of gossip, there is another major way in which the *Recherche* may be seen to be operating "shallowly" (an epithet which I use, as far as it is possible to do so, descriptively rather than as a value judgment). After alerting us to the fact that *signe* is one of the most frequently used words in Proust's novel, Gilles Deleuze gives the following pithy account of how "worldly" signs tend to operate therein: "The worldly sign appears as the replacement of an action or thought. It stands for action and for thought. It is therefore a sign which does not refer to something else, to a transcendent signification or to an ideal content, but which has usurped the supposed value of its meaning. This is why worldliness, judged from the viewpoint of actions, appears to be disappointing or cruel; and from the viewpoint of thought, it appears stupid. One does not think and one does not act, but one makes signs" (6). The example Deleuze offers is that of Mme. Verdurin's counterfeit laughter.

Proust's characters perform to the requirements of social form—even when they are being spied on in some of their most private moments. (The flagellation of Charlus is the book's climactic incident of sexual role-play.) Not that the shallowness of signs is lacking in meaning. On the contrary, it is often by the reading of physical movements that Marcel manages to divine the deepest psychological significance. The disturbing point is that one has to attend to the slightest gesture as if it were some runic scripture, just in case it should turn out to be a manifestation of the soul rather than a mere affectation. In many cases it will prove to be, simply, the latter.

Roger Shattuck has shown how insistently Marcel's viewpoint, for all its famous celebrations of smells and tastes, is fixed in the sense of sight; and, as such, how it constantly comments on visible surfaces: "it is principally through the science and the art of *optics* that he beholds and depicts the world" (6). The result is, of course, a shallowness of concern in one area, and a consequent displacement of depth: "The accumulation of optical figures in *A la recherche* gradually removes our depth perception from space and re-erects it in time" (43). It may be, then, that by distinguishing between the novel's spatial and temporal dimensions, we can recognize in the former—in its apparent shallowness, its concern with visible surface values—a conventionally camp narrative of the type that aspires to be mistaken for pure gossip.

However, there seems to me to be a more profoundly significant area in which Proust's camp operates in a distinctly Modernist manner and offers itself as an example to subsequent gay writers and artists. This is the way in which Proust's narrative technique marshals various groups of his readers, controlling what each group understands the text to mean, and thereby also taking control of the ways in which different readers relate to author, narrator, and characters.

It may be that Modernism forces us to consider including a depth model alongside, or within, our customary, prejudicial definitions of gossip as an entirely shallow affair. Patricia Meyer Spacks has suggestively referred to the "elegant form of gossip called psychoanalysis" (104). Indeed, many early texts from the mental health movement—I am thinking in particular of Krafft-Ebing's *Psychopathia Sexualis,* but others would do—sound as if they had issued, fully formed, from a perverse collaboration of Balzac and Feydeau. In Proust, gossip is very often a way of life—not just a pastime but a psychological necessity. It is also an art. For instance, Marcel's aunt Léonie, rendered idle by illnesses largely imaginary, keeps a stern watch from her window on all the movements of the people of Combray. If the delivery boy from Galopins passes with a pastry, she has to deduce for whom it is destined, or she sends her maid Françoise to find out. And if the street is so quiet as to offer no human subject to her curiosity, she is content to gossip about the village dogs (1:72–77).[1] Now, it may be that a woman who is reduced to gossiping about a dog is a pathetic case; but she is also, perforce, impressively creative, not least because she must conjure up, out of nothing, her own satisfaction. Anyone who has ever tried to gossip about a dog must have felt keenly the prospect, the probability, of disappointment: for there is no possibility of a canine rumor's eventually finding its way to its own victim's ears—and that is half the pleasure gone. Be that as it may, Léonie has passed beyond the point at which gossip satisfies as mere entertainment. It is life and breath to her, the *cogito* of Descartes rendered sociable: I think socially, therefore I am. That is why, as a character, Léonie is so crucial to Proust's project.

However, it is toward a more sophisticated definition of camp, rather than merely of gossip, that we must direct our work, in order to recognize beyond the social panorama of the *Recherche* a campness that is central to Proust's Modernism. After all, as I have been suggesting, camp is not necessarily superficial. Its shallowness is in struggle with depths, and not always to the latter's disadvantage. The glittering queen, for all her poise and all her noise, contains a complex case history, potential jailbird, and fodder for the mind-quacks. It is this unacknowledged side that gives the queen's jokes their edge and her torch-songs their poignancy.

Jonathan Dollimore has written about the kind of camp that "undermines the depth model of identity from inside, being a kind of parody and mimicry which hollows out from within, making depth recede into its surfaces. Rather than a direct repudiation of depth, there is a performance of it to excess: depth is undermined by being taken to and beyond its own limits" (310–11). I would add, however, that in the work of a writer like Proust, or of W. H. Auden after him, camp stratagems may have been adopted in affirmation of the depths of homosexual identity, in opposition to the shallows of heterosexual complacency. Thanks to the heterosexual tendency to misconstrue homosexual patterns of behavior and thought, we are able to live out the inner dimensions of our lives within the carapace of absurd stereotypes imposed on us by those who, in ignorance, are unable to appreciate that we have any depths at all. They want us shallow, so we act shallow. This compromise is both quiescent and defiant.

The source of most of the *Recherche*'s camp ironies is an apparent distance between the mind "behind" the book and the mind of the narrator: the gap between Marcel and Proust. So much depends, then, on what we know about Proust and what we must deduce about Marcel. The whole issue finds its focus in the inevitable question of sexualities. Most commentators have not felt shy of offering firm opinions in this area. George D. Painter's biography set up the standard account of the relationship between the author's psychology and that of his narrator: "In his novel Proust rejected his own inversion, and created the Narrator from the lost but real heterosexual part of his own divided nature" (313). Others followed this line, which obviously meant concluding that Marcel was at a greater distance than Proust from the book's proven homosexual characters: "The narrator himself is not a homosexual; he 'looks at' the maneuvers of the homosexual Baron de Charlus from outside" (Brée, 175).

Even recently, and even in studies that purported to examine the book's sexualities in depth, critics have continued to feel very sure of themselves on this issue: "The narrator of *A la recherche* is, of course, presented as heterosexually inclined" (Rivers, 16). In its acknowledgment that presentation is the nub of the issue, this is a step forward, but what we need to take into account is that Marcel presents *himself* as heterosexual, which proves nothing.

Even where the presence of homosexuality is acknowledged, many commentators feel that the book's "universality" quotient is at risk if one pays inordinate attention to its interest in a minority concern. For instance: "The issue is not homosexuality but the complex, contradictory motives that underlie any sort of love" (Splitter, 55). In sum, the usual critical line is most succinctly typified by this claim of Malcolm Bradbury's: "Marcel is heterosexual, Proust was homosexual" (142). This is to take Marcel's narrative, simplistically, at face value. It also, in its juxtaposition of those tenses, "is" and "was," implies that heterosexuality is of more immediate significance to today's reader than the homosexuality of a dead man. Alternatively, a transgressive camp "sensibility" (of both the author and a certain constituency of readers) might allow us to take the critically dubious step of treating a character—in this case the novel's narrator and supposedly its controlling consciousness—as a human being. It might sanction my own view that Marcel would have been far happier in a *ménage* with Robert de Saint-Loup than he ever was with Albertine Simonet.

What it comes down to is this. Does Proust want us to believe Marcel is telling the whole truth about himself? Is Proust hiding behind a crudely heterosexualized Marcel; or is he using a Marcel who crudely heterosexualizes himself, to reveal himself, Proust, as a man who has been having to *pass*? Could it be that Proust is that impossible, self-betraying creature, a closeted gay man who portrays himself as a closeted gay man? By showing himself in the closet, he comes out of it.

The more one dwells upon the supposed "heterosexuality" of Marcel, the more implausible it seems. If we decide, or pliably allow the critics to decide on our behalf, that Marcel is attracted only to women, and that this attraction is stable, we may eventually have to conclude that the whole novel is irreparably flawed by the fact that its narrator—in his very character as well as in the things he says—is incredible. The problem would not be, then, that Marcel is unreliable or evasive or mendacious, but far worse: in the central premise of the novel, the nature of its narrator (and, consequently, of its narrative), Proust himself has made an incompetent decision.

I am not willing to make this criticism—and I wonder how those critics who think that Marcel is monolithically heterosexual would answer it. Convinced, as I am, that he is *not* (that he is, at the very least, uncertain or not confident of his sexuality; or that he is bisexual; or even that he might be, as I have already suggested, gay), I find him a much more complex figure, and his narrative much richer, than such critics seem to suggest. All we can be sure of is that Marcel wishes us to *believe* he is heterosexual.

Let us, for a moment, take the whole argument to one of its logical conclusions. If Proust could fictionalize his chauffeur as Albertine, as all the critical material assures us, is it not possible that Marcel has done the same? Has Marcel imprisoned, not an Albertine whom he loves but suspects of being lesbian, but a boy whom he loves but suspects of being straight? He does, after all, refer to his Albertine as a work of art. Perhaps the book's greatest and most enduring joke is in the way the critics have fallen for this deception of Marcel's. The soul of discretion on this score, Marcel gives himself away only by his excessive interest in other people's homosexuality.

Say Marcel is a closeted homosexual. Eve Kosofsky Sedgwick argues that this reading is "banal." I am not sure what purpose this haughtiness serves: for the fact is that this reading, while potentially "banal" to a sophisticated, anti-homophobic reader, is anything *but* to those who have fought to resist it. Sedgwick does add, however, that she does not see how the closeted narrator can any longer be excluded from readings of the text; and she argues that the matter is raised to its "least bathetic" level when it forces us to ask what effect it has on the text's relation to its readers (223).

The outcome of all this speculation about Marcel (or should we call it gossip?) is a confusion of possibilities. If we refuse to allow dominant critical readings to preempt our relations with the text by enforcing a closure on many of its potential readings, we liberate ourselves into uncertainty. Since Proust is the pioneering promoter of the manifold nature of reality, this is an appropriate condition to be in. It is also, contrary to popular opinion, a vitally productive condition.

It is worth remembering that, whatever we conclude about his sexuality, Marcel is not only a bourgeois interloper in the beau monde, he is also an outsider and spy within the homosexual demi-monde, to which he gives the names of the Cities of the Plain, creeping down its corridors and peering through its oubliettes. Likewise the bourgeois or proletarian reader, on being "drawn into" the Hôtel de Guermantes; likewise the heterosexual reader, on "entering" Jupien's whore house. Their situation is somewhat akin to that of tourists mingling with residents. Whether straight or gay himself, Marcel is a fascinated homophobe. He learns a lot about, but rarely understands, the many inverts he meets. He teaches the ignorant reader; but there are many readers who know more about the subject than he. To the latter, he may prove either comical or intolerable. It is clear that to Proust he was both.

Biographies pinpoint a fundamental difference between Proust and his mother: "She was a woman who'd never shake hands with a valet or a footman; he was a man who often wished he could make love to men she'd never touch" (Hayman, 50). It is in the fusion of such contrary sensibilities that Proust generates the essential campness of the baron de Charlus: his involvement in the extremes of high and low life; the snobbery dictated by his social status, and the inverted snobbery dictated by his sexual inversion. It is the baron's social pride that makes him so apt a subject for sexual humiliation. Furthermore, Proust seems to have giggled privately at every use of the name he gave this character: Charlus was, in reality, a vaudeville performer who used to moonlight as a hustler.

Most of the book's jokes about, and signs of intolerance of, homosexuality occur around the figure of Charlus. It is, therefore, around him that cultural critics cluster when passing sentence on the status of inversion within the book. Gilles Deleuze says: "That Charlus is homosexual is an astonishment" (90). But to whom, and when, and why? Marcel is astonished, certainly. But the reader is not compelled to read signs as he does; indeed, we would be well advised not to. The closer we identify with him, the more hurt we will be on finding that, while he defends himself against suspicions of homosexuality, he is increasingly open about his interest in girls. Marcel's first instinct on losing Albertine is to take a little girl into his flat and sit her ("for some time") on his knee. When her parents lodge a complaint against him for corruption of a minor, he is saved from scandal and arrest by the fact that the head of the Sûreté also has "a weakness for little girls" (11:19–20, 36–38).

This predilection of Marcel's receives little critical comment. Indeed, one book glosses over the above episode as follows: "He takes home with him a little girl, who, however, only aggravates his grief" (Spalding, 12). This is misleadingly euphemistic, and yet not entirely inaccurate: for it clearly fits the spirit of Marcel's own account. He does not give the episode, in terms of space, much attention, so the critics follow. As with the question of his deep interest in all things related to homosexuality, the majority of commentators are content to take his version of himself at face value. I do not believe that this is what Proust expects of an informed and active readership.

To put the matter crudely, the episode with the little girl seems to be part of Proust's revenge for having had to represent Marcel as having the "universal" (white, heterosexual, male) proclivity of heterosexualism. The murkiness of Marcel's sex life is an elaborate and ponderous joke which, throughout the book, runs in parallel with, and to an extent undermines, the homophobic comedy about the baron de Charlus. One wonders how many straight readers are receptive to this bifurcation of comic points of view.

Why do heterosexual critics resist taking camp seriously? Of course, either because they are unaware that it exists except as something to do with men in frocks, or because it proposes the scandal of *a privileged gay consumer.* Whether there is any sociological truth in this—after all, there are perceptive and sensitive straight readers, just as there are obtuse gay ones—it has the ring of an aesthetic truth, at least to the extent that it is an assumption on which many gay artists and consumers operate.

Gérard Genette asserts that the topic of homosexuality "will remain for the reader as for the hero, until the opening pages of *Sodome,* a continent one-hundred times met but never recognized" (200). Insofar as it supposes that all readers are heterosexual, this is incorrect. It overlooks a continuous sequence of exchanges—behind, as it were, the narrator's back—between the author and those readers who are *in the know.* (I say "an exchange" because, although we cannot speak to the author, he does at least *expect a response* from us.) These implicit exchanges between Proust and the homosexual reader, from which the narrator is excluded, do not constitute some new fictional device to which only homosexual men are privy. The situation is much the same as exists whenever an aware reader is addressed by a less than totally reliable narrator. But what I am suggesting is that many of the exchanges between Proust and his readers exclude not only the narrator but also, whether literally or symbolically, the heterosexual reader. (A "symbolic exclusion" would be an instance when straight readers would perceive and recognize the exchange taking place, but know that they were being excluded from it all the same.) On reading this new literature of homosexuality, heterosexual readers should feel that universality is extracted from the text only at a price. It will cost them most of the subtler jokes.

How easily and routinely Proust manages this trick of maneuvering behind the backs of so many of his straight readers is proved by the obtuseness of straight critics' responses to certain key episodes. Think of the early moment when Marcel observes a muscular wave which ripples over M. Legrandin's hips outside Combray church, a "wholly carnal fluency" which draws Marcel's attention to "the possibility of a Legrandin altogether different from the one whom we knew" (1:169). Jack Murray, in his book *The Proustian Comedy,* notices a joke here, but laughs for what can only be described as, from the viewpoint of a gay reader, the wrong reason. He comments: "The snap of Legrandin's rumps [*sic*], particularly as enhanced by Proust's opulent and mock-ponderous description of it, is also the snap of revelation: Legrandin is a snob" (21). This perception is not incorrect, but neither is it the point that is being so palpably and carnally signaled. In fact, of course, the semiotic charge of Legrandin's backside lays bare the fact that he is homosexual. More specifically, he takes it up the arse.

There is a lot more to be said about this physical sign. For all that they are eloquent and unambiguous signs of sexual receptivity, passivity, such buttocks are also evoked as being predatorily, threateningly *active*. They represent, as it were, a volte face, the obverse of the cruising queen's ceaselessly roving and winking eyes: their role is to attract penises and then to receive them. Such buttocks are no more passive than a brilliant society hostess who attracts men into her salon. To be sure, it is they who travel while she stays put; but they minister to her pleasure, and whatever intelligence or beauty they bring is marked up to her credit.

To misread such signs is not just a question of misinterpretation, relating to textuality alone. It is also to misread Proust's readership as a cultural phenomenon, importantly consisting of people who share the author's sexuality. Later in the same book, Murray comments on Mlle Vinteuil's violation of her father's photograph: "for the overwhelming majority of readers, the sexual benefit of this scene for Mlle. Vinteuil will remain unintelligible" (102). The merit of this remark is that, at least, it recognizes a division in the novel's readers, between the "overwhelming majority" and a minority. It also seems to include an admission that the "overwhelming majority" of readers are at a disadvantage when reading the novel's key episodes of homosexual passion. So there is, after all, a kind of perceptive capitulation, here, to the insistent feeling that only a minority of readers are on Proust's wavelength. In fact, the "sexual benefit" of the photograph scene should be perfectly intelligible to anyone who has grown up as a homosexual in a heterosexual home.

Murray remarks again on the division between readers of different sexual orientations when he comments on the scene in which Charlus is finally disgraced by the Verdurins: "Charlus is unmasked—and in the cruelest way. Any homosexual, anxious that his dreadful secret not be known, must cringe at the exposure-fantasy that this melodramatic scene certainly depicts. Of course, the scene is more comical than horrifying for most readers, since Charlus, unwittingly, has unmasked himself long before this particular occasion. He just happens to have thought he was getting away with it until then" (148). Because all readers, even heterosexuals, are assumed by now to be in the know about the baron's sexuality, the scene does not offer the pleasure of revelation. Instead, according to Murray, it splits its readers into those who find it more comical than horrific and those who find it more horrific than comical. The former, "most readers," are those who do not "cringe at the exposure-fantasy"; since Murray cannot conceive of an out gay reader, they are all heterosexual. The major problem with this reading is that it unnecessarily splits the emotions. It seems to me that any nonhomophobic reader should be able to react to the episode with both laughter and extreme discomfort. Somewhere at the heart of this dual mood lies the bitter sweetness which is the aim of all seriously self-conscious camp. It is a mood of defensive pride that takes pleasure in the overcoming of homophobia. One may hate Charlus, but one aches with sympathy for his plight.

To analyze Proust's humor without taking into account its participation in homosexual camp is, simply, not to have seen the joke. Take the following as a typically incomplete summary: "Proust's humor is of another nature [than Socrates/Plato's]: Jewish humor as opposed to Greek irony" (Deleuze, 166). Proust was not, as it were, "actively" Jewish as he was actively (which is to say, passively) homosexual. To a similar extent, his participation in the codes and conventions of homosexual culture was more committed than his willingness to give much serious weight to his Jewish lineage. Confining ourselves to the question of humor, in short, there are more camp than Jewish jokes in his book. If such a percipient and distinguished reader as Gilles Deleuze can miss so much, the enormous scope for the deception of a heterosexual readership becomes fascinatingly clear. Camp is the "secret" that privileges the homosexual reader. What renders it effective is, precisely, the distance heterosexuals are determined to keep between themselves and the very idea of homosexuality. It is a distance leaving ample space for irony.

There are times in the novel when life in the salons, life at its most conventional and routine, seems to approach the conditions of *carnival* as delineated by Mikhail Bakhtin. This is a rigidly structured society in a perpetual state of collapse. The boundaries of gender, no matter how precisely they have been mapped by the society's moral cartographers, have become blurred. What is left of French aristocracy is a masked ball at which—as in a de Sade story—when a man dressed as a woman and a woman dressed as a man fall in love, the heterosexual orderliness and propriety of the affair that ensues occurs purely by chance. In carnival, transgression is necessary and virtue is contingent. How is it possible, then, in this milieu, for any event to provoke shock or outrage? When transgression is reacted to with a mere shrug—or with fake outrage, acted out like Mme Verdurin's laughter—moral authority exists in theory, in pantomime: in a disapproving frown, perhaps; or a clerical vestment; or in the written word.

Many, perhaps most, of the book's key propositions about love take the form of paradoxes.[2] They are clever; they amuse; they may even intimidate. This is not unexpected, coming from a homosexual author of the Modernist period. Proust takes his place in a strongly established position, one that shores up its strength with each utterance that resists the complacency of the

Doxa, "public opinion." As homosexual literature, this is dynamic and in-cisive; and it works well alongside the book's other "modern" experiments and preoccupations.

However, if we are to read the novel as a heterosexual text—which it is, certainly, the narrator's intention that we should, and which the great majority of critics continue to do without question—these paradoxes seem distinctly odd, ineffective, mannered, *dated.* Marcel shapes his opinions of the world according to a lapsed fashion, "decadent" already at the fin de siècle. In an invert of Charlus's generation, paradox may be seen as entirely "natural." In a man of Marcel's, who seeks to be taken for a lover of women, this mode of speech seems all the more affected, dandified. Charlus is a dandy, to be sure: he cannot help it. But Marcel, who can, seems to be *trying* to be like that. This is strange, for his paradoxes compromise him.

As does his loquacity. Gérard Genette is instructive on this issue, as on so many others. He says that the discourse of the *Recherche* is "sometimes so liberated from any concern with a story to tell that it could perhaps more fittingly be called simply *talking*" (167). Notwithstanding the length and ba-roque elegance of its sentences, it rambles wherever the association of ideas will take it. Unguardedly deviant and oblique, it keeps changing the subject, until the listener/reader is transported and overwhelmed by the sheer quantity of speech. It stands at the opposite end of a stylistic spectrum to the costive taciturnity of Ernest Hemingway, which so loudly proffers as its principal meaning "virility." By contrast, the logorrhoea of Proust declares itself hyper-sensitive to the point of effeminacy. Yet there is an extraordinary moment in *The Captive,* volume nine of the translation, when the narrator says, à propos of the homosexual Charlus, "it is almost impossible for men of his sort to hold their tongues" (9:57). This is after Marcel has been narrating continuously for more than 2,950 pages.

At the heart of Proust's contrariousness is his recognition that, while the smooth functioning of language depends on the closure of words' tendency to expand beyond definition, what language is used to express is open, unstable, and expansive. He expresses the point in terms of binaries, although his prac-tice actually demonstrates that many a given word has a plurality of "op-posites": "There is no idea that does not carry in itself a possible refutation, no word that does not imply its opposite" (11:256). Marcel too often forgets this, especially when he is pontificating about types. But the text, as it were, con-trives to remind us in spite of him. Proust's camp disruptions are often too profound to be compatible with Marcel's need to make definitive sense of his life.

Notes

1. Volume numbers and page numbers refer here and in subsequent references, to the Chatto and Windus edition of the Scott Moncrieff/Andreas Mayor translation of *Remembrance of Things Past*. Given its self-conscious elegance and unselfconscious eccentricities, the Scott Moncrieff translation has itself become an object of some interest to connoisseurs of camp.

2. A quick survey offers up the following: "we live in perfect ignorance of those we love" (5:388); "There is nothing like desire for preventing the thing one says from bearing any resemblance to what one has in one's mind" (6:60); "A person has no need of sincerity, nor even of skill in lying, in order to be loved" (9:142); "To be harsh and deceitful to the person whom we love is so natural!" (9:144); "we love only what we do not possess" (10:245); "love ... is a striking example of how little reality means to us" (11:207).

Works Cited

Barthes, Roland. *A Lover's Discourse: Fragments.* London: Cape, 1979.

Benjamin, Walter. *Illuminations.* London: Fontana, 1973.

Booth, Mark. *Camp.* London: Quartet, 1983.

Borrel, Anne, Alain Senderens, and Jean-Bernard Naudin. *Dining with Proust.* London: Ebury, 1992.

Bradbury, Malcolm. *The Modern World: Ten Great Writers.* London: Secker and Warburg, 1988.

Brée, Germaine. *The World of Marcel Proust.* London: Chatto and Windus, 1967.

Core, Philip. *Camp: The Lie that Tells the Truth.* London: Plexus, 1984.

Deleuze, Gilles. *Proust and Signs.* London: Allen Lane, 1973.

Dollimore, Jonathan. *Sexual Dissidence: Augustine to Wilde, Freud to Foucault.* Oxford: Clarendon Press, 1991.

Genette, Gérard. *Narrative Discourse.* Oxford: Blackwell, 1980.

Hayman, Ronald. *Proust: A Biography.* London: Minerva, 1991.

Jameson, Frederic. *Marxism and Form: Twentieth-Century Dialectical Theories of Literature.* Princeton: Princeton University Press, 1971.

May, Derwent. *Proust.* Oxford: Oxford University Press, 1983.

Murray, Jack. *The Proustian Comedy.* York, S.C.: French Literature Publications, 1979.

Painter, George D. *Marcel Proust: A Biography.* Vol. 2. London: Chatto and Windus, 1965.

Proust, Marcel. *Remembrance of Things Past.* Trans. C.K. Scott Moncrieff and Andreas Mayor. London: Chatto and Windus, 1970.

Rivers, J.E. *Proust and the Art of Love: The Aesthetics of Sexuality in the Life, Times, and Art of Marcel Proust.* New York: Columbia University Press, 1980.

Sedgwick, Eve Kosofsky. *Epistemology of the Closet.* New York: Harvester Wheatsheaf, 1991.

Shattuck, Roger. *Proust's Binoculars: A Study of Memory, Time, and Recognition in* A la recherche du temps perdu. London: Chatto and Windus, 1964.

Spacks, Patricia Meyer. *Gossip.* Chicago: University of Chicago Press, 1986.

Spalding, P.A. *A Reader's Guide to Proust: An Index Guide to* Remembrance of Things Past. London: George Prior, 1975.

Splitter, Randolph. *Proust's* Recherche: *A Psychoanalytic Interpretation.* Boston, London, and Henley: Routledge & Kegan Paul, 1981.

Degenerate Personality:

DEVIANT SEXUALITY AND RACE
IN RONALD FIRBANK'S NOVELS

WILLIAM LANE CLARK

In his critique of contemporary culture, *No Respect,* Andrew Ross attempts to disentangle the economic, cultural, technological, and social threads that led to the emergence of camp in the 1960s as a category of cultural taste whereby "sixties intellectuals were able to 'pass' as subscribers to the throwaway Pop aesthetic, and become patrons of the attractive world of immediacy and disposability created by the culture industries in the postwar boom years" (136). By positing a conflict between categories of "high" and "low" culture driven by postwar technology and prosperity, Ross argues that camp, which embraced the values of low culture, provided sixties intellectuals an opportunity to critique the "hermeneutics of depth and discrimination through which the New York Intellectuals had filtered extracurricular literary taste since the war." That is, critics such as Susan Sontag who could promote "pleasure and erotics" at the expense of "judgment, truth, seriousness and interpretation" engaged in a "flight from sincerity." This new intellectual stance differs markedly from the camp intellectual of the previous century who, according to Ross, "may well be a parody or negation of dominant bourgeois forms: anti-industry, proidleness; antifamily, probachelorhood; antirespectability, proscandal; antimasculine, profeminine; antisport, profrivolity; antidecor, proexhibitionism; antiprogress, prodecadence; antiwealth, profame." Such binarism fostered the *containment* of camp by virtue of its irrelevance, relegating it to the province of degeneracy, typified for the bourgeois dominant culture by a senescent, foppish aristocracy whose affectations the camp as pseudoaristocrat adopted. Yet in *Sexual Dissidence,* Jonathan Dollimore presents Oscar Wilde's camp, transgressive aesthetics precisely as a critique of the depth model and an attack on sincerity. Whatever cultural upheaval was wrought by two world wars and the rise of middle-class affluence and consumerism, the distance between Sontag and Wilde on the point of sincerity and moral seriousness is not as great as the span of a near century would suggest. Ross bases his analysis of sixties camp on a twofold challenge to establishment values: Pop values consequent to a mass-produced culture, and sexual liberation redefining masculinity and femininity. Redefinition of gender role was a crucial element of Wilde's transgressive aesthetics, which suggests the challenge of new sexualities began long before its manifestation in postwar society of the twentieth century. Mass-produced Pop culture, too, originated in the aftermath of the first war with the technology of cinematic filmmaking. At mid-point in the spectrum connecting the Victorian critique of Wilde on one end with the sixties reevaluation of moral seriousness on the other, Ronald Firbank wrote the first truly camp novels. Firbank's work both incorporated the transgressive aesthetics of Wilde, devaluing subjective identity and promoting sexual liberation, and anticipated the power of a yet nascent but growing mass-produced popular culture.

Ronald Firbank was a "degenerate," a personality in pursuit of celebrity. He was also a serious writer who displaced subjective narrative and created what were among the first "modern" novels of the twentieth century. A devotee of "low" culture, Firbank adored the cinema and its stars and introduced cinematic techniques into his writing. He similarly appropriated the style and techniques of another low form, "Negro" jazz, as structural devices in his novels. Cinema and jazz as degenerative forms of high culture perfectly matched the degenerate and "dangerous" personality Firbank created as the core of his writing. In Andrew Ross's lexicon, Ronald Firbank had *no respect.* Tinged by the colors of the decadence, both his personality and writing fit the description of the nineteenth-century camp intellectual drawn by Ross, especially the binaries regarding industry, family, masculinity, progress, and respectability. Yet respectability can hardly be categorized in simple opposition to *scandal,* as Ross's catalog. In truth, respectability subsumes the other categories (industry, family, masculinity, progress) as an ideology of bourgeois values. The ideology of Respectability from the nineteenth century to the present is the true subject of camp, challenged first by Wilde and attacked by Firbank. Respectability as the dominant culture's ideology contains the deviant by relegating transgressive individuals and behaviors to a subject culture "Other" than the homogeneous norm. The ideological complex of Respectability, driven by social Darwinian concepts of industry and progress, is threatened by an opposing value-complex of the Other, Degeneracy, typified by the regressive.

Respectability and Appearance

In *Nationalism & Sexuality: Respectability and Abnormal Sexuality in Modern Europe,* George Mosse describes the rise and eventual cultural hegemony of bourgeois values that galvanized around a nationalistic response to new concepts of "normal" and "abnormal" sexuality, as sex in the waning decades of the last century was removed from religious authority to become a principal subject of medical discourse. Deviant sexuality, previously categorized in terms of aberrant behaviors (e.g., sodomy, incest, bestiality), became redefined in terms of sexual "being," subjective identification *as* a homosexual, for example. Respectability as a sociopolitical ideology placed new restraints upon sexual behaviors, equating public identity with behavior: one's social identity is premised on one's behavior. Respectability, therefore, tied prescriptive gender roles to larger goals of national security and social progress. Degeneracy, perceived to be the greatest threat to national security in the xenophobic rationalizing of the Respectable majority, resulted from the insidious influence of "outsiders." Those outside the pale of Respectability included the urban poor, Jews, and people of color, and, most important, the sexual deviant, principally the "masturbator" and the homosexual.[1] Idealization of respectable type produced stereotypes of masculinity, femininity, and race by which the Other could be identified and contained. Even the onanist whose disapprobative, solitary vice was practiced unseen could supposedly be identified by visible manifestations of degeneracy in his appearance (Mosse 11). The Jew and people of color, of course, could be more easily identified (and contained) by perceived physical difference.

Oscar Wilde's *ur-camp* transgressive aesthetics, however, traded on the primacy of appearance in the dominate culture of respectability, insisting appearance and surface constitute the *only* value. The threat to the integrity of subject posed by Wilde's critique of depth attacked not morality per se, but the foundation upon which Victorian morality rested, Respectability. Firbank's consummate handling of camp grew from a thorough understanding of Wildean aesthetic theory, a nearly fetishistic reverence for Wilde and identification with his transgressive desire, and an amoral dismissal of the conventions that clustered about the ideology of Respectability.

By tying morality to gender stereotypes pre/proscribing behaviors (whether behaviors of dress, appropriate speech acts, physical gesture, sexual activity, etc.), the ideology of Respectability not only intimately affects individual nature, it also comprises subjective identity. By displacing subjective identity, Wilde's aesthetic theories jeopardize the dominant culture's control and containment. Distinguishing between morality and respectability, Jonathan Dollimore rightly perceives Wilde's targeting of the latter, noting that Wilde attacked "not so much conventional morality itself as the ideological anchor points for that morality, namely notions of identity as subjective depth," subverting "the essential categories of identity which kept morality in place" (68). Wilde's effect was subversion, because his use of paradox traded on inversion, a reversal of the dominant/subject binary that threatened the dominant pole by displacing its politicomoral norms, while leaving the binary relation in place. The outsider, the Other contained by recognition of its degeneracy and made *different,* became threateningly *proximate* in Wilde's aesthetic transgression. As Dollimore explains, Wilde's use of paradox allowed him to evade immediate censure from the dominant culture because his "transgressive desire is both rooted in culture and the impetus for affirming different/alternative kinds of culture." Thus it allows him to

> enact one of the most disturbing of all forms of transgression, namely that whereby the outlaw turns up as inlaw, and the other as proximate proves more disturbing than the other as absolute difference [which makes] abnormality . . . not just the opposite, but the necessarily always present antithesis of normality. It is an uncompromising inversion, this being the (perversely) appropriate strategy for a transgressive desire which is of its "nature," according to this culture, an "inversion." (15)

The ultimate linking of Wilde's transgressive aesthetic and his transgressive desire, both products of "inversion," however, assured his eventual downfall, as "inversion," Dollimore argues, "was being used increasingly to define a specific kind of deviant sexuality inseparable from a deviant personality" (67).

Although still required as a social "scheme" for comic value, Firbank reduced even more than Wilde the distance between the degenerate and the respectable by dispensing with the binary. There is no separation of degeneracy and respectability in the characters populating the Firbankian society because they are exponents of a single degenerate personality, Ronald Firbank. The Other in Firbank's world is not just an inlaw, disturbingly proximate, it reorganizes Respectability as Degeneracy. (Scandal in Firbankian society, for example, amounts to little more than lack of taste or misunderstanding of fashion.) This aesthetically confusing *reinscription,* in Dollimore's terms, may largely account for the lack of critical attention to Firbank's art.

The Critical Dilemma

One either *gets* Firbank or dismisses his art with objections to its preciosity and effeminacy.[2] Firbank has been since the first appearance of his camp novels in 1915 an *acquired* taste, appreciated largely by a cult of homosexual readers. The glittering complexity of Firbank's social representation with all its brilliant detail nonetheless presents the literary critic with at best only a core of etiolated plotless structure for analysis. E. M. Forster summed up the futility of critical analysis of Firbank's art by comparing the effort to stretching a butterfly on a rack. The gay insect rebukes his inquisitor's gross method by insisting that he "only exist[s] in [his] surroundings, and become[s] meaningless as soon as . . . stretch[ed] . . . upon this rack" ("Ronald Firbank," Horder 180). How does one analyze what is largely absent, what is only suggested, or examine the fleeting context of the gestural? Yet camp's increasing importance to the discourse of sexuality, gender, and sexual representation in the arts requires just such a practice.

Although Firbank's novels are steeped in sexuality, sexual activity is not described in a single page of his work. Edward Martin Potoker notes in a monograph on Firbank that although his writing may be "concerned with evil it is naughtiness that he really portrays. All behavior, particularly sexual behavior, is fun" (12). W. H. Auden similarly notes that "improprieties in Firbank are those of children playing Doctor behind the rhododendron bushes," whose suggested sexual acts are "infantile and polymorphously perverse" (1004). For it is not sexuality that drives Firbank's method, but rather gender appearance. And for Firbank's social universe, gender is only an illusion. His minority of male degenerates, powdered, pale, and langorous, serves for foil to a society of equally degenerate dominating women, exaggeratedly feminine signified, who seem often rapaciously heterosexual and simultaneously lesbian, even male homosexual, in their behaviors and desires. The cognitive confusion Firbank creates in his polygendered characterization of the social may well rest on the radical of drag. Heterosexuals, homosexuals, and bisexuals in Firbank's society are only so by appearance; all are in drag.

As Judith Butler convincingly theorizes, compulsory heterosexuality requires repetitive *performance* of gender-identifying acts to define itself against its antecedent, homosexuality.

> That heterosexuality is always in the act of elaborating itself is evidence that it is perpetually at risk, that is, that it "knows" its own possibility of becoming undone: hence, its compulsion to repeat which is at once a foreclosure of that which threatens its coherence. That it can never eradicate that risk attests to its profound dependency upon the homosexuality that it seeks fully to eradicate and never can or that it seeks to make second, but which is always already there as a prior possibility. (23)

This continual reconstitution of gender promotes an illusion of inherent sex-determined gender "being" that simultaneously stigmatizes and penalizes transgressive behaviors in a process of self-affirmation and authentication of the presumed essential state. Hence, prescriptive sexuality is driven not by a supposedly *natural* gender state, but by an artifice of repetitive, personal theatrics, as everyone is in drag. Rather than exploit gender roles by masculine/feminine reversal for comic and political effect, as it seems in its exaggeration of gender signification, camp actually exploits the fragile and constant *re*-cognition required by compulsory gender role prescriptions of self-affirming heterosexuality. The transgressive aesthetics of camp combine decentered desire and transgressive sexuality. The illusory crux of the camp method can be sought then not in the psychosocial homo/sensibility of gay men and lesbians who, through intentional transgression of gender repetition, engage the duplicity in prescribed heterosexuality, but rather in the larger society whose compulsory *re*-cognitive gender acts are mistaken as ontologically essential. The ambiguity of camp mirrors the ambiguity of constructed gender. Firbank's camp novels explore exclusively the illusion of gender stability in a nominally heterosexual society of wildly ambiguous gender identities and gender behaviors. With all principal characters in various complications of gender appearance, with no normative characterization to generate a moral base, with no narrative structure to provide closure and conclusive "meaning" to the social representation, the artificial world of Firbankian society can easily be dismissed as superficial and lacking artistic integrity, since acknowledging the validity of its representation threatens the "meaning" of the social model it describes.

Yet Firbank's method was appreciated by contemporaries such as Evelyn Waugh precisely for its *realism*.[3] The reality of the Firbankian world represents a society destabilized by performative gender that disavows the ideology of Respectability. If such a camp methodology represents heterosexual reality as a universal hypocrisy, what "norms" apply? The ambiguous characters in the Firbank camp novel can no more be perceived as "gay" than they can be as respectable heterosexual apologists. Camp, after all, as well noted by Sontag in her nonessay on the subject,[4] receives a death blow from the merest hint of moral earnestness, and Firbank was a slavish devotee of Wilde's aesthetic philosophy. Firbankian literary camp attacks the ideology of Respectability from the inside, deconstructing subjective identity and replacing it with degenerate personality.

Black Eros, Black Art

Firbank's second biography, Brigid Brophy, notes that his personality was marked by three salient "deviant" characteristics: homosexuality, a penchant for sexual flagellation, and transracial sexual desire, a trio of degenerate char-

acteristics that threatens Respectability. I have elsewhere examined the flagel-
lant/masturbatory and homosexual subtexts in Firbank's novels as they relate
to personality and as they challenge the presumptions and authority of the
respectable.[5] Despite the importance played by gender appearance and the
vagaries of sexuality, to both his work and the nature of camp, however,
Firbank's fascination with people of color and black culture is that degenerate
aspect of the deviant personality most important toward elucidating style and
structure in his writing.

It is difficult to look back to the second decade of this century without the
lens of political correctness distorting perception. Despite the unfortunate title
of his best-known novel, *Prancing Nigger* (the original title, *Sorrow in Sunlight*,
preferred by the author and used in the English publication, was replaced by
Carl Van Vechten for its first, and American, publication), and his widespread
use of *nigger*, Firbank can hardly be considered racist. Firbank identified with
blacks as "others" in the binary of degeneracy/respectability so intensely that
Brophy came to describe his affinity as "Negroism of the mind." "Firbank," she
declares, "was a violently racially prejudiced man: in favour of the black races,"
and elsewhere concludes that "the Negroes in his books are so deeply created
from Firbank's self that his pro-Negroism is without taint of condescension or
paternalism" (174–75). Significantly, the "Negro" figure in Firbank's camp
projects popular culture and sexual liberation—those twin impetuses Ross
perceives as triggering the eruption of camp in the sixties.

Fashion and style so intimately affect the subject of camp that they are the
single common link between camp's otherwise confounding division into separate form—camp acts and camp objects. Objects may become camp when
excess or want of style in other cultural periods exaggeratedly contrasts with
current fashion. Incongruities of style in current fashion (for example, pastiche: simultaneous reference to different style periods or other art forms) are
the building blocks of camp, as well. For the respectable Eurocentric participant in the dominant high culture, fashionable expressions of subject low
cultures have no meaning *inside* art. In the words of Eulalia Hurstpierpoint,
matriarch in a female Firbankian resort Valmouth, they are, like men for her,
"unglimpsable." Black culture, as well as people of color, were equally unglimpsable in the early decades of the century unless portrayed as stereotype
and denigrated as comic. But black culture was newly "fashionable" at the
time, due to the burgeoning influence of the Harlem Renaissance in America
and the serious interest in African art taken by French intellectuals. As a
fashion, American jazz constituted the most widespread expression of African-
American culture, especially in the United States and France. Although Firbank never visited the United States, he spent a great deal of time in both

France and North Africa and reputedly visited Haiti. Through the efforts of Carl Van Vechten, he participated in the Harlem Renaissance. Firbank's passion for jazz and his love of "coloured entertainments" according to Brophy, were "a source of amusement to his friends and of discreet suspicion to his acquaintance" (174). Adopting the methods of jazz composition, Firbank subverted the form of the English novel by disrupting plot and developing verbal mosaics that rely upon contextual relation and improvisational technique for integral form. In the process, he created black characters who functioned not as stereotype or clowns of the subject culture, but as normative elements in the inverse world of camp.

Although in her critical biography Brophy perceptively argues that music plays an informing role in the construction of some novels, she emphasizes the neoclassical and baroque musical forms, describing *Vainglory,* for example, as a form of prelude and fugue. Jazz, however, especially the ragtime and Dixieland popularized in Firbank's day, makes a more convincing model. Jazz does bear a certain similarity to the *technique* of the baroque that comes from the shared improvisation on themes, the constant development and restatement of initial melodies. Both forms rely on virtuosity as well. The primary distinction between the work of Bach and that of King Oliver, however, arises from a difference in the *kinds* of structures generated by the musical forms. The fugue, despite its elaborate improvisation on theme, remains a closed and balanced work. Jazz, on the other hand, like Firbank's novels, depends on spontaneity, individual contribution to the overall piece by immediate improvisation, and the violation of form, as in the syncopation of meter in the rag. What is more important, jazz creates a frisson of sexual energy. It is this effect of jazz, its perception by the Respectable as racial/sexual/degenerate, that underlies Firbank's use of it in his camp.

Jazz Composition

Firbank's reconceptualization of the novel, which replaced subjective identity with the artifice of personality, depended on his unique method of literary composition. He prepared his manuscripts by carefully arranging plot elements written on separate large cards. Plot structure in Firbank's work consequently develops mechanically, rather than organically, from the interrelated arrangement of discrete elements instead of through causal linear progression. Brophy describes the novels as "emotional and linguistic motifs" arranged according to the "logic of design rather than the logic of narrative and characterization" (67). His method thus elevated style over structure and approximated musical composition. The primacy of style in the design of Firbank's

novels reorients representation in the same way Cubism, for example, rear-
ranges the constituent planes of an object, in achieving a multiple perspective
of simultaneity. Even today, Firbank's readers are as puzzled by his innovations
as Braque's and Picasso's early viewers were by their paintings. Van Vechten
aptly noted in a review of a Firbank novel that "the cubists are remembered.
Firbank plays Picasso's violin. The decorations serve more than their purpose"
("Ronald Firbank," Horder 163). The apparent cacophony of jazz provides a
musical parallel to Firbank's writing, discrete elements (either instrumental or
thematic) colliding in dissonant simultaneity, resolving in emergent design.

Firbank frequently comments on jazz in his novels. In *Caprice* he presents
an underlying black/white radical to its form.

> By the Buddha shrine, festively decked with lamps, couples were pirouetting
> to a nigger band, while in the vicinity of the buffet a masked adept was holding a
> clairaudience of a nature only to be guessed at from afar. An agile negro melody,
> wild rag-time with passages of almost Wesleyan hymnishness—reminiscent of
> Georgia gospel-missions; the eighteenth century in the Dutch East Indies—
> charmed and soothed the ear. (*Complete Ronald Firbank* 405–6)

What the narrator describes in the style of the jazz music can be applied as well
to Firbank's own disrupted rhythms of speech that produce the puzzling cohe-
sive disintegration typical of his artistic structure. The (black) "wild rag-time
passages" combine with (white) "passages of almost Wesleyan hymnishness"
in the plasticity of negro melody. The stately rhythmic progress of white Meth-
odist hymnody composed for a congregational unified voice vies with the
exuberant individual and "wild" voices of the jazz instrumentalists, twisting
the still perceptible melody in both directions. The tension between individual
(black) anarchy and the (white) order of ensemble playing by the jazz band
arrests straightforward and linear development of themes. The disintegrative
challenge of spontaneous improvisation to the jazz melody results in a series of
anticlimax in the jazz composition that constantly subsides with each virtuoso
performance blending back into the whole. Firbank's form imitates the jazz
composition, playing on the potential disintegration of the whole as opposed
to the elaborate development of formal constituent elements that in the fugue
produces a balanced, closed structure of variations.

Firbank uses jazz techniques in language as well as overall composition and
structure. Ragtime was the current fashion in American jazz and the first style
exported to Europe by way of Paris, where Firbank likely developed his attraction for the music. The challenge to order in ragtime is most apparent in the
violation of rhythm that results from syncopation of the measure. Firbank
imitates this jazz effect in the constant retardation of syntactical flow with

inverted word order and narrator interruption. Mrs. Yaj provides an example of syncopated effect in *Valmouth:* " 'Wears her horse,' the elder Negress demanded, 'a rose?' "(*Complete Ronald Firbank* 418). As his most notable syntactical peculiarity, this style of dialogue produces hesitation in the flow of words that approximates the rhythms of ragtime jazz. Although the passage will subsequently be examined more thoroughly, the following dialogue from *The Flower beneath the Foot,* reflects the technique.

> "I suppose I'm getting squeamish! But this Ronald Firbank I can't take to at all. *Valmouth!* Was there ever a novel more coarse? I assure you I hadn't gone very far when I had to put it down."
> "It's *out,*" Mrs. Bedley suavely said, "as well," she added, "as the rest of them."
> "I once met him," Miss Hopkins said, dilating slightly the *retinae* of her eyes. "He told me writing books was by no means easy!" (*Complete Ronald Firbank* 532)

The rapid staccato crescendo of the first speaker's declamatory single clauses is punctuated by exclamation as it rushes to a full stop. Mrs. Bedley's response, however, is *suave* in its dipping retardation, making a rolling four-part delivery of a single sentence replete with improvisational inflection in tone to its weightiest word, *out.* The lilting iambs that shape the separated short clauses retard the movement with the emphasized second foot. The third speaker, also in sympathy with the maligned writer, continues the sense of syncopation by narrator insertion between her two sentences of the halting near cessation of flow that employs the syncopated device. Appending the adverb to the participle stalls the rhythm while underscoring the effect of the dilatory, in reference both to the speech patterns and to Firbank's novels, as well as to the physically impossible, intentional retinal dilation of both eyes, affected by the speaker. Had she merely "widened" her eyes, the effect would diminish and the meaning implied for the whole would lose its clarity.

The conventions of jazz melodies, distorted, ruptured, at times dissonant, may so override the melody line that a listener accustomed to the conventions of song discerns only the noise. The raucous effect of jazz produces a sense of cacophony that requires some familiarity with its conventions to perceive the structure and trace the melodic thread. The style of Firbank's dialogue produced similar perceptions of "noise" to readers accustomed to the conventions of the nineteenth-century novel. Firbank introduced the English reader to a form of jazz writing that put soloists in ensemble. Reviewers attacked what they dismissed as affected "snappy dialogue" and declared it impossible to make sense of, or identify speakers in, extended multivoice conversation. John Anthony Kiechler accounts for the technique, appropriately comparing Firbank's method to musical orchestration: "Repetitive, monotonous phrases like 'he retorted,' 'he said' were primed to a minimum, and are sometimes missing altogether. He consciously avoided intrusive analysis of character in the dialogue sections. And the result was the masterly presentation of a magpie chattering crowd. Firbank's attitude seems to have been literally to 'score' the conversation for a full complement of voices" (59).

White Society and Black Culture

The most significant influence on white interest in African-American art arose from the new stereotype of blacks as "primitive" and "natural." Robert Coles and Diane Isaacs in a recent revaluation of the Harlem Renaissance argue that the primitive cult among artists, writers, and intellectuals in white society became an intellectual revolution "to remake values for a more decent humankind" based on the natural model of the black man ("Primitivism as a Therapeutic Pursuit,"in Singh, Shiver, and Brodwin 26). John Cooley makes a similar argument in evaluating primitivism's role in white society's re-creation of the African American. He cites the work of e. e. cummings, Gertrude Stein, Sherwood Anderson, Carl Van Vechten, and Waldo Frank as attempts to create a new image of the black

> as another kind of primitive; for them blacks were "naturals." First of all blacks were regarded as childlike and their lives were simplistic. Nor was this a defect to these white writers, for one of the notions that runs through the 1920s is the ideal of "salvation by the child," as Malcolm Cowley expressed it. Another idea which gained popularity during the 1920s was "living for the moment" (or, as we would say today, "living existentially"), and with it a demand for greater creativity, for new and simpler styles of expression. A strand of sensuality also stretches across the decade, and with it a cry to imprison reason and restore the body to its rightful place. To these white writers, blacks symbolized those qualities so striking for their absence from white America. ("White Writers and the Harlem Renaissance" in Singh, Shiver, and Brodwin 18)

Such qualities were equally absent from English society as well. Yet Firbank attached the new black type to personality as one more aspect of positive degeneracy. Blacks in Firbank's novels refract the verbal, social, and sexual sophistication of the driving camp personality behind all characterization. Unlike the gender/gender role confusion typifying camp characterization based on the drag persona, the stability of black characters consistently counters the flux of Firbankian society. The inversion of the Respectable/degenerate binary in the social model allows Firbank to portray the black as "respectable" for comic gain and without pleading moral seriousness. The difference between black characterization and the naughty sexuality of other characters is a matter of erotic appreciation, not necessarily that of the reader, but assuredly that of the author. Although the new black type integrates in his multifaceted camp personality, Firbank's *self*-identification with blacks carries over into the characterization; he can make fun of himself, his homosexuality, and his erotic attraction to other races, but not of the black man or woman. Firbank never exaggerates physical characteristics for comic effect, nor trades on racial stereotypes of the mammy, the pickininny, or the tom. Firbank's identification with blacks is typified in his creation of such characters as Blanche Negress in *The Princess Zoubaroff*, whose racially binary name, perhaps, reflects the author's sense of self. The emblem of the "white Negro" is scattered over nearly all the novels. Blacks occur in subtext as type, as well as in full characterization.

Black as Type

The black type in subtext evidences positive erotic value, even in the midst of the all-encompassing degeneracy of the sexualities making up Firbankian society. In *The Flower beneath the Foot,* for example, Firbank, homosexuality, and interracial sexual attraction appear in relation to each other in the bookstore scene where several ladies from the English colony on the island kingdom of Pisuerga have gathered to borrow English-language books from the makeshift library of the shopkeeper, Mrs. Bedley. Firbank's style requires a rather lengthy excerpt.

> "Have you read *Men—My Delight*, Bessie?" Miss Hopkins asked, "by Cora Velasquez."
>
> "No!"
>
> "It's not perhaps a very. . . . It's about two dark and three fair men," she added vaguely.
>
> "Most women's novels seem to run off the rails before they reach the end, and I'm not very fond of them," Mrs. Bedley asserted.
>
> "*The Passing of the Rose* I read the other day," Mrs. Montgomery said, "and *so* enjoyed it."
>
> "Isn't that one of Ronald Firbank's books?"
>
> "No, dear, I don't think it is. But I never remember an author's name and I don't think it matters!"
>
> "I suppose I'm getting squeamish! But this Ronald Firbank I can't take to at all. *Valmouth*! Was there ever a novel more coarse? I assure you I hadn't gone very far when I had to put it down."
>
> "It's *out*," Mrs. Bedley suavely said, "as well," she added, "as the rest of them."
>
> "I once met him," Miss Hopkins said, dilating slightly the *retinae* of her eyes. "He told me writing books was by no means easy!"

Mrs. Barleymoon shrugged.

"Have you nothing more enthralling, Mrs. Bedley," she persuasively asked, "tucked away?"

"Try *The Call of the Stage,* dear," Mrs. Bedley suggested.

"You forget, Mrs. Bedley," Mrs. Barleymoon replied, regarding solemnly her *crepe.*

"Or *Mary of the Manse,* dear."

"I've read *Mary of the Manse* twice, Mrs. Bedley—and I don't propose to read it again."

"_____?"

"_____!"

Mrs. Bedley became abstruse.

"It's dreadful how many poets take to drink," she reflected.

A sentiment to which her subscribers unanimously assented.

"I'm taking *Men are Animals,* by the Hon. Mrs. Victor Smythe, and *What Every Soldier Ought to Know,* Mrs. Bedley," Miss Hopkins breathed.

"And I *The East is Whispering,*" Mrs. Barleymoon in hopeless tones affirmed. (532–33)

Miss Hopkins's inquiry of the availability of *Men—My Delight,* a novel by a woman but about two dark and three fair men, is given a scandalous quality by the speaker whose attenuated description ("It's not perhaps a very . . .") suggests a (homo)sexual theme. The vague disclaimer to a group of proper ladies implies that the book with a title evocative of interracial sexual pleasure (*My Delight!*) may not be very respectable, although, protests aside, the ladies select equally suggestive titles. That Miss Hopkins might have insight into the theme of the book is supported by her personal connection with the disreputable Ronald Firbank, whose objectionable novels are all *out,* as Mrs. Bedley suavely notes. Miss Hopkins's interest in male homosexuality is reaffirmed as well in the selection of the two books she finally decides to borrow, the suggestively titled *Men are Animals* and *What Every Soldier Ought to Know.* Mrs. Barleymoon reemphasizes the connection between race and erotics by selecting *The East is Whispering.* Firbank's fascination with people of color may partly be due to an *orientalist* penchant, an appreciation of Islamic art and architecture, and an attraction to North African boys. *Santal,* a noncamp novel, for example, portrays plaintively the idealized death of a beautiful Arab boy. The Eastern culture of Islam, with even greater restrictions on female autonomy than those imposed by Western respectability, is well known for a degree of receptiveness to male homosexuality among young males, and Firbank, born in the nineteenth century, stands midway in a continuum of homosexual English writers from William Beckford in the preceding century to Joe Orton in the twentieth century, who enjoyed this aspect of the East, especially the culture of northern Africa. As "Greek" was code for Wilde and his time, "the East" served Firbank's generation.

The black as natural, erotic type is a figure in many of the novels, especially used to contrast with the straitened meanness of Respectability. Sally Sinquier, whose disastrous flight to the London stage from the middle-class home of her cleric father and dourly proper mother supplies the plot of *Caprice*, is trapped in the world of respectability. Her entrapment is clear in the description she provides of her existence that begins in the bastion of respectability, the church: " 'I was born in the sleepy peaceful town of Applethorp (three p's), in the inmost heart—right in the very middle,' Miss Sinquier murmured, tucking a few wild flowers under her chin, 'of the *Close*' " (*Complete Ronald Firbank* 321). As a budding degenerate, Sally is fascinated by the sexual, the exotic, and foreign. She has several romantic reveries in which she casts herself as exotic. She makes her decision to flee Respectability after sympathetically attempting to "obliterate" the canon's Sunday sermon from his mind by reciting parts of *Ozias Midwinter*, an erotic poetic lament of a white man for a "Negress." The poet presents the black as a cultural mixture of African and Indian with references to "Congo serpents" as well as "Madras handkerchiefs," a composite Firbank uses in representing the nonwhite Other in his black figures. The recitation requires, she insists, that "one ought *really* to shake one's shanks!" although her father asks her to forego the choreography in deference to the sabbath. This slang expression refers to the popularity of African-American inspired "race" dances such as the black bottom, the buck and wing, the Charleston. Race and sex perfuse this opening episode, as Mrs. Sinquier is in turn disgusted and frightened by the linking of the two, referring to blacks as "scandalous topsies that entrap our missionaries." Shuddering at the memory of "those coloured coons" who reveled at the palace fete the previous year, "roaming all night in the Close," she recalls looking from her window the following morning to be shocked by "an old mulatress holding up the baker's boy in the lane." As one of the self-contained, discrete elements of design making up the multipartite structure of the novel, this introductory passage establishes the social scheme universal in Firbank's social representation. Representatives of the Respectable dominant culture, when confronted by a *proximate* rather than *contained* deviant/degenerate Other, become comically confused by the confrontation with representatives of the subject culture. That the "close" itself (the word suggests religious, nominal, and spatial values) is violated by interracial sexuality speaks to the *proximal* danger of the degenerate threat to the Respectable order of the Sinquier household. In the world of respectability there is nothing natural about sexuality and everything frightening in interracial sexuality.

The scheme of subject/dominant culture confrontation overlays all the novels, including the one novel set in an all-black tropical island, where the culture conflict elides into white Negroism. Although *Prancing Nigger* presents an entirely black society, it is one indistinguishable from all Firbankian social representation. The central degenerate/Respectable scheme frames the "Negress" Mrs. Mouth and her ridiculous aspirations to place her daughters in Society. Her trust in fortune telling cards and her liberal notions of sexuality, however, contrast with her husband's decidedly English-style conservatism and religiosity. As a Respectable figure, he is petulantly Wesleyan, his hero Wilberforce. In this "white" representation of a black society, the sole character representing the "natural" or "primitive" black, daughter Miami's boyfriend, Bamboo, is left behind when the Mouth family moves to Cuna-Cuna to enter Society. He remains outside the action in the edenic, but appropriately named, small town of Mediavilla.

Mediavilla, exotic natural garden, fails Mrs. Mouth in two ways. Not only is there no Society for her girls to establish social reputation, the "number of ineligible young men or confirmed bachelors around the neighbourhood was a constant source of irritation." Firbank conflates "natural" sexuality with homosexuality in his fantasy of an unspoiled "negro" community as alternative to white society. The first description of the place occurs within the first two pages of the novel and includes, in addition to the expected depiction of exotic tropical flowers, the picture of a couple "strolling towards the sea, two young men . . . with fingers intermingled." The "ineligible" males are often associated with butterflies, as are gay men even today, and especially so Ronald Firbank, who described himself in a famous meeting with Siegfried Sassoon as "Pavlova, chasing butterflies" (Hoare 117). Miami's farewell to Bamboo before departing for Cuna-Cuna, a scene in which she desires once more to "snatch away" his crimson loincloth, is filled with homoerotic descriptive elements: "Boats with crimson spouts, to wit, steamers, dotted the skyline far away, and barques, with sails like the wings of butterflies, borne by an idle breeze, were bringing more than one ineligible young mariner back to the prose of shore" (*Complete Ronald Firbank* 599).

This humorously inflated, empurpled style continues throughout the Mediavilla chapters, exaggerating the idyl. The colors of the homosexual demimonde and the Decadence (mauve, lavender, iris, violet) tint nearly all description. The waters on which the island boys sail to tryst with passengers or seamen from white society, for example, is the Violet Sea lying between Mediavilla and Cuna-Cuna, its name underscoring the personal nature of this romantic fantasy for Firbank's own interracial desires. All the island attends the Mouth family's going-away party where "all iris in the dusk, a few loosely-loinclothed young men had commenced dancing aloofly among themselves," a group Miami discovers to include her younger brother, Charlie, "a lad who preferred roaming the wide savannah country after butterflies with his net to the ever-increasing etiquette of his home." Charlie's nascent "ineligibility" and sexual orientation become even clearer in contrast to the newly established "white" regimen of household decorum. Social respectability in Mrs. Mouth's view comes only from education and by learning the manners of white society. Her reveries while still in Mediavilla include dancing in the arms of a blond foreigner. And the dancing at the party is wildly jazz: "The latest jazz, bewildering, glittering, exuberant as the soil, a jazz, throbbing, pulsating, with a zim, zim, zim, a jazz all abandon and verve that had drifted over the glowing savannah and the waving cane-fields from Cuna-Cuna by the Violet Sea, invited, irresistibly, to motion every boy and girl" (604).

As in the majority of Firbank's novels, plot closure is a truncation of narrative by some tragic event. None of Mrs. Mouth's family members adapts well to the exotic new requirements of Society. As her son joins the homosexual demimonde of "wonderful boys" in the city of Cuna-Cuna, and her second daughter becomes first a mistress to a wealthy bachelor of high social standing and eventually a prostitute, Mrs. Mouth's resilient attempts to place Miami are met with frustration from both Society and her daughter, who pines for her "natural" love in Mediavilla. A naif, Bamboo could never be sufficiently educated to fit into Society, and he never reaches Cuna-Cuna though he makes a desperate attempt. He, tragically, is eaten by sharks while sailing to Cuna-Cuna, the sad news of which drives Miami in despair to enter a convent instead of Society.

Black Characterization

Valmouth, that coarse novel unfit for a lady reader in *Flower beneath the Foot,* uses both the type and the character in its presentation of the black figure. Valmouth is quintessentially British, a wealthy resort town inhabited by Anglo centenarians, principally women, most of whom are sexual flagellants. The novel is homoerotic in tone, and the aged female denizens parody stereotypical aging homosexual "queens" in their obsessive preoccupation with desirable young boys and handsome men, a subject that dominates their elaborate all-female dinner parties in equal measure with flagellation. The only nonwhite characters in the novel are the mysterious Mrs. Yaj and her even more mysterious niece, Niri-Esther, character and type of women of color, respectively. Valmouth society has an upper and lower class. The upper class is dominated by Mrs. Hurstpierpoint and Mrs. Thoroughfare, matrons of Hare-Hatch House. The lower is headed by the ancient Granny Tooke, whose dairy farm is home to a strapping shepherd lad, David, and his naive sister, Thetis, who pines for the seawandering Dick Thoroughfare, a virile young man of multiple interests, which include Thetis, Niri-Esther, and his fifteen-year-old "middy-chum" Jack Whorwood. Lady Parvula de Panzoust, like Mrs. Yaj and Niri-Esther, temporarily inhabits Valmouth, the guest of the Hare-Hatch House matrons. Cosmopolitan, a sexual sophisticate, she is a foil for the equally wise Mrs. Yaj.

In the ancient community of Valmouth, moribund and enlivened only by fetishistic behaviors, religious and sexual, Mrs. Yaj functions as a rejuvenating agent. A masseuse, she utilizes an array of masturbatory sexual toys in her massage technique to "end off wid a charming sensation." She first appears roadside as the two dames of Hare-Hatch House see her from their carriage carrying "something that looked to be an india-rubber coil" which prompts Mrs. Hurstpierpoint's scandalized response, "Those appliances of hers—; that she flaunts!" The purpose to which Mrs. Yaj puts these implements of her trade becomes clear in the exchange between the women, whispered in the presence of a priest who occupies the carriage with them.

> "In massaging her 'cases,' " Mrs. Thoroughfare *sotto-voce* said, "I'm told she has a trick of—um."
> "Oh?"
> "And of—um!"
> "Indeed?" (*Complete Ronald Firbank* 389)

Perhaps the oldest inhabitant of Valmouth, Granny Tooke looks forward to Mrs. Yaj's visits, calling them her "vibro days." Mrs. Yaj takes justifiable pride in having restored the oldster "to all the world's delight." Philosophizing endlessly on sensual pleasure and the nature of love, Mrs. Yaj resolves the crisis of senescence for her patrons and figures prominently in the resolution of plot, procuring a virile lover for Lady Parvula, providing Captain Dick with a "Negress" bride, uniting the two social spheres by sexual rejuvenation, integrating the subject Other into the most proximal relationship with the dominant culture, the Hare-Hatch House family.

As exponent of the novel's organizing personality, Mrs. Yaj comes closest of all Firbank's black figures to his identification with people of color. Although she seems to be Indian, she is in truth representative of all negritude, an element in the degenerate complex associated with homosexuality and masturbation. She is another version of Blanche Negress and perceives little difference in the races. "De skin . . . may vary, but de Creator ob de universe has cast us all in de same mould," she tells Lady Parvula. Although she can weep at the erotic poetry of Tagore when recited by Niri-Esther, she herself recites a Blake couplet in explaining herself to the inquisitive Lady Parvula: "My mother bore me in the southern wild / And I am black, but O! my soul is white." She is a universal black figure, geographically unrestricted. When asked what part of the world is home, she insists her home is "here," meaning Valmouth, but describes her family as "geographically scattered." Her mixed family is Indian, perhaps African, and Tahitian, and includes brothers, one of whom is a "lady-killer" and has three wives, the other of whom has a "pash-on" for bananas, making a "Cult" of his job as fruit inspector, and has no interest in women. Lady Parvula recognizes her match in Mrs. Yaj and mouths Firbank's racial views in her estimation of Niri-Esther. "Lady Parvula de Panzoust, alone, a sure connoisseur of all amative values, was disposed to allow the Negress her dues, divining those ethnologic differences, those uneasy nothings, that again and again in the history of the world have tempted mankind to err" (412–13).

In contrast to the decrepit denizens of Valmouth, Lady Parvula and Mrs. Yaj, though both elderly, evidence a similar liveliness associated with their complete understanding of love. Although the Englishwoman's knowledge has significant breadth, it remains circumscribed by its Eurocentricity. Her curiosity about love in other cultures prompts her to question Mrs. Yaj in detail. The masseuse, on the other hand, never questions Lady Parvula. She has attended the greatest ladies in white society, including the duchess of Valmouth, which impresses Lady Parvula who so admires the duchess, "you'd almost say she was a man." Lady Parvula speaks several European languages. Mrs. Yaj, who knows an equal number of foreign tongues, surprises Lady Parvula by speaking perfect French. Her response to the Englishwoman's surprised question "You know French?" is a matter of fact "Like ebberything else!" John Anthony Kiechler's analysis of erotic alienation and language in Firbank's novels concludes that characters frequently only overcome their disconnectedness when speaking French, what Kiechler calls Firbank's "erotic language." French for Mrs. Yaj, however, is but a small part of her comprehensive knowledge of love, life, and human relations, describable only as *everything else.*

Unlike Mrs. Yaj, the Negro-as-character, Niri-Esther reflects less the personality behind the characterization, being a Negro of type. She is portrayed as "natural" and behaves "instinctively." Surrounded by an air of mystery, her very physical nature seems incomprehensible to others. "Advancing with undulating hesitation," the narrator describes Niri-Esther's entrance at one point, "the young black girl brought with her a something of uttermost strangeness into the room." Decidedly lesbian in characterization, Mrs. Yaj contrasts with her heterosexual niece who before appearing at Valmouth has already married Valmouth's most desirable male, Captain Dick, whom she is to wed at novel's end in a second, Christian ceremony. It is clear that Niri-Esther will never fit the expectations of her new social order, despite her potential integration by marriage. Her perspective is natural rather than social, moving her to see the subject and not the artistry in the suggestive Hare-Hatch House sculpture of a hermaphrodite, which she delightedly and repeatedly spanks to the chagrin of her new in-laws. The final emblem of her natural distinction from the social expectation, and her association with Firbank's sense of his own "natural" sexuality, occurs in the ultimate paragraph of the work when she is discovered missing as the wedding ceremony begins: "But Niri-Esther had run out of the house (old, grey, grim, satanic Hare) into the garden, where, with her bride's bouquet of malmaisons and vanessa-violets, she was waywardly in pursuit of—a butterfly" (477).

Though the natural may prove impervious to social regimen, her effect on the flagellant lesbian Mrs. Hurstpierpoint is as noticeable as the effect of her aunt on old Granny Tooke. With increasing desire for Niri-Esther's beauty, Mrs. Hurstpierpoint, childless dowager, undertakes the child rearing of Dick and Niri-Esther's first child and increasingly identifies with the mixing of race. By novel's end she wears a black veil, to Mrs. Thoroughfare's consternation, in an attempt to appear more appealing to the child who is frightened by white faces, an attempt to appear more appealing as well, perhaps, to the desirable Niri-Esther and assuredly to herself. Mrs. Yaj and Niri-Esther, invading a decrepit white society, quicken it with sexuality, stimulate it with love, and finally transform it. Mrs. Hurstpierpoint, reputable scion of that society, transforms ultimately into another version of idealized type, Blanche Negress.

The White Negro

The degenerate complex comprising Firbank's camp personality is exploded in its three major elements to organize and structure his literary restatement of it in his novels. Characters thus refract the deviant triad masturbator/homosexual/Negro to the degree they draw from one or more of the constituent elements of the transgressive personality. On one hand, sexual identity as projected personality retains an ambivalence (orientation is inconclusive in characters simultaneously homosexual and heterosexual), since the source of sexual identification resides in illusive gender performance, which is by necessity repetitive and consequently variable. Transracial identification, on the other hand, ties personality to an actual subject culture defined not only by its proximal threat of degenerative otherness, but also by its physical differences and its deviant behaviors.

Whereas camp cloaks the sexual projections of transgressive personality, allowing a sympathetic reader to read one side of ambiguous characterization and yet forestalling censure by providing the antagonistic reader equally plausible meaning(s), the projection of white/Negro characters creates problematics for social vérité, and risks the insertion of a moral agenda into an amoral camp world. Firbank solves the problem in some ways by setting his characters in novels with fantasy locales of indeterminate cultural mix. Aldous Huxley writes of Firbank telling him he was traveling to the West Indies "so as to collect material for a novel about Mayfair" ("Osbert Sitwell," Horder 73). Firbank's preface to the American edition of *The Flower beneath the Foot* claims the novel "is really Oriental in origin, although the scene is some imaginary Vienna," and concludes with the paradoxical statement: "Ah the East. . . . I propose to return there, some day, when I write about New York." The chimeric topography of Firbank's settings allows him to present members of the dominant Anglo culture as colonials in what otherwise appears to be English society, the English "colony" in Pisuerga in *The Flower beneath the Foot*, for example. The cultural and social mix of the indeterminate Firbankian locale reduces as well the primacy of race in the deviant subject culture when projected as personality. Deemphasis of physical racial characteristics, recognizable signs of stigma to contain the racial Other in the dominant culture, consequently elevates the deviant import of the race. Projections of the proximate Other, the Negro in white society, do not take the form of miscegenation, or a blending of physical characteristics, they occur in characters with deviant "Negro" behaviors, whether the characters are black or white. Removed from the physical, "negroism" becomes a matter of mind and behavior.

Racial distinctions are maintained, but, as with inconclusive sexualities, they appear illogically simultaneous. In the prelapsarian locale of Mediavilla, where society lays no claim, characters may be simultaneously black and white. A "sable Negress out of Africa" at the going-away party for the Mouths vaunts her exotic foreign extraction, viz., African, by repeatedly saying "I'm Irish, deah." Half Irish himself, and identified with blacks, Firbank may be inverting the emblem of the white Negro in this case. In the more recognizably Anglo society of Cuna-Cuna, however, social stigma may still accrue along racial lines as with the cat Snowball who has *again* "dropped black kittens."

Deviant sexuality and race are most notably joined in the character of Blanche Negress from Firbank's only play, *The Princess Zoubaroff*. Her name most aptly fits Firbank's personal interracial desire; she is homosexual, a novelist whose works include *Lesbian, or Would He Understand,* and by name is both black and white. The play, unlike the novels, is insistently socially programmatic and can serve as a critical tool for reading the novels. Although it is Wildean in its use of paradoxical dialogue (Wilde and Douglas appear idealized in character), Brophy traces its social program to Shavian origins (497–500). Without the refractory play of personality that creates the structural design of the novels and provides a variety of readings for meaning, the play straightforwardly presents the problem of a possible homosexual social contract in the failure of heterosexuality for all of the characters. The Princess Zoubaroff, whose record of heterosexual union is dismal, having divorced six times, has established by the final curtain a lesbian convent to which all the women, including Blanche, subscribe. The two leading males, abandoned by their wives, set about at play's end to raise an infant boy, the casual issue of an unfulfilling marriage, as a gay couple. In the spare form of drama, Firbank unmistakably hovers over the resolution of the problem of homosexuality in society in the guise of a lesbian, white Negro novelist. But Blanche Negress as surely stands behind his literary camp conception, as well. As the principal aspect of the driving camp personality that is Ronald Firbank, the white Negro no less determines the interrelation of sexual transgression(s) and interracial desire in his novels than in the play. The white Negro, in the shadow of the outré personality projections of masturbation and homosexual desire, which is the naughty sexuality that gives Firbank's camp novels their most identifiable quality and tone, however, nearly eludes identification. Although there are no social moral problems to be resolved by camp in the novels of Ronald Firbank, the white Negro in all its manifestations: character, type, and fashion, offers one approach to critical analysis and gives the student of Firbank's camp an opportunity to pin the butterfly.

Notes

1. In addition to Mosse's study of gender, morality, race, class, and nationalism, related arguments can be found in Carol Dyhouse, *Girls Growing Up in Late Victorian and Edwardian England* (London: Routledge & Kegan Paul, 1981); *Manliness and Morality: Middle-Class Masculinity in Britain and America 1800–1940,* ed. J.A. Mangan and James Walvin (New York: St. Martin's Press, 1987); and Frank Mort, *Dangerous Sexualities: Medico-Moral Politics in England since 1830* (London: Routledge & Kegan Paul, 1987).

2. Anthony Powell's preface to *The Complete Ronald Firbank,* for example, confesses his own critical impotence with a caveat to the reader echoed in nearly every other serious attempt to understand Firbank's work: "Ronald Firbank is not a writer to be critically imposed by argu-

ment. . . . Either you find entertainment—even food for thought—in the Firbankian Universe, or you do not" (p. 10).

3. Waugh's essay, "Ronald Firbank," can be found in Mervyn Horder, ed., *Ronald Firbank: Memoirs and Critiques*, pp. 175–79.

4. Susan Sontag's seminal essay on the subject of camp, "Notes on Camp," is one of the collected essays in *Against Interpretation* (New York: Farrar, Straus and Giroux, 1966).

5. William Lane Clark, "Subversive Aesthetics: Literary Camp in the Novels of Ronald Firbank" (Ph.D. diss.), George Washington University, 1991.

Works Cited

Auden, W. H. "Ronald Firbank and an Amateur World." *The Listener* (June 1961).

Brophy, Brigid. *Prancing Novelist: A Defense of Fiction in the Form of a Critical Biography in Praise of Ronald Firbank.* New York: Harper and Row, 1973.

Butler, Judith. "Imitation and Gender Insubordination." In *Inside/Out: Lesbian Theories, Gay Theories*, edited by Diana Fuss. New York: Routledge, 1991.

Dollimore, Jonathan. *Sexual Dissidence: Augustine to Wilde, Freud to Foucault.* Oxford: Clarendon Press, 1991.

Firbank, Ronald. *The Complete Ronald Firbank.* London: Gerald Duckworth and Co., 1961.

Hoare, Philip. *Serious Pleasures: The Life of Stephen Tennant.* London: Hamish Hamilton, Ltd., 1990.

Horder, Mervyn, ed. *Ronald Firbank: Memoirs and Critiques.* London: Duckworth, 1977.

Kiechler, John Anthony. *The Butterfly's Freckled Wings.* Bern: Francke Verlag, 1969.

Mosse, George. *Nationalism & Sexuality: Respectability and Abnormal Sexuality in Modern Europe.* New York: Howard Fertig, 1985.

Potoker, Edward Martin. *Ronald Firbank.* New York: Columbia University Press, 1969.

Ross, Andrew. *No Respect: Intellectuals and Popular Culture.* London: Routledge & Kegan Paul, 1989.

Singh, Amritjit, William Shiver, and Stanley Brodwin, eds. *The Harlem Renaissance: Revaluations.* New York and London: Garland Publishing, 1989.

"The Kinda Comedy that Imitates Me":

MAE WEST'S IDENTIFICATION WITH
THE FEMINIST CAMP

PAMELA ROBERTSON

Most debates on camp equate it with gay male taste and then proceed to explore camp's effectiveness as a form of opposition for a gay subculture.[1] Insofar as camp has been attributed a political function, that function seems to have depended entirely upon its articulation within a gay male subculture. While recognizing camp's appeal for "straights," most critics argue that "something happens to camp when taken over by straights—it loses its cutting edge, its identification with the gay experience, its distance from the straight sexual world view." Women, in particular, have been excluded from discussions of camp because women, lesbian and straight, are perceived to "have had even less access to the image- and culture-making processes of society than even gay men have had."[2] And women have argued that by its preference for blatantly misogynistic images of female excess, camp merely reproduces signs of patriarchal oppression, just as gay camp reproduces gay stereotypes and reinforces gay male oppression. By most accounts, then, the only authentic form of camp is gay and generally misogynist.

Camp, however, offers feminists a model for critiques of sex and gender roles. This essay argues for the role of women as producers and consumers of camp, using Mae West's star text as an example. I aim to de-essentialize the link between gay men and camp, which reifies both camp and gay male taste, and to underline camp's potential for asserting the overlapping interests of gay men and women, lesbian and straight. I do not deny the historical phenomenon of camp and its alliance with gay subculture. But I suggest that camp as a structural activity has an affinity with feminist discussions of gender construction, performance, and enactment and that, therefore, we can examine a form of camp as a feminist practice. In taking on camp for women, I reclaim a female form of aestheticism, related to female masquerade, which articulates and subverts the image and culture-making processes to which women *have* traditionally been given access.

In 1971, when *Playboy* asked Mae West to define camp, she responded: "Camp is the kinda comedy where they imitate me."[3] West's self-reflective definition of camp could be taken as an assertion of her own role as a producer of camp, or of a style compatible with camp taste; in other words, "Camp is the kind of comedy that imitates the kind of comedy I produce." However, for a 1970s audience, West's quote would point not simply to her status as a producer of camp, but also to her role as camp object: "Camp is the kind of comedy that makes fun of Mae West." That *Playboy*, the self-proclaimed arbiter of swinging sixties and seventies male heterosexuality, should be celebrating camp at all could only occur after the 1960s exposure and subsequent mainstreaming of gay camp taste, marked by Susan Sontag's influential "Notes on Camp" in 1964. At the same time, *Playboy*'s interest in Mae West as both an aged sex symbol and a camp icon represented the sublation of Mae West into what she referred to as "the Mae West character." From West's "comeback" in the late 1960s to her death in 1980, at the age of eighty-seven, she was not so much a star as a pop culture celebrity, the icon "Mae West," who was discovered by a new generation of viewers on late-night TV and in repertory theater festivals. The essence of "Mae West," a "cheerfully extravagant vulgarity,"[4] consisted of a few easily imitated traits—the hip-rolling swagger, look-'em-over stares, and outrageous double entendres—and epitomized the camp sensibility for both gay and straight audiences.

As Andrew Ross observes, "the camp effect" occurs at the moment when cultural products (for instance, stars, genres, fashions, stereotypes) of an earlier moment of production have lost their power to dominate cultural meanings and become available "in the present, for redefinition according to contemporary codes of taste."[5] West's late camp effect depended upon a shared assumption that West herself was obsolete and outmoded. As a 1970s celebrity, West enacted and became a one-dimensional misogynist joke. West's camp effect depended on her continuing to promulgate an image of herself as a sex symbol, with a seeming disregard for her age, pairing herself romantically with the youthful Timothy Dalton in *Sextette* (1978) and insisting on her own youthful appeal: "If you didn't know me, you'd think I was twenty-six."[6]

Neither West nor her audience seemed able to differentiate between the Mae West personae of the 1940s theatrical comeback, the 1950s Vegas rock-and-roll muscleman act, the 1970s caricatures of *Myra Breckinridge* (1971) and *Sextette*, and the initial 1930s film career, let alone her earlier vaudeville and theatrical career.[7] West's late high-camp popularity relies upon, but necessarily obscures, her earlier career—particularly the ten films she made between 1932 and 1943 which forged "the Mae West character." But, by examining her early film career in its historical context, we find West as a 1930s star producing a very different camp effect from that of her later career(s).

West was already a deliberate anachronism in the 1930s. Her most successful films, like her chief theatrical successes, were set in the Gay Nineties. Rather than nostalgically invoking the past, West used the 1890s setting to expose the ideological contradictions of women's roles in the 1930s. She parodically reappropriated the live entertainment traditions of burlesque and female impersonation to create an ironic distance from the gender stereotypes supported by these traditions, thus putting into question contemporary stereotypes.

In 1933, William Troy of *The Nation* described West: "Miss West's acting style is at once both traditional and burlesque. Unfortunately, there is a certain confusion possible here because one means both that Miss West's style is in the tradition of burlesque, or burleycue, and that it is a burlesque of that tradition."[8] Most accounts agree that West never appeared in burlesque. By the 1920s, burlesque was synonymous with cooch dances and stock shows centered around the display of the female body, and by the end of the 1930s, burlesque no longer existed except as a euphemistic misnomer for nightclub strip shows.[9] Still, Troy rightly situates West in the "tradition of burlesque" inasmuch as that tradition, from the late 1860s until the turn of the century, covered a number of forms of comic entertainment, including parodic critiques of various types of theatrical entertainment and acting styles, as well as inversions and exaggerations of sex and gender roles.

Robert C. Allen argues that nineteenth-century burlesque was encoded as a subversive form specifically about, and critical of, female representation and the relationship of women onstage to women in the real world. Burlesque was the most thoroughly feminized form of entertainment in the history of the American stage—women played all roles, male and female. Burlesque parodically redefined—and resexualized—the forms of theatrical feminine spectacle which had largely been relegated to "respectable" and "artistic" living pictures and ballet. The burlesque performer was distinguished from her female counterparts in girlie shows, tableaux vivants, and the ballet by her awareness of her own "awarishness"—the directness of her address and her complicity in her own sexual objectification. According to Allen, because the sexy spectacle of burlesque consisted of male impersonation and direct female address, it "provoked desire and at the same time disturbed the ground of that desire by confusing the distinctions on which desire depended."[10]

Early in her career, West imported the rhetorical directness and "awarish" sexuality of burlesque into small-time vaudeville. As a vaudeville performer, she gained notoriety for her transgressively sexual song-and-dance style, "her enchanting, seductive, sin-promising wriggle."[11] West modeled her 1913 solo comedienne act as "The Original Brinkley Girl" in part on Eva Tanguay, known for her uninhibited antics, sexual transgressiveness, and "I Don't Care" theme song.[12] Tanguay, however, was able to achieve stardom in vaudeville only by rechanneling the transgressiveness of burlesque through the grotesque, thereby containing her threat.[13] West reactivated the spirit, if not the letter, of burlesque not simply by becoming a female grotesque, but by merging burlesque with the styles of female impersonation and camp.

West has frequently been compared to a female impersonator. Most accounts locate the original comparison with the gay critic Parker Tyler who called West a female impersonator in 1944, when she left Hollywood. He thereby equated her camp effect with her decline as a film star.[14] The comparison generally partakes of camp's misogyny—West seems like a female impersonator because she appears to be a grotesque, a man in drag, a joke on women, and not a woman. Some feminist critics, however, have taken on the comparison to claim West's style as an instance of deliberate and ironic female masquerade.[15] These retrospective comparisons point usefully toward a crucial element of West's persona, but typically fail to acknowledge that West actually modeled herself on contemporary female impersonators.

According to her biographers, the other major influence on West's solo act besides Tanguay was the female impersonator Bert Savoy, who combined two types of female impersonation—the comic dame and the sex or double entendre act—and whose signature line was "You must come over."[16] In 1934, at the height of West's stardom, George Davis of *Vanity Fair* compared West to Savoy:

> Miss West, long have I loved you. Ay, long before *I'm No Angel.* Long before *Diamond Lil.* Long, even, before your first great play, *Sex.* . . . I can pay you no greater tribute, dear lady, than to say it has healed the wound in my heart caused by the death of the one and only Bert Savoy. I love you, Miss West, because YOU are the greatest female impersonator of all time.[17]

Davis's extravagant tribute suggests that contemporary audiences could recognize West's affiliation with the tradition of female impersonation and that this aspect of her persona, like her use of burlesque, was developed before she got to Hollywood. Whether West copied Savoy directly or not, evidence from West's playscripts suggests that in creating "the Mae West character" she not only modeled herself on female impersonators but also explicitly understood their style as camp.

West wrote a total of eleven plays, eight of which were produced before she went to Hollywood. In Hollywood, she was credited with writing at least her own dialogue, if not entire screenplays. Although all West's pre-Hollywood scripts contain some characteristics of the West film persona, only *Diamond Lil* (1928), the star vehicle that took her to Hollywood, seems to join these characteristics to the double entendre and aestheticism so crucial to later West characters. West's earliest scripts, *The Ruby Ring* (1921), *The Hussy* (1922), *Chick* (1924), *Sex* (1926), and *The Wicked Age* (1927), all feature a sexually aware, powerful female, but this character primarily functions as a comic vamp and/or good-bad girl. In the short sketch, *The Ruby Ring,* West's character Gloria proves for a bet that she can get five men to propose to her in less than five minutes each by using a different vamp method on each. For "Alonzo Mosquite of the wild and wooly west," Gloria decides to be romantic "according to all the rules of the Amalgamated Vamp's Union." She uses "baby vamp" stuff on an old man, "Theda Bara" for a professor, and so on.[18] *The Hussy* works the same routine into a straightforward love story about a gold digger with a heart of gold. *Sex* and *The Wicked Age* are melodramas which depict, respectively, the self-sacrifice of a Bowery prostitute unwilling to ruin the man she loves by exposing him to her past, and the downfall of a cold-hearted gold digger. These plays contain themes that will recur in West's later works—love as a performative technique, men as "suckers," jewelry as measure of love's value, West as friend and counselor to subordinate women, and the conflict between female sexuality and society—but the dialogue contains almost none of the word play associated with West.

The characters in West's scripts who sound most like West's film persona are the gay men in *The Drag* (1927) and the female impersonators in *The Pleasure Man* (1928). West wrote both plays, but did not act in either one. *The Drag* is a serious attempt to represent the plight of homosexuals in a hypocritical society through a quasi-medical and juridical discourse, but most of its power and verve center around the drag ball and the dialogue of its gay characters. The play features a bevy of "queens" who express their desire and sexual identity through witty double entendres.[19] Grayson, a construction worker, serves as straight man, in a double sense, for the gay men in the play whose lines presage those of West's own film characters. Clem, who calls all men "she" and "molls," says: "Yes, I'd love to stay and see your wonderful construction. But we have other plans." Another character, Winnie, echoes Savoy's tag line ("You must come over") and anticipates West's famous "Come up and see me sometime" when he says: "So glad to have you meet me. Come up sometime and I'll bake you a pan of biscuits" (II, 8).

West described the flamboyant and witty style of the drag queens and female impersonators as camp. In the backstage drama, *The Pleasure Man,* West clearly identifies the performance style of female impersonators as camping. Stage directions note the entrance of the female impersonators onstage with the shorthand: "Boys camp—enter through [central door fancy]" (I, 13). Here, the verb *camp* suggests that the actors will mime some activity which will effectively mark these characters as female impersonators. Later, when the lead man assaults a woman, one female dancer asks if anyone heard a scream and another dancer responds: "No, you heard them queens next door, campin'" (II, 20). Throughout the play, the "campin'" of the impersonator Bird of Paradise and his "manleykins" consists of witty performative exchanges which express homosexual desire: "Paradise, did you ever have a platonic love affair?" "Yes, but his wife found it out" (I, 24). Like the homosexual dialogue in *The Drag,* the dialogue attributed to the female impersonators and identified as camping anticipates West's wisecracks to a degree that most of her own theatrical roles do not.

In these playscripts, West aligns "campin'" with Wildean aestheticism, as well as with verbal activity. In *The Pleasure Man,* references to dandies and aestheticism serve as a joking, coded language for the in-crowd of homosexuals. When a straight performer expresses concern about the peculiar proclivities of his partner who makes lampshades, the stage manager Stanley, identified as "the Beau Brummel," says: "He's all right—nearly. There's no harm in lampshades. He's just an aesthetic type" (II, 20). Descriptions of the ball gowns in *The Drag* join aestheticism to gay camp practice and emphasize the relation between gay and female aesthetics: "Wait until you see the creation I'm wearing, dearie. Virginal white, no back, with oceans of this and oceans of that, trimmed with excitement in front" (II, 4). This description, which emphasizes effect over detail, parodies the lingo of female fashion design and, to paraphrase Wilde, asserts the primacy of style over sincerity in "matters of grave importance."

In a curious half-truth, Ethan Mordden describes West's personality as "the gay style exposed to the outsider."[20] Mordden recognizes the gay style in West, but misunderstands, I believe, what her use of gay style exposes. West did not simply copy gay style; she also linked certain aspects of gay culture to aspects of a female sensibility. West modeled herself on a camp gay style because she believed that gay men were like women, not only because she adhered to inversion models of homosexuality, but also because she believed that gay men and women were similarly oppressed by straight men. As Bird of Paradise says, taking a stand against the "pleasure man" who assaults a woman he impregnated and abandoned: "If you're a man, thank God I'm a female impersonator" (II, 2, 24). West impersonates gay men and female impersonators not to expose the gay style, but to exaggerate, burlesque, and expose stereotypical female styles as impersonation.

We can see elements of the female impersonator in West's fetishistic costumes—like the drag queen Clem, her costumes are excessively ornamental and "trimmed with excitement." For example, in *She Done Him Wrong,* West wears a tight black Edith Head design with sequins on the bodice, off-the-shoulder feathers, and white satin birds accentuating the bust. She foregrounds the fetishistic character of her costumes to the point of parody, in gowns that play upon female stereotypes, like the Travis Banton spider dress worn in *I'm No Angel.* The 1890s corsetted silhouette exaggerates and constricts the woman's body, fetishizing the bust and hips in a caricature of the female form.

In part, as a female female impersonator West represents an instance of ironic female masquerade. Using Joan Riviere's 1929 essay, "Womanliness as Masquerade," many feminists have pointed to the feminist utopian possibility of masquerade. Mary Ann Doane, for instance, sees the masquerade as an opportunity for a form of "double mimesis" in which a woman flaunts and exaggerates her femininity to reveal the performative activity of gender and sexual identities and to deprive stereotypes of their currency.[21] According to Doane, drag and other forms of cross-dressing are fully recuperable and can reinscribe gender identities—insofar as the surprise and incongruity of drag, at least in its comic use, depend upon our shared sense that the person behind the mask is *really* another gender. In opposition, the concept of the masquerade offers a more radical parodic potential. The surprise and incongruity of same-sex female masquerade consist in the identity between the gender of the masquerade and the performer—she plays at being what she is always already perceived to be.

The concept of the masquerade, then, provides a useful preliminary model for feminist camp. To understand the masquerade in terms of camp, however, we must realign the concept of the masquerade with the activities of drag and cross-dressing. West's female masquerade is mediated through gay discourses on femininity and needs to be understood in the context of gay practices of drag and cross-dressing. Recognizing this, Ramona Curry describes West's female masquerade as a modified form of gender reversal or drag. While arguing for a feminist reading of West as a female female impersonator, Curry claims that West represents an instance of deliberate female masquerade through her embodiment of masculine characteristics, as a "phallic woman" and as a "female displaying a male displaying a female."[22] West's masquerade does respond to drag, and this means it can be read as camp. But I argue that that response can only be described as feminist because it parodies drag by *replacing* and *displacing* it with the hyperbolization of the feminine through the masquerade—and not because West represents masculine characteristics behind the female masquerade. Female impersonators absorb and displace a female aesthetic: West recuperates this aesthetic *as* a female aesthetic. She parodically reappropriates the image of the woman from male female impersonators so that the object of her joke is not the woman, but the idea that an essential feminine identity exists prior to the image: she reveals that feminine identity is always a masquerade or impersonation.

At least in her early career, however, West not only parodies female stereotypes and images but also embodies and identifies with them. To read her impersonation as wholly ironic, one must ignore her status and appeal as a sex symbol and deny her affiliation with the female tradition of burlesque. The two-sidedness of her impersonation demonstrates the porousness of pleasure, the locally overlapping features of passivity and activity, affirmation and critique, which constitute camp.

For a 1930s audience, West embodied a complex and contradictory image of female sexuality which relied undeniably on gay camp, but merged the effects of gay camp with female burlesque to produce a form of feminist camp available to a female as well as a gay camp audience. The epithets attached to West in the 1930s point not only to her camp qualities ("the world's best bad actress," "the greatest female impersonator of all time"), but also to her sexual allure ("the Empress of Sex," "Queen of Curves," "Siren of Sex and Sensation," "Hollywood's Number One bachelor gal") and to the transgressive quality of her sexuality ("the bad girl friend of the world," "the first lady gangster," "the feminine Babe Ruth of the screen"). West was simultaneously sexy and a parody of sex; she was both a sex object and a sexual subject.

West's complicated star image depended heavily on her anachronistic employment of 1890s settings. From her first starring role in *She Done Him Wrong* (1933), West was identified with the 1890s. Advance publicity for *Belle of the Nineties* (1934), her fourth film, and the third with a Gay Nineties setting, featured just a silhouette drawing (towering head-dress, exaggerated curves, trailing gown, parasol) identifiable simultaneously as generic nineties fashion and as West, with the caption "Coming events cast their shadows before." Publicity for *Goin' to Town* (1935), her first starring role with a contemporary setting, underscored the close identification between West and "the Mauve Decade" by insisting on the film's modernity ("down-to-the-minute modern") while detailing the absence of Gay Nineties effects ("there isn't a pearl gray derby or a handle-bar mustache to be found"), and juxtaposing a photo of West in a 1935 Travis Banton design with a line drawing of a spare nineties silhouette.

In part, West evokes the fashions and entertainment forms of the nineties nostalgically, but, at the same time, she renders both the period and the nostalgia outmoded. Although her look was associated with the nineties, West's attitudes were recognized as decidedly modern. A *Time* review of *Klondike Annie* (1936) reflects how essential this disjunction was to her star image and appeal: "As usual, the comedy depends mainly upon the incongruity between Mae West's up-to-date wisecracks and their *fin de siecle* background."[23]

The gap between mise-en-scene and social mores serves to exaggerate West's cynicism and distances her from contemporary film stars and screen stereotypes. Contemporary fan magazines sometimes positioned West as a rival to thirties sex symbols, especially Garbo and Dietrich.[24] But reviewers also took West's cynicism as a welcome and critical relief from the maudlin seriousness of these screen vamps:

> She as made our old-fashioned vampires, those mysterious, pallid, emaciated, smoky-eyed females appear as futile as they usually are in real life.[25]

> Mae West is the first and real Waterloo of the Garbo and Dietrich schools of sultry, languorous, erotic emotions . . . her healthy, Amazonian, audacious presentation of the ancient appeal known as sex has made the world-weary, secretive charm of Greta and Marlene appear feeble by comparison.[26]

By these accounts, West represents at once healthy sexuality and uninviting cynicism. She opposes and ridicules the vamps' style making it seem "futile" and unrealistic. Other sex symbols were both sexy and funny, but the way in which West blended sex and humor parodied the very notion of sex symbols.

West's camp effect depends partly on this disjunction between social mores, and also, more pointedly, upon the gap between outmoded 1890s live entertainment traditions and Depression-era film and music styles. Sometimes West anachronistically inserts blues and jazz numbers into the Gay Nineties. In *She Done Him Wrong,* for instance, she sings the 1930s blues-influenced "I Wonder Where My Easy Rider's Gone" and "A Guy What Takes His Time"; but she also sings the period song "Silver Threads Among the Gold," with an accompanying Irish tenor; and she merges various traditions in a jazzy update of the period song "Frankie and Johnny." By incorporating multiple styles, she recodes the period songs to give them a sardonic thirties flavor and tone; and she distances the viewer from the thirties songs by recontextualizing their racy cynicism.

When West performs numbers suited to the Gay Nineties setting, she parodically reworks them in a burlesque of burlesque itself. *Belle of the Nineties* contains West's most extensive parody of burlesque entertainment. In it, she plays Ruby Carter, the "Queen of all Entertainers" and "the Greatest Sensation of our 19th century," a "St. Louis Woman" who transfers her act to New Orleans. Ruby's first number, "My American Beauty," "the most beautiful act" her emcee has ever had the "privilege to offer," consists of Ruby, in a shiny, clingy dress, posing before and "becoming" a giant butterfly, a vampire bat, a rose, and a spider, until finally, torch in hand, she personifies the Statue of Liberty—all of which, according to the song, represent different aspects of this American beauty. Ruby shifts her weight a bit from left to right, in true West style, but can't be said to perform anything—instead, she silently enacts and impersonates a series of feminine stereotypes. This number, however, functions like Doane's "double mimesis" to make these poses, and the tropes they represent, incredible, literally fantastic. The act's excessive build-up and amazingly enthusiastic reception seem ridiculous in relation to what Ruby actually does, especially since the other six performances Ruby gives, which feature Duke Ellington and anachronistically insert Depression-era blues and jazz into the Gay Nineties, demonstrate West's genuine and unique talent as a singer. "My American Beauty" anachronistically retrieves the form of 1840s girlie shows in which women posed as living statuary—which, in turn, were revived in 1890s films like Edison's *American Beauties*, featuring the American flag, an American beauty rose, and a woman.

In playing upon the gap between 1930s and 1890s entertainment forms, West's films both depict and render outmoded the gender segregated world of nineteenth-century popular entertainment. As Kathy Peiss has pointed out, at the turn-of-the-century, middle-class forms of leisure witnessed the emergence of a female audience; but women's participation in popular venues (like the circuses, saloons, variety shows, and sports events depicted in West's films) was still severely limited due to the cost as well as the content, still linked to the masculine saloon culture.[27] Female performers were culturally coded as prostitutes, and working-class women who wanted to attend these popular events often functioned as "charity girls," exchanging sexual favors for male attention, gifts, and a good time.

Miriam Hansen has emphasized how the "maximally inclusive" world of mass and consumer culture in the cinema gave women access to horizons of experience previously unavailable to them. She cites the Corbett-Fitzsimmons fight which surprised exhibitors by drawing huge crowds of women who were able for the first time to see half-naked men boxing.[28] In *Belle of the Nineties*, Ruby not only attends a boxing match, where she is clearly the only female spectator, but she also determines the outcome of the fight by slipping one of the boxers a mickey. The scene of the boxing match at once represents female exclusion from this sphere and undermines it, by drawing the film's female audience into it and by giving Ruby access to and control over it.

The 1890s "Mae West character" in film is almost always a performer and sometimes a gold digger/charity girl, but covertly, of course, she is a prostitute. Her role as performer functions as code for, and is seen as of a piece with, prostitution. Lady Lou of *She Done Him Wrong* makes the connection explicit by referring to herself as the "finest woman who ever walked the streets." West undoubtedly downplays her characters' transgressiveness and criminality to suit Hollywood mores, but, in her roles as a performer, she reveals the contradictions of working-class women's roles in society. "The Mae West character" may function as a kind of prostitute, a victim of the social and gender hierarchy in the public sphere, reliant on her physical attributes for luxuries; but she also undercuts that role by manipulating her place in the public sphere.

Functioning as an autonomous agent in the public entertainment sphere, West's character suggests the possibility of breaking free from prescribed roles for women in all spheres, and especially in relation to sex and marriage. As Colette described her: "She alone, out of an enormous and dull catalogue of heroines, does not get married at the end of the film, does not die, does not take the road to exile."[29] Although, due to pressure from the Production Code Administration, the West character must usually get married at the end of each film, she believes in marriage "only as a last resort."[30]

An equally important part of West's star text, and one that goes hand-in-hand with her sexual autonomy, is West's constant battles with the censors.[31] According to Curry, due to her transgressive image, West played "a unique iconographic role in the public discourse of the period about movie morality and censorship."[32] In part, her camp employment of double entendre was a conscious effort to deflect the censors. Joseph I. Breen, the director of the Production Code Administration, stated the difficulties of censoring West in a memo to his staff: "Lines and pieces of business, which in the script seem to be thoroughly innocuous, turn out when shown on the screen to be questionable at best, when they are not definitely offensive."[33] West was a frequent target of theater and film censors not simply because of her sexual explicitness, but also because "censors feared the independence and freedom of Mae West."[34] She was "the alarm clock that awakened the cleaner-uppers" because "she made amorous dallying appear entirely too funny."[35]

The fan discourse about Hollywood's efforts to censor West focused on whether the "real" Mae West was like the characters she portrayed. West's publicists attempted to dissociate their star from her characters, offering as evidence her clean lifestyle.[36] In response to this effort to clean up her image, however, Gladys Hall of *Motion Picture* claimed that if fans got the impression that West was not like her characters "the most glamorous and the most gaudy woman in the world today will step back into the ranks of 'just another blonde'" and "if Mae West goes Pollyanish, she is ruined."[37] A fan letter to

Movie Classic asserted the difference between the star and her characters: "It is my opinion that any woman who doesn't like Mae West is not using her common sense and doesn't stop to realize that Miss West is not at all the character she portrays on screen." But, this same letter suggests that fans might identify with the star through her characters: "And, too, many women would give their right arms to be Miss West."[38] West's "awarish" and transgressive sexuality was taken at once as a pose or joke and as a real source of power—and fans, especially female fans, could identify with both.

I argue that West's female fans identified with her and that this identification was a camp practice. In a recent essay, Jackie Stacey criticizes reductive models of identification assumed in psychoanalytic film theory and offers instead a model for broader cultural and social dimensions of identification in the cinema.[39] She distinguishes between two basic kinds of conscious social identification. The first consists of identificatory fantasies related to the cinematic context that involve fantasies about the relationship between the identity of the star and the identity of the spectator. The second consists of identificatory practices that take place outside the cinematic context and involve the audience in some kind of self-transformation to become more like the star. Here, I would like to emphasize the female spectator's extracinematic practices of copying, consumption, and imitation, and her cinematic identification with West as spectacle; I claim that, for West's female fans, these were camp practices. Without access to female fans' own comments about West, I rely on promotional materials, production statements, and fan magazine discourse. I contend that these materials helped mediate the female fans' understanding of West and made it possible for fans to subvert the image-making processes to which women have traditionally been given access—namely, an aesthetics of femininity related to fashion, consumption, spectacle, and performance.

Alexander Walker claims that West's "films never made fans out of that all important female audience."[40] Reviews and articles of the time, however, assert again and again the importance of West's female audience. Although West was a sex symbol, and potential rival, she appealed to women as a friend who understands them. In her films, her character frequently functions as counselor to subordinate women, like the fallen Sally in *She Done Him Wrong*, whom she counsels on men and whose shame she ameliorates with the worldly wisdom that "when women go wrong, men go right after 'em." Fans could sympathetically identify with West as a woman not unlike themselves. Leo McCarey, who directed *Belle of the Nineties*, claimed: "Women like her as well as men. Mae understands the psychology of her own sex."[41] Elza Schallert concurred: "Any red-blooded he-man can understand Mae. . . . His lush, full-blooded sister understands her, too—and likewise becomes her pal."[42]

At the same time, fan discourse emphasized West's difference from her female fans, especially with respect to body type. This contributed, in part, to West's promotion as a friend to women. As Madame Sylvia of *Photoplay* put it, they didn't resent her "because she was so far removed in physical type from the modern woman of today, that they figured she wouldn't be serious competition."[43] But, women also presumably desired West's curves and wanted to be more like her. An article in *Motion Picture* noted the "influence of Mae West" in creating a "new deal in feminine film figures."[44] The article proclaimed the new curvaceous styles to be " 'IT' with the bones covered." *Vogue* magazine featured a photo of West in her corset with West's claims that the corset was "a return to normal"; "a ladies way of saying that the depression is over," and a recognition that women need heft, confidence, vitality, and stamina.[45] For Colette, West's plumpness was of a piece with her independence, so that when West lost some weight, she mourned it as "a violation of principle."[46] West popularized plump female figures to such a large degree that the Central Association of Obstetricians and Gynecologists congratulated her and called her style "a boon to motherhood";[47] although Madame Sylvia, on a less congratulatory note, accused women of using West as an "elegant alibi" for letting themselves get too fat.

In her autobiography, West claimed that she wrote the play *Diamond Lil* in order to appeal to a female audience who, she felt, would be attracted to the fashions and glamour of an 1890s mise-en-scene.[48] When West brought Lil to Hollywood in the enormously successful *She Done Him Wrong*, Edith Head's Lady Lou outfits started a fashion craze toward a return to the frills, plumes, ruffles, and proportions of the Victorian era.[49] In addition to this extracinematic identificatory process of copying and consumption, female spectators could also identify with the cinematic spectacle of the costumes, enjoying them in themselves, apart from their narrative context.

Similarly, fans could identify with the spectacle of West herself. Noting that reviewers and spectators sat through *She Done Him Wrong* two or more times, while others waited to get in for a first viewing, Jay Brian Chapman claimed that its appeal resided in the spectacle of personality:

> This tendency to hold seats means just one thing to seasoned showmen and critics. Experience has taught them that when an audience likes a picture because of its story, it does not remain to see the show a second time, which tends to spoil the plot's effect. It is when the star's personality is the attraction that seat-holding becomes a nuisance.[50]

The plots of West's films could not account for her extraordinary popularity. Because West's character changed very little from film to film, it was her personality that functioned as the attraction. It is "the Mae West character" that appeals and it operates as an extranarrative attraction, justifying the melo-dramatic plots which serve as a mere pretense for the star's wisecracking personality and hip-rolling swagger.

Female fans, attracted to this spectacle of personality, engaged in the extra-cinematic camp practice of playfully imitating West. Stacey differentiates be-tween copying, which reflects a desire to look like the star, and imitating, which involves a partial taking-on of the star's identity, by replicating her behavior and activities. Female spectators identified with and imitated West's cynical attitude and her mannerisms. West described herself as "the woman's ego": "When women'd be leaving the theater at intermission, you'd see them sort of walking like the Mae West character, you know, giving an attitude—and the talk, too."[51] According to one fan magazine, when the Mayfair nobility gave parties, they gave Mae West parties, and "everyone from Mayfair duchesses to kindergarten tots" imitated her cynical style, repeated her wisecracks, and replicated her gestures.[52] Imitating West gave women imaginary access to her autonomy, transgression, and humor; and it enabled them to create an ironic distance from their own roles. Like West's female female impersonation, their imitations created a "double mimesis," which was at once a form of identifica-tion with West and with her masquerade.

The 1970s camp effect of *Myra Breckinridge* and *Sextette* channeled and dif-fused West's transgression through her construction as a grotesque figure, which disqualified her as an object of erotic desire and distanced her from a female audience. In contrast, in the 1930s, West demonstrated that camp can create an alliance, rather than further division, between women and gay men. Rather than a misogynist joke, "the kinda comedy where they imitate me" was a practice of camp identification between the female spectator and West. Through cinematic and extracinematic identificatory fantasies and prac-tices, West's female fans gained access to a form of camp that enabled them to distance themselves from sex and gender stereotypes and to view women's everyday roles as female impersonation.

Notes

I wish to thank Miriam Hansen, Corey Creekmur, Jay Schleusener and the members of the Gay and Lesbian Workshop at the University of Chicago for making invaluable suggestions on this article. I'd also like to thank Ramona Curry for making her dissertation available to me.

1. See, for instance Richard Dyer, "It's Being So Camp as Keeps Us Going," in *Only Entertain-ment* (New York: Routledge, 1992), 135–48; Jack Babuscio, "Camp and the Gay Sensibility," in *Gays and Film,* ed. Richard Dyer (1977; London: British Film Institute, 1980), 40–57; Andrew

Britton, "For Interpretation—Notes against Camp," *Gay Left* 7 (1978/79); Mark Booth, *Camp* (London: Quartet Books, 1983); Philip Core, *Camp: The Lie that Tells the Truth* (New York: Delilah, 1984); and Michael Bronski, *Culture Clash: The Making of Gay Sensibility* (Boston: South End Press, 1984), 40–46.

2. Dyer, "It's Being So Camp," 12, 11.

3. Robert C. Jennings, "Mae West: A Candid Conversation with the Indestructible Queen of Vamp and Camp," *Playboy,* January 1971, 78.

4. Ibid., 74.

5. Andrew Ross, "Uses of Camp," in *No Respect: Intellectuals and Popular Culture* (New York: Routledge, 1989), 139.

6. George Eells and Stanley Musgrove, *Mae West: The Lies, The Legend, The Truth* (London: Robson Books, 1984), 268.

7. On this point, see Joan Mellen, "The Mae West Nobody Knows," in *Women and Their Sexuality in the New Film* (New York: Horizon Press, 1973), 243.

8. William Troy, "Mae West and the Classic Tradition," *The Nation,* 8 November 1933, 547–48.

9. For an account of the history of burlesque, see Robert C. Allen, *Horrible Prettiness: Burlesque and American Culture* (Chapel Hill: University of North Carolina Press, 1991).

10. Ibid., 129, 148.

11. Quoted in Robert C. Toll, *On with the Show: The First Century of Show Business in America* (New York: Oxford University Press, 1976), 226; and Carol M. Ward, *Mae West: A Bio-Bibliography* (New York: Greenwood Press, 1989), 9.

12. Eells and Musgrove, *Mae West,* 35.

13. Allen, *Horrible Prettiness,* 273. Most accounts of Tanguay describe her as a sort of frantic madwoman.

14. Parker Tyler, *The Hollywood Hallucination,* cited by Tyler in his introduction to John Tuska, *The Films of Mae West* (Secaucus, N.J.: Citadel Press, 1973), 10–11.

15. See, for instance, Miriam Hansen, "Pleasure, Ambivalence, Identification: Valentino and Female Spectatorship," in *Stardom: Industry of Desire,* ed. Christine Gledhill (New York: Routledge, 1991), 277; and Ramona Curry, "Power and Allure: The Mediation of Sexual Difference in the Star Image of Mae West" (Ph.D. diss., Northwestern University, 1990), 257–320 and passim. Although she refers to early appreciations of West as a female impersonator, Curry focuses primarily on gay camp readings of West as an impersonator from the 1960s onward.

16. Eells and Musgrove, *Mae West,* 36.

17. George Davis, "The Decline of the West," *Vanity Fair,* May 1934, 82.

18. Library of Congress manuscript, 11. Hereinafter, all playscript citations will be in text.

19. West recruited about fifty chorus boys from a Village hangout for homosexuals. During rehearsals, she let the performers "cavort and carry on" as much as they wanted and during the play's run much of the dialogue was ad-libbed (Eells and Musgrove, *Mae West,* 65–66).

20. Ethan Mordden, "No One's Woman: Mae West," in his *Movie Star: A Look at the Women Who Made Hollywood* (New York: St. Martin's Press, 1983), 123.

21. See Joan Riviere, "Womanliness as Masquerade," in *Formations of Fantasy,* ed. Victor Burgin, James Donald, and Cora Kaplan (London: Methuen, 1986), 35–44. The article was first published in *The International Journal of Psychoanalysis* 10 (1929). For the introduction of the concept into film studies, see Mary Anne Doane, "Film and the Masquerade: Theorizing the Female Spectator," *Screen* 23, nos. 3–4 (1982): 74–87, and "Masquerade Reconsidered: Further Thoughts on the Female Spectator," *Discourse* 11, no. 1 (1988–89): 42–54; and Claire Johnston, "Femininity and the Masquerade: *Anne of the Indies*" in *Jaques Tourneur,* ed. Claire Johnston and

Paul Willeman (Edinburgh Film Festival, 1975), reprinted in *Psychoanalysis and Cinema*, ed. E. Ann Kaplan (New York: Routledge, 1990), 64–72. See also Stephen Heath, "Joan Riviere and the Masquerade," in Burgin, Donald, and Kaplan, *Formations of Fantasy*, 45–61; and Judith Butler, *Gender Trouble: Feminism and the Subversion of Identity* (New York: Routledge, 1990), 43–57.

22. Curry, "Power and Allure," 389.

23. Review of *Klondike Annie, Time,* 9 March 1936, 44.

24. For example, Jay Brian Chapman, "Is Mae West Garbo's Greatest Rival?" *Motion Picture,* July 1933, 28–29, 76–77; Kenneth Baker, "War Clouds in the West?" *Photoplay,* December 1933, 47, 109; and Constance Champion, "Katherine Hepburn, Mae West—and Sex Appeal!" *Motion Picture,* March 1934, 28–29, 87–88.

25. Leo McCarey, "Mae West Can Play Anything," *Photoplay,* June 1935, 126.

26. Elza Schallert, "Go West—If You're an Adult," *Motion Picture,* May 1933, 32.

27. Kathy Peiss, *Cheap Amusements: Working Women and Leisure in Turn-of-the-Century New York* (Philadelphia: Temple University Press, 1986), 142–45.

28. Miriam Hansen, "Adventures of Goldilocks: Spectatorship, Consumerism and Public Life," *Camera Obscura* 22 (1991): 52.

29. Colette, "Mae West," in *Colette at the Movies: Criticism and Screenplays,* trans. Sarah W. R. Smith, ed. Alain and Odette Virmaux (New York: Frederick Ungar, 1980), 63.

30. This ambivalent and transgressive attitude toward marriage and women's roles was a keystone for West's star discourse. West married only once, secretly, in 1911, but separated from her husband, Frank Wallace, within a year. Later, at the height of her stardom, when Wallace made their marriage public, she denied the story as a kind of tabloid blackmail attempt, saying that hundreds of men had claimed to be her husband. She wisecracked: "Marriage is a great institution. As I've always said, no family should be without it." See Kirtley Baskette, "Mae West Talks About Her 'Marriage,'" *Photoplay,* August 1935, 40.

31. During her initial theatrical career, *Sex*—which had been listed as one of New York's "dirt shows"—was the cause of West's being jailed, on the count of producing an immoral play. *The Drag* was forced to close out of town after West and her manager, James Timony, acquiesced to claims that it would "upset the city." *The Pleasure Man* was tried for being immoral, indecent, impure, and obscene, but the jury was unable to reach a verdict.

32. Ramona Curry, "Mae West as Censored Commodity: The Case of *Klondike Annie,*" *Cinema Journal* 31, no. 1 (1991): 67.

33. Quoted in Eells and Musgrove, *Mae West,* 280. The Production Code Administration focused on scripts, rather than performance.

34. Leonard J. Leff and Jerold L. Simmons, *Dame in the Kimono: Hollywood, Censorship, and the Production Code from the 1920s to the 1960s* (New York: Grove Weidenfeld, 1990), 40.

35. William F. French, "What Price Glamour?" *Motion Picture,* November 1934, 29.

36. See, for instance, Edward Churchill, "So You Think You Know Mae West," *Motion Picture,* July 1935, 49, 70–71; and William French, "'It's All in Fun,' Says Mae West," *Movie Classic,* December 1934, 27, 70.

37. Gladys Hall, "The Crime of the Day in Hollywood," *Motion Picture,* January 1934, 28.

38. Mrs. Beulah Leake of Brooklyn, "Defending Mae West" (First Prize Letter), *Movie Classic,* March 1935, 10. Although fan letters may not be reliable, as a published document this forms part of West's star discourse.

39. Jackie Stacey, "Feminine Fascinations: Forms of Identification in Star-Audience Relations," in Gledhill, *Stardom,* 141–63. Christian Metz adopted the psychoanalytic terminology of three registers of identification (primary, secondary, and partial) for cinematic identification. See

Christian Metz, *The Imaginary Signifier: Psychoanalysis and the Cinema,* trans. Celia Britton, Annwyl Williams, Ben Brewster, and Alfred Guzzetti (Bloomington: Indiana University Press, 1977), 1–88. The cultural and social forms Stacey highlights relate most closely to the psychoanalytic category of secondary identification—identification with an actor, character, or star. For a thorough analysis and summary of the psychoanalytic concept of identification in film studies, see Anne Friedberg, "A Denial of Difference: Theories of Cinematic Identification," in Kaplan, *Psychoanalysis and Cinema,* 36–45.

40. Alexander Walker, *The Celluloid Sacrifice: Aspects of Sex in the Movies* (London: Michael Joseph, 1966), 74.

41. McCarey, "Mae West Can Play Anything," 127.

42. Schallert, "Go West," 32.

43. Madame Sylvia, "Is Mae West Skidding on the Curves?" *Photoplay,* November 1936, 86.

44. Ruth Tildesley, "Curves! Hollywood Wants Them—And So Will You!" *Motion Picture,* July 1933, 34–35.

45. Cecelia Ager, "Mae West Reveals the Foundation of the 1900 Mode," *Vogue,* 1 September 1933, 67, 86.

46. Colette, "Mae West," 62.

47. Review of *I'm No Angel, Time,* 16 October 1933, 34.

48. Mae West, *Goodness Had Nothing to Do with It* (Englewood Cliffs, N.J.: Prentice-Hall, 1959), 106–7.

49. Ward, *Mae West,* 57.

50. Chapman, "Is Mae West Garbo's Greatest Rival?" 76.

51. Richard Meryman, interview with West, *Life,* 18 April 1969, 62C.

52. Hall, "Crime of the Day," 70.

The Critic as Performance Artist:

SUSAN SONTAG'S WRITING AND GAY CULTURES

MARCIE FRANK

—I think the main question people have is, creature, what is it you
want?
—Fred, what we want, I think, what everyone wants, is what you and
your viewers have—civilization.
—But what sort of civilization are you speaking of, creature?
—The niceties, the fine points, diplomacy, standards, tradition—that's
what we're reaching toward. We may stumble along the way but, civilization, yes, the Geneva Convention, chamber music, Susan Sontag,
yes, civilization. Everything your society has worked so hard to accomplish over the centuries—that's what we aspire to. We want to be
civilized.

[In *Gremlins 2: The New Batch* (dir. Joe Dante, 1990), one of the creatures
drinks brain hormone and is interviewed as the spokesperson for the species.
His voice is done by Tony Randall.]

D. A. Miller begins his review of Susan Sontag's *AIDS and Its Metaphors* with
a telling citation of Sontag, who, in an interview, expressed her disappointment at the book's reception by scientists and AIDS experts.[1] She would have
preferred it to have been recognized as a "literary *performance* [having] more
to do with Emerson than with Randy Shilts" (emphasis added). Miller explains
what he calls "the phobic quality of Sontag's writing" in her book on AIDS by
characterizing it, rightly, as a consequence of the status she gives to her writing.
Sontag's book concentrates on the metaphors of AIDS at the expense of people
with AIDS. She is interested in demystifying the metaphors used to discuss
AIDS even as she claims that her writing is, itself, immune—if not from metaphor, then from the disease. Sontag's writing is "phobic," Miller argues, because writing obviously is not subject to disease. Sontag's attitude betrays

panic in the privilege it proclaims for the purity of writing. But the status that Sontag claims for her writing, that it is a "literary performance," is not new to the AIDS book.

Sontag has claimed performative status for her writing from the beginning of her career. In the note to the paperback edition of *Against Interpretation*, published in 1967, Sontag presents herself as a novelist rather than a critic, thereby highlighting her "literary performance[s]": "The articles and reviews collected here make up a good part of the criticism I wrote between 1962 and 1965, a sharply defined period in my life. In early 1962 I finished my first novel, *The Benefactor*. In late 1965 I began a second novel. The energy, and the anxiety, that spilled over into the criticism had a beginning and an end."[2] Defining her critical achievements as an interlude between novelistic endeavors, Sontag states that the value her essays may possess lies in "the extent to which they are more than just case studies in [her] own evolving sensibility" (*AI* viii). However, this claim is about her "evolving sensibilities." Insofar as she implies that the value of her essays increases because she is a novelist, Sontag is being disingenuous. Moreover, the essays generally have been regarded more highly than the novels, which may lead us to reject her attempt to evaluate her essays.[3] Nevertheless, we need to investigate her underlying assumption: that there is a relation between her sensibility and her goals as a critic. This relation pervades her critical writings; to elucidate it is also to describe how her writing constitutes a performance.

Perhaps the most memorable intersection of Sontag's sensibility and her "literary performance" occurs in the "Notes on Camp" where she describes her critical goal: "to name a sensibility, to draw its contours and recount its history" (*AI* 276). In the five paragraphs that introduce the "Notes on Camp," Sontag reflects on the task she has assumed and sketches a justification of the form her writing takes: "To snare a sensibility in words, especially one that is alive and powerful, one must be tentative and nimble. The form of jottings, rather than an essay (with its claim to a linear, consecutive argument), seemed more appropriate for getting down something of this particular fugitive sensibility" (*AI* 277). Her introductory remarks end in a dedicatory flourish that establishes both her aspirations and her high standards. "It's embarrassing to be solemn and treatise-like about Camp. One runs the risk of having, oneself, produced a very inferior piece of Camp. These notes are for Oscar Wilde" (*AI* 277). Inferior or not, Sontag acknowledges that in the service of analyzing it, she has herself become a producer of camp. In fact, the essay ends as it begins, with Sontag recognizing that to describe the conditions for appreciating camp is to produce camp. In the fifty-eighth and final note, Sontag summarizes her accomplishments. She identifies "the ultimate Camp statement: it's good because it's awful. . . . Of course, one can't always say that. Only under certain conditions, those which I've tried to sketch in these notes" (*AI* 292). It is telling, however, that her acknowledgment of her production or performance of camp is ambivalent. Although her essay attempts to identify the analysis of camp with its performance, this production carries with it no guarantee of aesthetic excellence.[4] As we will see, trying to supply the missing guarantee drives Sontag's critical career in the directions it takes.

In her study of Sontag, Elizabeth Bruss makes a crucial observation about the shape of Sontag's career: she notices that the early concern with "sensibility" is displaced in *On Photography* and *Illness as Metaphor* by more impersonal terms like "photographic seeing" and "Ideology" (*Beautiful Theories* 231). But how do we get from one to the other? Elizabeth Hardwick suggests that the shift in Sontag's career from "sensibility" to "ideology" is measured in the shift from "spiritual" to "fascist."[5] Her apparently neutral summary of Sontag's familiar claims characterizes the range of Sontag's interests: from the "spiritual style" of the films of Robert Bresson, which is "cool, impersonal and reserved," to the "fascist style" of Leni Riefenstahl, which is "dramatic, grandiose, orderly, communal and tribal." Hardwick's point is that Sontag's interest in style proposes this symmetry between "spiritual" and "fascist": both are styles of filmmaking; both are modified by a series of evocative adjectives. In fact, in a later essay, "Fascinating Fascism" (1975), Sontag returns to the question of camp; in the context of discussing Riefenstahl, she repudiates it.

In this essay, I argue that the linchpin in Sontag's shift from sensibility to ideology is camp. In note #37 of "Notes on Camp," Sontag describes three sensibilities: "The first sensibility, that of high culture, is basically moralistic. The second sensibility, that of extreme states of feeling, represented in much contemporary 'avant-garde' art, gains power by a tension between moral and aesthetic passion. The third, Camp, is wholly aesthetic" (*AI* 287). In 1975, Sontag renounces the high valuation of the "wholly aesthetic," condemning it as dangerously porous because it can be injected with politically abhorrent meanings. But her repudiation is less a contradiction of her earlier position than it might appear. In fact, the two attitudes are consistent. Sontag's shift from "sensibility" to "ideology" is structured by her understanding that criticism is a "literary performance." She expresses her idea of performance paradigmatically in "Notes on Camp," where it has an explicit relation to gay subcultures. Sontag's desire to give her writing the status of a "literary performance" remains constant throughout her career and this critical stance derives from a (disavowed) relation to gay subcultures; in both the instances that she embraces camp and those in which she repudiates it, she assumes that there is a special relation between gayness or gay culture and performativity.

Sontag's dedication of "Notes on Camp" to Oscar Wilde and her interspersing of some of Wilde's epigrams among her own numbered entries, a gesture Elizabeth Hardwick characterizes as an audacious "incorporation" of Wilde (*A Sontag Reader* xiii), suggest that a comparison between Sontag's and Wilde's understanding of the role of the critic would elucidate Sontag's complicated attitude toward criticism as a "literary performance."

In "The Critic as Artist," Oscar Wilde explodes the false dichotomy between a "critical" faculty and a "creative" one when he proposes that criticism is autobiography.[6] As Wilde's speaker, Gilbert puts it, "the highest criticism really is the record of one's own soul. It is more fascinating than history, as it is concerned simply with oneself. It is more delightful than philosophy, as its subject is concrete and not abstract, real and not vague. It is the only civilised form of autobiography" ("The Critic as Artist" 68). Wilde's understanding of criticism seems to offer a model for Sontag. Indeed, Sontag's statement, "A sensibility (as distinct from an idea) is one of the hardest things to talk about" (*AI* 275), is reminiscent of Gilbert's more forceful assertion, "It is very much more difficult to talk about a thing than to do it" ("The Critic as Artist" 60). But Sontag appropriates Wilde selectively.

If she seems to adopt Wilde's blithe sublation of the opposition between objective observation and subjective investment or participation, Sontag also retreats from a full embrace of the autobiographical, offering in its place coy gestures that intensify her personality. She adopts Gilbert's critical watchword: "It is only by intensifying his personality that the critic can interpret the personality and works of others" ("The Critic as Artist" 78). She thereby replaces Wilde's understanding of critical practice by a notion of "literary performance."

The paradoxical terms by which Sontag characterizes her position as a critic in her introduction to "Notes on Camp" illustrate her misappropriations of Wilde. On the one hand, she represents herself as an intrepid investigator, embarking on a difficult, and therefore rewarding, task: "A sensibility (as distinct from an idea) is one of the hardest things to talk about; but there are special reasons why Camp, in particular, has never been discussed. . . . Camp is esoteric—something of a private code, a badge of identity even, among small urban cliques" (*AI* 275). On the other hand, she is significantly less detached than her anthropological tone might suggest. Commenting on the dearth of discussions about camp, she declares, "To talk about Camp is therefore to betray it" (*AI* 275). How can the discussion of a sensibility constitute a betrayal? The affect of the term, "betray[al]," illustrates, but does not explicate, Sontag's investment in camp.

Sontag quickly transforms her contradictory position into the famous announcement of her critical qualifications:

> I am strongly drawn to Camp, and almost as strongly offended by it. That is why I want to talk about it, and why I can. For no one who wholeheartedly shares in a given sensibility can analyze it; he can only, whatever his intentions, exhibit it. To name a sensibility, to draw its contours and recount its history, requires a deep sympathy modified by revulsion. (*AI* 276)

Initially, her claim to critical expertise seems to overcome the opposition between the critic as objective observer and the critic as participant in terms that are similar to Wilde's. However, the contrast Sontag draws between analyzing and exhibiting a sensibility reinscribes the polarity and privileges analytical detachment. Furthermore, initially, it seems that her contradictory reactions to camp—being both attracted and repelled—enable her as a critic. But a closer look reveals that while her attraction to camp may give her the knowledge to talk about it, it is her revulsion that qualifies her as a critic.

Even more paradoxically, Sontag's critical position expresses her ambivalence about performance. She wants to limit the performance of sensibility even though her own writing is the performance of her sensibility. She suggests that the acceptability of performance is a matter of degree: if an unspecified degree of involvement in a sensibility is necessary, "wholehearted sharing" disables analysis. Significantly, the terms she chooses to limit performance are moral: "no one who wholeheartedly shares in a given sensibility can analyze it; he can only, *whatever his intentions,* exhibit it" (emphasis added). Too much participation in a sensibility turns one into an inadvertent exhibitionist. Both betrayal and exhibition are overloaded terms whose moral resonances measure the distance between Sontag and Wilde.

Rejecting the autobiographical mode as exhibitionism, Sontag does not identify the characteristics that allow her to know camp. Instead, she produces her revulsion as a badge of the average, which offers the reader grounds for identifying with her. Her statement, "To talk about Camp is therefore to betray it" (*AI* 275), constitutes readerly curiosity as voyeurism, but both our voyeurism and her betrayal are transvalued by averageness. Sontag supplies information about camp that is both ostensibly not otherwise available and appropriately "modified by revulsion"; this supply yields the moral gain of self-edification: "If the betrayal can be defended, it will be for the edification it provides, or the dignity of the conflict it resolves. For myself, I plead the goal of self-edification" (*AI* 276). "Our" identification with her revulsion allows us to be edified by proxy.

Sontag's motives for evading the autobiographical are now perhaps clearer: the autobiographical mode would stymie the moral transvaluation of betrayal and voyeurism into edification because it would explain Sontag's investment in camp in other terms. Evasion grounds Sontag's critical position as a moralist. The hip knowingness that her writing exudes results from an intensification of personality, but her retreat from the autobiographical means that the sources of this knowledge are mystified even as she purports to analyze them.[7]

By criticizing Sontag's desire to produce "literary performances," I am not advocating antitheatricalism; I am noting a paradoxically antitheatrical slant in Sontag's endorsement of the theatrical.[8] After all, it is Sontag's understanding of performance that allows her to write her groundbreaking essay on camp. Furthermore, by holding Wilde's definition of criticism as autobiography over Sontag's head, I do not mean to suggest that what is missing from Sontag's writing is information of a private nature. When Wilde has Gilbert say that criticism is autobiography, I do not take him to mean "private" or "personal." The fact that Gilbert is a character dramatized by Wilde in "The Critic as Artist" both invites and complicates taking him as an autobiographical figure. Nevertheless, Wilde's wholehearted embrace of the theatrical means that his practice of criticism as autobiography works in the following way: when Wilde talks about himself, he can talk through himself (or through Gilbert's talking about himself) about issues of aesthetic valuation and meaning. What I would require of Sontag, then, is not a confession about her investments in camp, but rather a fuller embrace of critical practice instead of performance, that is to say, a fuller embrace of autobiography. By ostensibly suppressing herself in order to talk about "other things," by acting on an antitheatrical valuation of "detachment" or "impersonality," all she manages to do, paradoxically, is to draw attention to her desires to be a "literary performer."

In taking camp as the paradigm of performance, Sontag transforms Wilde's depiction of the critic as artist into the critic as performance artist. The position of the critic as a performance artist allows Sontag to equate the analysis of camp with the production of it at the same time that it also provides her with a covert position of morality from which she can supply the otherwise absent guarantee that her productions will be of aesthetic quality. In "Fascinating Fascism," Sontag turns to the political register in order to enforce that guarantee by explicitly moral means.

Whatever we may want to make of the claim from "Notes on Camp" that "Camp taste, is above all, a mode of enjoyment, of appreciation—not judgment" (*AI* 291), we need to see the continuities with the pronouncement Sontag makes in "Fascinating Fascism": "Art which evokes the themes of fascist aesthetics is popular now, and for most people it is probably no more than a variant of camp" (*A Sontag Reader* 320). "Most people," she seems to be saying, currently can't recognize fascism because they (mis)take it for camp.

> Fascism may be merely fashionable, and perhaps fashion with its irresistible promiscuity of taste will save us. But the judgments of taste themselves seem less innocent. Art that seemed eminently worth defending ten years ago, as a minority or adversary taste, no longer seems defensible today, because the ethical and cultural issues it raises have become serious, even dangerous, in a way they were not then. (*A Sontag Reader* 320–21)

What has changed so substantially between 1964 and 1975 to raise such an alarm? In note #2 of "Notes on Camp," Sontag had claimed that "it goes without saying that the Camp sensibility is disengaged, depoliticized—or at least apolitical" (*AI* 277). In 1975, however, Sontag seeks to recuperate the political valences of what, in 1964, she depicted as resolutely "apolitical." The paragraph from "Fascinating Fascism" that I just cited continues: "The hard truth is that what may be acceptable in elite culture may not be acceptable in mass culture, that tastes which pose only innocuous ethical issues as the property of the minority become corrupting when they become more established. Taste is context, and the context has changed" (*A Sontag Reader* 321). Could the critical change between 1964 and 1975 be the politicization, after Stonewall, of what had seemed to Sontag to be a purely aesthetic phenomenon, namely, camp? If so, then perhaps Eve Kosofsky Sedgwick's recent description of Allan Bloom's defense of the canon is relevant: in defending "that curious space that is both internal and marginal to the culture"—the bohemian elite—Bloom offers "an unapologetic protection of the sanctity of the closet."

> The modern, normalizing, minoritizing equal rights movement for people of varying sexual identities is a grave falling-off, in Bloom's view, from the more precarious cultural *privilege* of a past in which "there was a respectable place for marginality, bohemia. But it had to justify its unorthodox practice by intellectual and artistic achievement."[9]

Like Bloom, Sontag wants to protect a bohemian elite, but her desire to do so operates only as long as the aesthetic and apolitical "quality" of its artistic productions can be guaranteed. In "Notes on Camp," camp was "at least apolitical" (*AI* 277); in "Fascinating Fascism," Sontag brings a full-blown moral vocabulary masquerading as politics to ensure that if gay culture won't stay apolitical, it is guaranteed to be marginalized, or worse.

Interestingly, Sontag's "political" solution is already apparent in "Notes on Camp." In entry #51, Sontag makes explicit the relation between gay culture and camp:

> The *peculiar* relation between Camp taste and homosexuality has to be ex-
> plained. While it's not true that Camp taste *is* homosexual taste, there is no
> doubt a *peculiar* affinity and overlap. Not all liberals are Jews, but Jews have
> shown a *particular* affinity for liberal and reformist causes. So, not all homosex-
> uals have camp taste. But homosexuals, by and large, constitute the vanguard—
> and the most articulate audience—of Camp. (*AI* 290, emphasis added)

In parenthesis, Sontag explains the analogy between the peculiarity of homosexual taste and the particularity of Jewish morality.

> (The analogy is not frivolously chosen. Jews and homosexuals are the outstand-
> ing creative minorities in contemporary urban culture. Creative, that is, in the
> truest sense: they are creators of sensibilities. The two pioneering forces of
> modern sensibility are Jewish moral seriousness and homosexual aestheticism
> and irony.) (*AI* 290)

In entry #52, Sontag asserts that the social marginalization of both homosexuals and Jews is what makes them more creative; both groups are motivated
by their search for legitimation and acceptance by society: "The Jews pinned
their hopes for integrating into modern society on promoting the moral sense.
Homosexuals have pinned their integration into society on promoting the
aesthetic sense. Camp is a solvent of morality. It neutralizes moral indignation,
sponsors playfulness" (*AI* 290). After Stonewall, it would no longer have been
possible for Sontag to characterize homosexuals' sociopolitical interest as primarily to sponsor playfulness nor to propose "integration" as their goal. It
could no longer be said of a gay movement agitating for legal and political
recognition that it advocated a purely aesthetic sense.

But Sontag is not the only one, who, in 1975, sought to recuperate the
political valences of the things she had described in purely aesthetic terms in
1964. Like Bloom, Sontag's use of political terms to protect the bohemian elites
should be seen in the context of a general reaction to the 1960s.[10] It is instructive to consider Sontag's always slightly avant-garde development alongside the
shift in the literary academy from the sixties to the eighties from formalist to
political criticism of all stripes. We now know that it probably was never
possible to call any phenomenon "purely aesthetic." What then becomes salient is the inadequacy of the political terms Sontag chooses.

In "Fascinating Fascism," Sontag seeks to identify the features of a fascist
aesthetic. On the one hand, she presents the fascist aesthetic as no different
than a sensibility, but on the other hand, she relies on the term "fascism" to
produce the moral outrage that will differentiate sensibility from ideology.
Sontag turns from sensibility to ideology on ostensibly moral grounds. Under-
writing the morality, unfortunately, is homophobia. Whereas in "Notes on

Camp," camp reveals "a mostly unacknowledged truth of taste: [that] the most refined form of sexual attractiveness consists in going against the grain of one's sex . . ." (*AI* 279), in "Fascinating Fascism," "once sex becomes a taste, it is perhaps already on its way to becoming a self-conscious form of theater, which is what sadomasochism is about" (*A Sontag Reader* 325). Here is the same antitheatrical bent that constitutes Sontag's ambivalence toward performance in "Notes on Camp"; the terms are simply more explicit.

In "Fascinating Fascism," after discussing the rehabilitation of Reifenstahl, which she calls "First Exhibit," Sontag turns to "Second Exhibit," a book of photos called *SS Regalia* that she uses as the point of departure to decry the erotic uses to which Nazi paraphernalia have been put. In the closing line, Sontag offers the most memorable instance of the essay's hysterical rhetoric: "The color is black, the material is leather, the seduction is beauty, the justification is honesty, the aim is ecstasy, the fantasy is death" (*A Sontag Reader* 323). Each clause repeats the structure of the previous one, but instead of providing clarification, each equation merely increases the vehemence of tone. The scene she unfolds before the reader can only become spectacular, however, after Sontag has affiliated sadomasochism with homosexuality. Notice the progression in this paragraph:

> In pornographic literature, films and gadgetry throughout the world, especially in the United States, England, France, Japan, Scandinavia, Holland and Germany, the SS has become a referent of sexual adventurism. Much of the imagery of far-out sex has been placed under the sign of Nazism. Boots, leather, chains, Iron Crosses on gleaming torsos, swastikas, along with meathooks and heavy motorcycles, have become the secret and most lucrative paraphernalia of eroticism. In the sex shops, the baths, the leather bars, the brothels, people are dragging out their gear. But why? Why has Nazi Germany, which was a sexually repressive society, become erotic? How could a regime which persecuted homosexuals become a gay turn-on? (*A Sontag Reader* 323)

How did we get from meathooks and motorcycles to gay turn-ons? Through Nazi paraphernalia, of course! Moreover, the insinuating logic of the list of locations in which we might find erotic gear—"sex shops, baths, leather bars, brothels"—makes it clear that the "people dragging [it] out" are gay men. Sontag equates gay male sexuality with sadomasochism, and, more damagingly, sadomasochism with an imputed "fascism" that is equivalent to Nazism.

Sontag's attempt to repoliticize what she had placed in the domain of the purely aesthetic founders on two substitutions: the confusion of moral for political categories (notable especially in her use of the term "fascist"), and the substitution of her own literary or critical performance for the phenomenon she discusses, and ultimately, for a critical practice.

Like D. A. Miller, Elizabeth Hardwick recognizes the ways in which Sontag's writing promotes the assimilation of her subject matter to her own sensibility. Unlike Miller, however, Hardwick has nothing but praise for this tendency: "The camp sensibility is not a text to be held in the hand. The only text is finally this essay [of Sontag's] . . . [with] its incorporation of the exemplar of the camp mode—the epigrams of Oscar Wilde."[11] At its most extreme, Sontag's writing involves the replacement of camp as a phenomenon by Susan Sontag herself. As Miller points out in the review I cited at the beginning, although Sontag at first affiliates camp with gay performance, she almost immediately repudiates the connection, severing camp from homosexuality, and putting "the claim to camp's origination . . . up for grabs. Someone else could invent Camp, and who better than the author of this manifestly inventive and authoritative essay?"[12]

Sontag's statement that the value of her essays lies in the extent to which they are more than case studies in her own evolving sensibilities to the contrary, we need to recognize that her description of the modern sensibility is no more and no less than a description of her own development.

> Somewhere, of course, everyone knows that more than beauty is at stake in art like Reifenstahl's. . . . Backing up the solemn choosy formalist appreciations lies a larger reserve of appreciation, the sensibility of Camp, which is unfettered by the scruples of high seriousness: and the modern sensibility relies on continuing trade-offs between the formalist approach and Camp taste. (*A Sontag Reader* 320)

This characterization recapitulates the moves Sontag has made from "Notes on Camp" to "Fascinating Fascism." It is Sontag herself who blurs the boundary between Reifenstahl's Nazi propaganda and the leather paraphernalia of sado-masochism. The main claim of "Fascinating Fascism," that camp lacks the moral seriousness necessary to prevent the resurgence of fascism, only makes sense, if it does *at all*, in the context of Sontag's earlier claims about camp. And from this point of view, we can see that Sontag's descriptions of camp have more relevance to her own career than to any other phenomena.

"Sensibility," the key term in her writings of the sixties, is the conceptual grid through which Sontag poses the problem that most sustains her interest to this day: how to connect "culture" to tradition and history. From the perspective offered on "Notes on Camp," first by "Fascinating Fascism," and later, by *AIDS and Its Metaphors,* we can see that by sensibility, Sontag means gay performance—one that first needs to be rehabilitated by her imitation of it in "Notes on Camp," and then requires the ideological correction by moral inoculation she attempts to give it in "Fascinating Fascism."

Notes

1. D. A. Miller, "Sontag's Urbanity," *October* 49 (1989): 91–101.

2. Susan Sontag, *Against Interpretation and Other Essays* (New York: Delta, 1967), vii. Further page references are given in the text.

3. Elizabeth Bruss notices that "Sontag's creative efforts have few ardent admirers and many detractors. [Moreover t]hough she is frequently cited, it is rarely for her fictions or her films." See Bruss's *Beautiful Theories: The Spectacle of Discourse in Contemporary Criticism* (Baltimore: Johns Hopkins University Press, 1982), 203–80, for a thorough examination of the relations between Sontag's critical, novelistic, and filmic endeavors. Further page references are given in the text.

4. Accounts of camp that differ from Sontag's influential one include Philip Core, *Camp: The Lie that Tells the Truth* (New York: Delilah, 1984), and Michael Bronski, *Culture Clash: The Making of Gay Sensibility* (Boston: South End Press, 1984).

5. See Elizabeth Hardwick's introduction to *A Susan Sontag Reader,* (New York: Farrar Straus and Giroux, 1982), ix–xiii. Further page references are given in the text.

6. Oscar Wilde, *Selected Writings* (New York: Oxford University Press, 1961), 38–119. Further page references are given in the text.

7. Elizabeth Bruss expresses what is most likely Sontag's rationale for evading autobiography: "Purely personal or private experiences are not at issue, as the enforced personality of *Illness as Metaphor* makes clear by refusing anywhere to raise the spectre of Sontag's own cancer (lest the analysis miss its public targets and shrink into a piece of private and unrepeatable heroism)" (*Beautiful Theories,* 232).

But D. A. Miller offers a powerful critique of Sontag's one powerfully "personal gesture—a resonant unsentimental account of the cancer that spurred her to write *Illness as Metaphor*" that appears in *AIDS and Its Metaphors.* Her account

> is doubly dislocated by the exactions of impersonality. In the first place, she is only able to confess her private interest in that "little book" [13] now that the interest, no longer current, has evolved into "a classic essay," the jacket reminds us—without the benefit of such confession; and secondly, in the new little book where the story is interpolated, it necessarily acquires a new meaning—if Sontag wrote about cancer metaphors because she had cancer, then she writes about AIDS metaphors because . . . she had cancer = does not have AIDS. ("Sontag's Urbanity" 97)

For Miller, Sontag's inscrutability "makes the question of her relation to the [epidemic] all the more urgent to pose." Though I put less of a premium than Miller on confession, we are both interested in the consequences of its omission.

8. On condemnations of the theater, their motivations, and their history from Plato to the twentieth century, see Jonas Barish, *The Antitheatrical Prejudice* (Berkeley: University of California Press, 1981). For the relation between "theatricality," "anti-theatricality," and art criticism, see Michael Fried, *Absorption and Theatricality: Painting and the Beholder in the Age of Diderot* (Berkeley: University of California Press, 1980).

9. Eve Kosofsky Sedgwick, "Pedagogy in the Context of an Antihomophobic Project," *South Atlantic Quarterly* 89, no. 1 (1990): 150.

10. In "Periodizing the Sixties," Frederic Jameson locates the beginning and end points of the period called "the sixties" in 1957 and 1972–74 respectively. Jameson contextualizes the shift in academics from philosophy to "theory" among other transitions such as those in world economic organization. Sontag's shift from sensibility to ideology can be seen as an idiosyncratic

version of the larger changes Jameson describes. Frederic Jameson, *The Ideologies of Theory: Essays 1971–1986* (Minneapolis: University of Minnesota Press, 1988), 2:178–207.

11. In Hardwick's introduction to *A Susan Sontag Reader,* this perception follows from her astounding homophobic account of *Against Interpretation,* in which she identifies the "aesthetic irregularities" with which Sontag means to unsettle, such as " 'Camp,' science fiction and the film *Flaming Creatures,*" as the "bright poisonous poppies [that] flame about Simone Weil, Levi-Strauss and Camus" (xiv).

12. Miller, "Sontag's Urbanity," 93.

"You Don't Have to Say You Love Me":

THE CAMP MASQUERADES OF
DUSTY SPRINGFIELD

PATRICIA JULIANA SMITH

> We live, I regret to say, in an age of surfaces.
> —Oscar Wilde, *The Importance of Being Earnest*

> You always wanted me to be something I wasn't,
> You always wanted too much.
> Now I can do what I want to, forever,
> How am I gonna get through?
> —Pet Shop Boys and Dusty Springfield,
> "What Have I Done to Deserve This?"

During the peak years of her career, Dusty Springfield presented herself in an admixture of oxymoronic and seemingly incongruous roles, particularly those of the "Great White Lady" of pop and soul, the "Queen of the Mods," and the prototypical female drag queen. When one considers her in these larger-than-life roles, and her subsequent fall from fame into a cycle of personal and public disaster that would befit any tragedy queen worthy of the name, one might well ask, "What becomes a [semi-]legend most?" Yet when one considers Mary Isobel Catherine Bernadette O'Brien, the bespectacled, tomboyish convent schoolgirl and closeted lesbian underlying this fantastic and even fictional persona, one must ask instead, "What's a girl to do?"

While it seems a truth universally acknowledged today that the "Swinging Sixties" were an era of great sexual license that liberated everyone's libido from the restraints of bourgeois morality, the sexual freedom the decade brought forth was primarily for the benefit of heterosexual males. Although this now-mythologized neoromantic revolution also granted heterosexual women and, to some lesser extent, gay men more sexual emancipation than they had previously known, in the pre–Women's Liberation years those who were neither male nor straight remained at best nonentities and at worst monsters, particularly in the ultramacho and generally homophobic world of rock music. One of the great pop culture icons of the British Mod music and fashion scene was, nevertheless, a lesbian, although few of her fans—themselves for the most part sexual outlaws—were completely aware of Dusty Springfield's "bent" sexuality.

Through a metamorphosis stranger than most fiction, Mary O'Brien—a proper, middle-class British Catholic girl of Irish descent, somewhat unsocialized and seemingly destined for a career as a librarian—became the flamboyant Dusty Springfield, the idol of a cultural movement that, ironically, had little to do with her own existence. In the fantastic Mod ethos of swinging London, however, one generally could be almost anything, no matter how extreme or incongruous, except oneself—particularly if one's own true self were queer. As a result, Dusty Springfield paradoxically expressed and disguised her own "unspeakable" lesbianism through an elaborate camp masquerade that metaphorically and artistically transformed a nice white girl into a black woman and a femme gay man, often simultaneously. In doing so, this individual who had placed herself outside mainstream British society subverted fixed ideas of identity by assuming the personae of two oppressed and excluded groups. Thus, consciously or otherwise, Dusty Springfield blurred the distinctions of race, gender, and sexuality just as she did those between life and art and those between reality and artifice.

Such camp masquerades are hardly new to or uncommon in lesbian culture; critics have noted similar semiotic modes in other areas of lesbian art, particularly literature.[1] Yet Dusty Springfield's gender- and race-bending antics in the already extreme world of rock music and popular culture are not only as elaborate as and far more vivid than any we are likely to uncover in the more conventional (i.e., respectable) arts, but are also capable of affecting and influencing a wider and more varied audience through the mass media. Unlike the lesbian disguises one encounters in the "higher" sister arts, Dusty Springfield's palimpsest was not a premeditated strategy set in motion from the outset of her career; rather, her amalgam of fictive identities and facades grew in complexity and extremity over time and in direct proportion with rumor, innuendo, and consequent public pressure regarding her sexual "inclinations."

In January 1964, a seemingly new and unknown voice became a frequent presence on American airwaves. "I Only Want to Be with You" was among the flood of recordings released in the United States in the first wave of the so-called British Invasion spearheaded by the Beatles; it was, in fact, the first recording of this period by a British artist other than the Beatles to reach the American Top Twenty. This was not, however, Dusty's first American musical success. Two years earlier, as a member of the Springfields, her brother's traditional folk/country combo, she enjoyed a Top Twenty hit with "Silver Threads and Golden Needles," which showcases her distinctive voice in a brief solo passage. Yet, despite the Springfields' high visibility and popularity in Great Britain, they remained, after this isolated success, nameless and faceless to American audiences and were therefore virtually forgotten by 1964. Consequently, fans of "I Only Want to Be with You" quite understandably failed to make the connection.

Unfamiliar, then, with the identity and appearance of the androgynously named singer, American listeners formed various misconceptions about her nationality, race, and even gender. The initial impression of Martha Reeves, lead singer of the 1960s Motown girl group Martha and the Vandellas, is typical: "When I heard her on the radio, I just assumed she was American and black. Motown signed up nearly all the best talent at that time, and I remember being a little surprised to find she was with a different label—and I was absolutely astounded when I finally saw her on TV."[2] Dusty's name and husky timbre, however, led some less astute listeners to imagine that the contralto voice that made her first hit so compelling was that of a young and probably black male. Lloyd Thaxton, who was host of a popular Los Angeles television teen music program in the early 1960s, awkwardly confessed to her on the air that he had expected his guest, whom he had not seen before the show, to be a man. As gauche as this statement may now seem, his error was not completely unreasonable. Recordings by black male rhythm-and-blues singers who had adapted the high tenor voice of gospel music to a popular format—and who frequently bore non-gender specific names (e.g., Smokey Robinson, Frankie Lymon, Garnett Mimms, Jewel Akens)—were relatively common during the late fifties and early sixties. Similarly—and ironically—through Dusty's indirect influence this mode was once again transferred, some two decades later, across lines of gender and race and embodied in the great drag queen of punk-rock soul, Boy George.[3]

Dusty's fascination with American soul music and identification with black female singers provided the foundation not only for her vocal disguise but also for the visual masquerade that eventually made her a role model for British drag queens. Publicity photos taken of the Springfields before her metamorphosis, show a redhaired Dusty in high-collared, full-skirted gingham dresses embellished with starchy cravats and voluminous petticoats, a countrified version of the quintessential nice (i.e., repressed, artificial, and asexual) white lady of the cold-war era. While visiting the States with the Springfields in 1962, Dusty discovered the various black girl groups then popular and eventually adopted not only their vocal styles but also their fashions. The high beehive hairstyles, heavy mascara, and false eyelashes favored by the Ronettes, the Crystals, and the Marvelettes soon became Dusty's own trademark and a sign of her complete break, in late 1963, with the Springfields and what she later called "that happy, breezy music" with which she "[wasn't] at all comfortable" (O'Brien 28).[4]

Nearly three decades after its release, her first British solo album, *A Girl Called Dusty*, provides a veritable catalog of subversive lesbian camp.[5] The cover photograph shows the "new" Dusty smiling boldly into the camera and outfitted casually in denim jeans and a man's blue chambray work shirt. Yet if Dusty appeared thoroughly butch from the shoulders down, she is virtually a parodic femme from the neck up, displaying exaggeratedly backbrushed and suggestively mussed-up peroxided hair, heavy black kohl mascara, false eyelashes, and bright frosted-pink lipstick. This vampy overkill completely shatters any naturalistic illusion of femininity and creates a highly ironic lesbian resignification of the gay man in drag. In like manner, her musical repertory undergoes an equally dramatic evolution. The disc consists primarily of her interpretations of hits by American black women vocalists, including the Supremes, Dionne Warwick, and, particularly, the Shirelles.[6] Conversely, the hyperbolically melodramatic "My Colouring Book" portends her future drama queen "arias," while her impassioned cover version of Lesley Gore's "You Don't Own Me" provides yet another recording of this prefeminist anthem which has been a lesbian favorite over the decades.[7] The most impressive and complex lesbian resignification of soul music in this collection, however, is her cover of Inez and Charlie Foxx's "Mockingbird." The original, sung by the brother-and-sister duo, is a playful call-and-response based on a traditional nursery rhyme, and it parodically laments the difficulties and disappointments of heterosexual romance. In her version, though, Dusty herself becomes a "mocking bird" who takes the parody a degree further. She demonstrates, lest anyone assume otherwise, that she, unlike Inez Foxx, can do without her brother, and, through recording overdubs and a startling display of a female baritone voice, she sings the male part to her own female lead.

Although her record company was no doubt pleased with the commercial success of the new Dusty Springfield, a certain nervousness about the playful incongruity of her style and deviance from the model of the conventional British female vocalist creeps into the liner notes of her record albums, in both their British and their American configurations. Lucy O'Brien observes that the "tradition[al] British female singer with the reassuring 'girl-next-door'

Dusty as androgyne: femme from the neck up, butch from the shoulders down. Photo: Michael Ochs Archives.

image . . . was the kind of girl who'd listen to your problems and make you a cup of tea" (45). Dusty's best-known contemporaries (e.g., Cilla Black, Sandie Shaw, and Petula Clark) "went for the bright, clean, fun-loving look" (44), and "were commonly viewed as dolly birds who simply sang what was put in front of them" (47). Moreover, the white female vocalist, whether British or American, was inevitably caught in a web of contraries. Singing the joys and sorrows of heterosexual love, she needed to present an image of sexual availability to her male audience while maintaining the decorous asexuality required of middle-class white women. Simultaneously, for her female audience (who, after all, formed a considerable portion of the record-buying public) she was called upon to replicate the friend in whom one could confide rather than the sexual rival who would steal one's boyfriend.

Conversely, the black woman and her music symbolized sexual freedom and power to middle-class white audiences—and thereby provided a means of subversively articulating unspeakable sexuality for a lesbian. This identification with fellow female outsiders also gave the lesbian a sense of connection nonexistent in her own very limited cultural context. Val Wilmer, a noted photographer of the 1960s British pop scene, a jazz and blues critic for the British music journal *Melody Maker,* and later an outspoken lesbian feminist writer, explains from her own perspective the appeal that African-American culture held for British lesbians in the 1960s: "However 'progressive' the individual might be, she . . . would have to be rooted. And it's that rooting, so vital to life's continuity, that is missing, being deliberately destroyed with little to replace it . . . in contemporary white British society and culture. Small wonder I've often felt more at home elsewhere."[8] Dusty's publicists, themselves facets of this "contemporary white British society and culture," had a vested interest in promoting her as part of their own "unrooted" cultural context. They were hard pressed, then, to reconcile a blues-singing and covertly lesbian white woman with conventional public expectations. Accordingly, blended into the banal and irrelevant information typical of 1960s publicity notices and fan magazine journalism, several basic "facts" are repeatedly emphasized on the covers of virtually every album Dusty Springfield released before her 1968 masterwork *Dusty in Memphis.* The public is reminded, for example, that Dusty was a member of the wholesome Springfields, is the product of a middle-class family and a Catholic education, and that her *real* name is Mary—which calls to mind not only the Blessed Virgin but also all that is safe and pure. At the same time, her publicists go to great lengths to extol her "eccentricity"—a term often employed in explaining away what might otherwise be identified as queerness. Dusty, we are told, is a lovable goon who keeps a pet monkey, slides down banisters, plays practical jokes, and vents her pent-up anxieties by smashing cheap dishes. In light of such odd yet thoroughly trivial peculiarities, her penchant for rhythm-and-blues—as well as the much-noticed absence of a "boyfriend"—could be dismissed as more of the same. This would, ideally, reassure the public that Dusty, despite her newly acquired blues vocal style and her radically artificial "feminine" appearance, was still a "nice" if adorably eccentric white girl—and therefore a harmless one.

The truth, nevertheless, will come out, even if only obliquely. Amidst the collected trivia that constitute the liner notes for *A Girl Called Dusty*, a rather startling bit of information appears. A smarmy narration of her schoolgirl days and her early attempts as an amateur performer ends with the revelation that her convent school jazz vocal combo "was brought to a sudden and unhappy end by the geography mistress who banned them from the school concert as she felt that their use of deep purple lighting during a hip version of 'St. Louis Blues' had an erotic effect."[9] Considering that her record company certainly had no desire to "out" Dusty in 1964, this narrative becomes a puerile and not terribly original indulgence in ridiculing the sexual repression of nuns, thus distancing Dusty from their "prudery" and giving her the illusion of sexual availability while paradoxically reemphasizing the propriety and sexual distance of the convent—and its product. The male writer of this piece either conveniently overlooks the intrinsically homoerotic ethos of the convent (upon whom, after all, would her performance have "an erotic effect"?) or appropriates it for a peculiarly heterosexual male variety of voyeuristic titilation.

Whatever the purpose, this "factoid" becomes a double-edged discourse that many lesbians readily recognize. Convent school homosociality and its subsequent ramifications in the lives of those who have experienced it have been a commonplace in Western culture and discourse since Diderot's *La Religuese*. That Dusty manifested such homosociality in her early solo performances is undeniable. Videotapes of her on the mid-sixties weekly British television program "Ready Steady Go" clearly demonstrate that she directs her performance to and interacts closely with the female portion of her audience—while admiring males keep a respectful distance. According to Charlotte Grieg, Dusty represented to her adoring schoolgirl audience "the height of decadence" and "suggested all sorts of unknown indulgences and pleasures," making her the subject—and, very likely, the object—of many adolescent female fantasies.[10]

In gathering her court, initially composed of teenaged girls but later predominantly young gay men, Dusty approximated the Queen Bee (or Queen B[ulldagger]) figure common in and peculiar to African-American lesbian fiction and culture. SDiane A. Bogus describes this prototype as "a female blues singer who bonds with other women," and who, through "her role as a musical artist, [becomes] a central figure in the community at large," moving and leading her audiences to a collective and even cathartic emotional response. Equally significant as the Queen Bee's sway over her followers is her unorthodox sexual behavior, "her bisexuality, her multiple relations, her liaisons, her lesbianism, and questionable heterosexuality—whatever we call her romantic involvements" (287).[11] Moreover, although generally not a particularly or conventionally feminine woman, she frequently dresses as a femme, or in some paradoxical admixture of butch and femme attire—as Dusty does on her early album covers. Yet if the qualities and conditions of the Queen Bee's reign are, as Bogus suggests, inextricable from those of African-American culture and community, the social, economic, and even psychological pressures informing the life of Mary O'Brien and the career of Dusty Springfield were, unquestionably, those of white middle-class British society. These pressures—and the inevitable limits on any artist attempting to create an art form rooted outside of her or his own culture—eventually redirected Dusty from the role of Queen Bee to that of another sort of pop culture monarch—the drag queen.

The release of *Ev'rything's Coming Up Dusty,* her second album, in September 1965, marked the first significant change in her career. To signal that Dusty Springfield had become a major and universal star, Philips, her recording company, presented *Ev'rything's Coming Up Dusty* as an extravaganza in every sense, from its lavish packaging, replete with a gatefold sleeve and photo-filled booklet insert, to its often excessively orchestrated musical arrangements. Over the eighteen months between her album releases, Dusty's public persona and position as an artist had gradually evolved from that of the youthful, insouciant, and safely rebellious "girl called Dusty" to that of a more serious performer who attracted a wider (i.e., an older and more affluent) audience. This modification in style, manifested in both her music and her sense of fashion, not only simultaneously promoted and contradicted her youth-movement image as the "Queen of the Mods" virtually omnipresent on British teen-oriented television programs throughout 1964 and 1965, but also represented a stunningly covert, albeit campy, expression of lesbian sensibility by means of inversion and antithesis.

After the success of the soulfully upbeat "I Only Want to Be with You" and its nearly identical follow-up "Stay Awhile," the conventional wisdom of the recording industry dictated that Dusty, like all female vocalists of the time, demonstrate another—and possibly safer—side of her artistry by releasing a series of so-called ballads, the typically slow and generally melodramatic fare commonly associated with heterosexual romantic love.[12] Moreover, in a period in which recording artists' royalties were relatively low and performers' publicity and travel expenses were deducted from their earnings, Dusty's handlers increasingly pushed her into both the cabaret and supper-club circuit and the family-oriented "light entertainment" television variety series. These were, at the time, the only truly lucrative venues in Great Britain for women performers who, unlike their group-based male counterparts, had the added expenses of wardrobe, cosmeticians, and hired musicians. Not surprisingly, their clientele required a more socially conforming style of performance and fashion than that presented by an eccentric, blues-singing white girl.

Accordingly, that she might be all things to all audiences, Dusty's subsequent single releases and the repertoire of her second album included a greater number of dramatic lost-love laments and more sanitized family fare, balanced with a proportionate offering of rhythm-and-blues material and songs that amazingly combined elements of both these seemingly opposite modes. *Ev'rything's Coming Up Dusty*, for example, juxtaposes cover versions of Aretha Franklin's "Won't Be Long," Baby Washington's "That's How Heartaches Are Made," and Mitty Collier's "I Had a Talk with My Man" with Anthony Newley's "Who Can I Turn To?" and an embarrassingly exotic rendition of "La Bamba," a souvenir, no doubt, of her Springfield days. Simultaneously, her ballad releases increasingly manifested bathetic emotionality and overblown musical arrangements, suggesting that if a lesbian were required to give voice to the heartbreak of heterosexuality, she would subvert the process by exaggerating it to the point of absurdity through high camp.

Her ironic approach to this excessive sentimentality can be readily discerned in a videotaped "Ready Steady Go" performance of "Losing You," a Tom Springfield composition that served as her British follow-up to "Stay Awhile." After participating with American singer Gene Pitney in a frenetic, high-speed, gender-bending mimed rendition of "Twenty-Four Hours from Tulsa," Dusty, assuming an attitude that can only be described as amused embarrassment, allows Pitney to escort her, gallantly if awkwardly, to center stage in a seeming satire of conventional heterosexual decorum. Responding to this travesty, she misses the first line of her lip-synched performance ("How many tears do you cry if love should break your heart in two?");[13] then, after glancing at an audience who regard both her and her song with great seriousness, she giggles through the song's equally heartrending second line ("How many tears will I cry now that I know I'm losing you?"). The rest of the song is delivered with camp grandiosity as Dusty displays elaborate mock melodrama, bemused divalike aloofness, and little connection between the lyrics sung—or, rather, mimed—and her stage actions. Consequently, she inverts the bitter, self-pitying irony of the song's concluding line, "I won't mind losing you," turning it into a comic statement of fact.

This deployment of camp parody eventually extended to her performing attire as well. During the early stages of her solo career, Dusty earned the appellation "Queen of the Mods" from admirers and detractors alike by setting fashion standards for her adolescent female fans. Often purchasing her clothing from the same relatively inexpensive retailers as her audience, not only did her fans dress as she did, but she as they did. Indeed, during one television performance she discovered a fan in the audience wearing a dress identical to hers—they had both purchased them "off the rack" from Marks and Spencer, a British department store comparable to J. C. Penney. As she was propelled into the world of cabaret and its older, more sophisticated audiences, however, she found it necessary to assume the evening-gown wardrobe characteristic of the chanteuse.

Within two years of her liberation from the restrictive pseudofemininity to which she was subject as the lady singer of the Springfields, she was, ironically, compelled to assume the role of an "unnatural woman" once again, only now in a more elaborate and glitzy mode. In doing so she took as her role models the most unnatural women of all, the drag queens. By 1966, Dusty Springfield impersonations had become standard fare for British drag queens—while Dusty, in turn, impersonated them: "Her own image was becoming more outrageous and difficult to control. She took tips from male drag queens, learning what kind of mascara lasted longest, and how to apply the heavy eye shadow. 'Basically, I'm a drag queen myself!' she said later" (O'Brien 83).

Dusty learned far more from drag queens than mere cosmetology. To succeed in her attempt to gain a wider audience while retaining her earlier following, and to blur the distinctions between reality and projected fantasy, she assumed the drag queens' epistemology of camp, a philosophy best articulated by Oscar Wilde: "We should treat all the trivial things of life very seriously, and all the serious things of life with sincere and studied triviality."[14] In this manner, the marginality of the lesbian became a joke the outsider herself controlled.

The masquerade allowed the closeted aspect of Dusty's persona not only an outlet but an identity as well, albeit that of a gay man. While the status of lesbians in pre-1970s Britain might seem privileged when compared with the legal persecution to which gay men were subjected, the very criminality of male homosexuality gave it definition and even an aura of outlaw glamour, unlike the relative invisibility and nonidentity of lesbians during the same period.[15] Moreover, the dichotomy between drag queens' public and private lives often paralleled the disjunctions in Dusty's own experience. Val Wilmer describes the double existence of her drag queen friends—among the few "safe" friends for lesbians in the British entertainment industry—during the mid-1960s: "On stage, these men could be sad or hilarious by turns, but they seemed to revel in the insults and coarse badinage. . . . Backstage, though, it was a different story. . . . [They] drank heavily, were nervous and self-deprecatory. One covered his nervousness with bluster but they really were stereotypical queens for whom life was probably a lonely existence" (161).

Clearly, the lonely, nervous, and self-deprecatory Mary O'Brien ever present in Dusty Springfield found kindred spirits in these outcasts from respectable society. At the same time, paradoxically, Dusty's adoption of drag allowed her a mode of purely lesbian expression in a context in which no lesbian aesthetic existed. At a time when mini-skirts and revealing bodices were the standard attire for fashionable women, particularly those constantly in the public eye, Dusty effectively deflected the heterosexual male gaze through her elaborate and concealing guise of gowns, wigs, false eyelashes, and cosmetics.

This masquerade could not completely reconcile Dusty to the alien atmospheres of the cabaret and family entertainment. She therefore sought a trump card that would allow her to exert control over her own career. Her means to this end was the recording of a relatively arcane Italian popular song refitted with English lyrics by the grand con-man of sixties pop, Simon Napier-Bell, and "Ready Steady Go" producer, Vicki Wickham.[16] "You Don't Have to Say You Love Me" was a phenomenal international success, topping sales charts throughout the English-speaking world and continental Europe. In creating this triumph, she quite consciously embellished her drag queen persona with yet another facet of gay male camp—sheer melodrama. "I chose 'You Don't Have to Say You Love Me' because it's commercial," she frankly admitted, adding "it's good old schmaltz" (O'Brien 83). Yet the success of this recording resulted not from her appeal to the lowest common denominator of public taste but rather from the artistic balance she maintained in its performance. What set it apart from pure tragedy-queen kitsch is that she, like any grand diva, treated this work of somewhat dubious artistic merit with the integrity and creative energy one would bestow upon an aria. For better or worse, "You Don't Have to Say You Love Me" firmly established Dusty Springfield as *La Prima Donna Assoluta* of Pop.

Throughout this period, Dusty continued to push her drag queen image to even greater extremes, donning ever more extravagant gowns and appearing in complex combinations of wigs, chignons, falls, and other hairpieces. However outrageous and attention-getting this masquerade may have been, it had, as do all divided lives, very definite limits. Although she had established a considerable and supportive gay male following with whom she enjoyed some sort of mutual sympathy and identification, Dusty nonetheless faced tremendous professional and personal frustration. While relishing this new and greater

Dusty as female drag queen: feeling like an unnatural woman. Photo: Michael Ochs Archives.

success, she continued to seek the woman-centered ethos and identification with fellow female outsiders available to her only through the music of American rhythm-and-blues "girl groups."

As she became increasingly unable to bridge the gap between disparate musical modalities, her artistic output became radically inconsistent both in kind and in quality, as evinced by her disappointing third album. The ironically if aptly titled *Where Am I Going?* is a chaotic jumble of divergent and conflicting musical and visual styles. Packaged to evoke a Carnaby Street Mod trendiness that was, by 1967, giving way to hippy sensibilities, the cover displays a thoroughly campy photo of Dusty, standing knock-kneed in a mini-dress and wearing a flower-bedecked straw hat. The title, issuing forth from her mouth in a cartoon-style balloon, is rendered in orange and magenta psychedelic lettering—despite the absence of anything in the repertoire even remotely resembling the then-nouveau acid rock. The pretentious sleeve notes, which pointedly demean the irrelevant "information" dispensed on her earlier album covers, merely reiterate it—only less coherently. The product inside the package is equally confused. While soul selections predominated on previous album releases, here they are not only bogged down by over-orchestration but also outnumbered by Broadway musical songs and syrupy, lugubrious ballads, including the Jacques Brel–Rod McKuen tearjerker, "If You Go Away," replete with an interpolated passage spoken in her best schoolgirl French. The album's release was met with critical indifference and poor sales, marking the first of many low points in Dusty Springfield's career.

Within months of this dismal commercial and artistic failure, Dusty launched the project that would secure her lasting critical acclaim and assure her place in rock posterity, even through her long period of relative obscurity. Early in 1968 she entered into a long-sought contract with Atlantic Records, a major American purveyor of rhythm-and-blues music since the 1940s. She traveled to Memphis to cut an album at American Studios, where Aretha Franklin habitually recorded. Not only was this done at Aretha's studio; it also was recorded with Aretha's musicians and with Aretha's backing vocalists, the Sweet Inspirations, and produced by Aretha's producer, Jerry Wexler. Although overdetermined a priori by the in absentia presence of the Queen of Soul, the sessions resulted in what is beyond question her finest recording, *Dusty in Memphis.* Lauded by American pop music critics, who had heretofore considered her a somewhat more interesting member of the same league as her compatriots Petula Clark and Cilla Black, the album brought her a new American following among white and black audiences alike and established her as a "credible" artist at a time when "authenticity" and sociopolitical relevance were becoming the criteria for both critical and popular success.

Paradoxically, her greatest musical triumph was also the beginning of her downfall. During the recording sessions she was self-conscious in a "foreign" environment, and her dealings with Wexler, who maintained authoritarian control in the studio, became increasingly strained. If Wexler did not create her reputation as a neurotic, demanding, and "difficult" woman, he has certainly perpetuated it through numerous public statements over the years. The sessions were also charged by rumors of her sexual "perversity." Pianist Bobby Woods, in an incredible admixture of absolute candor, "good old boy" gaucherie, and unreflecting homophobia, describes the atmosphere in the studio: "It was a kinda icky situation. I didn't want to get too close to it. At that time people didn't dare come out of the closet. In the country where I came from, if someone found out someone was homosexual you either got hung [sic] or ran out of town. It was that strong. I was a naive Southern Baptist boy. I'm not judging her, that's between her and the Almighty" (O'Brien 156).[17]

Dusty in Memphis also carved a complete dichotomy in her recording career and in her modes of masquerade and style. As Atlantic issued the album in the United States, Philips, which remained her British label, regarded her new grittier soul style with disapprobation and, perhaps, unspoken racism. British audiences, therefore, were treated to *Dusty . . . Definitely,* a collection of easy-listening ballads packaged with a photo of the artist smiling demurely and semi-reclining in a lavish canary-yellow sequined gown. In place of the soulful "Son of a Preacher Man," the initial hit single from her American album, Philips released "I Close My Eyes and Count to Ten," a piece of ersatz grand opera accompanied by Liberace-style piano and symphony orchestra. Divided between two recording companies in two countries, Dusty's masquerade was irrevocably bifurcated. She was a "blue-eyed soul singer" for her American audiences; in Britain she remained a female drag queen. Never again would she—or could she—negotiate both identities simultaneously.

Although under contractual obligation to record three albums for Atlantic, she did not return to Memphis for a projected second set of sessions with Wexler and his associates. Instead, she recorded the optimistically titled *A Brand New Me* under the auspices of Leon Huff and Kenneth Gamble, pioneers of the 1970s "Sounds of Philadelphia." A recording of considerable merit in its own right, *A Brand New Me* proved a moderate commercial success after its American release in 1970. In Britain, however, where it was released as *From Dusty . . . With Love,* the album fared poorly, plagued not only by Philips's underpromotion but also by the self-competition resulting from the almost simultaneous re-release of *A Girl Called Dusty.*[18]

Dusty had heretofore been a major British star with a modest American following; now, as her British popularity began to wane, she was at the peak of her success in America. But rather than utilizing her newfound American acclaim to its utmost potential, her ever-conservative management chose to construct the next phase of her career according to the model deployed in Great Britain several years before. Although Dusty's favor with American critics and audiences was based on her unique soul stylings, she was booked for engagements in Las Vegas, America's ultragrandiose version of the cabaret and supper-club circuit. Finding herself in a venue that historically has provided a congenial atmosphere for any number of performers who have presented variations of the drag queen figure (e.g., Liberace and, in his final stages, Elvis Presley), Dusty, conceivably weary of the masquerade she had virtually embodied, felt repulsed by the ethos of the gambling capital of the universe and returned to England in a rage of discontent.

Soon after this homecoming, Dusty startled the public by answering the unspeakable question that had dogged her since the beginning. In an interview printed in the London *Evening Standard,* she utterly demolished the image of asexuality her publicists—and perhaps she herself—had long and carefully cultivated: "A lot of people say I'm bent, and I've heard it so many times that I've almost learned to accept it. . . . I couldn't stand to be thought of as a big butch lady. But I know that I'm as perfectly capable of being swayed by a girl as by a boy. More and more people feel that way and I don't see why I shouldn't" (O'Brien 106).

Although rock stars could, as a rule, have publicly unorthodox sex lives with near impunity by 1970, virtually no highly visible popular performer had—or would—make a public admission of his or her still-taboo homosexuality.[19] Val Wilmer posits that "although there is just as much lesbian and gay activity among musicians as in any other sector of society," the music industry has in practice tended to be "a rather conservative world, particularly in its expectations of how women should behave" (168). When considered in this historical context, the sheer courage—if not the downright recklessness—informing Dusty Springfield's coming out is nothing short of amazing. At the same time, her own fear of being perceived as a "big butch lady," as well as her statement that "I could never get mixed up in a gay scene because it would . . . undermine my sense of being a woman" (O'Brien 107), are indicative of the internalized homophobia that many if not most lesbians suffered. In 1970 Women's Liberation and Gay Liberation were still in their infancies and had yet to make significant inroads into the social consciousness of the general public in Britain and America.

Whether intentionally or not, this gesture of candor allowed Dusty Springfield to unburden herself of both a masquerade and a career that had become untenable. Trends in popular music had shifted in the early 1970s; the primary emphasis was on the "socially conscious" singer-songwriter, while "simplicity" and "naturalness"—albeit essentially artificial—informed rock sensibilities. Having based her career on being much that she was not and nothing that she in fact was, Dusty found no place for herself in this new rock order and was left feeling that "I had run out of things to do . . . I could feel the rot setting in" (O'Brien 107). When the storm of controversy over her sexuality subsided, Dusty Springfield simply and quietly disappeared from the music scene.

Late in 1972, relocated in Los Angeles and freed from further contractual obligation to Atlantic Records, she returned to the recording studio, hoping to begin a new phase of her career. Instead she experienced a fifteen-year cycle of even more ineffectual management, abortive comeback attempts, and record company bankruptcies, along with recurring bouts of drug and alcohol abuse, hospitalizations, abusive relationships, and suicide attempts. Her tragedy queen persona of the 1960s had become a self-fulfilling prophecy in the 1970s.

While Dusty drifted in the demimonde of West Hollywood, seemingly forgotten by the public, she nonetheless maintained the loyalty of a large gay following. Her 1978 album *Living Without Your Love* was no more successful commercially—and certainly less successful artistically—than any of her other recordings between 1970 and 1987, yet it is noteworthy for "Closet Man," a surprisingly open song through which she publicly acknowledges her long-faithful gay supporters. Recorded at a time when Anita Bryant was leading her fundamentalist Christian cohorts in a crusade of legislative gay-bashing, the song declares that homosexuality (discreetly referred to as "it") is "older than religion, and quite honestly more fun"; and while Dusty and her chorus repeatedly assure her listener that "your secret's safe with me," she nonetheless encourages him to "come out into the light."[20] Despite suffering from the same musical blandness that afflicts the entire album, this song is remarkable for the singer's courage in recording it, a courage few other artists then demonstrated.

While her recordings throughout this long period of relative obscurity were, without exception, commercial failures, Dusty Springfield was not without her artistic successes in these years. The most notable of these is the 1982 album *White Heat*, which she coproduced. The first recording over which she exerted any significant artistic control and an attempt to present herself in a serious, noncampy manner, *White Heat* is a compelling work in the techno-pop genre then being pioneered by such gender-benders as the Eurythmics, Prince, and Culture Club. The sexually forthright songs that constitute its repertoire are a far cry from the pathos and melodrama of "You Don't Have to

Say You Love Me" and demonstrate, perhaps for the first time, Dusty Springfield's musical persona as subject rather than object. Although it demonstrated
considerable artistic merit, *White Heat* is the most obscure of her recordings.
Lost in a maze of record company financial failures, it remained unreleased in
England, unpromoted in the United States, and, consequently, unsold and
unknown virtually everywhere.

Despite the severity of the ensuing disappointment, Dusty made one more
comeback attempt in 1985, this time at the urging of gay British supporters.
When this, too, failed, with even more acrimony and embarrassment than her
many previous forays, she quietly retired from the music business, returning to
California to live and work on a ranch devoted to the preservation and rehabilitation of wild animals defanged, declawed, and subsequently abandoned
by owners who had attempted to domesticate them. Perhaps seeing a metaphor for herself in these maimed creatures, she used her past fame to gain
publicity for her newfound cause. It was, then, with considerable reluctance—
and allegedly a year of delays—that she accepted the offer of the Pet Shop Boys,
a newly popular and "pervy" British techno-pop duo, to record "What Have I
Done to Deserve This?" This collaborative single ultimately returned her to
fame and the top of the popular music charts.

All of which returns us to the two rhetorical questions posed at the beginning.
The answer to the second question, "What's a girl to do?"—especially when the
last thing she can do is be herself—should, by now, *be obvious.* Yet even while
Dusty Springfield was missing from the public eye, she remained a cult figure,
not only to her 1960s devotees, but to a new generation of gay and lesbian
fans as well. And this leads us back to the first question: "What becomes a
[semi-]legend most?"

From the 1970s to the present, an unofficial Dusty Springfield fan club, most
of whose members are gay men, has persisted in England.[21] Lucy O'Brien
suggests that these men find a reflection of themselves in Dusty, and respond
particularly to "her warmth, vulnerability, and a stage show that is . . . camp in
its melodrama" (127). For her smaller but equally loyal lesbian following,
identification with Dusty and her music, while just as personal, has had, as Val
Wilmer suggests, sociopolitical undertones as well: "I was sure of a welcome,
confirmation as well [from her music], years before any of us became aware
just how much such self-expression is necessary for spiritual survival. With
Dusty in Memphis on the [tape] deck I felt safe. She was something of a lesbian
icon, a singer we thought of as one of our own" (314).

That Dusty was indeed "something of a lesbian icon," may well account for
her popular resurrection. Although the heterosexual women who have tradi-

tionally served as the popular tragedy queen icons of gay male culture (e.g., Judy Garland, Edith Piaf, Marilyn Monroe) have often died prematurely and unnecessarily, the figure of the lesbian heroine is that of a survivor—and Dusty, perhaps in spite of herself, proved to be that after all. Having regained her fame through the success of "What Have I Done to Deserve This?" Dusty returned to England to enjoy her *new* status as a living legend for a *new* era of rock musicians and fans.

During the years of Dusty's absence important aspects of the social dynamics and gender politics of rock changed. Although the rock world remains a predominantly heterosexual and male field, openly lesbian performers such as k. d. lang and Phranc have made their mark. At the same time, a sufficient number of gay men—whether techno-pop wizards such as the Pet Shop Boys or Erasure, who transformed the seventies disco sound into a witty and intelligent synthesizer-based art form, latter-day tragedy queens such as Marc Almond and Morrissey, or dance bands turned gay militants such as Jimmy Sommerville's band, the Communards, or Frankie Goes to Hollywood—have exerted significant influence on the shape and direction of contemporary popular music.

Dusty, for her part, after returning to England, continued her famous ironic camp, making television commercials for the British orange juice industry, thus playing Anita Bryant with a decided twist. She has also resumed her recording career. Her 1990 album, *Reputation,* although not released in the United States, proved moderately successful in England and enormously popular on the Continent, particularly in Germany. Many of the songs on this album explore the problematic nature of secrecy and the dichotomy between public and private life, situations all too familiar in gay and lesbian life. "Reputation," for example, while not specifically autobiographical, addresses the absurd burdens imposed by the need to maintain a false public persona. "In Private" and "Nothing Has Been Proved" (the theme song of the film *Scandal*) both directly address the psychological and social perils of keeping sexuality secret, and, along with "Born This Way," contain suggestive and indirect allusions to homosexuality for the cognoscenti. There are remarkably few instances of gender specificity on the album, but those that do occur are in songs written by Neil Tennant and Chris Lowe of the Pet Shop Boys. In articulating their lyrics, Dusty, ever the lesbian *en travesti,* can be seen in the subject position of a gay man addressing a male lover and thus retains, even now, this aspect of her 1960s masquerade.

For Dusty Springfield, then, all has come full circle. In a 1988 interview, she assessed the signs of her newly regained fame: "I'm terribly proud. You know,

I've always been ripe material for the drag queens. In England, they love to do me. I went out of fashion for a while, because I wasn't very visible. But I know things must be going well, because they are starting to do me again!"[22]

Although a middle-aged lesbian diva in drag is something of an anachronism in a music scene that includes such bands as Gaye Bykers on Acid or God and the Lesbians from Hell, Dusty's contribution to popular culture is still obvious. Most of the queer boy bands of contemporary rock music, as well as such androgynous or sexually ambiguous women performers as Annie Lennox, Allison Moyet, Chrissie Hynde, and even Madonna, demonstrate, the musical, visual, or aesthetic influence of Dusty Springfield, one of the very first women in rock who dared to "strike a pose."

Notes

This paper was presented in a modified form at the Fifth Annual Lesbian and Gay Studies Conference at Rutgers University, 2 November 1991. I wish to thank Diana Fuss, Monica Dorenkamp, and Ed Cohen for giving me a public forum for this project, as well as Robert Arambel, Julie Isaacs, Jack Kolb, Colleen Jaurretche, Liz Wood, and Asif Zaman for providing vital information or assistance in my research. Most of all, I am indebted to Corinne Blackmer for her constant support and words of advice, and also for her endurance, if not patience, while I played Dusty Springfield records for hours on end.

1. The intersections of racial and sexual "passing" in texts by lesbian authors are discussed in Adrienne Rich, "The Eye of the Outsider," in *Blood, Bread, and Poetry: Selected Prose, 1979–1985* (New York: W. W. Norton, 1986); Lillian Faderman, *Surpassing the Love of Men* (New York: William Morrow, 1981), and *Odd Girls Out and Twilight Lovers* (New York: Columbia University Press, 1991); and Corinne E. Blackmer, "The Inexplicable Presence of the Thing Not Named" (Ph.D. diss., University of California, Los Angeles, 1992). Discussions of various historical aspects and applications of camp and masquerade as gender subversions may be found in Marjorie Garber, *Vested Interests: Cross Dressing and Cultural Anxiety* (New York: Routledge, 1992); Terry Castle, *Masquerade and Civilization: The Carnivalesque in Eighteenth-Century English Culture and Fiction* (Stanford: Stanford University Press, 1986), and "Marie Antoinette Obsession," in *Representations* 38 (Spring 1992): 1–38; Kristina Straub, *Sexual Suspects* (Princeton: Princeton University Press, 1992), and Julia Epstein and Kristina Straub, eds., *Body Guards: The Cultural Politics of Gender Ambiguity* (New York: Routledge, 1991).

2. Lucy O'Brien, *Dusty* (London: Sidgwick and Jackson, 1989), 63–64. Further references are to this edition and are noted within the text.

3. Boy George and his alter ego George O'Dowd manifest uncanny parallels with Dusty Springfield/Mary O'Brien. A gay British Catholic of Irish descent, he grew up trapped in a world in which his sexual orientation and his affinity with black, white, and Asian women could only be expressed through masquerade. Ultimately he created what was certainly the most elaborate and campy identity ruse in popular music, one that easily surpassed Dusty's own. His performance

persona, which might best be described as Elizabeth Taylor in the guise of a Rastafarian/Hasidic Jewish geisha girl *qua* soul diva, along with his widely publicized series of personal disasters and subsequent fall from public grace, firmly established him as the Dusty Springfield of the 1980s.

4. The numerous photographs of Dusty that appear in *Melody Maker*, the British music weekly, between 1962 and 1964, indicate that these most visible signs of Dusty's characteristic public persona developed during this period, rather than occurring as part of an overnight transformation in 1955, as Lucy O'Brien asserts in her information-filled if cautiously superficial biography.

5. *A Girl Called Dusty* (Philips BL7594, 1964) is substantially different in content from her first American album, which bears the cumbersome title *Stay Awhile—I Only Want to Be with You* (Philips PHM 200–133, 1964). In the fashion of the day, the American release included material previously released as singles while the British issue did not. As a result, the songs that make up *A Girl Called Dusty* are divided between her first American album and its follow-up, released a year later and simply entitled *Dusty* (Philips PHM 200–156, 1965), and are augmented with material released separately in the United Kingdom. The observations I make here regarding the British album are nevertheless applicable to these two American releases. The covers of *A Girl Called Dusty* and *Dusty* are identical, while the photograph gracing the cover of *Stay Awhile—I Only Want to Be with You* is obviously a product of the same session, as the singer appears in the same clothing in both photos.

6. A similar observation could be made of the Beatles' first album, recorded earlier in 1963. With John Lennon singing "Baby It's You" and Ringo Starr singing "Boys," one might speculate if, like Dusty, the Beatles also entertained a secret desire to be the Shirelles.

7. For a discussion of the significance of "You Don't Own Me" and insights into the lives and careers of two other singers who enjoy icon status with lesbian audiences, see "Lesley Gore on k. d. lang . . . and Vice Versa," in *Ms. Magazine*, July/August 1990, 30–33.

8. Val Wilmer, *Mama Said There'd Be Days Like This: My Life in the Jazz World* (London: Women's Press, 1989), 307. Further references are to this edition and appear within the text. It is noteworthy that Wilmer's 1964 photograph of Dusty Springfield performing on "Ready Steady Go" serves as the backdrop for the publicity shot of the Pet Shop Boys used in promoting "What Have I Done To Deserve This?"

9. John Frantz, liner notes to *A Girl Called Dusty*.

10. Charlotte Grieg, *Will You Still Love Me Tomorrow: Girl Groups from the 50s On* (London: Virago, 1989), 97. Correlatively, the hazards of purely heterosexual adolescent female fantasies about Dusty Springfield—or those that fail to see the camp irony inherent in her performances—are well illustrated in Kate Jennings's "Dusty Springfield Grows Up," in *Save Me, Joe Louis* (Harmondsworth: Penguin Books, 1988). I thank Liz Wood for bringing this text to my attention.

11. SDiane A. Bogus, "The 'Queen B' Figure in Black Literature," in *Lesbian Texts and Contexts: Radical Revisions,* ed. Karla Jay and Joanne Glasgow (New York: New York University Press, 1990), 278, 282, 287. As Bogus implies here, the Queen Bee's "homosexuality" is rarely defined precisely. An examination of Dusty's few and guarded statements about her own sexuality indicates that she has generally tended to define her involvements vaguely and virtually has never "named names."

12. I would suggest that this strategy on the part of record companies is inextricably linked with the repressed sexuality of the early 1960s. Dances—for which records, more often than not, provided musical accompaniment—were among the few safe and acceptable public expressions of sexual desire and activity. Hence the commercial demand for recordings suitable for slow dancing, regardless of artistic considerations, was doubtlessly high.

13. Tom Springfield and Clive Westlake, "Losing You" (Springfield Music, 1964).

14. Robert Ross in Dialogue with Wilde, 1895," in *Wilde: Comedies*, ed. William Tydeman (London: Macmillan, 1982), 41.

15. Although male homosexual activity was outlawed and punishable by imprisonment from the 1880s until the early 1970s, lesbianism has never been a criminal offense in Great Britain. For a discussion of the rationale governing this legislative disparity and the impact of this legal "non-existence" on British lesbians, see Sheila Jeffreys, *The Spinster and Her Enemies: Feminism and Sexuality, 1880–1930* (London, Henley: Pandora Press, 1985).

16. Wickham, who has been Dusty Springfield's manager since her 1987 comeback, also masterminded the 1970s transformation of the rather undistinguished girl group Patti LaBelle and the Bluebelles into the campy and flamboyant disco-drag queen combo Labelle. For an insightful analysis of the creation of Labelle, which is in many ways analogous to the evolution of Dusty Springfield's public persona, see Grieg, *Will You Still Love Me Tomorrow*, 175–79.

17. It is noteworthy that Woods, aside from this particular matter, actually admired her (see O'Brien 99).

18. From the release of *Dusty in Memphis* to the present, Phonogram (the international recording conglomerate that includes Philips) has countered virtually all of Dusty Springfield's comeback attempts and releases of new (and generally American) recordings with reissued old material, forcing her to compete with her earlier (i.e., more popular) image and musical output.

19. It is worth noting in this context that Elton John and David Bowie, who eventually made public statements of their bisexuality, were still only moderately successful performers in 1970. Both came out to the public in the mid-1970s, when, at the height of their respective careers and at a time when the disco craze provided greater visibility for gay men in the popular music industry, their established popularity deflected much of the resulting "fall-out" and allowed both to survive relatively unscathed.

20. D. Foster, E. Mercury, D. Gerrard, "Closet Man" (Cotaba Music/Midnight Wizard), on Dusty Springfield, *Living Without Your Love* (United Artist Records UA-LA936-H, 1978).

21. Dusty Springfield's legendary status among gay men, even those who were not yet born at the height of her fame, as well as her ability to bridge both gender and racial dichotomies, is illustrated in Philip Saville's 1988 film *Wonderland*. In it, a half-black gay British teenager on the run from the authorities informs a middle-aged gay opera singer—with great seriousness—that although he had never met a star, he had smelled one: his aunt had caught a perfumed handbag that Dusty Springfield tossed into the audience during one of her 1960s performances. Similarly, the gay bar performance of "I Only Want to Be with You" by a sexually ambiguous singer in Neil Jordan's 1992 film, *The Crying Game*, demonstrates the continuing influence of Dusty Springfield and her work in the British gay subculture.

22. Brant Mewborn, "Wishin' and Copin' with Dusty Springfield," *US Magazine*, 2 May 1988, 59.

"It's My Party and I'll Die If I Want To!":

GAY MEN, AIDS, AND THE CIRCULATION OF CAMP IN U.S. THEATER

DAVID ROMÁN

Over the telephone, Bob, a playwright, tries cheering up Robin, his ex-lover who has AIDS. Robin, however, is interested in neither nostalgia nor comfort. "If you have to do something," he explains, "write me a funny AIDS play."[1] So ends *Pouf Positive* (1987), Robert Patrick's short and powerful one-act that concludes his epic oeuvre *Untold Decades*. Patrick, of course, grants his character's request by offering *Pouf Positive* as that same "funny AIDS play." Robin's acerbic and witty monologue, of which the entire play is composed, self-consciously articulates a set piece of theater criticism, calling for a theater that extends beyond the tragic classical realist dramas that characterize the majority of plays about AIDS produced by gay men. Through Robin's request, Patrick also reminds audiences that the seemingly incongruous, indeed audacious, pairing of AIDS and humor need not run counter to a politics of representation set forth by AIDS and/or gay activists. In fact, 1987, the year Patrick wrote *Pouf Positive,* was also the year that Larry Kramer—author of the celebrated AIDS play *The Normal Heart*—shifted gears and inaugurated the spectacularly effective and often seriously funny AIDS theatrics, the direct action AIDS activist organization ACT UP (AIDS Coalition to Unleash Power).[2]

If 1987 marks a turning point in AIDS activism, it also marks a participatory and simultaneous transition in the history of the drama of AIDS. *Pouf Positive* stands as the first AIDS play based entirely on what we familiarly and awkwardly term *camp,* incorporating the survivalist strategies of the earlier, pre-Stonewall gay model of responding to oppression, violence, and discrimination with post-Stonewall outrage, irony, and wit. Whereas earlier staged productions representing AIDS and people with AIDS worked from the universalist impulse invested in soliciting both sympathy and understanding,[3] Patrick's aim, not unlike ACT UP's own, is to focus on the anger and to anger the focus against the limited discursive fields by which we live with, and struggle against, AIDS.

Although by 1991 ACT UP had expanded to include more than fifty chapters in the United States alone, American theaters have less successfully expanded their interrogation of how gay men and AIDS have been represented by such institutions as the media, biomedical science, and the state.[4] My interest here is both to examine how gay playwrights and performers position themselves against these representations, what I call the masterplots of dominant culture that construct mythologies about gay men and AIDS, and to provide a critical practice of reading in the light of AIDS these formations and representations of a gay subject. Specifically, I'm interested in the efficacy of the recent (re)circulations of camp on contemporary U.S. stages as a strategic intervention in the battles surrounding the representations of gay male identity and AIDS. Such an analysis necessitates questioning the implications of the white subject positions of those who are producing and are produced in the process of such an enterprise as "gay" theater, especially since these are the models that circulate within, and frequently inform, the ideology of not only the extended "gay community," but often and even more problematically, the larger mainstream audience. I will focus on three different contemporary productions: Terrence McNally's *The Lisbon Traviata*, Lypsinka's *I Could Go On Lip-Synching*, and the Sodomy Players' collaborative performance of *AIDS! The Musical!* Looking at the techniques and manifestations of these three very different productions may lead to useful speculation on the discourses by which gay men, at least in the theater, fashion selves in relation to AIDS and establish a language by which to address the vexed and multilayered relationships shared as a result of AIDS. Although only one of the plays actually concerns itself with AIDS, all three plays position a gay response to the epidemic, trigger various impulses in gay and mainstream spectators, and, when read collectively, suggest the role that camp has begun to play on American stages as well as in a popular culture fissured by the issue of AIDS.

I. Domestic Quarrels (or the Operas of Everyday Life): The Lisbon Traviata

"You can say all you want about Maria, no one's ever accused her of causing AIDS." — *The Lisbon Traviata*

In the initial New York production (1985) of Terrence McNally's *The Lisbon Traviata*, the play concludes with the troubled diva-identified protagonist Ste-

West Coast production of Terrence McNally's *The Lisbon Traviata*, directed by John Tillinger. Photo by Janet Van Ham.

phen stabbing his lover, Mike, who is breaking up with him. In the critical moment of Stephen's performance, he provides his own soundtrack; first Maria Callas's "Sempre Libre" from Verdi's *La Traviata* and then her "Humming Chorus" from Puccini's *Madame Butterfly*. It is in one of these operatic moments—re-enacting the role of women in opera, in which Catherine Clément argues "women sing their perpetual undoing"[5] that Stephen stages his own dénouement. McNally revised the ending for the second production (1989), in part he admits because critics were disturbed by the bloodiness of the finale, and in part because he simply "hadn't gotten it right."[6] In the second version, Stephen neither stabs Mike nor spins the Puccini aria. Instead, the lovers have "a terrible, tremendous moment between them. The only sound is Maria Callas singing *La Traviata*."[7] Yet, one year later, in what McNally views as the definitive version of the play, he restored the violent conclusion of the first production, albeit in a slightly modified form, focusing less on the Jacobean qualities of the finale and more on the nuances of Stephen and Mike's relationship and Stephen's friendship with his opera cohort, Mendy.

The instability of McNally's text, evident in its various editions, suggests the difficulties of staging gay relationships and friendships, but even more points to McNally's struggle with the available discursive means of staging gay relations, gay subjectivity, and death in the late 1980s. That is, *The Lisbon Traviata* enacts the same problematics of representation spurred by Patrick's *Pouf Positive* and ACT UP; the play attempts to reconstitute the means by which gay men, in particular, articulate both singular and collective identities at the same moment that dominant cultural institutions exercise a horrific refusal to recognize any such voices.

Although *The Lisbon Traviata* hardly mentions AIDS, McNally does not avoid the subject entirely. Rather, AIDS informs the reality of its protagonists as a shadow that threatens to intercede at any moment; it is the woeful component that underlines the play's tragic capabilities. Like Violeta's consumption in Verdi's *La Traviata*, AIDS in *The Lisbon Traviata* provides the means by which opera's grand dénouements can be realized. Both *Traviatas* are, after all, about love.

The tragedy embedded in *The Lisbon Traviata*, however, emerges from the comic first half of the play, which highlights the friendship between Stephen and Mendy, the uproarious camp who, while unloved, has found some sense of solace and companionship in the recordings of Maria Callas. In the argot of high camp, Stephen and Mendy spend the earlier part of the evening dishing various divas, recordings, concerts, and, occasionally, mutual acquaintances, passing the time listening to opera before Stephen's tenuous date with a young waiter sometime later that evening:

> STEPHEN: Are you still looking for that *Medea?*
> MENDY: Here's Dallas, the first La Scalas with Lenny, Covent Garden, the night she met Onassis, *O notte tremenda, notte d'orrore,* but where's the last La Scala?
> STEPHEN: Mendy, I don't want to hear *Medea.* Any of them. I hate *Medea.* I loathe *Medea.* I despise *Medea.*
> MENDY: Even with Maria?
> STEPHEN: Even with Ethel Merman. It's boring music.
> MENDY: Maria was never boring.
> STEPHEN: She was in *Medea.*
> MENDY: You're going to hell for that.
> STEPHEN: I already have. I'm just here on a pass. (18)

It is during these moments that the play's major themes unfold. While the two skirt around the issues that are really at stake in their lives, Stephen casually mentions how he has just acquired a rare and pirated recording of Callas's 1958 Lisbon performance of *La Traviata*, which the obsessive Mendy insists he must hear—immediately. And here is where the personal drama begins to disclose its presence—the coveted recording is at Stephen's apartment, where Stephen's soon-to-be ex-lover is entertaining a date, someone who cares very little for opera, although ironically he may have actually heard Callas's performance as a boy growing up in Lisbon.

The first act centers on this dual tension underlying the play's major theme of loneliness and the need for intimacy: Will Mendy ever hear the Callas recording? How will Stephen cope with his lover's new fuck buddy? Mendy, who admits that he is "too much for some people," wants to be loved, but lacking love, finds comfort in the grand passions of opera and his unwavering fidelity to La Divina. Stephen is less resigned than Mendy; he sees his relationship with his lover, which began with an intensity worthy of opera, as a kind of real-life equivalent to the grandly expressed couplings in the operatic canon.

While the play's title would indicate that McNally's master plot is the Verdi opera, it becomes clear as the work develops that McNally positions his play in relation to all opera. And although it would seem that the elevated place that opera holds in the arts (for many, opera is the apex of refined cultural tastes) is what defines these urban gay men, it is essentially opera that undoes them. Opera, and the diva-identification of its enthusiasts, pushes the comic matrix of the first act toward the tragic conclusion of the final act. For this is precisely the ideology of all opera, as Clément eloquently argues in her important feminist critique of the art form: "But beyond the romantic ideology, lines are being woven, tying up the characters and leading them to death for transgression—for transgressions of familial rules, political rules, the things at stake in sexual and authoritative power. That is what it is all about" (10).

For Clément, the only lament available for women is death: "that is opera's innermost finality" (22). Clément's insights into the sex and gender systems encoded in opera point to what many feminists theorists from Gayle Rubin to Luce Iragaray and Eve Kosofsky Sedgwick have called the traffic in women between men.[8] Patriarchal masterplots involve women as the symbol that is passed between men in the homosocial negotiations that provide the constraints by which patriarchies exert their hold over women. Yet women are not the only ones undone by opera; a quick perusal of opera plots and themes demonstrates how any deviation from the reigning ideologies are aestheticized, contained, or indeed destroyed. Feminist analysis may clarify the equally problematic phenomenon, evident in The Lisbon Traviata, whereby gay men assume a tragic identification with and thereby appropriate the place of women in the patriarchal economy shared by opera and Western culture in general.

Gay men, as McNally's play reminds us, have a peculiar relation to patriarchy. Although gay men are neither true upholders of ideological constructs of masculinity and power, nor true reflections of women's position as construed by dominant culture, male same-sex orientations undergo a process by which dominant cultural practices can define, and hence confine, them.[9] In this process, same-sex unions are most often categorized under the familiar rubric of the perverse and/or monstrous. Facing the no-win situation of identification within a binary sex/gender system of difference, McNally's characters find recourse in the abstracted although highly gendered subjectivity of the tragic heroine. While Mendy and Stephen attempt to negotiate an identity that is based on, but not limited to, sexuality—that is a sexuality that is not itself essentialized—they aspire to an identity that finds cultural recognition in the highly aestheticized stylizations of difference in the world of opera. On one level, this process seems to connect with the dynamics of all bourgeois drama and to precipitate the result that Bertolt Brecht finds most loathsome of classic realist theater—namely, cathartic release. Or, to put it in another way, in the world of opera Mendy and Stephen find a means to counter what Adrienne Rich calls compulsory heterosexuality, the oppressive mechanism of a dominant Western conception of normative behavior and sexuality.[10] Yet Stephen seems unaware that these same operatic ideals are defined by the ideology of compulsory heterosexuality. Notice how Mendy comments on Stephen's process of identification, as Stephen describes his first meeting with his lover:

STEPHEN: The moment I saw him, even before he'd seen me, before we were introduced, I knew he was going to be the one. He was my destiny and I was his. I saw my future flash before me and it was all him. It was like the first act of *Carmen.* Don José sees her, she throws him the acacia flower, and his fate is sealed.

MENDY: Carmen isn't gay.

STEPHEN: She is when a certain mezzo's singing her.

MENDY: What did Mike throw you?

STEPHEN: Wouldn't you like to know?

MENDY: I love your choice of role models, Carmen and Don José. They were a fun couple.

STEPHEN: We're turning into . . . who? I can't think of anyone who ends happily in opera.

MENDY: Hansel and Gretel. (20)

Mendy's continual undercutting of the master plot that Stephen uses to situate his own relationship indicates that he, at least, recognizes the pitfalls of compulsory heterosexual identification. However, Mendy himself finds no effective means to resist the pervasive ideological discourse of perversity that accompanies nonheterosexual identification. Given the context of AIDS that permeates this play, such perversity, moreover, is associated with death. Both

Mendy and Stephen are unable to fashion selves that allow them a means to express, let alone pursue, their desires. If Stephen finds voice in the heroines of opera, Mendy's modus operandi is drawn from the divas who sing them.

In sum, Stephen and Mendy find refuge in opera, either in the heroines of the plot or in the tragic lives of the women who sing them. But this place of refuge is itself oddly diseased, contaminated by the associative miasma of identification. Opera undoes the women characters caught in the negotiations between men, it undoes the women who sing them, and it undoes the gay men who identify with either. Identification can only lead to alienation, marginalization. There is no entrance into this system where the lament is not death.

The language by which Mendy and Stephen give voice to their desire, moreover, is formulated around the camp argot of a historically specific subset of the urban gay male experience—a survivalist strategy deployed against a society that, as social historian Allan Bérubé explains, "questioned [gay men's] status as men, stereotyped them as effeminate, and harassed them for their sexuality."[11] Mendy and Stephen spend hours volleying in their own campy stichomythia, one punctuated with the learned details of opera, establishing a zone where they seemingly control the social and discursive spaces that determine their relationship. Yet the discourse of camp, rather than providing Mendy and Stephen a pivotal language with which to articulate their anxieties about intimacy, relationships, and AIDS, ends up eradicating any possibility of emotional depth in their dialogue.

By the end of the drama, Stephen has murdered his lover and Mendy is locked in his apartment. Mendy, at least, now owns the coveted Lisbon *Traviata* recording. But what is Mendy's future? "All great beauties are finally alone. Look at Maria, that apartment in Paris became her tomb," Stephen explains to Mendy early on, telling us more about Mendy's own future than of hers (21). In *The Lisbon Traviata*, McNally stages characters locked in the gridlock of master plots and their resulting archetypal pathologies. McNally, in his own struggle to write a play that demonstrates what might be called the operas of everyday life, fails to let his characters, gay men in the midst of an epidemic, recognize that opera is opera and everyday life something much more negotiable than either Mendy or Stephen can fathom. Instead of searching for the enabling subversion of identity, sex, and gender categorizations, what Judith Butler calls "gender trouble,"[12] McNally seems to see no place for subversion within the possibilities of gay identity. The fact that in this finale, Stephen's lover—a doctor and the only character in the play with any AIDS awareness—lies dying suggests that gay male identities are further threatened within the world of the play. In *The Lisbon Traviata*, McNally posits contemporary gay identity in the mode of tragic spectacularizations of love, loss, and death.

II. *"Read My Lips: Lypsinka and the Politics of Nostalgia"*

"What I call nostalgia, a lot of people call
'post-modernism.'"—John Epperson

John Epperson's brilliant claim (in the epigraph above)[13] to the terrain of current theoretical interrogations of popular culture immediately positions his camp-infested one-person tour de force, *I Could Go On Lip-Synching,* as a resounding site of origination. Epperson's drag persona, Lypsinka, is strategically situated within the matrix of camp and nostalgia on the one hand, and the politics of discursive narrative productions of the self on the other. His show is a self-described "parody of a cheesy Las Vegas lounge act" (19). Epperson continues:

> When people find out that I'm a "female impersonator"—a term I don't particularly like—they ask "Who do I do," and I tell them I don't do anyone. I made up my own character. I made an elaborate soundtrack of all these different voices and Lypsinka is all those people rolled into one. She's also a living cartoon, very animated, very high energy. It's a very stylized form of theatre and because it's so artificial and ritualistic, it approaches performance art. But I just see it as plain entertainment with a unique twist. Everything is lip-synched, even the dialogue. I don't utter a word.[14]

Epperson, whose career as Lypsinka began in the downtown clubs of Manhattan, has since met with wide critical acclaim. *I Could Go On Lip-Synching* has been reviewed favorably in the mainstream press and continues to have financial success throughout the country. Currently, Madonna is a financial backer.

The curious phenomenon surrounding Lypsinka's achievement, however, has less to do with Epperson's obvious talent and more with the commodification of camp that his work implies, its recirculation in both gay and mainstream venues, and Epperson's insistence on its apolitical appeal. Just as in *The Lisbon Traviata,* in *I Could Go On Lip-Synching* camp is staged in all its excess. Furthermore, Lypsinka's *I Could Go On Lip-Synching* reminds its spectators, and in particular, its gay audiences, of camp's availability in fashioning an identity in relation to, and perhaps even in spite of, societal mechanisms that normalize compulsory heterosexuality.

Despite this deconstructive edge, the ruling impulse behind *I Could Go On Lip-Synching* is anchored in the politics of nostalgia. On the one hand, Epperson demands from his audience a type of cultural literacy that is similar to that which McNally presumes in *The Lisbon Traviata.* Both Epperson and McNally present diva identification as a familiar, if not the defining, trope for gay men of a certain class and education. Thus, recognizing opera heroines, sopranos, lounge acts, and Hollywood icons is the litmus test for the ideal spectator.

Many gay men do share the vocabulary of Mendy, Stephen, and Lypsinka;[15] but many others do not, and that suggests the class and racial barriers these productions generate. On the other hand, the very nature of Epperson's production—Lypsinka never speaks—necessitates that the spectator identify with these voices from the past. If the combination of camp discourse and opera trivia enabled the audience of The Lisbon Traviata to speculate on the efficacy of camp's discourse in relation to AIDS, the glamour-based iconography of I Could Go On Lip-Synching is staged as the only operable mode available for gay men to begin imagining a voice from which to sing. In other words, since Lypsinka never speaks, the audience is given no choice other than identifying with and then contextualizing the prerecorded voices that give shape to the performance. Revival, Lypsinka seems to be saying, equals survival. It is precisely this enforced nostalgia that permeates the entire production.

Specifically, the show itself serves as a brief but concentrated lesson in the endless litany of tragic torch singers, spunky Hollywood actresses, glitzy showbiz girls, and syndicated TV heroines of the Eisenhower era, who have served, for many years, as fetishized icons for some gay men. Epperson indulgently marches in an outrageous diva-ridden parade consisting of nearly thirty female voices from the archives of American popular culture: Natalie Wood to Phyllis Diller, Pearl Bailey to Cyd Charisse. He offers this mass blitzkrieg of hyped femininity so that the spectator can participate in the icon-shaping that the show encourages; that is, as Lypsinka, Epperson writes himself into the very same diva fascination by which he/she holds his audience unconsciously complicit. The structure of the narrative invites the audience to witness the star-making machinery at work, tracing the trials and tribulations of Lypsinka as she embarks on her road to stardom. Epperson's artistry is a craft of self-consciousness; this mimicry of divas is interrupted only by the implicit desire that Lypsinka be recognized as a famous, legendary "voice" despite the audience's obvious awareness of Epperson's lip-synching. Indeed, as Lypsinka, Epperson exaggerates his lips with wicked, bewildered expressions mocking the formal constraints of lip-synching and further calling attention to the conventional rules of the genre.[16] Still, by the end of the performance, after having simulated various icons from the past, Lypsinka joins the ever-growing conga line of pop celebrity. The show concludes with Lypsinka's own arrival at the mythic landscape of stardom, or as the evening's program claims: "the well-worn comeback trail takes her from the burlesque to Vegas to Paris to, at last, a glorious career in Hollywood as the Lypsinka we know and love today."[17]

Although much could be said about the obvious gender blurring typical of female impersonation and its own complicated relation to camp, I would like to focus on the relationship between camp and nostalgia, especially since

Epperson himself sees them as central components of his show. *I Could Go On Lip-Synching* embarks on a retreat into history, one that may be best described as a hermetically sealed moment that precedes AIDS, and one that is additionally reinforced by the formal design of Lypsinka's performance. Nostalgia is first solicited from the coded icons Lypsinka mimics, and further triggered by the awareness of the historical marking of camp and drag in gay and lesbian history. For many gays, especially those who are older, Epperson brings up a familiar and important style, which may have lost its initial potency and immediate urgency. While the gay bar along with drag entertainment has long been essential for gays (and lesbians) as a refuge from the culture of the closet, since Stonewall gay men have had many more options for meeting and communicating. Furthermore, the social spaces where drag and camp were first assigned have expanded so that camp culture has now permeated the mainstream. Thus, Lypsinka (re)occupies that place in gay culture, and (re)provides that once flourishing space for gay men.[18]

I Could Go On Lip-Synching serves as a fantasy for a certain gay spectatorship yearning for the "simplicity" of life before AIDS. Lypsinka's choice of emulated icons supports this longing—although, in the process, Lypsinka alienates generations, classes, and ethnicities of gay men and lesbians who do not recognize Tallulah Bankhead, let alone Dolores Gray.[19] In many ways, Lypsinka's coded and specialized iconography and vocabulary validate the subject position of mainly older white gay male spectators. Lypsinka's own discursive narrative production of the self, based on camp and drag, furthermore recalls an earlier generation's strategy of self-defense: "[Camp] could simultaneously distance [gay men] from the humiliation they endured as social outcasts while creating an alternative moral order and culture in which gay men were in control. . . . These styles reflected the self-consciousness of some gay men as sexual or gender outsiders and helped them define themselves as 'insiders' of their own secret world" (Bérubé 86–87).

Whereas the nostalgic recollection of these strategies of self-defense and survival may serve a useful function for some spectators, even for a younger or unfamiliar gay spectator astute enough to recognize the historical significance of camp and drag, these memories also point to the problematics of camp's commodification in contemporary culture for gays and lesbians. The social significance of camp and drag, available to gay men and lesbians, may not be apparent to a mainstream audience. Mainstream spectators, some with no sense of gay and lesbian history, may leave with impressions that see gay men *as* entertainments. The success of drag on Broadway in such commercial hits as *Torch Song Trilogy, La Cage Aux Folles,* and even *M. Butterfly* demonstrates the demand by mainstream audiences for this type of gay performance, to such an extent, as Mark Gevisser argues, that "gay culture is presented to mainstream heterosexual America as a drag show."[20] The survivalist quality that so marks camp and drag for the gay spectator is reconfigured and depoliticized in the commodification process.

Epperson seems well aware of this market, exploiting the popularity of camp and drag for all his spectators. Lypsinka's performance marks a self-conscious retreat, for performer and gay spectator alike, into a pre-AIDS moment, recalling an era when camp and drag were, arguably, sources of empowerment and survival, as well as entertainment. On the one hand, it is admirable how Lypsinka proposes that these same modes of self-representation—camp and drag—which have always been available to gay men and lesbians, may in fact now be useful for gay people surrounded by AIDS. The politics of nostalgia, therefore, may enable a familiar, and ostensibly successful, battle for gay men fighting AIDS. Yet, on the other hand, there's something emphatically apolitical about Lypsinka. Epperson himself claims, "some people opt to be [political]. I don't. I set out to entertain."[21] From this perspective, the politics of nostalgia only lengthens the distance between past and present, locating nostalgia in the liminal plane of the neither here nor there. The spectator is brought to that location and asked to participate vicariously in Lypsinka's narrative production of the self, one based entirely on camp and nostalgia. Yet vicarious participation suggests a type of implication. Lypsinka suggests that we, too, seek that same self-conscious retreat into a glorified past, one fueled more by fantasy than by any claim of truth. Ask any of these same older gay spectators about these romanticized days of gay life before AIDS, for instance, and they will tell you that these were not all days at the beach, or, even, nights at the movies.

I Could Go On Lip-Synching is entirely located in this hermetically sealed zone of a mythical, glorious past. After all, Epperson only mimics: Lypsinka gestures wildly and widely but always invoking the politics of nostalgia. And yet, Epperson claims he is not at all political, "The closest I get to a political comment in my show is with Shirley Bassey singing 'This Is My Life' and then cutting to Norma Zinger singing 'This Is My Country' and then abruptly cutting into Tallulah Bankhead asking, '*What* have you been doing? What *have* you been doing?' " (Hilbert 44). This final number is punctuated throughout by Lypsinka's silly gestures—she clutches, like a purse, a box of *Life* cereal, guaranteeing that laughs, not necessarily ideas, are left with the spectators. Still, the assertion of Lypsinka's life in these final moments secures our response to the begging question, what have *we* been doing? In fact, Lypsinka answers the question for us. We, of course, have been watching her. And by the finale—Lypsinka's arrival and success in Hollywood—the answer becomes

clear, especially as we watch her *in* Hollywood, that lip-synching is the promoted voice, indeed the only available voice (if we can even call it one), for gay
men's success at the moment. The stunning and eerie epiphany of this ending
resonates as the curtain drops and the house lights brighten; the audience once
more returns to the streets of reality where silence, as we are all too often aware
of, does equal death.

To his gay audience, Epperson presents lip-synching as the only available
discourse, and divas as our only models. To survive in the grueling presence
of AIDS, gay men have few choices here: nostalgic retreats into a formulated and artificial collective memory; croonings with the coded beltings of a
tortured, but fabulous past; or most uncannily, lip-synching Lypsinka's own
lip-synching. By the end of the performance, Epperson has brilliantly staged
his own celebrity and gay men have one new diva to emulate, mimic, and
adore—Lypsinka herself. Such a proposition, to lip-synch Lypsinka, while
clever, seems odd—although perhaps that is just the point. In *I Could Go On
Lip-Synching*, camp circulates as a perpetually available site of origination; a
location to which gay men can retreat temporarily and reclaim that mythic
truth of identity and agency that may never have really been there in the first
place.

While Epperson positions camp as the mechanism that instigates a certain
apolitical nostalgia, AIDS activists at this point intervene with a radical cultural critique of nostalgia and its assumed frivolity with its READ MY LIPS
graphic, which fuses camp and nostalgia in order to serve their own purpose.
Along with various other agents in the late eighties, ACT UP participates in the
lip-synching phenomenon characteristic of the period. From Lypsinka to presidential campaigns, network television game shows to same-sex kiss-ins, at the
close of the decade U.S. popular culture is immersed in an unprecedented
fetish for lips. In part, this preoccupation derives from the insidious AIDS
hysteria of contagion and the popular misconception of HIV transmission
through kissing. If AIDS is just one player in a crisis of authority affecting the
nation, nonetheless the role of AIDS cannot be underestimated. In the spring
of 1988, for example, ACT UP New York staged the spectacular *Nine Days of
Protest* at various locations in New York City, Newark, and Albany as part of
the national action called forth by the recently established national AIDS
network, ACT NOW (the AIDS Coalition to Network, Organize, and Win).
The action was part of a nation-wide demonstration calling attention to the
various local and national issues that contribute to AIDS and AIDSphobia.
Same-sex kiss-ins emerged as one of the most successful tactics highlighting
homophobic responses to AIDS.

On April 29, 1988, ACT UP New York staged a kiss-in with a fact sheet,

"Read My Lips" designed by Gran Fury, 1988. Used by permission of ACT UP, the AIDS Coalition to Unleash Power, 496A Hudson St., Suite G4, NYC 10014.

WHY WE KISS, to educate the public on homophobia and AIDS. Among its five reasons, was the declaration that "we kiss as an affirmation of our feelings, our desires, ourselves." Gran Fury, "a band of individuals united in anger and dedicated to exploiting the power of art to end the AIDS crisis,"[22] produced posters of same-sex couples kissing declaring "Read my lips," now available nationally as T-shirts sold to help finance ACT UP.[23] The graphic used for the men's poster and T-shirt is a World War II photograph of two uniformed sailors kissing, with "Read my lips" strategically centered to capture attention and anchor the message. Later in 1988, in a presidential election, George Bush would boast his campaign slogan, "Read My Lips: No New Taxes" joining Lypsinka, Gran Fury, and the countless ACT UP members and supporters in the unending crisis of authority, discourse, and representation that the whole phenomenon of lip-synching indicates. To emphasize this specific cultural anomaly and its location in the public imagination, one need only recall that around this same time a popular network television game show "Putting on the Hits!" actually awarded prizes to contestants who best lip-synched familiar chartbusters on the airwaves.

The "Read my lips" men's graphic powerfully and cleverly recontextualizes the image of the two kissing sailors for an AIDS activist agenda. Just as Epperson reaches back into the archives of popular culture and pulls out Lypsinka, Gran Fury resurfaces with, as Andrew Ross has put in his discussion of camp, "the rediscovery of history's waste" (151). And just as Lypsinka speaks through voices from the past, the image of the two kissing World War II sailors gives voice to the activism of their eighties cohorts. Yet differences abide. In Lypsinka, a peculiar variation on the activist slogan Silence=Death seems to have taken effect. I have argued that in *I Could Go On Lip-Synching,* Epperson employs the politics of nostalgia and finds himself perpetuating a discursive paralysis that finds no exit, except as fantasy or diversion, for performer or spectator, in the inescapable context of AIDS. That camp and nostalgia can combine with an AIDS activist politics, however, is evident in the "Read my lips" graphic.

T-shirts and posters, of course, like Lypsinka, don't really speak. But as images that circulate like money in and out of diverse fields, they carry messages that can be relayed and easily consumed. The message of the "Read my lips" graphic is so simple that it literally instructs us how to respond. If, for gay men, reading Lypsinka's lips results in an inevitable "who's that girl?" bewilderment and positions the chapped lips of near forgotten divas as our only voice, the Gran Fury graphic solidly and audaciously reminds us that those (re)circulating sailor lips are ours to claim as well. And just as gay men leave Lypsinka's show encouraged only to proliferate Lypsinka's own production, a sort of "We Could All Go On Lip-Synching," gay men sporting the "Read my lips" graphic proliferate the kiss; giving voice to our desires, lips open for all to hear.

Many would argue that Lypsinka's show is more firmly in the tradition of gay performance as entertainment. And, indeed, there is much to be said for the utility of entertaining the troops in the age of AIDS.[24] Gay men, as Bérubé has documented, have a long tradition of staging camp as a means to entertain those on the front lines of war. Furthermore, to be constantly reminded of AIDS and its horrors could have an equally demoralizing effect for those who are in the midst of mourning. In fact, there are some gay playwrights who feel obliged to avoid the subject of AIDS entirely, seeing their responsibility during the epidemic as one of offering seemingly apolitical productions that provide a refuge from the reality of AIDS. "Who needs to see someone die of AIDS on stage? Who needs to have their heart broken again?" wonders playwright and producer John Glines.[25] The 1991 off-Broadway revival of Robert Patrick's 1964 play, *The Haunted Host*—one of the earliest openly gay plays—suggests the proliferation of the trend of both camp and nostalgia. And yet for many others convinced that representations and their larger ideological effects are the central agenda for gay and lesbian politics, the retreat into, or perhaps from, history has serious ramifications. Activist groups ranging from ACT UP and Queer Nation to GLAAD (Gay and Lesbian Alliance Against Defamation) go to great lengths to raise these issues of representation, holding both gays and straights accountable for the perpetuation, deliberate or inadvertent, of negative stereotypes and limited representations of lesbian and gay experiences. Productions as diverse as *The Lisbon Traviata* and *I Could Go On Lip-Synching* only fuel the current battle over representation precisely because of their availability to gay and straight audiences alike. Whether either play engages in AIDS issues directly or not, because they circulate within mainstream venues across the country the characters they represent inevitably participate in the ideological constructions of gay men that have come about in the age of AIDS. Regardless of any prefatory disclaimer or insistence on the performances' apolitical tactics, these productions derive from a larger, more complex cultural position that cannot be separated from the current politics shaping our responses to AIDS.

III. (In)House Music: Act(ing) Up in AIDS! The Musical!

"You've had the disease, you've been to the demonstration,
now see the musical!"—Promotional slogan for *AIDS! The Musical!*

The peculiar logic of the announcement for the Sodomy Players' production of *AIDS! The Musical!* rests on the presumption that attending their pushy pairing of AIDS and entertainment *is* the next step for AIDS activists. Such a strategy proved successful for the world premier of the production at Highways Performance Space in Santa Monica, California, on August 2, 1991. That

Even during a plague, there's a time to sing

AIDS! The Musical! books and lyrics by Wendell Jones and David Stanley, music by Robert Berg, choreography by Antony Balcena, directed by Alan Pulner. Photo by Suzanne Tallon.

the opening night performance was a benefit fundraiser for ACT UP/Los Angeles helped validate the producer's claim that seeing the musical was complicit with AIDS activist politics, thus guaranteeing its eventual sold out status.[27] But *AIDS! The Musical!* goes much further than simply subtle, crafty marketing strategies, for it locates, in the vexed and troubled arena of representation, a site where the issues facing lesbians, gays, and/or AIDS activists can be voiced and heard. Many of the people affiliated with the production are active members of ACT UP/LA, suggesting that *AIDS! The Musical!* is one more instance of the AIDS activist credo, "By any means necessary." Camp, too, prevails. Unlike *I Could Go On Lip-Synching* or *The Lisbon Traviata*, where camp emerges as a possible intervention into the crisis of (gay male) representation in the age of AIDS only to be subsumed by the larger ideological effects of either compulsory heterosexuality or the politics of nostalgia, *AIDS! The Musical!* manages to maintain both camp's outrageousness and its efficacy as a survivalist discourse. *AIDS! The Musical!* demonstrates how the theater can accommodate both entertainment and activism or, more precisely, how camp can serve AIDS activist politics through the medium of the theater.

The musical, written by Wendell Jones and David Stanley with music by Robert Berg, is described in its press release as "an all singing, all dancing, all queer voyage into a world of AIDS activism, new age gatherings, sleazy sex clubs, radical fairies, lesbian love, and fags bashing back!" It charts the emotional, spiritual, and political development of Thomas, a person with AIDS who, at the musical's opening, loses his lover, Bob, to AIDS. But before he dies, Bob opens the production exclaiming in his last words: "I always wanted death to be like a big musical with angels and songs."[27] Moments later, to diffuse the emotional charge of the character's death, the actor playing Bob shouts to the audience in true Brechtian fashion, "Ladies and gentlemen, sisters and brothers, girlfriends all, the Sodomy Players are proud to present *AIDS! The Musical!*" reminding us that what we are about to witness is only a production, a representation of AIDS. With the by-now-standard AIDS death out of the way in the very first number, a complete reversal of the operatic movement toward death evident in *The Lisbon Traviata*, the focus shifts to highlight the person living with AIDS and his picaresque wanderings through contemporary gay culture. At various points, performers break out in song either to give voice to their personal desires or to comment on the actions staged, therefore successfully manipulating any predictable audience response to the production's music. In order to challenge the prevailing ideology of AIDS perpetuated by dominant culture, *AIDS! The Musical!* employs activist tactics in both the thematic and the narrative aspects of the play, in its Brecht-based theatrics, and most effectively, through its employment of camp.

The major plot motivation centers on Thomas's madcap, Alice-in-Wonderland-like romp through the diverse currents that together may constitute "gay culture." While he endures the six-month lag for regular care through the county medical system, Thomas discovers and explores political activism, spirituality, violence, and healing in a gay and lesbian community torn apart by a decade of deaths and government indifference. On his journey, Thomas finds himself singing, dancing, and pulled in different directions by apolitical AIDS buddies, dogmatic political activists, skirted spiritual gay men, closeted talk show hosts, burnt-out ERA leaders, and an East Texas transsexual named Lurleen Devoreaux. The music spans popular styles that range from country western and Morrissey-like ballads to new age chants and rap. Supporting actors perform various characters who exemplify distinct facets of gay identity and together give life to the concept of a "queer community." In order to implant the concept that identity is both dynamic and performative, characters themselves, like the actors who play them, highlight different aspects of their identity at different moments, making it difficult to locate a fixed and assigned role. Thus, for example, the hunk whom Thomas meets at the Flesh Pit underground sex club directs him to the radical fairy gathering at the beach on the following day. Thomas travels to and from these divergent fields of gay culture to emerge by the end of the musical with an identity that builds from the best of all these queer locations. While the principal voyage is undoubtedly Thomas's, the writers show other characters in the same process of political and spiritual awakening. Lisa, a white lesbian and former ERA spokesperson, embarks on a journey of her own after meeting Vanessa, an African-American lesbian AIDS activist who rekindles Lisa's political activism. As the production unfolds, activists end up becoming more spiritual while spiritualists, in turn, become more political. Various identity markers are announced, appropriated, and fashioned in an on-going give-and-take by the characters. This is unlike the circles of lip-synching endlessly entrapped in Lypsinka's performance. The fluidity of identity construction in *AIDS! The Musical!* enacts a postmodern re-creative politics, rather than an imitative politics of nostalgia.

To their credit, Jones and Stanley insist on the complexity and paradoxes of gay life in the nineties, avoiding any overly romanticized notions of contemporary gay culture. Instead, the episodes are staged as fully dramatic contradictions. For example, at the first ACT UP/LA meeting Thomas attends (rendered entirely in rap), members argue vehemently and with malice, to such an extent that one actor comments, "AIDS, the spectacle, it's not so wonderful." Yet after such heated exchanges as, "You don't trust me / You disgust me," or the defenselike posturing of "ACT UP members aren't hostile to newcomers, just to each other," the feuding activists pull through to demonstrate against inadequate health care funding. The cacophonous members of the ACT UP/LA meeting that closes the first act—including the voices of women and people of color—find a collective voice in the "Paint the City" scene that begins Act 2. In one of the musical's most powerful scenes sung by the company, Thomas participates in his first ACT UP action—a covert operation to commit vandalism by painting bloody handprints on city property—and sings of the importance of the action with fellow activists:

> Paint the city, gonna paint the city, paint the city
> till it's dripping red.
> Paint for all the walking wounded, paint for my friends
> who're dead.
> Paint, paint, paint, paint the city
> Paint, paint, paint, paint the city red
>
> Paint for Larry, gonna paint for George,
> Paint for Henry, gonna paint for you.
> Cover this city in pain and anger
> Paint the truth to get our message through!
> Paint, paint, paint, paint the city
> Paint, paint, paint, paint the city red.

While the characters sing, they hang signs that carry such slogans as "Full Funding for AIDS Programs," "Stop Right Wing Fascists," and "Women's Right to Choose." Placards with the sketched faces of Jesse Helms, Lou Sheldon, William Dannemeyer, and George Bush, inscribed with such accusations as "killer," "shame," and "bloody," are painted and posted throughout the performance space during this scene. The effectiveness of this metatheatrical scene lies primarily in the reenactment of the ACT UP theatrics combined with the Brechtian explanatory, simple song.

Throughout *AIDS! The Musical!* voices sing from specific subject positions as well as from a communal chorus that, rather than obliterating differences, calls attention to the common goals among diverse members. The songs also vary in tone. In the evening's most impressive solo moment, Carlos, a PWA (person with AIDS), responds in song to his buddy's obsessive care-taking habits of providing everything but what he actually wants:

> Momma, I need a gun for my birthday
> Momma, I'm sure a gun could blow this tension away.
> This world is filled with sorrow and pain,
> I find it harder each day to maintain.
> The strength I need to help me stay sane . . .
> I'll pick the folks who have to scream "OWW!"
> When I shoot them with my gun POW!
> Momma I need a gun for my birthday.

The deadpan humor of the PWA singing "Momma I Need a Gun" is as poignant as it is outrageous and angry. The actor who sings the song also happens to be the company's most gifted singer, yet the director deflates the serious emotional intensity of the song's formal composition by having him employ campy gestures of trigger-happy fantasies of usurpation and anni- hilation. Anyone who hates queers or is made nervous by people with AIDS is shot. The conventional solo, standard in musicals as a means to convey the emotional depth of character and as the device to bring the spectator into the character's psyche, is so manipulated in the production of *AIDS! The Musical!* that spectators have no firm grounding from which to enter the emotional identification process typical of classic realist theater. Instead, spectators are left ciphering through the contradictions of the performance, constantly chal- lenged to speculate on the *issues* raised rather than on the *emotions* generated from the plot.

The Brechtian legacy invoked by the production's manipulation of conven- tional theater practices and devices places *AIDS! The Musical!* in the tradition of a political interventionist theater that demands that its spectators question the normalizing effects of dominant ideological institutions. Brecht's famous "alienation effect" distances the spectator from the mystification process by which dominant ideology maintains its grip on oppressive social conditions. While Brecht's concept of "epic theatre" directly challenges the class conditions perpetuated and secured by dominant culture, his ideas have long served various oppressed groups throughout the world. Recently, cultural materialist feminists have demonstrated the efficacy of Brecht's strategies for a theater embroiled in the representational restructurings of gender relations and gen- dered identities. Jill Dolan explains the potential of Brecht's ideas for such a project:

> Estranging the spectator from the conditions of life outlined by the representa-
> tion denaturalizes the dominant ideology that benefits from such "natural"
> social relations. Ideology circulates through a text as a meaning effect which can
> be deciphered by a spectator freed from the dreamlike state of passive receptivity.
> If the representational apparatus is ideologically marked, its material aspects
> must be brought into full view and denaturalized for the spectator's inspection.
> The mystification of social relations is exposed and the spectator is presented
> with the possibility of change.[28]

Although Dolan here is appropriating Brecht's ideas for her own feminist- based interrogation of the cultural conditions and representations of women in dominant culture, her use of Brecht provides AIDS activists with a material- ist model to employ in any theatrical intervention against the dominant scripts about AIDS. Brecht's ideas and Dolan's interpretation set the foundation for an AIDS activist critique of representational practices and their ramifications especially in, but not limited to, the theater.[29]

Within this critical framework, the political efficacy of *AIDS! The Musical!* becomes apparent. *AIDS! The Musical!* recuperates the class-motivated politics of Brecht's epic theatre and appropriates his concepts for an AIDS activist agenda. The intentional manipulation of the formal, compositional motifs of musical comedy, the shifting yet dynamic interplay of actor and role, and the informative educational basis of the production are mixed with the deliberate invocation of campy, outrageous humor. All combine to articulate an activist position in the representational crisis around AIDS. For the spectator, *AIDS! The Musical!* offers a location from which the various issues surrounding AIDS can be discussed, debated, and argued. Before the start of the second act, for example, a woman actor takes the stage to announce the continuation of the play, but before doing so she anticipates some of the questions spectators may have of the specific constituency the musical seems to ignore: "You know a lot of people have been asking us, 'Why don't you have any straight people in your show?' The answer is really very simple, 'Because we don't have to.' The media in this country has ignored homosexuals for years. This show is about that community. . . . Thank you, and now, Act II of *AIDS! The Musical!*"

Such a bitchy disregard for the straight but nonetheless marginalized population of women, people of color, and other minorities can be seen from one perspective as an unnecessary affront to people as horribly stigmatized by AIDS as "homosexuals" have been. My sense here, however, is that the playwrights are focusing instead on how one particular community—the diverse gay community of Los Angeles—copes with the epidemic. And unlike the majority of AIDS representations in the popular media—from Kimberly Bergalis to the melodramatic mothers in the television special "Our Sons"—which focus on "innocent" heterosexual "victims" or the responses of heterosexual siblings, *AIDS! The Musical!* refuses to accommodate the comforts of a nongay spectatorship by softening its queer elements. Such a direct confrontation succeeds, moreover, in raising the issues that inform our understanding of AIDS. Straights and gays leave the theater forced to consider both the dominant representations of AIDS in the media and the implications of excluding other communities affected by AIDS in any representation that invokes AIDS.

The most effective technique of disturbing our understanding of AIDS is directly addressed to the gay community that the creators of the musical want to depict and address. Indeed, the musical deliberately plays on this potential exclusion of in-house "others." First, while the major plot concerns Thomas, a white gay man with AIDS finding his own voice and sense of identity in the midst of the epidemic, the writers are astute enough to include other gay men who also have AIDS, including men of color. Yet the real *coup de theatre* (and the major political trump card) in *AIDS! The Musical!* arrives at its conclusion when we learn that Lisa, the lesbian activist and friend to Thomas, also has AIDS. Moreover, her illness has been overlooked by all of her friends, associates, and suggestively, her audience. The revelation that Lisa has AIDS offers its gay audience the sting of complicity in its own perceptions of AIDS. That women are dying for AIDS treatment is certainly, and unconscionably, one of the most disturbing unheard cries of the epidemic.[30] Jones and Stanley effectively introduce Lisa's diagnosis in order to challenge the effects of their own production. Lisa's AIDS diagnosis unsettles the musical's narrative trajectory which has centered on Thomas. In a brilliant moment of disturbance, the conclusion implicates the performance and its audience for focusing on Thomas at Lisa's expense.

Despite the effectiveness of *AIDS! The Musical!* for its specific lesbian, gay, and/or AIDS activist constituency, and even in its capacity as an educative, albeit voyeuristic, device for a nongay audience, the production has some of the same problems of representation as *The Lisbon Traviata* and *I Could Go On Lip-Synching*. Mainly, the concern falls on the efficacy of camp and its translatability for mainstream spectators. In the case of *AIDS! The Musical!* camp functions for its specific, self-proclaimed audience of gays and lesbians as an invigorating, informative, and in-house representation. Camp, in this sense, is utilized as yet one more Brechtian alienation-effect by which the performance maintains its politicized edge. Yet, for mainstream viewers unfamiliar with the coded survivalist strategies of a lesbian and gay community, or even unaccustomed to a radical theater, camp upsets the emotional leverage most associated with AIDS representations in the popular culture. From this perspective, camp solicits a very different distancing effect that results in a form of dismissal.

Moreover, in the commodification process of theater within a mainstream economy of late capitalism, the radical, upfront politics of camp that resonates in *AIDS! The Musical!* risks becoming neutralized. For example, in the review published in the *Los Angeles Times*, the critic Robert Koehler began by awarding the production the "Bad Taste Title of 1991."[31] While it could be argued that Koehler was engaging in his own campy repartee, this seems unlikely given the cryptic review that followed. On the one hand, he applauds the esprit de corps of the company—"You also have to chuckle over an evening that exudes the spirit of a Mickey Rooney–Judy Garland musical where the rallying cry is 'Hey kids! Let's put on a show!'" He also imagines the audience might undergo "terrific therapy" especially for those of us with the disease, or those of us who know anyone with the disease (who's left?). Yet, on the other hand, he faults the show for not living up to the aesthetic standard that he classifies under the aegis of "a real musical." In this regard, the major complaints are set against the casting, the score, and the overall "intent" of the production, as the following excerpts variously indicate.

> While the game plan is to attack the disease, public apathy, and the political enemies of gays and lesbians with wit and song, it's undercut by truly peculiar casting: The good voices are demoted to small, supporting roles, and the weak, often inaudible (due to the over-cranked volume of the taped score) sometimes tone-deaf voices are awarded with the leads. . . .
>
> It's a work-in-progress, and then some. Jones, Stanley and Berg are tossing around lots of ingredients right now, but they haven't decided what it is they are actually cooking. . . .
>
> But now that they Jones, Stanley and Berg have pushed down the barrier that says you can't treat AIDS comically, they have to get down to the hard business of crafting a real musical.

However valid this critique of the cast's talent as singers may be, the critic misses the deliberate and camp aspect of such casting. He also misses the potency of the writers' obvious agenda—clear to the majority of its gay audiences—that a different type of theater as well as a new spectatoral relationship to the material elements of production are necessary to engage the audience critically on the issue of AIDS. Rather than letting the spectator revel and be drawn in by the virtuosity of voice (think of Mendy and Stephen listening to Maria Callas), the casting of nonsingers, or amateur voices, in prominent roles ensures a catharsis-free engagement with the issues addressed throughout the performance. Furthermore, much of the camp element is stressed in these (tone-deaf) moments. Humor, too, emerges from such deliberate shrills. Camp in *AIDS! The Musical!* informs both the narrative elements of the plot and its production.

Rather than seeing the Brechtian-based and interventionist performative strategies employed as a means to interrupt the mystification processes of AIDS by the mainstream media, this review, itself published in the mainstream media, only reifies the very power structure that systematically obscures any radical AIDS agenda. The radical politics of AIDS activists are reduced to the infantalized attention-getting antics of the neighborhood clique. Unlike *The Lisbon Traviata* or *I Could Go On Lip-Synching,* where the material elements of the productions—costumes, sets, lighting—deliver the effects of finished and marketable products, *AIDS! The Musical!* relies on its work-in-progress–like quality to deliver its message. Its grittiness—in "peculiar casting," minimal setting, rehearsal-like tone, for example—contributes to its major intention: to politicize representations of AIDS from a gay and lesbian activist point of view. The sheer energy generated from the community-based collective that brings *AIDS! The Musical!* to the stage informs its audiences of the necessary fusions between art and life, camp and politics, performance and activism. At the end of the musical, cast members returning for their curtain call begin singing "Silence equals death! Action equals life! We are alive!" inviting members from the audience to join them in song and dance and opening up the performance space in a reminder that the activist performative gestures of the cast are available to anyone interested in fashioning oppositional images and representations for a group of people in the midst of crisis. The (in) house music engendered by the performance proliferates the possibility of further interventions in the representational struggles around AIDS that we all face in the 1990s—gays, lesbians, queers, straights, people of color, white people, women, men, and all the possible intersections of these identity markers.

In each of the plays discussed—*The Lisbon Traviata, I Could Go On Lip-Synching,* and *AIDS! The Musical!*—the imaginative impulses of the gay men who have created them inform audiences, particularly gay audiences, of the possible discourses available to us when faced with the omnipresence of AIDS. Each of these moments in contemporary theater, however situated around the issues of AIDS, participates in the constitutive role of ideology through the production and dissemination of our responses to the epidemic, and, by extension, in the degrees by which our own responses give shape to the ideological formations around AIDS. This participatory exchange or, rather, play between the formation of an AIDS ideology and the ideological forces that give shape to our responses to AIDS finds direct address in the theater where performative constructions of (gay male) identity and articulations of a (gay male) subject position are offered to the (gay male) spectator in a complex fusion of identification, entertainment, self-determining agency, and/or a call to action. The various possible positions for gay men that these three productions invoke—whether they be the problematic, and tragic, identification with the gendered master plots of compulsory heterosexuality; the paralysis of the politics of nostalgia; or the invitation to sing and act (up)—announce camp's availability in articulating and disseminating a gay male response to AIDS, however divergent its employment.

Near the conclusion of Robert Patrick's *Pouf Positive,* Robin the protagonist, announces to his playwright friend: "It's my party and I'll die if I want to!" (129), reclaiming an agency for gay men and all people with AIDS during the epidemic, and recirculating camp as a means to intervene in the dominant discourses governing AIDS representations. The theater, as Robin believes and Patrick insists, holds the capacity to service a community—in this case, gay men who are fashioning selves and communities to best cope with AIDS and its insidious mystifications in dominant culture. Mendy and Stephen, Lypsinka, and the characters of *AIDS! The Musical!* are, after all, only markers in the contemporary institutional and discursive practices that we engage as we confront the epidemic. McNally, Epperson, and the Sodomy Players Collective, however, participate in the larger ideological constructions of gay male representation and thus can inform that ideology as it takes shape.

As spectators, we too are involved in the production and distribution of the discourses that constitute the social phenomenon we call AIDS. In the theater, especially, our engagement involves a certain complicity that we must either entertain or resist. Our task is to locate our participation so that we can question it, and then formulate, in our own voices, the available avenues of opposition to the positions we eschew or the available courses of support for those we embrace. Camp, as one alternative, already points to the complexity of the situation of constructing selves, as well as to some of the possible pleasures. Such a project—to intervene in the dominant representations governing AIDS—must involve a serious interrogation of the discourses, imagined or available, by which we fashion our identities to counter AIDS. The goal to fight back and stop AIDS is, moreover, securable to all of us who participate in the collective and localized enterprise we call theater. No doubt, for many of us, it's the role of a lifetime.

Notes

This essay was written in Los Angeles during the summer of 1991. Discussions with Joe Boone, Doug Sadownick, and Doug Swenson helped enormously in formulating my ideas. I'm grateful for their continual support and friendship. I would also like to thank the editors of *Theatre Journal,* Bill Worthen and Janelle Reinelt, who first published this article in 1992; David Bergman for his many insights and longstanding encouragement; and my friends and cohorts in ACT UP/LA, especially Mark Kostopoulos who died of AIDS complications on 20 June 1992.

1. Robert Patrick, *Pouf Positive* in *Untold Decades: Seven Comedies of Gay Romance* (New York: St. Martin's Press, 1988), 212.

2. For Kramer's manifesto on AIDS activism see *Reports from the Holocaust: The Making of an AIDS Activist* (New York: St. Martin's Press, 1989). On the theatrics of ACT UP see Doug Sadownick, "ACT UP Makes a Spectacle of AIDS," *High Performance* 13, no. 1 (1990): 26–31.

3. For a critical reading of classic realist plays and AIDS activism see David Román, "Performing All Our Lives: AIDS, Performance, Community," in *Critical Theory and Performance,* ed. Janelle Reinelt and Joseph Roach (Ann Arbor: University of Michigan Press, 1992). See also the excellent study of the limits of classic realism, analyzed with a cultural materialist methodology, in Catherine Belsey, *Critical Practice* (New York: Methuen, 1980), and Jill Dolan, *The Feminist Spectator as Critic* (Ann Arbor: University of Michigan Press, 1988).

4. For comprehensive discussions of these issues, see Simon Watney, *Policing Desire: AIDS, Pornography, and the Media,* 2d ed. (Minneapolis: University of Minnesota Press, 1989); Cindy Patton, *Inventing AIDS* (New York: Routledge, 1990); and *AIDS: Cultural Analysis/Cultural Activism,* ed. Douglas Crimp (Cambridge: MIT Press, 1988).

5. Catherine Clément, *Opera, or the Undoing of Women,* trans. Betsy Wing (Minneapolis: University of Minnesota Press, 1988), 5. Further references to this work will be within the text.

6. McNally quoted in the *San Francisco Examiner,* 21 October 1990.

7. Terrence McNally, *Three Plays* (New York: Plume Books, 1990), 87. Further references to this edition will be within the text. An earlier version of the play is available in *Out Front: Contemporary Gay and Lesbian Plays,* ed. Don Shewey (New York: Grove Press, 1988). Sam Abel has documented the mainstream critical response to these different versions of McNally's play in his unpublished essay, "The Power of Death: The Politics of Genre, Sexuality, and Opera in *The Lisbon Traviata.*"

8. Gayle Rubin, "The Traffic in Women: Notes on the 'Political Economy' of Sex," in *Toward an Anthropology of Women,* ed. Rayna Reiter (New York: Monthly Review, 1975), 157–210; Luce Irigaray *This Sex Which Is Not One,* trans. Catherine Porter (Ithaca: Cornell University Press, 1985), and Eve Kosofsky Sedgwick, *Between Men: English Literature and Male Homosocial Desire* (New York: Columbia University Press, 1985); but see also Karen Newman, "Directing Traffic: Subjects, Objects, and the Politics of Exchange," *differences* 2(1990): 41–54.

9. See, for example, Michel Foucault, *The History of Sexuality:* Volume 1, *An Introduction,* trans. Robert Hurley (New York, Random House, 1978). Also of interest is Ed Cohen's essay "Legislating the Norm: From Sodomy to Gross Indecency," in *Displacing Homophobia: Gay Male Perspectives in Literature and Culture,* ed. Ronald R. Butters, John M. Clum, and Michael Moon (Durham: Duke University Press, 1989), 169–206.

10. Adrienne Rich, "Compulsory Heterosexuality and Lesbian Existence," in *The Signs Reader: Women, Gender, and Scholarship,* ed. Elizabeth Abel and Emily K. Abel (Chicago: University of Chicago Press, 1983).

11. Allan Bérubé, *Coming Out under Fire: The History of Gay Men and Women in World War Two* (New York: Plume Books, 1990), 86. See also Esther Newton, *Mother Camp: Female Impersonators in America* (Chicago: University of Chicago Press, 1979); Sue-Ellen Case "Toward a Butch-Femme Aesthetic," in *Making a Spectacle: Feminist Essays on Contemporary Women's Theatre,* ed. Lynda Hart (Ann Arbor: University of Michigan Press, 1989); and the chapter entitled "Uses of Camp" in Andrew Ross, *No Respect: Intellectuals and Popular Culture* (New York: Routledge, 1989). Further citations to these editions will be given within the text.

12. Judith Butler, *Gender Trouble: Feminism and the Subversion of Identity* (New York: Routledge, 1990).

13. Ken Dickman, "Lypsinka: The Real Voice of a Show Biz Phenomenon," *San Francisco Sentinel,* 18 July 1991, 19.

14. Ibid.

15. See, for instance, Michael Bronski, *Culture Clash: The Making of a Gay Sensibility* (Boston: South End Press, 1984), which unravels some of the investments gay men hold for opera and diva-identification.

16. On the formal designs of female impersonation and lip-synching see Newton, *Mother Camp,* as well as Morris Meyer's fascinating, more recent essay, "I Dream of Jeannie: Transsexual Striptease as Scientific Display," *Drama Review* 35 (1991): 25–42.

17. *I Could Go on Lip-Synching* program note, Callboard Theatre in Los Angeles, Spring 1991

run. For me, the irony of actually seeing the show in Hollywood only adds, as Lypsinka would argue (that is, if she were talking), to "the legend of Lypsinka."

18. This is not to say, of course, that camp and drag have lost their initial appeal. I am suggesting that Lypsinka's camp and drag are more readily familiar as the camp and drag of a lost era. The new radical drag of gays and lesbians is a deliberate departure from the earlier "apolitical" entertainment of piano bars and burlesque reviews. This newer drag, a topic outside my scope, is much more about the politics of visibility of current gay movements, although it needs to be noted that a radical drag and camp agenda has been operative way before the birth of any Queer Nation. On this concept, see Mark Thompson, "Children of Paradise: A Brief History of Queens," in *Gay Spirit: Myth and Meaning,* ed. Mark Thompson (New York: St. Martin's Press, 1987), 49–68.

19. I cannot stress enough how this resonates in the present. Not one of my students in the gay and lesbian studies seminar I taught recently knew who Tallulah Bankhead was or why she is significant to certain gay men.

20. Mark Gevisser, "Gay Theater Today," *Theater* 21 (1990): 46–51.

21. Jeffrey Hilbert, "The Politics of Drag," *Advocate,* 23 April 1991: 42–47. Further citations to this article will be given in the text.

22. Quoted from Douglas Crimp with Adam Rolston, *AIDS Demo Graphics* (Seattle: Bay Press, 1990), 55, 17. Crimp and Rolston document ACT UP New York's participation in *Nine Days of Protest.* I use their text as the base for my synopsis.

23. There is also a women's graphic for the "Read my lips" campaign. One image is a photo of a lesbian couple in a 1920s Broadway play and shows the two women yearning with desire but not kissing. After objections from women activists who claimed this image only perpetuated the invisibility of lesbian sexuality, Gran Fury offered the very sexy image of two women of color kissing. See Crimp with Rolston, *AIDS Demo,* 53.

24. Many of these "apolitical" entertainers—including John Epperson—generously participate in various benefits for gay and lesbian and/or AIDS organizations.

25. Glines is quoted in Michael Sommers, "Beyond Off-Broadway: Just What Is the State of Gay Theatre?" *Genre* (bi-monthly publication of Genre Publishing) (Summer 1991): 31.

26. *AIDS! The Musical!* ran at Highways (130-seat capacity) on 1–4 and 8–11 August 1991. Performances were sold out during the run.

27. All quotes from *AIDS! The Musical!* are from the unpublished script (book/lyrics by Wendell Jones and David Stanley), copyright 1991. I'm grateful to David Stanley for offering me a copy of the script for the purpose of this essay.

28. Dolan, *The Feminist Spectator as Critic,* 107. But see also the important work of Elin Diamond, Janelle Reinelt, and Sue-Ellen Case among others. Their essays have been published in various journals since the mid-1980s; see Dolan for a bibliography. On Brecht's concept of epic theatre, see Bertolt Brecht, *Brecht on Theatre,* trans. John Willett (New York: Hill and Wang, 1964).

29. A materialist AIDS activist criticism, which I have attempted to practice throughout this essay, considers the material conditions and social relations that construct the discourses by which the dominant culture speaks about AIDS. The goal of a materialist AIDS activist criticism is to destabilize the assumptions that underlie the dominant mythologies of AIDS. Intervention in the cultural inscriptions of AIDS is a political tactic meant to disrupt the ideology that continues to perpetuate oppressive social and institutional arrangements that contribute to the AIDS crisis.

30. On this issue, see The ACT UP/NY Women & AIDS Book Group, *Women, AIDS, &*

Activism (Boston: South End Press, 1990). Currently, AIDS activists are advocating for the expansion of the Center of Disease Control's definition of AIDS to include the opportunistic infections specific to women, inclusion of women (and people of color) to clinical drug trials, and research specific to women's health and healthcare.

31. Robert Koehler, review of *AIDS! The Musical!* in the *Los Angeles Times,* 7 August 1991, F9. All subsequent quotes are from this review.

"Kinky Escapades, Bedroom Techniques, Unbridled Passion, and Secret Sex Codes"

MATIAS VIEGENER

The national flowering of "underground" gay punk fanzines offers us a new map through alternative gay identities, recolonizing areas such as punk, drag, hardcore, camp, and SM. A challenge against "assimilationist" gays, they are a product of a generation of gay people *born after* Stonewall who have never known gay life without the specter of AIDS. In a play of nasty photomontages and true confessions, these magazines problematize what in the mainstream gay community has come to be regarded as oppositional politics and representations—the kinds of gay identities that are most often made available in the community itself. The identity embroidered by magazines like *Advocate* and *Gay Sunshine* and by writers like Rita Mae Brown or David Leavitt suggests that homosexuality is both natural and reasonable, different but symmetrical with heterosexuality.[1] This constellation of new fanzines, however, informs a quite different sensibility: queerness is both natural and unnatural, good and bad, reasonable and irrational. Rejecting bourgeois gay culture, gay punk subcultures develop out of the hardcore rock community and often pirate straight culture for their material, calling into question the oppositional "identity" politics of what has come to be called gay liberation.[2] The regimes of heterosexuality and gender are capsized by the 'zines insistence on gender as a performance open to subversion through the fusion of two once antithetical aesthetics, punk and camp.

Blending star lore, anarchy, camp sex, punk rock, and gender dysphoria in homemade packages that range in tone from harsh to arch, gay 'zines alter and appropriate images (publicity photos of actors, models, and politicians), fictionalize (and usually sexualize) histories of the stars, and subvert all the codes of "pure" desire, breaking down the distance between spectator and performer, reader and text, or audience and star. Some of their antecedents are pulp novels, photo-novellas, and slasher novels, such as those written by the fans of "Star Trek," which involve sadomasochistic scenes between Captain Kirk and Dr. Spock.[3] However, unlike movie fan magazines such as *Photoplay* or music magazines such as *Cream,* these fanzines serve no publicity function. The fandom designated here is distinct from its Hollywood form, marked, as in science fiction, by the "possession of a particular knowledge of the fanzine's subject, unavailable to the uninitiated."[4] Access to this knowledge is gained by knowing its code, the jargon, the symbolic values, and the allusions to obscure references.

These "underground" magazines are usually self-published and badly distributed; they are cheap, a dollar or two, and must usually be ordered by mail, one issue at a time, arriving in plain brown envelopes, "to accommodate your potentially oppressive environment."[5] Like straight fanzines, they are how gay punks speak "for themselves to themselves," a defense against misrepresentation in the established media; the main forum, not only for the communication about gay punk, but for its construction as well, they are the "means by which punk writes itself."[6] *Sin Bros.* from Los Angeles and *J.D.s* from Toronto, for example, are Xeroxed, folded, and stapled; many are unpaginated, typewritten or handwritten instead of laser-printed. *Thing* is a slicker black men's 'zine with a decidedly camp twist. *My Comrade* is a gay men's magazine that flips upside down to *Sister,* a lesbian magazine; both ends display many of the same models dressed in drag or leather (or both—musclemen in bras, for example) and often playing out multipage spreads styled like photo-novellas.[7] The work in these fanzines is either blatantly pseudonymous (one assumes the editors generate the writing) or, most often, from readers, which means they are unusually participatory, breaking down the boundaries between audience and artist. *Homocore* in particular has a frenzied section of letter exchanges, a kind of reader-response network; the editors and readers of all these magazines are highly conscious of the whole subgenre and refer to each other with regularity. There are frequent first-person narratives: "Tails from the Pit," "My Life as a Celebutante," and "I had Gay Sex with Bigfoot." This is low-tech desktop publishing with a nasty twist, street aesthetics in combat against corporate ones.

The style of these fanzines is graphically reminiscent of underground or punk graphics of the mid-1970s, while the content often joins sixties camp irreverence to the rancor and pessimism of gay pulp novels from the fifties. As in straight fanzines, the two typographic models are graffiti, seen in "magic marker" script, and the ransom note, typefaces taped together to form an

Minneapolis, MN.

homopunk USA

the homosexual fraternity reveals its hidden world

I'd hate to consider the possibility that since their demise Husker Du has become the stuff of legends, or god forbid, myth, but I've gotten more different versions of the same supposed story than reliable accounts of Christ's life the Vatican Council of Trent had destroyed, leaving us with a mere four from which to choose.

I've talked to people who swear they've slept with Greg Norton and people who "know him personally" & swear he's hetero and always despised Grant Hart's "aberrations". I've heard that Grant and Paul Osby from Otto's Chemical Lounge were lovers, that Grant and Dave Pirner from Soul Asylum were lovers. The only concensus I've gathered - the assertions everyone seems to agree on - are: 1) Grant Hart and Urban Guerillas' Maestro Larry Zahagian (he of the Pink, Heat-Seeking Moisture Missile fame) are both queer as proverbial 3 dollar bills and cut wide swathes through the behinds of underage male fans from coast to coast in this country and beyond. 2) No one knows of anyone or at least anyone who will admit to having slept with Bob Mould (except maybe Grant Hart, whose taste has always been suspect, anyway - "as long as it's warm & wet"). It would seem Mr. Mould has been relegated to his own asexual ministrations. Maybe that's why he gravitated to all that '60s hippie bullshit - he feels a bond of sorts with flowers - he sort of reminds me of a barren rose bush, you know? - kind of amorphous until pruned, not too pretty to look at, and definitely not to touch (but excellent training for composing railing, whining songs of angst). 3) That the Replacements (known around these here parts as the 'placemats', whatever their respective preferences (anything at least 100 proof), have always been 'too drunk to fuck'.

I'm afraid I haven't been a lot of help for your intended expose. You may just have to go to the Mountain, Mohammed, and in Grant Hart's case, the metaphor isn't too far off considering his corpulence of late. But you'd better hurry before the landslide: the last I saw of Herr Hart, he was backstage at a show my band was playing at with Toxic Reasons at the end of March, drawing cryptic, Freudian cartoons on an easel-held tablet of poster-sized newsprint, chewing on his hair and chanting some unintelligible mantras. He didn't seem a well man. Still, I'm sure he's a fine, fine individual.

Later, then

TEG

Thanks, Teg! Oh, by the way, I hear there's a fag in Toxic Reasons, too. True?

Sorry to break this to you, dudes, but Gay is Rad

anonymous message; the ransom note suggests a connection to terrorism and crime as well as a "documentary" intervention; graffiti functions as a kind of signature attached to a fictive creation, ironically grounded in the "real." Fanzine images, primarily photographs, are almost always cannibalized from other publications and often altered by graphics or collage. Aesthetically, gay fanzines link up to punk subculture more than any other; yet they work through different alliances and allegiances: *Sin Bros.* leans to the mod or pop/camp aesthetic, whereas *J.D.s* devotes itself to a more skinhead punk; *Homocore* combines hardcore rock and punk with radical fairies, while *Pansy Beat* and *My Comrade/Sister* invokes a New York underground club or glam-rock aesthetic.

All these magazines fuse punk with drag and camp sensibility and share a revisionist articulation of the social construction of gender, race, and sexuality. Clad in uniforms of leather, torn jeans, safety pins, and nasty haircuts (uniforms elaborated in local dialects of skateboards, pink triangles, lingerie, and false breasts), these new gay magazines impose a sharp break between those inside the subculture and those outside it. The eclecticism itself is hard to fig-

ure: junkie narratives, drag queen exposés, Jacobean revenge fantasies, photos of punks with their pants down, high-school locker fetishism, photomontages, "kinky escapades, bedroom techniques, unbridled passion and secret sex
codes."[8]

These publications promote a kind of festive combat: they employ style to
decenter a totalizing cultural hegemony. Style in this formulation involves a
reterritorialization, a vocabulary stolen from the master, which functions to
rehearse and sarcastically resolve cultural contradictions. On the one hand,
style generates a mark of difference, a code visible only to the initiated. On the
other, it signals a certain refusal. A classic example would be Jean Genet's
adaptation of the tube of vaseline, which moves from being the dirty object
that proclaims Genet's homosexuality to the world to being a kind of fetish for
him. The fetish function of style in this underworld is to subvert the codes of
the master. It is, as Dick Hebdige says, a kind of guarantee: of absolute visibility
and absolute hatred, projecting the abstraction of homophobia into a concrete, if provisional, symbolic structure.[9]

Like members of all subcultures, gay punks are highly conscious of their
placement within the margins of a greater mass culture whose function is as
much to oppress and control its consumers as it is to satisfy their needs. The
fascination with celebrities and the media, and in this case (from *Sin Bros.* no.
3) the homophobia and racism of Guns 'n Roses lead singer Axl Rose, generates work that plays on both high ("poetic") and low culture:

> You finally achieved your MTV fame,
> but I remember when you'd squeal my name.
> I first saw your zit-filled face
> in quite a different place.
> Fake I.D., The Rage, 1983.
> "Would you like to come home with me?"
> Bad hairdo from '75, fine-boned and petite,
> you really did like my big black meat.
> Now you play to the fears of this Reaganite nation,
> when Blueboy and Mandate turn your thoughts to masturbation.
> Thirteen year old girls may believe your rock star poses,
> But you'll always prefer my gun to their roses.[10]

This text spars with "outing" on the level of wish fulfillment, a strategy of
stylistic "reading," not political accusation. It plays on both the singer's erotic
appeal (filtered through the subliminal wish of the gay audience that all celebrities have a potential sexual availability) and his infamous homophobia—
strategically taken, as often before in gay movements, as a sign of his repressed
homosexuality. Axl Rose's dress and manner, stylistically rooted in the hard-

SAYS NOTHING TO ME ABOUT MY LIFE

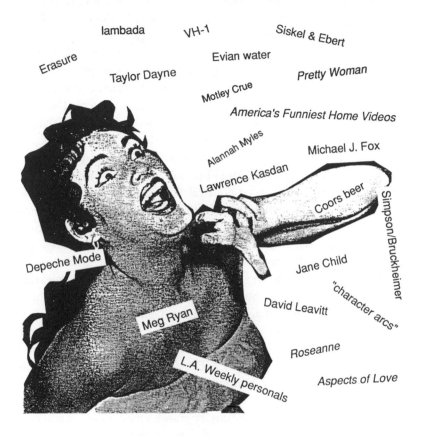

lambada   VH-1   Siskel & Ebert

Erasure   Evian water

Taylor Dayne   Pretty Woman

Motley Crue

America's Funniest Home Videos

Alannah Myles   Michael J. Fox

Lawrence Kasdan

Coors beer   Simpson/Bruckheimer

Depeche Mode

Jane Child

"character arcs"

David Leavitt

Meg Ryan

Roseanne

L.A. Weekly personals   Aspects of Love

core movement and expressing its most reactionary (homophobic and racist) tendencies, are identifiable derivatives of gay leather style. Rose's visual semiotics testify to the reappropriative power of all youth subcultures. Whereas queer punks are copying the juvenile-delinquent stylizations of straight punk, with its subliminal vampirelike homoeroticism, "straight" punks were originally attracted to gay leather and bondage accoutrements (especially piercing and tattooing), imitating "tactics pioneered by the sexual outlaws on the fringes of gay life."[11] References to these shifts in style and sexual identification ironically intensify the revenge enacted in the outing of the poem.

The Frankfurt School argued that all cultural forms in an era of bourgeois dominance are inauthentic, artifacts of false consciousness, the antithesis of genuine expressions of individuality and freedom. In his examination of popular music, Theodor Adorno claimed that its repetitious phrases and rhythms are essentially the same as the rhythms that administer the modern factory, so that pleasure in the former secures one's complicity in the latter.[12] The only way to resist such social control is by introducing the negative through forms of critical thought (and critical expressions of art) that oppose the ideologically dominant forms of popular thought and cultural experience. These negations must deny the essentially affirmative nature of culture and must critique the form and structure of bourgeois culture as well as its content. The Axl Rose poem is hardly a critical negation, though it is a stylistic one. Its closing, "But you'll always prefer my gun to their roses," signals a resistance and a kind of utopian return of the repressed, a guerrilla resurgence, and promises something more powerful (destructive and libidinal) than pop sentiment.

In gay fanzines, a spectrum of political activism from anarchist to libertarian is often clothed in costumes unfamiliar to a mainstream gay or straight audience. There are articles on ACT UP, on the Anarchists' Convention, on beauty pageant protests, and on Pro Choice rallies. The logic to these articles operates quite differently from what one sees in *Advocate;* it isn't just good, correct, and reasonable to be an activist for these causes: it is also pleasurable. It's cool. In a certain sense this merely rehearses what already exists within ACT UP, which has its singular manner of fusing fashion with function. These fanzines share ACT UP and Queer Nation's penchant for turning political issues into spectacles; for every direct or declarative challenge made against social hegemony, homophobia, and AIDS discrimination, another indirect one is lodged in terms of style. Homophobe Axl Rose is unmasked as a closet cocksucker, not just an ordinary one, but a tacky cocksucker with a bad haircut; conservative Senator Jesse Helms is transformed into a carnival stick figure, a lecherous Colonel Sanders. The contradictions in the political situation of gay people are formulated and "magically" resolved at the superficial level of style. The rigidity of compulsory heterosexuality, for example, is inverted through outraged accounts of the horrors of child-bearing heterosexuals in "Underground in the Land of the Breeders."

This attack on the "regime" of presumptive and compulsory heterosexuality also questions the much-policed gradations between acceptable manifestations of sexuality (heterosexual married couples) and the unacceptable ones (anal sex, prostitution, rape, incest).[13] One has merely to look at the gay movement's troubled relation to transvestism and pederasty to see these distinctions at work within an oppositional microcosm. One reaction to this appears in *Homocore* no. 4, an interview with the boyish cofounder of NAMBLA, the North American Boy Lover's Association, which reproaches the tendency of oppositional movements to ruthlessly divest themselves of their extremities, to sever the troubling parts of homosexuality or sexuality in general. And trouble, in the form of hustlers, transvestites, transsexuals, delinquents, or skinheads, is just what these publications court.

The codification of oppositional identities, a central enterprise in gay fanzines, takes place in the context of refusal and negation: "J.D.s like all girl gangs, had a code, for even among kids like these, there is a code. She denies her girlhood and flaunts her sex. . . . It's not easy to love a delinquent girl. She's vulgar, she's coarse. She despises the world."[14] From the outside, the encodement of these subcultures generates "noise" as opposed to sound, as Hebdige puts it, "an actual mechanism for semantic disorder: a kind of temporary blockage in the system of representation" (90). As a result the subcultures and their magazines are perceived by the gay mainstream as retrograde and unreadable: they're hard to love.[15] The texts themselves—stubborn, badly printed, often Xeroxes of Xeroxes and filled with aggressive, raw graphics—are opposed to the sense and sensibility of such mainstream gay publications as *Christopher Street* or *Advocate.* Clarity and universality are objects of contempt. The enemy is less heterosexuals than gay yuppies, or as the editor of *Bimbox* puts it, "crypto-fascist clones and dykes . . . telling us how to think."[16] They celebrate the useless fetish, the bad seed, the ugly adolescent; *Homocore*'s Tom Jennings states that "one thing everyone here has in common is that we're all *social mutants;* we've outgrown or never were part of any 'socially acceptable' categories. You don't have to be gay . . . any decision that makes you an outcast is enough."[17]

Sociologists have long defined traditional delinquent subculture as "not only a set of rules, a design for living which is indifferent to or even in conflict with the norms of 'respectable' adult society," but plausibly "defined by its 'negative polarity' to these terms."[18] The delinquent solution is a response to class structure, a way for working-class youth to gain the status references they have internalized from a middle-class culture. Although this can be seen in the "girl gang" story, the tone of the piece is infused with a campy self-consciousness, which indicates the way these representations go beyond traditional delinquency and into an "ultra-delinquency," a kind of parody of the delinquent (taken more from the position of the middle than the working class), whose violations "are not so much illegal as they are attacks on style and form."[19] The choice to be a punk is more than (and, arguably, less than) a political act; it breaks not only with straight culture but with delinquency as well, and its extreme stylization tells us that politics is intimately laced with both aesthetics and everyday life.

Punk's amalgamation of aesthetics and everyday life was one that escaped very few of its commentators; almost all of them link punk explicitly to the tradition of the avant-garde, noting that shock and defamiliarization, deliberate provocation, negation, and antigrammaticality dismantle the boundaries between art and real life, and attack the ideology of authority, the individual, and authorship.[20] But of course there are differences: punk lacks a certain critical self-consciousness, an intellectual, theoretical impetus, footing, or substructure, and offers no real materialist critique or at best a kind of charismatic anarchism. In a way punk is about not thinking, an attack against rationalism and its bourgeois valorization, which explains its appeal to intellectuals and graduate students. Punk is marked by its strong gesturalism, with graffiti being essentially the "pure punk" form, as it is "public, obscene, often mis-spelled and ungrammatical, generally reductive and emblematic (rather than symbolic or allusive)."[21] Its paradox is the contrast between its own urgency around anything concerning punk culture and its acute apathy toward sociopolitical improvement and political change. Punk art emphasizes power, obscenity, passion, incoherence, delirium and pure sensation "at the expense of refinement, order, logic, beauty."[22]

The question that haunts most of punk's commentators is whether the movement represents an eruption of genuine resistance or the ultimate in modernist capitulation to despair, decadence, and nihilism.[23] In their eagerness to see the movement as a straightforward negation of capitalism (and as an example of a genuine working-class movement), critics are often reduced to reading subcultural signs as explicit symbols and referents: "Swastikas, for instance, were not worn to indicate that punk was in agreement with fascist philosophy, but rather to remind society of the atrocities it permits."[24] Such readings often rely on simple denotation, ignoring the polyvalence of sign and context; they neglect the obvious mythologization at work, in the sense of Barthes's connotative level that refers to an empty signified, devoid of the historical authenticity of primary levels of significations and substituting for its bourgeois ideology. Punk artifacts are not just symbols of other things, they are objects within the system of punk (as antirational a system as dada). Its clothes for example—the coded emblems of chains, leather, belts—are not just the defilement of the motorcycle cop uniform; the safety pins are not just a comment on a crumbling society; the gestures of spitting and vomiting; the tattoo, the shaved head, and so on, all possess both a ritual emptiness and an emblematic plenitude within the subculture. The amount of speculation on *what punk means* is extraordinary, especially in contrast to the paucity of ink spilled on disco, which coincided with punk. Often these inquiries are more accurately a reflection of the critic's values and expectations, a feature that should be cautionary for any critic of punk, camp, or gay identity.

In reading these texts, artifacts, and objects, one must bear in mind that they are not just about punk, they *are* punk. This is not an ontological category, but a kind of performative category, albeit a very self-reflexive one, an ironic one that testifies to the constructedness of (all) such categories. It is an operation of style, a ritual in which there is no pretense of the natural or the rational; it uses the figure of masquerade to reveal that there is no essential or innocent identity to be concealed or unveiled. Gender becomes a kind of performance, a stylized repetition of acts, imbricated with the realms of class and sometimes race; this performative gender, in Judith Butler's terms, "is an 'act,' as it were, that is open to splittings, self-parody, self-criticism, and those hyperbolic exhibitions of 'the natural' that, in their very exaggeration, reveal its fundamentally phantasmatic status."[25] It is in this fashion that punk comes around the corner to meet the operations of drag and camp, which are more properly Butler's object. Punk moreover is enmeshed more directly with the issue of class, particularly in its assault on normative bourgeois values. One might say, in Tillman's terms, that if punk was a parody of juvenile delinquency, then gay punk is the parody of that parody, a commentary on the ironic position of the gay/lesbian being told that s/he is only a (poor) copy of the real thing, the heterosexual.[26] What this copy shows, in its "subversive laughter," is that the original, the heterosexual, the good, and the healthy are themselves "constituted as effects" and no more natural than the perverse/delinquent/homosexual.[27]

The queer 'zine stages or rehearses the kinds of contradictions endemic to postwar Western urban culture, particularly to youth: grow up / stay young, sex is good / sex is bad, be nice / be cool, follow upward mobility / go slumming, be modest / be shameless, be private / be public. Even the subcultural relation to authority and authorized codes, which revolves around the defer to/rebel from dyad, is one we've seen before; the encouragement to (limited) dissent can be said to be built to some extent into mass culture.[28] What is different is a questioning of gay identity that exists in a far more monological form of interdiction in society—there is hardly a "be gay" command echoed in mass culture. This affirmation is reserved for the post–Stonewall gay movement, whose configuration of identity is unsuitable to the queer punk constituency.

Much of the sixth issue of *J.D.s* is devoted to Kristy McNichol, the child actress who starred as the androgynous "Buddy" in the 1970 TV series "Family." The fourth page has "live" photos (taken off the TV screen) with the

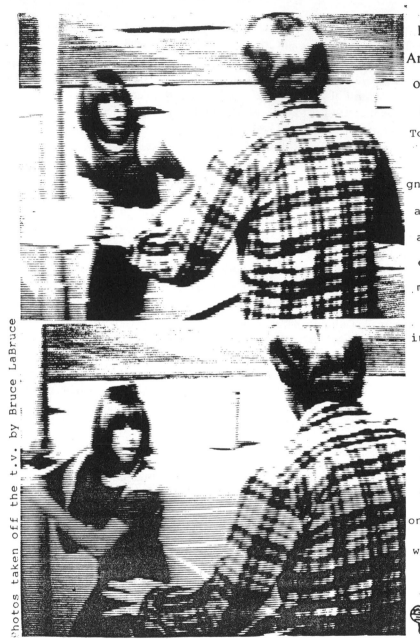

Buddy, t[...]

American [...]

on the ac[...]

series *F*[...]

Tomboy B[...]

uses h[...]

gnarly bo[...]

as a we[...]

against [...]

evil ch[...]

moleste[...]

rapist [...]

in a spe[...]

two-pa[...]

episod[...]

of Fam[...]

that ha[...]

chillir[...]

one-word [...]

which I [...]

rememb[...]

Photos taken off the t.v. by Bruce LaBruce

sidebar "Tomboy Buddy uses her gnarly board as a weapon against the evil child molester/rapist in a special two-part episode of 'Family' that had a chilling one-word title which I can't remember." The two sequential photographs show the man's plaid-clad back and Buddy's face as she swings the stick. They constitute a classic moment of seventies gritty "realism," showing the enlightened viewer how by facing evil, one can control it. The documentary quality of the photographs reflects the liberal, forthright spirit of the show, its self-effacing tendency to minimize spectacle in favor of conscientious realism.

On the page opposite the "live" photo there is an untitled and uncaptioned sketch, much like an unpolished Tom of Finland. It shows a short-haired girl hitching a ride as she stands on her skateboard, her breasts thrust forward, looking for trouble. Positioned in the same place as the attacker in the two Buddy photos is an androgynous skinhead "male," also in a plaid shirt. He has his hands on his crotch, and because the girl dominates the frame, it is unclear if he will threaten her or just urinate; looking further at his hips, it is very likely, though not definite, that he is a woman. S/he embodies a rewriting of "Family"—a postfeminist, postliberal paradigm in which it is conceivable that one might want to court danger or be the object of a "male" gaze. While hardly advocating rape or acquiescence to rapists, this sketch highlights two versions of possibly compatible desire, displacing the model of aggressive perversion victimizing normal sexuality. While the "live" photos demonstrate the tendency to reappropriate found material, the sketch underscores the main axiom of punk anarchism, which is *do it yourself*, whether taking up a guitar or a pencil. The dialogue of these two pages sets up a paradigm of gay identity around the poles of pleasure and danger, between enlightened understanding and guilty delight. It also wrestles with the distinctions of inside and outside, of defining the subculture by the terms of liberalism (moderating the social repression of "natural" desires) or by the terms of the subculture (the negation of cultural hegemony, sexual mores, and commodity culture through deliberate strategies of provocation and antigrammaticality).

The contradictions between liberal gay-tolerant culture and queer subculture come up later in the tragicomic Kristy McNichol centerfold spread. " 'Everyone thinks Kris is so innocent,' said her ex-housemate Ina Liberace. 'Deep down, there's trouble in that body.' " We are treated to Kristy trivia, such as the fact that "Family" lived in Pasadena, "the birthplace of [gay writer] Dennis Cooper." As she neared her eighteenth birthday, "she started acting less like a little adult and more like an adolescent." The final blurbs are about the palimony suit filed by her lover (Liberace's niece), which was the moment when McNichol's sexuality became a tabloid scandal and a public issue, linked to the earlier queer spectacle of Liberace's sexual identity. But the focus here is less on the "outing" than on the scandal, the presumptive closet in which the tomboy actress conspicuously stood both inside and out. While they all play with the closet, few of these fanzines make *coming out* the determinant of gay identity. This corresponds to an argument John D'Emilio has made against gay liberation's "overreliance on a strategy of coming out," which has "allowed us to ignore the institutionalized ways in which homophobia and heterosexism are reproduced."[29] Contained in the Kristy McNichol centerfold is the idea that because coming out is still not acceptable in mass culture, it is not useful to be "nice." Playing with the closet and teasing out the contradictions of sexual identity directly attack the bourgeois individualism and good manners implicit in coming out.

Kristy McNichol's position in this is as both a kind of guerrilla ingenue and a child victim of some nameless terrorism. The style of the layout, typewritten notes and pasted-together magazine excerpts, echo the "ransom note" theme recurrent in fanzine practice. McNichol's vacant expression is another familiar gesture in punk subculture, reiterating what critics characterize as the "self-effacement" of punk, the " 'blankness,' the removal of expression, the refusal to speak and be positioned," a kind of "conjunction of identity and displacement," an "evaporation of presence."[30] The astonishment these pages generate is a product of the strange blend of unselfconsciousness and hyperselfconsciousness.[31] The "trouble" here is both a form of provocation and the consequence of repression; McNichol's good tomboy Buddy was equally a repression of her sexuality and an acceptable expression of it, and her current confusion (or that expressed by the article's producers) oscillates between these poles. This oscillation of possibilities built in to the reading effectively undoes any "repressive hypothesis" that culture and the law operate through the (cultural) repression of "natural" drives. Likewise, it plays both with and against the interpretation of homosexuality as a gender dysfunction.

The McNichol saga offers us an anatomy of the desexualized "lesbian" identity built by the post-Stonewall movement of the 1970s. The actress's mute face is covered by Xerox lines and copier dirt, almost effacing her. The kind of gay identity constructed by *Gay Sunshine* is rendered particularly untenable: the "naturalness" of being gay, of celebrating ("good") gay sex. McNichol's surprised, melancholy face shines through the Xerox dirt, a metempsychosis of her pure, onscreen life with her troubled afterlife. Once the archetype of the adult child, she becomes the emblem of the childish adult who won't or can't behave. The superimposition of generations signals a refusal of a monological sexual identity. As Holly Hughes puts it, "I feel so much of lesbian experience has been represented in this really *precious,* sentimental, gooey way—like a lesbian Disneyland."[32] The queer punk constituency demands the chance to be

Once upon a time she was TV's whiz kid, a winner of two Emmys in her role as Buddy, the all-American tomboy on the acclaimed series *Family*.

As McNichol neared her 18th birthday, she started acting less like a little adult and more like an arrested adolescent. She found herself behaving like someone half her age.

"No one could look at me as this person who was in trouble...

"I almost feel like I'm from another family," says Kristy McNichol's problem proved harder to hide.

Though McNichol did go back and finish the film a year later, the rumors were flaring out of control.

"I didn't know the word *no*"

"Everyone thinks Kris is so innocent," said her ex-housemate Ina Liberace. "Deep down, there's trouble in that body."

DID YOU KNOW?

That the Lawren of "Family" li in Pasadena, California, the birthplace of Dennis Cooper?

! ! ! ! ! !

That Laticia "Buddy" Lawren a.k.a Tizzy-li: a.k.a. Kristy is an avid ski and lesbian?

! ! ! ! ! !

That Ina Libera Liberace's nie once slapped Kr with a pali suit?

Kristy McNichol

Buddy

bad, to be unnatural and perverse, choosing the gender dysphoric underworld in place of a hegemonic absorption into the normalizing eye of mass culture; precisely by confronting mass culture with its own inconsistencies, these 'zines make a spectacle that is neither entirely within the margins nor in the mainstream. This kind of terrorist negation preserves a space for social alterity that works against the Disneyfication of queers.

The evocation of a kitsch-laden image (the tomboy on a 1970s television series), the play on gender, and the emphasis on taste and its subtleties are all rudiments of camp, perhaps the oldest strategy for articulating homosexual sensibility in modern Anglo-American culture. Its primary mechanism is the insertion of an old, tired image into a new context, recycling history's waste, which is usually a product of an earlier mode of production that has lost its power to produce viable cultural meaning. Andrew Ross calls it "a re-creation of surplus value from forgotten forms of labor," a theft of the product—or a theft of control of the product's *meaning*—from its original producers (in this case, the television media).[33] The control of the image's meaning is seized by the newcomer, with the "original" meaning gleaming through like a palimpsest, marking only a partial break at best with the logic of cultural capital.

Camp here becomes an operation of taste, of reading, a making of fine distinctions in the domain of a mass or pop culture that equalizes all things; it takes the determination of meaning from the product's producer and gives it to the critic or reader, a variant on what Barthes called a writerly text. Camp has been said to reside "largely in the eyes of the beholder," or as the editors of *Thing* put it, in a "nudge and wink."[34] This plays on the distinction of those inside the subculture—in this case the savvy post-seventies queer—and those outside. This distinction underlies the political deployment of camp, both because of its engagement with the commodification of taste and because camp contains "an explicit commentary on feats of *survival* in a world dominated by the taste and interests of those whom it serves."[35]

Camp has been called "the lie that tells the truth" and "the heroism of people not called upon to be heroes" by Philip Core, and described by Christopher Isherwood as "expressing what's basically serious to you in terms of fun and artifice and elegance."[36] In both these statements there emerges an oxymoron, but moreover, a chiasmus: a crossing of contrasting elements, a poetic transit. Mark Booth says "to be camp is to present oneself as being committed to the marginal with a commitment greater than the marginal merits."[37] Again, what is evident is a similar sense of disproportion, an antirational structure that uses elements of style to claim positions not available within the dominant grammar of meanings.

Within this contestation, the primary type of the marginal in society is the

traditionally feminine. Thus the issue of gender lies at the core of camp production, offering us a highly nuanced way to talk about sexual difference.[38]
While this is most often read in terms of men in drag as women, the Kristy
McNichol centerfold recasts this in girl as boy *and* in child as adult and adult as
child; it plays on the camp irony between real-life performance and melodramatic lives,[39] and appends to this the gender trouble inherent in the figure of
the tomboy, a kind of supplement to the stable roles of boy and girl. The
question of whether the actress was a tomboy or was impersonating one
becomes unanswerable.

Camp demonstrates gender performance; it highlights the constructedness
of gender and cultural objects. It denaturalizes. Its impulse is to make fun *out
of* something very serious to its constituency, rather than making fun *of* it. And
if, as Mark Booth says, camp is a matter of self-presentation rather than of
sensibility, this is because it is always predicated on an audience (17). Jack
Babuscio claims camp style "signifies performance rather than existence. . . .
the emphasis shifts from what a thing or a person *is* to what it *looks* like; from
what is being done to *how* it is being done" (44). If camp aesthetics treat life as
theater, it is in part because identity is treated as a role, especially for gays and
lesbians who can only survive by *passing,* pretending to be heterosexuals. By
changing the normal and natural into style and artifice, camp might be said to
change the "real, hostile world into one that is controllable and safe."[40] But
camp's manifestation in the Kristy McNichol story also reverses this charge,
trading the controllable, safe worlds of established gay identity (cast as a kind
of paradoxical closet) for a more troubled world of gender dysphoria—one
that just as strongly assaults the regime of presumptive and compulsory heterosexuality. Gender becomes an act whose very repetitiveness is the basis for
the institutions of heterosexual identity, and the recognition of this iterative
act always (already) opens it to parodic decentering.

The fanzines I've examined here without exception demonstrate an unusual
cultural fusion, uniting punk and camp, two once-antithetical aesthetics. This
antigrammaticality explains the initial charges of unreadability levied against
the fanzine. They play on the contradictory *ethics* of these two aesthetics, on
punk as male signifier (against a "feminized" bourgeois culture), as working
class, aggressive, gestural, and reductive, characterized by crude thinking and
"poor" theater. Camp is counterpoised by its ethics of the feminine, its stress
on connotation over denotation, its higher class position, its passivity, its
expansiveness, and its sense of the spectacular. The practice of camp is linked
to metaphor, while punk's affinities are to metonym; one expands while the
other shrinks meaning; one is rereading, the other is rewriting (if we accept
graffiti as the "purest" punk form). Although punk archetypally trades in

social apocalypse, camp is postulated in social anomie; together they play between the Nietzschean poles of violence and laughter. Taken literally, punk's ambiguous promise is especially Nietzschean, a reformulation of society, a revaluation of all values. Faced by the amount of speculation on what punk means, characterized especially by the celebratory anarchism of Greil Marcus, one must ask if punk fundamentally deploys itself against meaning at all, whether it insists on a radical breakdown of meaning. And if punk is about the truancy of meaning, isn't camp about its superabundance, about reading the overdetermination of cultural signs? Camp's seriousness consists of *reading style seriously* against content. Punk's seriousness is constituted defensively against the class structuring of bourgeois consciousness. Thus both camp and punk wrest meaning from the control of abstract, hegemonic, and normative agencies; while both treat meaning as a play of signs, a game of varying intensity, they both recognize meaning's social negotiations, and indeed issue precisely from volatile sites of social contestation.

In this respect it may be most useful to see punk and camp as ethics rather than aesthetics, ethics that deploy style to both make and unmake sense. Punk's refusal to speak and be positioned, its evaporation of presence, and its self-effacement, like camp's hypertrophic presence, its theater of gender identity, unveil the illusion of normative heterosexuality to be, in Judith Butler's terms, "nothing other than a parody of the *idea* of the natural and the original."[41] If we accept the charge that punk, like the avant-garde, fell short of any developed considerations of gender, sexuality, and gender identity, perhaps its pollination by camp bridges that gap. Certainly, punk directly addresses issues of class (and race) that camp tends to skirt. If punk is indeed without the intellectual basis of critical negation so requisite to academic notions of resistance, it is characterized by a gestural negation, a "crude thinking." In contrast camp is oddly affirmative, what Sontag calls an aesthetic of love. Their synthesis, however, addresses *banality* in a configuration quite different from the core modernist avant-garde gesture of transgression; they embrace the banal, they refigure its pervasive physiognomy.

To interpret these publications without undue scholarly violence necessarily propels me to consider the need for a new intellectual cultural politics, one geared particularly to examine the very tenuous zones of resistance within the all-consuming paradigm of postmodernism. To examine the reformulation of gay identity in North America largely requires that we supplement the models of deprivation (such as Marxist class struggle) or *lack* (as in that posited by psychoanalysis) with the models of excess (as proposed by Situationists, for example).[42] These latter are predicated on a culture of surplus production and overdetermined cultural meaning, where in Baudrillard's terms the map precedes the territory, a culture of affirmation in which control operates through the induction of desire and where countercultures are subject to a repressive tolerance. Such a cultural politics recognizes that oppressed classes (relative to their class position, especially), are motivated by the desire to consume, the desire to desire, buy, and own, and not necessarily to rebel. This is beyond the traditional academic, like E. D. Hirsch (author of *Cultural Literacy*), who would never read *Sin Bros.*, or would at best, say yes or no to *Sin Bros.* It is beyond the role of the organic intellectual, like Susan Sontag, Richard Dyer, or Michael Bronski, who would read *Sin Bros.* in order to say yes, that it represents the interests of a rising class. What we need is a kind of postorganic intellectual who would not deny the place of an organic kind of advocacy, not allow a "no" to be imposed, to always say yes politically, while measuring other expressions of negation and affirmation *which don't necessarily make sense,* which defy rules of grammar.

The current proliferation of gay fanzines signals a shift in the relation of knower to known and a resistance to rationalization. Anchoring gay identity to the shifting sands of the "natural" in these times may be perilous. The logic of reasonable nature is being used to clean the air and ban malathion but also to prevent women's abortions; to question the authority of the A.M.A. over collective knowledge of the human body but also to make provisions for quarantining all gay men; embedded in these strategies is a refusal to see how sexuality is cultural, not natural, or at best to think of homosexuals as having "natural" drives bridled by cultural limits. Nature may become the last refuge for scoundrels in the nineties—its rhetoric, with all its attendant middle-class valorizations, whether in the form of antivivisectionists, the Greens, or the Family Values Coalition—spurring wildly various political agendas. In these appeals to nature and reason, the line between utopian and authoritarian grows perilously thin. What these fanzines articulate is a crisis in identity formation (one of representation), in knowledge of oneself and one's sexuality, and the recognition that knowledge easily ceases to be a liberation and becomes a mode of surveillance.

Notes

The author wishes to thank Danny Babcock, Liz Kotz, and Dick Hebdige. This paper was originally presented at the Fourth Annual Lesbian, Gay & Bisexual Studies Conference at Harvard University, October 28, 1990. Portions of this essay originally appeared in *Afterimage* 18, no. 5 (1991): 12–16. The addresses of the fanzines discussed in this article are: *Homocore,* c/o World

Power Systems, P.O.B. 77731, San Francisco, California 94107; *My Comrade/Sister,* 326 E. 13th, #15, New York, New York 10003. *Sin Bros.,* P.O.B. 618, N. Hollywood, California 91630; and *J.D.s,* P.O.B. 1110, Toronto, Ontario, Canada M5C 2K5.

1. The earliest American homophile magazines, *ONE* and *Mattachine Review,* stressed how "homosexuals were just like anyone else except for their sexual orientation"; *Advocate* added "pride in difference" to this same "longing to be a part of the mainstream" (Michael Bronski, *Culture Clash: The Making of Gay Sensibility* [Boston: South End Press, 1984] 146–47).

See Dennis Altman, *The Homosexualization of America* (Boston: Beacon Press, 1982), for an analysis of the effects of post-Stonewall gay "identity politics" on the model of ethnic minority communities. See also John D'Emilio, *Sexual Politics, Sexual Communities: The Making of A Homosexual Minority in the United States, 1940–1970* (New York: Monthly Review Press, 1983).

2. See David James, "Hardcore: Cultural Resistance in the Postmodern," *Film Quarterly* 42, no. 2 (1988–89): 31–39. Straight hardcore music mounted "a deliberately anachronistic attempt to sustain early punk's negativity against its diffusion and assimilation by the music industry as various forms of new wave. The entirely recalcitrant music provided a besieged subculture with the basis for defensive rituals in which the sonic (and other forms of) violence and the obstinate antiprofessionalism that signaled rejection of overproduced corporate rock also informed strategies of negation and antigrammaticality for everyday self-presentation . . ." (35).

3. An excellent survey of "Star Trek" slasher novels can be found in Constance Penley, "Brownian Motion: Women, Tactics and Technology," in *Technoculture,* ed. Constance Penley and Andrew Ross (Minneapolis: University of Minnesota Press, 1991).

4. Dave Laing, *One Chord Wonders: Power and Meaning in Punk Rock* (Philadelphia: Open University Press, 1985), 14.

5. Tom Jennings, *Homocore* masthead. Citations from 'zines are a bibliographer's nightmare; many have no dates or page numbers and authors are often uncredited.

6. Virginia Boston, *Punk Rock* (New York: Penguin, 1978), 14. David James, "Poetry/Punk/ Production: Some Recent Writing in LA," in *Postmodernism and Its Discontents,* ed. E. Anne Kaplan (London: Verso, 1988), 178.

7. For descriptive surveys of queer fanzines, see Dennis Cooper, "Homocore Rules," *Village Voice,* 4 September 1990, 92; Bill Van Parys, "Fag Rags Come of Age," *Advocate,* 6 November 1990, 70–72; Wickie Stamps, "Queer Girls with an Attitude," ibid., 20 November 1990, 56–57; Adam Block, "The Queen of 'Zine," ibid., 75.

8. *My Comrade/Sister,* Summer 1989, n.p.

9. Dick Hebdige, *Subculture: The Meaning of Style* (London: Methuen, 1979), 1–19. Further citations will be given within the text.

10. i.i. cummings, "Axl Greased," *Sin Bros.* 3 (January/February 1990): 17.

11. Craig Lee, "Getting Down With the Third Sex: Gay Post-kids Build a Scene of Their Own," *L.A. Weekly,* 20 July 1990, 56.

12. Theodor Adorno, "On Popular Music," *Studies in Philosophy and Social Science* 9, no. 1 (1941).

13. See Gayle Rubin's "Thinking Sex," in *Pleasure and Danger: Exploring Female Sexuality,* ed. Carole S. Vance (Boston: Routledge & Kegan Paul, 1984), 267–319.

14. G. B. Jones, "Gang Girl," *J.D.s,* no. 5, n.d., n.p.

15. *J.D.s* received a scathing indictment from Toronto's leftist art magazine *Fuse* and was refused distribution at the Montreal Anarchist Bookstore and Glad Day Bookstore, a world-famous gay bookstore in Toronto. See *Homocore,* no. 1 [1988?], 4.

The resistance queer 'zines first met has largely disappeared, as the style and provocation of the 'zines have been taken up by the mass media. Witness, in this respect, the use of 'zine aesthetics and kinkiness in Madonna's book, *Sex* (New York: Warner, 1992).

16. Quoted in Cooper, "Homocore Rules," 92.

17. Tom Jennings, "Rude Noises from the Editor/Censor," *Homocore*, no. 3 (February 1989), n.p.

18. Albert Cohen, "The Delinquency Subculture," in *Juvenile Delinquency*, ed. Rose Giallombardo (New York: Wiley, 1976), 108. Cohen's article dates from 1958.

19. Robert H. Tillman, "Punk Rock and the Construction of 'Pseudo-Political' Movements," *Popular Music and Society* 7, no. 3 (1980), 170.

20. See Tricia Henry, *Break All Rules: Punk Rock and the Meaning of a Style* (Ann Arbor: UMI Research Press, 1989), and "Punk and Avant-garde Art," *Journal of Popular Culture* 17 (Spring 1984): 87–97; Laing, *One Chord Wonders*, 76–79; and Greil Marcus, *Lipstick Traces* (Cambridge: Harvard University Press, 1989).

21. "The attraction of punk culture to graduate students, to upper middle class, white, well educated men and women (despite the fact that they were often the target of punk tirades), was a curious phenomenon . . ." (Jon Lewis, "Punks in LA: It's Kiss or Kill," *Journal of Popular Culture* 22 [Fall 1988]: 90). See also 89.

22. Larry McCaffery, "Kathy Acker and 'Punk' Aesthetics," in *Breaking the Sequence: Women's Experimental Fiction*, ed. Ellen G. Friedman and Miriam Fuchs (Princeton: Princeton University Press, 1989), 220.

23. In addition to sources cited in note 20, see Hebdige, *Subculture*; James, "Hardcore: Cultural Resistance in the Postmodern," and "Poetry/Punk/Production." See also Bruce Dancis, "Safety Pins and Class Struggle: Punk Rock and the Left," *Socialist Review* 39 (May–June 1978); Dave Laing, "Interpreting Punk Rock," *Marxism Today* 22, no. 4 (1978): 123–28; Robert Christgau, "A Cult Explodes—and a Movement is Born," *Village Voice*, 24 October 1977, 57, 68–74; Simon Frith, "Beyond the Dole Queue: The Politics of Punk," ibid., 77–79.

24. Henry, *Break All Rules*, 80.

25. Judith Butler, *Gender Trouble: Feminism and the Subversion of Identity* (New York: Routledge, 1990), 147.

26. See Judith Butler, "Imitation and Gender Subordination," in *Inside/Out: Lesbian Theories, Gay Theories*, ed. Diana Fuss (New York: Routledge, 1991), 20–21. Also to be considered here is Fredric Jameson's argument about the postmodern logic of pastiche, a kind of parody of parody, without an underlying origin. See "Postmodernism and Consumer Society," in *The Anti-Aesthetic: Essays on Postmodern Culture*, ed. Hal Foster (Port Townsend, Wash.: Bay Press, 1983), 114.

27. Butler, *Gender Trouble*, 146.

28. Habermas argues that all countercultures are subject to a "repressive tolerance." Advanced capitalist societies avoid a legitimation crisis by uncoupling the sociocultural systems from the political-economic system, so that culture becomes a "private reserve" of meaning which cannot be had in the world (Jurgen Habermas, *Legitimation Crisis* [Boston: Beacon Press, 1972]).

29. John D'Emilio, "Capitalism and Gay Identity," in *Powers of Desire: The Politics of Sexuality*, ed. Ann Snitow et al. (New York: Monthly Review Press, 1983), 111.

30. Henry, *Break All Rules*, 97; Hebdige, *Subculture*, 28; James, "Poetry/Punk/Production," 164–65.

31. Another page devoted to McNichol (41) has "live" photos of her trapped in a dessert factory, peering through the bars as her brother (who is alleged to be gay himself in a letter from Dennis Cooper on the same page) comes to the rescue.

32. "An Interview with Holly Hughes," *My Comrade/Sister,* Winter 1990, n.p.

33. Andrew Ross, "Uses of Camp," *Yale Journal of Criticism* 2, no. 1 (1988): 14.

34. Jack Babuscio, "Camp and the Gay Sensibility," in *Gays and Film,* ed. Richard Dyer (London: British Film Institute, 1977), 41; "What Is Camp?" *Thing,* no. 3 (n.d.): 27.

35. Ross, "Uses of Camp," 9. Susan Sontag, by contrast, saw camp as essentially "apolitical," an aesthetic of "failed seriousness" ("Notes on Camp," *Against Interpretation* [New York: Farrar, Straus and Giroux, 1966], 277.

36. Philip Core, *Camp: The Lie that Tells the Truth* (New York: Delilah, 1984); Christopher Isherwood, *The World in Evening* (London: Methuen, 1954).

37. Mark Booth, *Camp* (New York: Quartet, 1983), 18. Further references to this work will be given within the text.

38. According to Carol-Anne Tyler's "Boys Will Be Girls: The Politics of Gay Drag," in Fuss, *Inside/Out,* 32–70, camp's gender politics are more problematic than I allow. Camp is "a relationship with an absent 'other' as phallic M/Other" (59). This absent other guarantees a kind of plenitude, full self-presence, and knowledge by the offer of the phallus. "Camp (like mimicry) functions complexly by dragging in many differences at once that are all too easily articulated with phallic narcissism in a symbolic which is really a white, bourgeois, and masculine fetishistic imaginary" (62).

39. Babuscio defines camp irony as "any incongruous contrast between an individual or thing and its context or association," such as "masculine/feminine," "youth/(old) age," "sacred/profane," "spirit/flesh," "high/low status." "At the core of this perception of incongruity is the idea of gayness as a moral deviation" ("Camp and the Gay Sensibility," 41).

40. Bronski, *Culture Clash,* 42.

41. Butler, *Gender Trouble,* 31.

42. Certainly, with the exception of Greil Marcus, all the commentators on punk have based their analyses on the model of deprivation and reaction. Sontag's essay is likewise postulated on camp as the reaction formation of an oppressed class, a counterpart to Jewish moral seriousness.

On the Situationists, see Marcus, *Lipstick Traces,* and Elisabeth Sussman, ed., *On the Passage of a Few People over a Rather Brief Moment in Time* (Cambridge: MIT Press, 1990). See also Guy Debord, *Society of the Spectacle* (Detroit: Black and Red, 1977).

STYLE AND HOMOSEXUALITY

Fake It Like a Man

KEVIN KOPELSON

CALLER 1: So what do you look like?
CALLER 2: Well, I think I look a lot like Tom Cruise.
CALLER 1: (*straining for credulity*) Well, you don't *sound* like him . . . but let's go with it.

The gay critic, we'll call him "Mary," who shared this phone (s)ex-change with me has asked that I not reveal his name. I think I understand Mary's anxiety. I wouldn't want *my* colleagues to know I subscribe to that particular party line. (Gay critics aren't supposed to act *too* gay.) Nor would I want them to think I see myself as Tom Cruise. (I'm not that attractive.) But unlike Mary, unlike many of us, I would like them—you—to know I can't, or feel I can't, carry off any of the identificatory impersonations that make me gay. I would also like you to know I can't, or feel I can't, carry off the impersonations that make me a gay critic. As a gay man, I do, in fact, want to look like Tom Cruise. (I've had a thing for him ever since I saw *Risky Business*.) As a gay critic, however, I try to sound like Oscar Wilde (my favorite queer martyr). I also try to sound like Eve Kosofsky Sedgwick (my favorite queer diva). Of course, as I imagine you can tell, I don't sound anything like them. And that's, as Stuart Smalley would instruct, if not convince, himself, okay. Because even though I can't quite carry off these impersonations (I don't even do Stuart Smalley very well), like Mary, who came to be where he needed to "go," I can still manage to carry on.

At this point, you may not want me to carry on. You probably find my introductory paragraph upsetting. Gay critics, after all, aren't supposed to be *too* campy. Nor are we supposed to be *too* solipsistic. If I were a drag queen, I could proclaim myself "fabulous" and not be thought unladylike. As a gay critic, however, I can't go around saying "I'm *so* fascinating." That would be "unprofessional." But I *am* fascinating. I'm at least as fascinating as the phenomena I write about. And, let's face it, I'm a lot more fascinating than most of the phenomena I read about. My sexual and critical performance anxieties, for example, are, if I do say so myself, simply spellbinding. But you're upset. I won't say another self-indulgent word. I will, however, do what gay critics do best. I'll explore, in a thoroughly "professional" manner, the social dis-ease of which my own anxieties are, in large part, symptomatic. Or will I? As you can tell from my choice of texts, which happen to concern Wilde, Cruise, and Sedgwick, my exploration is a form of self-exploration. Let's just hope it also speaks, howsoever inadvertently, to *your* anxieties.

Opera Glasses

Theorists of gender and sexuality as performative suggest we are all prone to four related anxieties. We should beware: (1) having to perform a gender or sexuality; (2) performing a gender or sexuality badly; (3) performing an inappropriate gender or sexuality; and (4) performing an inappropriate gender or sexuality badly. But where are the cultural markers of these anxieties? "How," as Judith Butler asks, "are troublesome identifications apparent in cultural practices?"[1] We can begin to answer these questions by reading Gilbert and Sullivan's *Patience* (1881).

Patience attests to performance anxieties one and two. This comic opera involves a number of homosocial rivalries and problematic travesties. Two self-styled "aesthetes"—Archibald Grosvenor, an "idyllic" poet, and Reginald Bunthorne, a "fleshly" poet based on Wilde—vie for the love of Patience, a dairy maid. Together with a group of dragoons the poets compete for the love of twenty "rapturous maidens." The dragoons do in fact win their love, but only by imitating Bunthorne's aestheticism, which, like Wilde's, is itself an imitative "sham."

> A languid love for lilies does *not* blight me!
> Lank limbs and haggard cheeks do *not* delight me! . . .
> In short, my mediaevalism's affectation,
> Born of a morbid love of admiration.[2]

And Grosvenor succeeds in wooing Patience, but only by pretending to be ordinary and unaesthetic.

> A commonplace young man,
> A matter-of-fact young man,
> A steady and stolid-y, jolly Bank-holiday
> Every-day young man! (203)

These rivalries and travesties signify that homophobic men like W. S. Gilbert read homosexual artificiality as indicative of heterosexual artificiality, that, as Butler puts it, the "imitative effect of gay identities works . . . to expose heterosexuality as an incessant and *panicked* imitation of its own naturalized idealization."[3] Gilbert's Bunthorne is a false aesthete but a true homosexual. No one, including Bunthorne himself, regrets his loss of Patience to Grosvenor and of the rapturous maidens to the dragoons.[4]

> BUN: In that case unprecedented,
> Single I must live and die—
> I shall have to be contented with
> With a tulip or li*ly!*
> (*Takes a lily from button-hole and gazes affectionately at it.*)

> ALL: He will have to be contented
> With a tulip or li*ly!*
> Greatly pleased with one another,
> To get married we decide,
> Each of us will wed the other,
> Nobody be Bunthorne's Bride! (207)

This conflation of homosexuality and Wildean aestheticism (Bunthorne's "walk down Piccadilly with a poppy or a lily in [his] mediaeval hand" is an unmistakable allusion to Wilde), although vague enough not to be defamatory, is deliberate (174). "In satirizing the excesses of these (so-called) aesthetes," early audiences were told by producer Richard D'Oyly Carte, "the authors of *Patience* have not desired to cast ridicule on the true aesthetic spirit, but only to attack the *unmanly oddities* which masquerade in its likeness."[5] But of what is true male homosexuality, according to the logic of *Patience*, a poor imitation? Is it an inappropriate and bad copy of the right sexuality (the "true" and "manly" aestheticism of Ruskin and Morris), or an inappropriate and bad copy of the wrong gender (Bunthorne is a "Francesca da Rimini, miminy, piminy, / *Je-ne-sais-quoi* young man" [204])? The dragoons, true heterosexuals who try but fail to enact Bunthorne's pseudoaesthetic homosexuality, seem to think it both. They move like aesthetic men, "in stiff, constrained, and angular attitudes" (197), and dress like aesthetic women, in "cobwebby grey velvet . . . trimmed with Venetian leather and Spanish altar lace, and surmounted with something Japanese" (171). Goons in drag, they swagger *and* swish. But if this travesty implies that true heterosexuality, unlike true homosexuality, is nonperformative, Grosvenor's travesty theorizes both as equally imitative. Whereas Bunthorne is a homosexual who pretends to be heterosexual, to want to marry Patience, Grosvenor is a *heterosexual* who pretends to be heterosexual. His true "commonplace" drag, unlike the dragoon's false pseudoaestheticism, is both convincing and appropriate. Grosvenor, however, is only one of two "commonplace" heterosexuals in *Patience*. One dragoon, a lieutenant, purports to be "commonplace" as well—to be neither "particularly intelligent, . . . remarkably studious, . . . excruciatingly witty, . . . unusually accomplished, [n]or exceptionally virtuous"—but due to his rank and wealth (he "has the misfortune to be a duke, with a thousand a day" [167]), is not. His all too true heterosexuality is a poor and insufficiently "commonplace" imitation of Grosvenor's.

But what about the women? What does *Patience* indicate about female performance anxiety? It suggests that men would like to believe there is no such thing. Although the rapturous maidens are as pseudoaesthetic as Bunthorne,[6] Patience is completely artless. She neither imitates nor impersonates anyone, which may explain why the opera is named after her. Patience is the quintessential natural woman, a figure of whom men like Gilbert and Sullivan, if not men like Wilde, grew increasingly fond the more they sensed that femininity, like masculinity, is nothing more than a masquerade.

Dark Glasses

Unlike *Patience*, *Risky Business* (1983) attests to anxieties two (performing a gender or sexuality badly) and three (performing an inappropriate gender or sexuality). This film represents the sexual constitution of high-school senior Joel Goodsen. Joel (Tom Cruise) becomes a full-fledged heterosexual, or "man," by asking himself "what the fuck?" and becoming a pimp, by assuming the "risk" of selling women to male classmates. He also purports to heterosexualize his customers, each of whom, he promises, will "walk like a man." One sign of Joel's new subjectivity is misogynist and antiaesthetic. He accidentally cracks his mother's precious crystal egg. Another sign is a fashion accessory, Joel's stylish black "Wayfarer" sunglasses—a mod look soon sported by millions of Cruise fans. (I bought mine as soon as I left the theater.) But if the Ray-Bans signify Joel's (white) male heterosexuality, they also signify the disconnections upon which that subjectivity now depends. Grosvenor reads as heterosexual even though he has closer ties to Bunthorne's aestheticism than to the dragoons' militarism. Joel, however, comes of age in an age of overwhelming transsexual anxiety. Unlike Grosvenor, he must avoid extraneous identificatory alliances. He must avoid eye contact with undesirables. He tries, for example, to lock Jackie, a black transvestite, out of his house. But not only does

Jackie force his way in, he also offers Joel the key to normative adult masculinity. Jackie, who represents the wrong gender, the wrong race, the wrong sex, and, presumably, the wrong sexuality, gives Joel the name and number of Lana, the sexy young prostitute who becomes Joel's business partner and, it would seem, his first "girlfriend." Like Jackie, however, Lana makes Joel very nervous. She is a "sexpert" who may neither find Joel's sexual performance satisfactory nor want to be his "girlfriend."

> LANA: And, you got a girlfriend to boot.
> JOEL: Do I? Well, do I?
> LANA: What do you think?
> JOEL: I don't know, you tell me. Yes? No? Maybe?
> LANA: Yes. No. Maybe.

Risky Business also features three of Joel's cohorts. Glenn, who is unpretentious and promiscuous, would appear to be quintessentially heterosexual, were it not for the film's strategic use of "Mannish Boy," sung by Muddy Waters with considerable irony: "I could make love to you, woman, in five minutes time, / Ain't that a man!" Miles, who is pretentious and virginal, who shuns the risks toward which he constantly urges Joel, is trapped in a boyhood that no one would mistake as even "mann*ish*." Neither Glenn nor Miles, however, is as problematic as Barry (Bronson Pinchot). Just as Joel's heterosexuality is compromised by his furtive contact with Jackie, Barry's heterosexuality is compromised by his own fussy aestheticism, which, unlike the false pseudoaestheticism of the dragoons in *Patience,* is neither parodic nor homophobic. When Barry ogles every prostitute who enters Joel's house, Muddy Waters supplies an explanatory lyric: "I'm a man." But when Joel hastily reassembles his parents' étagère, Barry offers a disquieting critical intervention: "I would put all the Chinese things together, and the Greek on a separate shelf. I don't think you should mix centuries." In other words, there is something very gay, something gay *identified,* about Barry's imitation of heterosexuality. Which doesn't surprise me. There is something very gay about all of Pinchot's nongay characters. There is even something very gay about Pinchot's own (nontheatrical) heterosexuality. Like Barry, Pinchot remains a nerve-racking signifier of the extent to which heterosexuals read as homosexual, of the extent to which they emulate gay style. As well he should.

However, if heterosexuals impersonate homosexuals, homosexuals impersonate heterosexuals. I'm not the only gay man to have worn black Wayfarers in 1983, a fact to which *Sticky Business* (1984), a porn video derived from *Risky Business,* bears witness. *Sticky Business,* like *Risky Business,* attests to performance anxieties two and three, but does so from a gay perspective. Just as the film represents the heterosexual constitution of Joel Goodsen, the video represents the homosexual constitution of Mike, a teenager who, like Joel, dons Ray-Bans, dances in his underwear, hosts a profitable sex party, and becomes sexually active (sells his "virgin ass" for two thousand dollars). And just as Joel suspects he is no good at heterosexuality, at having a "girlfriend," Mike can't even pretend to enjoy his abysmal gay debut, can't keep himself from sizing up the situation with characteristic perspicuity: "It hurts." (Or is Mike lying? He wouldn't be the first pseudovirginal hustler to fake pain in order to approximate a client's sexual script.)

Sticky Business also features the homosexual seduction of Mike's friend Cory, an effeminate boy who is too closeted to join the party, by Matt, a noneffeminate boy who sees through Cory's heterosexual act. At first, the two make love while watching, or listening to, a straight porn video, which suggests that their gay sexuality, like *Sticky Business* itself, is a bad copy of a nongay original. And even after they stop attending to the video, a cessation that coincides with their sodomitical congress, Cory, who notwithstanding his femininity is playing the role of masculine top to the hilt, delivers a line that Matt might find disorienting. "Take it like a man," Cory tells him, "just the way I like it." How can someone being sodomized take it like a man? Isn't submission to phallic penetration supposed to be effeminate? If Cory has learned anything from that video, shouldn't he tell Matt to take it like a woman? Not necessarily. For one thing, *Sticky Business* was made at a time when many gays were questioning the heteroerotic equation of sexual "passivity" with femininity and sexual "activity" with masculinity. Matt is less effeminate than Cory because, as a bottom, he is presumed to play the more manly, powerful role. For another, Matt, who seems nonplussed, who even congratulates Cory on his successful, if somewhat inappropriate performance (the exclamation "just the way I like it" suggests that Cory is a bottom), correctly infers that, in his case, "take it like a man" *does* mean "take it like a woman"—something Mike, by the way, refuses to do. Because Cory is really saying, regardless of Matt's evident pleasure: "Don't complain, you're not supposed to enjoy this."

Despite their similarity, *Risky Business* and *Sticky Business* tell different stories about performance anxiety three. The consequences of heterosexual emulation of homosexual style and homosexual emulation of heterosexual style are, of course, neither identical nor symmetrical. Western culture requires heterosexual but not homosexual purity. Heterosexuals are to abjure homosexual identification, if not homosexual, homoerotic, and homosocial conduct. Homosexuals, however, are both forced to occupy closets (to *act* straight) and encouraged to explore heterosexuality (to *be* straight). Western culture also envisions homosexuality as, in essence, a bad imitation of heterosexuality. It deploys an inversion model gays and lesbians have co-opted and transfigured. So whereas heterosexuals do disavow homosexuality and homosexuals do disavow heterosexuality, homosexuals are less likely to be disconcerted by inappropriate identifications.[7] Which is why, even though both are incongruous, Barry's gay aestheticism is more upsetting than Cory's macho posturing. Gay male tops are supposed to act butch. Straight boys, however, are not supposed to fancy figurines.

White Glasses

Unlike *Risky* and *Sticky Business,* Eve Sedgwick's essay "White Glasses"[8] attests to anxieties three (performing an inappropriate gender or sexuality) and four (performing an inappropriate gender or sexuality badly). Sedgwick is a nongay woman who bonds with gay men, a breast cancer survivor who sees herself as a person with AIDS. Hers, she writes, is an "identification that falls across gender, . . . across sexualities, across 'perversions' " (198), an identification best symbolized by her remarkable eye wear:

> The first time I met Michael Lynch, I thought his white-framed glasses were the coolest thing I had ever seen. It was at the MLA Convention, in New York, in 1986. My first thought was, "Within two months, every gay man in New York is going to be wearing white glasses." My second thought: "Within a year, every fashion-conscious person in the United States is going to be wearing white glasses." My instant resolve: "I want white glasses first." (193)

Eventually, Sedgwick does locate a pair of Lynch's signature "patio-furniture" frames, a pair that, unlike Joel's disconnective Ray-Bans, promises to bridge the gender/sexuality gap that separates her from her new friend. Unfortunately, the glasses no longer signify "Michael Lynch": "The white of the glasses means differently for a woman, for a man. The white of the glasses is two things, after all. White is a color—it is a pastel. White the pastel sinks banally and invisibly into the camouflage of femininity, on a woman, a white woman. In a place where it doesn't belong, on Michael, that same pastel remains a flaming signifier" (197).

Although Sedgwick seems to have no compunction about performing an inappropriate gender and sexuality—she is too queer to maintain categorical distinctions she has spent much of her professional life deconstructing—she is quite anxious about performing gay male sexuality badly. She would like to be flamboyant, to be, like Lynch's white glasses, "a flaming signifier," but can't control how her self-styled sexuality is received. Even poststructuralists, contrary to popular belief, know their audience.

> Now, I know I don't "look much like" Michael Lynch, even in my white glasses. Nobody knows more fully, more fatalistically than a fat woman how unbridgeable the gap is between the self we see and the self as whom we are seen; no one, perhaps, has more practice at straining and straining to span the binocular view between; and no one can appreciate more fervently the act of magical faith by which it may be possible, at last, to assert and believe, against every social possibility, that the self we see can be made visible as if through our own eyes to the people who see us. (197)

The irony of course is, if not that Sedgwick makes a better gay man than most gay men, then that she makes a better gay critic, especially of writers like Wilde, than most gay critics. Sedgwick may require "magical faith" to make us *see* her as she sees herself, but she doesn't need any to make us *read* her that way. Her textual performances alone are good enough to make us conceive of her as a gay man—even though she doesn't look the part. Think of Montserrat Caballé. She can't dance. She's as big as a house. But she *sounds* like Salome—and, for an opera queen, sound, or, more to the point, *inimitable* sound, is all that matters. Which is why, I suppose, when I heard "White Glasses" at a lesbian and gay studies conference in the Spring of 1991, *my* instant resolve, upon which, needless to say, I acted immediately, was: "I want white glasses, too." I had a "magical faith" that, if properly accessorized, I could make people see me, if not read me, as Eve Sedgwick. But I never got to do this gay male impersonation of a nongay woman's impersonation of a gay man. Because, in the end, I didn't buy "patio-furniture" glasses. I bought white-framed Wayfarers, a style that, as it turns out, suggests neither Cruise nor Sedgwick. Which may be just as well.

Notes

1. See Judith Butler, *Gender Trouble: Feminism and the Subversion of Identity* (New York: Routledge, 1990); and "Imitation and Gender Insubordination," in *Inside/Out: Lesbian Theories, Gay Theories*, ed. Diana Fuss (New York: Routledge 1991), 13–31; citation is from 27.

2. W.S. Gilbert, *The Savoy Operas*, vol. 1 (London: Macmillan, 1957), 173. Further references to this edition will be within the text.

3. Butler, "Imitation," 22–23.

4. Compare Jack Point's tragic loss of Elsie Maynard to Colonel Fairfax in *The Yeomen of the Guard* (1888).

5. Geoffrey Smith, *The Savoy Operas: A New Guide to Gilbert and Sullivan* (London: Robert Hale, 1983), 98 (emphasis added).

6. The *Times* reviewer noted that "the poetry of Reginald Bunthorne is totally unlike anything published by real poets in England [and that] the dresses and colours of the rapturous maidens . . . would scarcely pass muster in an aesthetic drawing-room" (25 April 1881, 10).

7. Cf. Butler, "Imitation,": "it is not something like heterosexuality or bisexuality that is disavowed by the category [homosexual], but a set of identificatory and practical crossings between these categories that renders the discreteness of each equally suspect" (17).

8. Eve Kosofsky Sedgwick, "White Glasses," *Yale Journal of Criticism* 5, no. 3 (Fall 1992): 193–208. Citations from this essay will be placed in the text.

Homosexual Expression and Homophobic Censorship:

THE SITUATION OF THE TEXT

MARTY ROTH

And when, upon the day of my arrival, a second William Wilson came also, I felt angry with him for bearing the name and doubly disgusted with the name because a stranger bore it, who would be the cause of twofold repetition, constantly in my presence and whose concerns, in my ordinary routine of school business, must inevitably, on account of the detestable coincidence, be often confounded with my own.

—Edgar Allan Poe, "William Wilson"

Because homosexuality has lacked a sanctioned discourse of its own, the "homosexual text" has had to conceal itself within the folds of a dominant discourse and conceal itself so skillfully that it could forestall any insinuation of its presence while still revealing itself through the mantling.[1] Until very recently, works that avowed same-sex passion have engaged in an intricate alternation of passing and coding, concealment and revelation. As Proust writes of the Parisian sodomites, "all of them obliged to protect their own secret but having their part in a secret shared with the others."[2]

These assertions are tautological since I am defining homosexuality as a condition that cannot enter language in earnest. The discourse I try to describe accepts its homosexuality as a pathology: Freud, for example, "enchains" and "encloses" homosexuality within the oedipal system as neurosis, because "in patriarchy, homosexuality can only be neurotic, can only be Oedipal failure."[3] Because of this baffled condition, these texts are as likely to express homophobia as homosexuality (if the division can even be made). What homosexuality is made aware of is its oppression, and homophobia is made aware of its excessive interest. The love that dare not speak its name infects even the original homophobic text: "the hall porter [at the Albermarle] handed him [Wilde] a card from the Marquess of Queensbury that said: 'To Oscar Wilde, posing as a somdomite.' In rage or ignorance the marquess had mispelled the key word."[4]

The revelation of this secret in the texts I am writing about is, by all accounts, a subtle, shifting, almost indeterminate style of signification. Parker Tyler writes that "it comes uninvited—circumstances bring one up against its unspeakable possibilities and all signs sneak into place"; Guy Hocquenghem writes, "Homosexual encounters are fixed by members of a secret fraternity which is visible only through the signs they exchange and which, for a brief moment, troubles the limpid serenity of the social structure"; and Harold Beaver writes that "homosexuals, like Masons, live not in an alternative culture but in a duplicate culture of constantly interrupted and overlapping roles. Every sign becomes duplicitous, slipping back and forth across a wavering line."[5] This textuality is far from the flamboyance of camp, which requires, according to Andrew Britton, "the *frisson* of transgression," a "sense of perversity in relation to bourgeois norms." The texts I speak of are not at all rebellious but most respectably constrained, one might even say terrorized by the possibility of a homophobic response. Camp, on the other hand, is outrageously manifest, but its excess can hypnotize: "It was Wilde's most paradoxical pose to mask his homosexuality by outbidding W. S. Gilbert's caricature, outbunthorning Bunthorne in velvets and lilies and bows, to suggest that he could not be what he seemed to be, when that is exactly what he was."[6]

It should not be surprising that the critic who took the play of semiotic codes as his subject was gay. Roland Barthes theorized homosexuality surreptitiously in writings like "The Grain of the Voice" (1972), *The Pleasure of the Text* (1973), and "Vocabulary" (1989) where "dragging" becomes a critical concept.[7] Harold Beaver cites a nightmare that Barthes recounts in *Fragments* (1977) as a coded presentation of homosexuality's exemption from the discourses of culture, a nightmare

> of a loved one falling ill in the street and, in his agony, asking for drugs. But everyone passed by and sternly refused, despite my frantic comings and goings. His anguish mounted to such an hysterical pitch that I reproached him, only to realize, a little later, that this person was me. Of course. Of whom else does one dream? I implored all the languages (the systems) passing by, who ignored me. Vociferously, *shamelessly*, I appealed for a philosophy that would "comprehend me"—would "embrace me."[8]

Freud's early bisexual model of individual development provides an obvious paradigm for how heterosexual texts contain and conceal homosexual texts. Homosexual discourse could even be theorized as a structural inevitability—textuality printing out the ontogeny of sexuality. Robin Wood writes, "if Freud was correct—and I see no reason to suppose otherwise—we should expect to find the traces of repressed homosexuality in every film, just as we should expect to find them in every person, usually lurking beneath the surface, occasionally rupturing it."[9]

In the first part of this essay, I want to survey three reasonably clear modes of homosexual coding (the homosexual writing that is *not camp*): cross-writing, displacement, and erasure. This is a rough set of strategies, and, as one might expect, the boundaries are blurred; in fact, the three techniques have a way of turning into one another.

Cross-writing involves reversing the gender or sexuality of the subject or the valence of the predicate. According to John Boswell,

> changing the gender of pronouns has been popular at least since Michelangelo's grandnephew employed this means to render his uncle's sonnets more acceptable to the public; and scholars have continued the ruse even where no one's reputation was involved: when the Persian moral fables of Saa'di were translated into English in the early nineteenth century, Francis Gladwin conscientiously transformed each story about gay love into a heterosexual romance by altering the offending pronouns. As late as the mid-twentieth-century, the *ghazels* of Hafiz were still being falsified in this way.[10]

The examples Boswell gives are only homophobic, but any number could be found in homosexual writers: as M. de Charlus describes one of his affairs, he recasts it pronominally—"I spring like a little usher . . . into the same car as the little person herself, of whom we speak in the feminine gender only so as to conform with the rules of grammar (as we say, in speaking of a Prince, 'Is His Highness enjoying *her* usual health')." Cross-writing is also called the "Albertine" strategy after Proust's admission to Gide that Albertine was modeled on a boy. Because of the William Beckford scandal, Byron "changed the gender of the dead beloved in his 'Thyrza' poems, which were a lament for John Edleston." Walt Whitman changed his poem, "Once I Pass'd Through a Populous City" before publication to alter the line "I remember only the man who wandered with me there for love of me" to "I remember only a woman I casually met there who detain'd me for love of me." Emily Dickinson changed gender-marked pronouns in her love poems before publication. Wilde heterosexualized his sonnet "Wasted Days," which began, "A fair slim boy not made for this world's pain," "into the better-known 'Madonna Mia'—beginning with 'A lily girl, not made for this world's pain.' "[11]

Crossing, as cross-reading, also takes place at the site of the reader without any manipulation of the text. There need be no structural or linguistic invitation. Most heterosexual fictions are sexually malleable: "once there [at the movies]," Richard Dyer remembers, "we could use the films—especially those *not* directly offering us images of ourselves—as we chose. We could practice on movie images what Claude Lévi-Strauss has termed *bricolage,* that is, playing around with the elements available to us in such a way as to bend their meaning to our own purposes."[12] Willa Cather, in works such as *The Lovely Lady* and "The Old Beauty," expresses the deep fascination of her male narrators for "lovely ladies." Even though women authors were expected to reproduce masculine imperatives in fiction, the presence of a woman author renders the fiction unstable, shifting it back and forth across the elusive line between heterosexuality and homosexuality, as the gender of the lover shifts between male and female.

Texts that *displace* homosexuality shift the locus of erotic energy to some acceptable form of male collaboration like sports, business, or adventure; or to some acceptable discourse: writing of Horatio Alger's tales, Michael Moon points out the congruence between the Christian rhetoric used by the older benefactors and an outlaw "rhetoric of seduction." In Henry James's tale, "The Collaboration," a French poet, Vendemer, and a German composer, Heidenmauer, become artistic collaborators, and this costs the Frenchman his fiancée because her mother cannot abide Germans. The tale is nominally devoted to the incompatibility between art and nationalism and, so positioned, the partnership can safely be described as a "monstrous collaboration," perverse, an abyss of shame and suffering, an "unnatural alliance," and an "unholy union." The reason given for the breakup is "*les femmes. . . .* they've a mortal hatred of art."[13]

The displacement of homosexuality into art is not merely an item in a series but one of the original names of the game, as Walter Pater, Henry James, Marcel Proust, and Oscar Wilde declare. Homosexual literature entered European culture en masse as aesthetic displacement. A substantial body of homosexual literature made its appearance during the fin-de-siècle as work officially lacking any relevant subject matter, concerned only with art for its own sake.[14]

Aestheticism often asks to be read homosexually. Pater's well-known exhortations in *The Renaissance,* which have been the cornerstones of a formalist university education, make gay sense: "*all art constantly aspires towards the condition of music.* For while in all other kinds of art it is possible to distinguish the matter from the form . . . yet it is the constant effort of art to obliterate it"; and "to burn always with this hard, gemlike flame, to maintain this ecstasy, is success in life." In the James tale, it is the sanctity of art that is said to motivate the reckless abandon with which the two men throw themselves into their collaboration and their indifference to the personal suffering it may involve.[15]

The aestheticization of homosexuality can also be read as the meaning of Willa Cather's "Paul's Case," not only within the tale but also in the outside commentary where a fiction of homosexual youth only gets read as a story about aesthetics, the overriding value of sensitivity to art.

Displacement in the form of sublimation was the destiny foretold for homosexuality by Freud. In his commentary on the case of *Senätsprasident* Schreber, he wrote that "homosexual tendencies are not . . . done away with or brought to a stop; they are merely deflected from their sexual aim and applied to fresh uses. They now . . . help to constitute the social instincts, thus contributing an erotic factor to friendship and comradeship, to *esprit de corps* and to the love of mankind in general."[16]

The love "triangle" is a conventional figure for heterosexuality, but in her book *Between Men* Eve Kosofsky Sedgwick identifies it as a primary figure for homosexual love. Expanding René Girard's work on triangular relationships in literature, she regards heterosexuality as dyadic; in its triangular form it is already subverted. The triangle sets up a dynamic shuttle for containing, distributing, displacing, and confusing homosexual and heterosexual energies because "in any erotic rivalry, the bond that links the two rivals is as intense and potent as the bond that links either of the rivals to the beloved." As Rictor Norton points out, the homosexual ambience of the love triangle, "even in modern television situation comedy . . . can still be detected by the fact that one of the men is not merely a strange interloper, but in nearly every case *the best friend* of the other."[17]

Norton names a second technique of displacement after Marlowe's unfinished poem "Leander," where the attention of the reader is diverted from a story of Leander's love for the priestess Hero "to a subplot involving the rape of Leander by Neptune, who mistakes him for Ganymede." The subplot is more interesting than the plot, "coming much closer to Marlowe's own sexuality, but it is still contained within an acceptably heterosexual frame."[18] In Rouben Mamoulian's *Queen Christina,* the two units are jammed together. The film begins as the story of a woman-loving woman who dresses in men's clothes and moves without any sense of rupture into the story of a grand heterosexual passion.

The relationship between the homosexual text and a larger category of the literature of the oppressed can also be figured as displacement. The homosexual text can easily pass itself off as a story about other deviancies, in Whitman's *Franklin Evans,* for example, as a story of alcoholism but one in which the language, particularly in the opening plea to the reader, "fits" homosexuality.[19]

Homosexuality can be displaced to the metaphoric or stylistic level as well as to a subplot. The following figure, for example, appears in Stendhal's *Ar-*

mance, one of the works identified by Jean-Paul Aron as erasing homosexuality and substituting impotence: "his was one of those minds which their natural pride places in the position of a girl who appears without rouge in a drawing room where the use of rouge is general; for the first few minutes her pallor makes her appear sad." Melissa Knox has described James's style as "decoration for the sake of decoration, piled on top of the narrative, which it sometimes obscures. . . . [he] seems to be using words and phrases the way a woman uses cosmetics and jewelry—to decorate, conceal and ultimately call attention to himself."[20]

"There is a social mechanism," Guy Hocquenghem writes, "forever wiping out the constantly renewed traces of our buried desires. One simply has to think about what happens with an experience as widespread as masturbation to realize how powerful this mechanism is: everybody has masturbated, yet no one ever mentions it, not even to their closest friends." The most basic form of textual *erasure* is the destruction of language: "Sappho's story provides the best-known example of systematic obliteration."

> [Deletion] may range from the omission of a single word which indicates gender (as is common where the original would reveal that the love object in the *Rubaiyat* is in fact male) to an entire work, like the *Amores* of Pseudo-Lucian, which Thomas Francklin excised from his translation because it contained a dispute about which sex was preferable as an erotic focus for males.[21]

If, in the cross-written text, the gender of the pronouns or the valence of the predicate is switched, in the erased text the pronouns are indeterminate. Homosexuals can make their love poetry "universal by hiding the gender of the beloved in neuter pronouns," a form of passing that Norton calls "pronoun pathology."[22] Such as aesthetic of indeterminacy haunts the songs of Cole Porter. By refusing to mark gender in his lyrics, Porter produces a situation where the heterosexual and homosexual text coincide. Unlike the other major lyricists of the period, Porter either leaves his pronouns open throughout the song ("Easy to Remember," "Everytime We Say Goodbye," "I Love You," "You Do Something To Me") or, if he has to make a heterosexual resolution, holds it off as long as possible. Unlike Ira Gershwin's "Somebody Loves Me," where the fourth line stipulates gender—"I wonder who she can be"—a song like "I Get a Kick Out of You" leaves one poised between hetero- and homosexuality until the very end when it is forced to conclude (ambiguously even then), "Flying too high/with some guy/in the sky." "Night and Day" foregrounds this habit by featuring the ungendered form of the pronoun: "A voice within me, keeps repeating, 'you, you, you.' "[23]

Erasure may disfigure a work in a form of amnesia. In the fictions of

Horatio Alger as read by Michael Moon, for example, a strong homosexual resonance is simply ignored or elided: culture exercises a hypnotic function so that what is patently there is not registered, for some readers, for some time. According to Arthur Laurents, the screenwriter of *Rope,*

> we never discussed, Hitchcock and I, whether the characters . . . were homosexuals, but I thought it was apparent. I guess he did too, but it never came up until we got to casting. . . . Eventually John Dall and Farley Granger played the boys, and they were very aware of what they were doing. Jimmy Stewart, however, who played the teacher, wasn't at all. And if you asked Hitchcock, he'd tell you it isn't there, knowing perfectly well that it is. He was interested in perverse sexuality of any kind, and he used it for dramatic tension. But being a strong Catholic, he probably thought it was wrong.

Although Glenn Ford remarked in an interview that he and George Macready "knew we were supposed to be playing homosexuals" in *Gilda,* director Charles Vidor laughed, "Really? I didn't know the boys were supposed to be that way!"[24]

But homosexuality is never really erased from the stories it has once inhabited; understanding of its presence flickers on and off like the lights on an old-fashioned movie marquee. It can also be present and absent in a more categorical way, as a fiction that is allowed epistemological status for a while and then peeled off as a falsity and thrown away (without a backward glance or a second thought). Vito Russo writes that "three of the first four American releases to deal with homosexuality in a major way used it only as the subject of a false accusation made against ultimately heterosexual characters: *A View from the Bridge, Walk on the Wild Side, Advise and Consent,* and *The Children's Hour.*" Whereas cross-writing allows one to preserve the illusion that the fiction of the text is heterosexual, this mode of erasure indulges the belief that the fiction is homosexual and then crosses at the last moment. In James Fenimore Cooper's *Jack Tier* and Bayard Taylor's *Joseph and His Friends* (as in Shakespeare's *Twelfth Night*), a homosexual love affair that has occupied most of the text is inverted, in the first by having the beloved be a woman in a pants role and in the second by having the lover swerve aside slightly and marry his friend's look-alike sister.[25]

In these instances, homosexuality is both present and absent, and that circumstance makes its condition in the text analogous to that of the fetishistic film signifier itself, dedicated, according to Christian Metz, to concealing and revealing the body of desire. Homosexuality is revealed only to be concealed through disavowal and concealed only to be revealed through the mechanism of the symptom: "seeking to conceal his homosexuality, James cultivates a style that expresses it."[26] Homosexuality in the movies has traditionally been governed by an outrageous oxymoron whereby actors like Edward Everett Horton, Franklin Pangborn, Eric Blore, and Grady Sutton absolutely were not and certainly were homosexual men.

There have been various attempts made to stabilize the homosexual text. Genres and tropes have been put forward as certain signs of homosexual presence—the Arcadian pastoral, the bathing scene, and the *formosus puer* or beautiful boy. George Stambolian and Elaine Marks ask if there is "a distinctly homosexual imagination or relationship to creativity," a homosexuality typology, topography, intertextuality, or homosexual discourse. Michel Foucault has offered a structural proposition: the experience of heterosexuality

> has always consisted of two panels, on the one hand, the panel of courtship in which the man seduces the woman, and, on the other hand, the panel of the sexual act itself. . . . In contrast the modern homosexual experience has no relation at all to courtship. . . . This is why the great homosexual writers of our culture (Cocteau, Genet, Burroughs) can write so elegantly about the sexual act itself, because the homosexual imagination is for the most part concerned with reminiscing about the act rather than anticipating it.[27]

Christine Rochefort regards homosexual literature as part of a larger other, the literature of the dominated, where homosexuality exchanges easily with "the whole of the third world culture" and women's literature (which dooms it to renewed invisibility). As Rochefort describes this vast cross-writing project, it clearly involves an attenuation of meaning: "it is difficult not to distort one's thinking in using the language of the oppressor. One must almost write as if twice removed, frame everything in irony and derision."[28]

But the distinction *heterosexual/homosexual* was always in a state of collapse, and this further interferes with a readable topography. As Eve Sedgwick has written in her recent book *Epistemology of the Closet,* "the violently contradictory and volatile energies . . . in our society show over and over again how preposterous is anybody's urbane pretense at having a clear, simple story to tell about the outlines and meanings of what and who are homosexual and heterosexual," and she lists twenty-six random ways in which individuals can be sexually differentiated.[29]

To assert manliness, for example, is not to assert heterosexuality but to assert heterosexuality or homosexuality indeterminately. The films most devoted to manliness most eliminate or marginalize women, create any number of occasions for the spectacular display of the body, and stage passion and physical contact between men. Parker Tyler sees the exaggerated heterosexuality of Wilde's *The Importance of Being Earnest* as an index of its homosexuality, and Bosley Crowther, reviewing *Goldfinger,* "identified the super-masculine pose of James Bond as 'what we're now calling homosexual sarcasm.' "[30]

I want to end by trying and failing to read a homosexual text—failing because the work has no other story to tell, other, that is, than the story of its own interference. The work is Vincente Minnelli's *The Bad and the Beautiful,* and it is a cross-written text by a homosexual Hollywood director about a successful Hollywood producer of melodramas.[31] It is an uncommon work for Hollywood because it treats an unlikable hero who is both unpaired and overpaired. The primary relationship shifts between the producer Jonathan Shields and two men and a woman (the woman is in the middle)—Fred Amiel, a director; Georgia Lorrison, the dipsomaniac daughter of a famous actor; and James Lee Bartlow, a southern college professor turned scriptwriter. Insofar as the title tells us that the film's central story is about Jonathan and Georgia it lies; the film is neatly divided among the three relationships, and no one is featured more than the others. At the end of the film, all three "lovers" are still available to Jonathan.

Jonathan is narcissistic and manipulative; his careerism leads him to violate every friendship and betray every trust. The film, then, is the story of a hero's improper behavior, and the paradox on which it opens also spells disgrace: Jonathan has won five Oscars but cannot raise five cents on his name. We are never told why Jonathan must break off relations with people who are attracted to him, but, paradoxically, those he betrays are not only unharmed but actually benefit by his immorality. Jonathan remains an enigma, his deep character too complex to exhibit.

The film opens as heterosexual parody with Fred on a dolly tracking down to a supine beauty in a low-cut dress. And this mode is sustained throughout by Lana Turner who plays Georgia, particularly in her scenes with a "burning" method actor like Kirk Douglas. Because of her low self-esteem and her drinking problem, she makes a terrible screen test, and, as a consequence, everyone is allowed to say that she is a wretched actress: Jonathan ("I've been trying to find one decent foot of film on you. Is there any?"), the English director ("The girl is impossible, wooden, gauche, artificial"), the studio public relations man ("She stinks"), and the associate producer ("The test was atrocious, for nothing you get nothing").

Almost all the heterosexual romances in the film are ruthlessly stage-managed by Jonathan.[32] At the beginning of the film, he "marries" Fred and a woman, Kay, at the beach: "It's time you two made it legal. . . . Just tell him yes, Kay. . . . I just happen to have a ring with me"; and he arranges to get a sluttish leading man, Victor "Gaucho" Ribera, to act for him by providing him with a woman. When Gaucho tries to return the favor, however, the exchange is curiously elided: Gaucho comes into his office tossing over the keys to his new car. He points the car out to Jonathan, and we see that Lila, a sultry starlet, comes along with it. He holds up the keys and asks, "How would you like to drive it around the block? It's as smooth a ride as you will ever have," but Jonathan says he's too busy.

The relationship between Jonathan and Georgia is severely one-sided: she languishes for him but his interest is only professional, that is, he must woo her in order to restore her self-confidence as an actor.[33] This connection, however, is superimposed upon an earlier, passionate relationship between Jonathan and Georgia's father: "He gave me my first drink at thirteen, at fourteen my first cigar, and when I was fifteen—he taught me the facts of life. He was a great actor—and a great man," and Georgia adds, "He was a rat, and a drunk." Georgia later says, "Careful, Mr. Shields, you're looking at me but you see my father."

What Jonathan must teach Georgia is how to be glamorous. She apparently lacks this sense of the fullness of the female self which Jonathan (like George Cukor or Vincente Minnelli) possesses. He finally turns Georgia into a great actor, directing her in a love scene that galvanizes everyone on the set. This is the film that constitutes the scandal of the opening, a film that is defective for other (unstated) reasons. Rather than release a "bad" movie, he buries it and bankrupts himself.

In order to free James Lee to write this important movie for him, Jonathan must first get his interfering wife out of the way. He arranges to have Gaucho occupy Rosemary while he sequesters himself in a mountain cabin with her husband. After Gaucho crashes his plane, killing himself and Rosemary, the two men become very intimate: in one scene, Jonathan sits on the arm of James Lee's chair, a hand on his shoulder: "She's dead and you're alive. You can't do anything about it and neither can I. Let's get to work"—and sweet music fills the frame. A montage follows and James Lee says in a voiceover, "without Jonathan, I don't know what I'd have done those next few months. He put me to work and kept me working." We see Jonathan packing his pipe, putting it in his mouth and lighting it for him. Jonathan later betrays his responsibility for Rosemary's death, but he is far from repentant and justifies his behavior in a harsh misogynist outburst: "she was a fool, she wasted your time, she wasted you."

Male relationships are marked as erotic. The bond between Jonathan and Fred has a sparkle that the relationship between Jonathan and Georgia lacks.

After their accidental meeting at the funeral of Jonathan's father, Fred is driven to seek out Jonathan and goes to his empty mansion. He finds that he can talk confidentially to Jonathan and immediately confesses that he can't advance his career because he's tongue-tied when it comes to selling himself, but, he admits after a pause, "I'm not so tongue-tied with you"—a line repeated later, "Ah, I could always talk to you." The bond between Jonathan and James Lee is intimate in another way: Fred loves or likes Jonathan at first sight, James Lee dislikes and grows to hate Jonathan before he succumbs to his charm. After the collapse of Jonathan's empire, James Lee wants to take *him* away to a cabin by a lake: "I've taken a cabin in Tahoe. I'm gonna finish my new book, and you're coming along. I work better with you around." Jonathan agrees eagerly, and that is when he betrays himself—as if he can't accept the possibility of their being together.

When the picture is finished, Jonathan drops out of sight. We have been told that he always experiences a black depression when he completes a picture. When this was set up early in the film, it figured heterosexual disgust: in the drive along the beach that ends with Jonathan and Fred impulsively breaking into the Lorrison mansion and meeting Georgia for the first time, Jonathan tells Fred, "When I work on a picture, it's like romancing a girl. You see her, you want her, you go after her . . . then the let-down, the after-picture blues."

When Jonathan does not come to the cast party, Georgia goes to his mansion with a bottle of champagne. He tells her of his depression as if it were a shameful thing—"After a picture's finished, something happens to me. It gets worse, I can't help it"—and tells her repeatedly to leave. She will not be warned off, and as she hugs him, a shadow eclipses their faces, the shadow of a drunk and smirking Lila on the stairs. In a movie that is patently false but hysterically valid, Minnelli insists on casting the shadow of an unworthy lust over the face of "true love." In a dead voice, Jonathan says to Georgia, "Now will you go back," and then, in an extraordinary burst of rage, he cries out, "Stop looking like that. . . . Maybe I like to be cheap once in a while. Get that look off your face, who gave you the right to turn me inside out and decide what I'm like?"

I cannot extract a buried story from Minnelli's film because no homosexual story ever gets told although its presence is felt everywhere. The text's energy goes into the activities of crossing, displacing, and erasing the master text. At the point of recovery, however, it is finally unclear what has been lurking in the folds. Is it another text or is it merely the text of interference? Or is it the wasting of the text as Harold Beaver says of the homosexual himself: "Like a cannibal, it might be charged, he exploits all ideas, messages, and roles by orgiastically wasting their content merely for the form, the vicarious fantasy, and then wearing them like a feather, or foreskin, in his cap."[34]

Notes

1. Homosexuality "scarcely put two words together until the bourgeois triumph of the Second Empire: there is no organized expression, no body of concepts for this dangerous subject matter. When it expresses itself through the language of the day, it does so almost imperceptibly in legal reports or very furtively, very elliptically in medical treatises. The reporters, the magistrates, the practitioners who evoke these 'nauseating phenomena,' dwell upon their reluctance to discuss the matter and complain that their pens are being defiled" (Jean-Paul Aron and Roger Kempf, "Triumphs and Tribulations of the Homosexual Discourse," in *Homosexualities and French Literature: Cultural Context/Critical Text*, ed. George Stambolian and Elaine Marks [Ithaca: Cornell University Press, 1979], 141–42). See also Louie Crew ("the inability to speak in one's authentic voice is a recurrent theme of homosexual literature"); he quotes Whitman's line, "the word unsaid must stay unsaid, though there was much to say" (Crew and Rictor Norton, "The Homophobic Imagination," *College English* 36, no. 3 (1974): 274; and D. A. Miller: "with homosexuality as with nothing else, what is connoted may not be denoted" ("Anal *Rope*," *Representations* 32 (Fall 1990): 119.

2. Marcel Proust, *Cities of the Plain*, vol. 2 of *Remembrance of Things Past* (New York: Random House, 1927), 15.

3. Guy Hocquenghem, *Homosexual Desire* (London: Allison and Busby, 1978), 59, 65, and 99.

4. Ted Morgan, *Maugham* (New York: Simon and Schuster, 1980), 37; see also Crew and Norton, "Homophobic Imagination," 273.

5. Parker Tyler, *Screening the Sexes: Homosexuality in the Movies* (New York: Holt, Rinehart and Winston, 1972), 107; Hocquenghem, *Homosexual Desire*, 75; and Harold Beaver, "Homosexual Signs (*In Memory of Roland Barthes*)," *Critical Inquiry* 8, no. 1 (1981): 105.

6. Andrew Britton, "For Interpretation—Notes against Camp," *Gay Left* 7 (1979); and Jack Babuscio, "Camp and the Gay Sensibility," in *Gays and Film*, ed. Richard Dyer (London: British Film Institute, 1977), 41.

7. Roland Barthes, "Vocabulary," *Semiotexte* 4, no. 1 (1989): 206.

8. Beaver, "Homosexual Signs," 115. According to John Mowitt, Barthes "once fantasized about writing a book on homosexuality," but never did. He never placed "his theory of the text explicitly in the service of gay scholarship, and this despite the fact that during the 1970s such scholarship was beginning to flourish within the West. Rather than conclude, however, that this represents some failure of nerve or lack of commitment on his part, I would argue that Barthes' critical practice was, in fact, engaged in such scholarship, but in a way that reflects his characteristic propensity for reconceptualizing issues" (*Text: The Genealogy of an Antidisciplinary Object* [Durham, N.C.: Duke University Press, 1992], 132).

9. Robin Wood, "The Homosexual Subtext: *Raging Bull*," *Australian Journal of Screen Theory*, no. 15–16 (1983): 59.

10. John Boswell, *Christianity, Social Tolerance, and Homosexuality* (Chicago: University of Chicago Press, 1980), 18.

11. Proust, *Cities of the Plain*, 10; Rictor Norton, *The Homosexual Literary Tradition: An Interpretation* (New York: Revisionist Press, 1974), 296; Seymour Kleinberg, "Homophobia in English Culture," *Review*, no. 8 (1986): 142; Robert K. Martin, *The Homosexual Tradition in American Poetry* (Austin: University of Texas Press, 1974), 4; Karen Keener, "Out of the Archives and Into the Academy," *College English* 44, no. 3 (1982): 309; and Norton, *Homosexual Literary Tradition*, 23.

12. Dyer, *Gays and Films*, 1.

13. Michael Moon, "'The Gentle Boy from the Dangerous Classes': Pederasty, Domesticity, and Capitalism in Horatio Alger," *Representations* 19 (Summer 1987): 88; and James, *The Complete Tales*, ed. Leon Edel (Philadelphia: J. B. Lippincott, 1962–65), 428–30, 418.

14. This gets confused in commentary with an almost essentialist alliance between homosexuality and art: "deprived of their own distinctive codes, homosexuals make art itself into their distinctive code" (Beaver, "Homosexual Signs," 106); or "homosexuals have pinned their integration into society on promoting the aesthetic sense" (Susan Sontag, *Against Interpretation and Other Essays* [New York: Farrar, Straus and Giroux, 1966], 290).

15. Walter Pater, *The Renaissance* (New York: Modern Library, n.d.), 111 and 197; and James, *Complete Tales*, 425.

16. Freud, "Psycho-Analytic Notes on an Autobiographical Account of a Case of Paranoia," *Standard Edition* (London: Hogarth Press, 1958), 12:61.

17. Eve Kosofsky Sedgwick, *Between Men: English Literature and Male Homosexual Desire* (New York: Columbia University Press, 1985), 20; and Norton, *Homosexual Literary Tradition*, 145. The homosocial triangle can also be found in psychoanalysis in the joke structure of Freud and, in anthropology, in the exchange of women between two males as interpreted by Claude Lévi-Strauss and Luce Irigaray: because heterosexual trading takes place "mainly or even exclusively among men," homosexuality is not "deviant and marginal to the established order, but rather . . . its endogamous basis" (Herbert Blau, "Disseminating Sodom," *Salmagundi*, special issue: "Homosexuality: Sacrilege, Vision, Politics," nos. 58–59 [1982–1983]: 234–35).

18. Norton, *Homosexual Literary Tradition*, 99.

19. Roger Austen, *Playing the Game: The Homosexual Novel in America* (Indianapolis: Bobbs-Merrill, 1977), 8.

20. Aron and Kempf, "Triumphs and Tribulations of the Homosexual Discourse," 142; Stendhal [Marie-Henri Beyle], *Armance* (Greenwich, Conn.: Fawcett, 1960), 26; and Melissa Knox, "*Beltraffio*: Henry James's Secrecy," *American Imago* 43, no. 3 (1986): 215, 221.

21. Hocquenghem, *Homosexual Desire*, 35; Keener, "Out of the Archives," 74–75; and Boswell, *Christianity*, 19.

22. Martin, *Homosexual Tradition*, 108; and Rictor Norton, cited in Jacob Stockinger, "Homotextuality: A Proposal," *The Gay Academic*, ed. Louie Crew (Palm Springs, Calif.: ETC, 1978), 145.

23. Unlike Berlin, Gershwin, or Hart, Porter also forces the voice to shift into falsetto, or "girl," as in the third verse of "Night and Day."

24. Vito Russo, *The Celluloid Closet: Homosexuality in the Movies* (New York: Harper and Row, 1981), 94, 78.

25. Ibid., 136; and Austen, *Playing the Game*, 7–10.

26. Knox, "*Beltraffio*," 221.

27. Stambolian and Marks, *Homosexualities*, 27–28, 24; and James O'Higgins, "Sexual Choice, Sexual Act: An Interview with Michel Foucault," *Salmagundi* (1983): 18–19.

28. Christine Rochefort, "The Privilege of Consciousness," in Stambolian and Marks, *Homosexualities*, 108, 109.

29. Eve Kosofsky Sedgwick, *Epistemology of the Closet* (Los Angeles: University of California Press, 1990), 54, 23. In his monograph on Leonardo da Vinci, which attempts to chart the difference between homosexual and heterosexual, Freud also stages the collapse of that difference in a personal narrative drama. In his self-fictionalization, Freud alternates between postures of feminine fear and helplessness and masculine control. The essay ends with a homosexual confession: "like others I have succumbed to the attraction of this great and mysterious man" ("Leonardo da Vinci and a Memory of His Childhood," *Standard Edition*, 11:84).

30. Tyler, *Screening the Sexes,* 36–37; and Russo, *Celluloid Closet,* 155.

31. Minnelli's biography is not clear about "whether he was gay or genuinely bisexual. But his creation of a particular style of cinema is sufficiently striking to merit attention. While Cocteau's Gaystyle is classical, Minnelli's is New York rococo, all curlicue, penthouse chiffon and the New Look" (Noel Purdon, "Gay Cinema," *Cinema Papers* [Australia] 10 [1976]: 118).

Minnelli divided himself between musicals and melodramas, the staples of cinematic camp, but these two genres also divide as the camp and the homosexual text. "A set of still frames from *American in Paris* alone," Purdon writes, "would provide a catalogue of the classic gestures and facial expressions of camp" (118), and Minnelli's *The Pirate* is totally given over to camp, a consequence, perhaps, of the double influence of Minnelli and Cole Porter (Porter is able to slip "flaming" and "masculinity" into the same line at least twice).

32. "True" heterosexual passion is framed as a quotation: the theater where the sneak preview is held is showing *Anna Karenina* with Fredric March and Greta Garbo.

33. Jonathan thus performs within the film what Minnelli had to do outside it: "my challenge was to make her portrayal a series of short curves [because Turner could not act over any length of time]. I wouldn't allow her to indulge her insecurities as an actress, and I called on many ruses and subterfuges to extract a performance from her" (Vincente Minnelli, *I Remember It Well* [London: Angus and Robertson, 1975], 254.

34. Beaver, "Homosexual Signs," 100.

Roland Barthes:

TOWARD AN *"ÉCRITURE GAIE"*

ROBERT K. MARTIN

> The political significance of writing is not simply a matter of political
> content or of an author's overt political commitment but also of the
> work's engagement with a culture's literary ordering of the world.[1]

Jonathan Culler's summary of Roland Barthes's position on politics in *Writing Degree Zero* might be adapted easily to represent Barthes's position on his own homosexuality or on sexuality in general: the sexual significance of writing is not simply a matter of sexual content or of an author's overt sexual commitment (or orientation), but also of the work's engagement with a culture's literary ordering of the world. This would indeed be the position enunciated by Barthes late in his life in the preface to Renaud Camus's *Tricks*, that one can write homosexually without writing homosexuality. Homosexuality is a style, not a subject matter. (As Lee Edelman puts it, arguing for a historically based rhetorical criticism, "the sphere of lesbian and gay criticism need not be restricted to the examination of texts that thematize gay sexuality or dramatize homosexual desire.")[2] Barthes's work envisages the creation of an *écriture gaie*, parallel to the *écriture féminine* that his theoretical writings also helped define.

It is not surprising that this important issue has gone almost entirely unnoticed in the reception of Barthes. Although two of the most important postmodern theorists—Barthes and Michel Foucault—were homosexual, the question has been elided in their reception both in France and in North America. Since Barthes in particular only occasionally writes (transitive) homosexuality, it has been easy not to see his sexuality as a crucial part of his art. This has not, of course, precluded some of the most vitriolic attacks on Barthes, which have been grounded precisely in cultural homophobia.

The most offensive of these attacks came in a 1986 review of *The Rustle of*

Language in the *New York Times Book Review,* by Harold Brodkey, tellingly titled "A Totalitarianism of Pleasure." Brodkey's target is largely that mythologized bogeyman, the 1960s, whose "failure . . . as a way to live or govern or think leaves us in a general wreckage of language (and doctrine),"[3] but he makes Barthes his particular target, while totally misrepresenting him as "a figure on the barricades" in 1968. The reasons for the particular scorn of Barthes become clearer when Brodkey denounces Barthesian pleasure (by which he means bliss, in fact) as the product of a "vicarious street boy" created by "Sade, Genet and Gide." However outrageous Brodkey's attack, it at least has the merit of recognizing the role of sexuality in Barthes where other readers have been silent, and of situating Barthes's origins in the Paris of 1968, the moment at which he parted company from Michel Foucault, choosing what we might call utopianism over cynicism. As Steven Ungar has put it, "where Foucault goes on to trace the disappearance of the individual within discourse, Barthes seeks to reassert the possibility of individual utterance as an act of resistance against such disappearance."[4] Barthes's proclamation of the death of the author referred only to the institutional power of the Author, and in no way prevented him from writing ever more in the confessional mode.

Although the "utopian" side of Foucault is always there—in his work for gay liberation and the liberation of prisoners and mental patients—it is increasingly muted in his later work. He nonetheless continues to suggest the existence of an unmediated being, one not yet or classified. Such a being is, for instance, the homosexual before homosexuality, before the creation of the "espèce" out of the "pratique."[5] Such a being is also Foucault's Herculine Barbin, capable of being read as male or female. The fluidity of his/her identity suggests a self yet to be made, or constantly remakeable, ultimately *polysémique.* Barthes had of course found such a subject a number of years earlier in the hero/heroine of Balzac's *Sarrasine.* It is here that Barthes and Foucault largely part company, for Barthes's response to the events of 1968 is to turn ever more toward a visionary poetics of sexual affirmation that seeks to employ language as a tool for the recuperation of the erotic. Barthes's utopianism has, as always, a strong echo of Fourier as well as Sade and is constituted at the level of body and language (*langue*).

Drawing on a Foucaldian analysis of discourse for his understanding of the plight of the artist who misreads Zambinella's sexuality because he lacks the code provided by the social context, and sharing a Foucaldian distaste for an inquisitive science of sexual power, Barthes looks toward the rediscovery of a radical social potential in the sexually ambiguous, and links this to the resistance of the unshaped to the forces of a shaping world. Far from viewing Zambinella as *lacking,* as the castrated male, as some critics have argued,

Barthes celebrates a supplément, the protean being of a sexuality that eludes capture and that constantly reasserts itself through language. This state is represented for Barthes by the neuter, a term as lacking in French grammar as in conventional sexual binarism. Although the term may evoke absence, for Barthes it is the middle ground, an *au-delà* of masculine and feminine, so striking in a language where every object must have one of two genders.

Barthes's radical critique of textuality, which decenters the text by constantly redirecting our attention to its margins, is part of a larger strategy of sexual politics that aims at replacing copulation by masturbation, production by pleasure, meaning by connotation. To what is ordinarily thought of as politics, Barthes has added both the politics of sexuality and the politics of literary form. Barthes's sexual/literary politics are directly related to the discovery at the center of *S/Z*, what we might call the reappropriation of sexual ambiguity. Along with Foucault, Barthes demonstrated the arbitrary nature of sexual definition, the extent to which our sexualities are shaped by the larger social discourse. This endeavor is important for both Foucault and Barthes as a way of validating what has been thought of as a "marginal" sexuality, and replacing it at the center of Western history and art. Their work is the most important aspect at the present time of an attempt to establish and define the nature of a homosexual language.

Stressing the role of these male critics in an attack upon patriarchal language and culture is by no means meant to suggest that the homosexual critique is the only way of challenging that traditional authority. Obviously much of what I say about the strategies of Barthes could be said of many feminist and postmodernist theoreticians as well. Indeed what is important is the recognition of the ways in which male authors and critics, working within a patriarchal tradition, may nonetheless begin a subversive critique of that tradition through an exploration of the potential of male homosexuality.[6] The very structures of that sexuality, its (at least potential) absence of the creation of an *other* who is always object of desire and never subject, offer the possibility of creating a language and politics of mutuality.

This potential in the work of Barthes and of Foucault has been neglected by the cultural process of silencing that has operated to desexualize them. Of course, to some extent, the silencing is accomplished in their texts themselves, in the ways Barthes or Foucault elides his own sexuality. However reluctant they have been to define themselves *as* homosexuals (a reluctance related not only to *pudeur* and a French claim to nonchalance about sexuality, but even more to the questioning of fixed definitions themselves, particularly in the light of Foucault's understanding of the disciplinary power of sexual categories), they have certainly provided the means for establishing what one may think of as a gay reading of the texts. In the case of Barthes, this may be seen most clearly in his emphasis on "the Goddess Homosexuality" in *Roland Barthes par Roland Barthes* (68).[7] But despite such clues, the process of critical reception has operated to obscure this element, to straighten Barthes out, to take the orgasm (*jouissance*) out of the text.

What I term the "later" works of Barthes date from the publication of *S/Z* in 1970.[8] In that work Barthes clearly moves away from the structuralist positions with which he had been associated. On the very first page of *S/Z* Barthes rejects the concept of a single structure that underlies all works. The structuralist position is flawed, Barthes argues, because it denies the "différence" of each text. Against the practice of searching for the ideal, he calls for a critical practice that can "remettre chaque texte, non dans son individualité, mais dans son jeu" (9).[9] This recognition of the playfulness of the text is part of a strategy against interpretation, as Susan Sontag called it, one in which the ascribing of a meaning to a text is to be supplanted by recovering "de quel pluriel il est fait" (*S/Z*, 11).[10] Barthes's plural text is radically egalitarian, for it is not a matter of finally determining which access is the principal one, whether we accede to the text best by psychoanalysis, or theology, or politics. The number of systems of meaning is infinite, and hence there can be no determination of narrative structure or final meaning: "pour le texte pluriel, il ne peut y avoir de structure narrative, de grammaire or de logique du récit" (12).[11] Barthes's central assertion of play (here *jeu*) is the basis for his break with his own structuralist past, as well as with the dominant practice of French literary criticism, and lays the groundwork for his late critical texts.

My view of this sharp break in Barthes's career runs counter to the view expressed by Jonathan Culler, who argues that "much of what was heralded as 'post-structuralist' was in fact already conspicuous in structuralist writings" (78). However, since Culler acknowledges a major shift in Barthes's thinking as of *Le plaisir du texte*, the argument is perhaps not terribly important, a simple matter of shifting the date of the change a few years. But what I take to be Culler's error is also instructive, since it indicates a misperception about *S/Z*, one that permits it to be read as, in Culler's terms, "an intertextual construct, the product of various cultural discourses" (85), and hence ignores both the status of the text as parody and the role of Barthes's exploration of the fluidity of sexual definition. *Sarrasine*, the story that *S/Z* "analyzes," is itself concerned with sexual power, particularly that of the visual and the verbal, and with the absence at the heart of a socially constructed sexuality. Barthes's tactic, and it is a brilliant one, is to connect the act of sexual penetration with that of textual penetration. In the place of a teleological, vertical reading, we have a horizontal reading of notes to notes, diagrams, and appendices. The castrato male/

woman at the heart of Balzac's tale thus becomes a model for the sexually diffuse self that is to be freed into its own polymorphous polysemy, as for the deconstruction of a phallocentric economy of narrative and erotics.

The concept of play is central to Barthes's thinking not only as a matter of style, but more important, as one of politics, what we may call, adopting Marianne DeKoven's phrase, "the politics of linguistic structure." As she puts it, "our language is distorted . . . not by the male itself, but by the dominance of the male over the female, the Father over the Mother: conscious over unconscious, symbolic over presymbolic, signified over signifier."[12] The play of language is restored by the liberation of the signifier from its service to a unitary signified. The signifier enjoyed in its own right is the phallus released from aggression and production, treasured as a source of pleasure (*jouissance*) rather than as means to control, linguistic or social. For Barthes the restoration of play is an ultimately serious business: "l'enjeu de cette hiérarchie est sérieux: c'est retourner à la fermeture du discours occidental (scientifique, critique ou philosophique), à son organisation centrée, que de disposer tous les sens d'un texte en cercle autour du foyer de la dénotation (le foyer: centre, refuge, lumière de la vérité)" (13–14).[13] We must listen closely to Barthes's terms here, and indeed listen to their connotations as well as denotations. The hierarchy denotation/connotation is a system of closure based on the concept of the center. Language gathered around its center of meaning is like the family gathered around its fire, worshipping its *lares et penates*. Barthes's "foyer" is an indication of the degree to which Western systems of meaning are part of a larger structure of power. The point for Barthes is to decenter that circle, not so much to put out the fire as to disperse it.

As connotation replaces denotation, meaning is no longer situated *within* but rather *alongside*. A fraternity of meanings comes to supplant the traditional hierarchy of meanings, based upon the oedipal and patriarchal. In this regard, one can see the links between Barthes's project and that of Robbe-Grillet, especially in his rewriting of *Oedipus* in *Les Gommes*. As words come alive and point to themselves rather than to a meaning *behind* them, so the larger structure of narrative is challenged. The equivalent to connotation at the level of narrative is digression, which Barthes places in opposition to what he terms the "discours du savoir" (19).[14] Digression is of course a form of deferral, or the trope, as Patricia Parker reminds us, of *dilatio*. To digress is to delay, to extend, to prolong: it amounts to a foreplay made over into play itself. If meaning, or knowledge, is the goal of language, then digression seems an obstacle, a way of delaying access to truth, or the achievement of climax. Viewed sexually, Barthes's notions of connotation and digression amount to a valorization of sexual play, to a reclamation of the body, radically different from the use or performance value of traditional patriarchy, however, since it is divorced from a functionalist meaning- or production-orientation.

We may, in other words, consider Barthes's as a utopian socialist vision of language, by seeing the connections between the linguistic concept of the signified, as a representative of a Western Logos, the literary concept of the narrative, with its progress toward climax or conclusion, and the economic/political concept of capital invested, and labor employed, for productivity. Our neglect of the playful, the digressive, the masturbatory, is analogous to our construction of a society of production. Thus our concern for a sexuality of use (all that is perverse that leads to no production) is an integral part of a social and linguistic system. Barthes begins his attack on this system at the level of language, for how can one possibly undertake to transform a society when the very language we employ reflects the values to be put into question? In this view, language is hardly neutral, and, far from being a mere matter of style, it is at the heart of our thinking and is at its base imperialistic. It is the role of "écriture" for Barthes to challenge this power of knowledge, by substituting the multiple for a unitary, the pleasurable for the productive, and thereby achieving a fluidity not of meaninglessness but of endlessly expanding meanings, rather than the simple "truths" of the dominant discourse: "Seule l'écriture, en assumant le pluriel le plus vaste possible dans son travail même, peut s'opposer sans coup de force à l'imperialisme de chaque langage" (212).[15]

The challenge to a unitary model of truth takes on particular importance in *S/Z*, Barthes's study, via Balzac, of sexual definition. Here narrative and sexuality are linked, both in the source and in the commentary. The narrator's tale seeks to reveal the truth (the absence that is a truth) and to exchange that truth for sexual service: a tale for a tail, or dare we say *un conte pour un con*. To know the truth is to have sexual power, indeed as Barthes suggests (42), to be the phallus. But if that truth is that there is no truth, that there is no phallus, then the sexual bargain must of course fail. The absent sex, the castrated male, the central void become in Barthes's rereading indications of a world lacking a central truth, to which all can be referred, at a metaphysical level, or a narrative without a conclusion, in literary terms (indeed, Barthes calls attention to Balzac's lack of closure in the tale's final line, "Et la marquise resta pensive":[16] instead of conclusion there is ellipsis). Balzac's story is particularly appropriate to Barthes's purposes since we as readers so easily fall into the trap of the meaningful. We are carried along wanting to know the answer to the mystery of the old man, and we seek that answer in an explanation of La Zambinella: is he or isn't she? Sarrasine's insistence upon *knowing*, like Oedipus', leads only to his own death.

Barthes's title places emphasis upon sexual/textual fluidity, and thus puts into question the most fundamental of all our dualistic structures. Sarrasine's own name is androgynous, since a French reader would expect the masculine form "Sarrasin" or the feminine "Sarrazine." The play upon s/z is thus a play upon mirror images, the social construction of gender out of the opposing self, as well as an allusion to the interplay of Barthes/Balzac. Neither Sarrasine nor Zambinella, neither s nor z is of fixed sex. Insofar as Sarrasine loves her, and sees in her ideal feminine beauty, Zambinella is a woman. She becomes a man again when Sarrasine discovers what she does *not* have; his essence becomes that which he lacks. This play upon sexuality suggests that Barthes's game is not merely to question our epistemology, but to assert a triumphant poly-morphous perversity as well. At the heart of Western art, in its idealization of women, there is a travesty/travesti(e).

Barthes's *mise en question* of gender definition obviously links him to a feminist critique of the definition of woman as other by lack. But it is also part of a strategy for claiming a plural sexuality, in which s flows into z, and back again. Like most French critics of the 1970s, Barthes conceives of sexualities rather than sexuality, and homosexualities rather than homosexuality.[17] In *Roland Barthes par Roland Barthes,* Barthes's outrageous critical study of him-self, the emphasis on the plural is linked to an attempt to deny sexual duality, and an important source of Barthes's linguistic concerns is located in this search for the transgression of boundaries:

> Qui sait si cette insistence du pluriel n'est pas une manière de nier la dualité sexuelle? In ne faut pas que l'opposition des sexes soit une loi de Nature; il faut donc dissoudre les affrontements et les paradigmes, pluraliser à la fois les sens et les sexes: le sens ira vers sa multiplication, sa dispersion (dans la théorie du texte), et le sexe ne sera pris dans aucune typologie (il n'y aura, par exemple, que *des* homosexualités, dont le pluriel déjouera tout discours constitué, centré, au point qu'il lui apparaît presque inutile d'en parler). (73)[18]

To pluralize and decenter meaning, to multiply the sensitive signifier are forms of challenging a system based on the oppositions male/female and straight/gay. Just as Zambinella is neither male nor female and at the same time both male and female, so the dichotomy heterosexual/homosexual is seen to be a matter of social construction. Barthes's thinking here joins the social con-structionism of Foucault to his own utopianism: significantly Barthes's tense in this passage is the future. The dominant discourse is deconstructed, or in Barthes's perfectly chosen word, un-played (Larousse: déjouer, faire échouer un projet, une intrigue). The stakes are considerable: if there is no center there can be no other, no difference when all is difference. Barthes's writing of the seventies thus stands apart from the dominant discourse of gay liberation with its assumption of fixed identity and its oppositional model; it is of course "paradisiaque," as it calls forth a world of continuous and undifferentiated pleasure(s).

Barthes uses Balzac's text to show the falseness of the male/female dichotomy and suggests instead that the characters in the tale may be distinguished by their relationship to castration. The castration of which he speaks is of course largely figurative, since Barthes adopts a Lacanian notion of the phallus, as the agent of empowerment. To be a Phallus is to be empowered, whereas, paradoxically, to have or possess the phallus is to be disempowered (42). Barthes thus works a change upon the Lacanian scheme, by making the receiver of the phallus, the biologically female, the "passive" male, hold power over the other's phallus. He also draws upon the concept of the gaze to subvert gender definition as it is inscribed in mythology and art, through the figure of Endymion. Barthes points out that the penetration of Endymion by the moonlight amounts to a "double inversion," punning of course on the term "inversion": "quoique féminine, la lune est active; quoique masculin, le garçon est passif" (*S/Z* 77).[19] Although social discourse ascribes masculinity to sunlight and femininity to moonlight, here the moonlight, figure of imagination and dream as opposed to science and knowledge, becomes the agent of power, but its object is no longer woman but the androgynous or castrated boy. The union of the phallic woman and the castrated man becomes Barthes's figure, out of Balzac, for a triumphant polysexuality in which all limits are transgressed.

Barthes's project is indeed part of a strategy of liberation, but he shifts that liberation from the signified to the signifier. To overcome the power of the phallus, one must see how it is inscribed in our discourse, how fully we have accepted a language of power through knowledge. Balzac's sculptor becomes for Barthes a perfect figure of the desire to unmask, to continually probe further to a presumed final truth, at the center of which is located "le vide." Zambinella's castrated self, neither male nor female, is the unwritten text of the world. But insofar as art takes on a realistic or mimetic goal, it seeks to possess the truth. It is not surprising then that we have made such an important figure out of the artist and his naked model, for it is the function of the artist to penetrate even further until he possesses the object of his desire, makes it over into the work of art. Barthes's phrases show how clearly this is a desire at once epistemological and sexual: "L'artiste sarrasinien veut déshabiller l'apparence, aller toujours *plus loin, derrière* en vertu du principe idéaliste qui identifie le secret à la vérité: il faut donc passer *dans* le modèle, *sous* le statue, *derrière* la toile" (128).[20] But at the heart of the mystery is the mystery. There is no final meaning, no ultimate signified, but only an infinite series of signifiers, offering a ground for play. The only profit, as Barthes puts it in a telling metaphor, is ludic.

If *S/Z* is Barthes's renunciation of structuralism and his acknowledgment of the sexual metaphor for artistic or philosophical knowledge, his next work, *Le plaisir du texte*, takes a poststructuralist position for granted (it is itself deliberately fragmented, offering only the conventional and false order of its index, in which alphabet and page numbering coincide!). *S/Z* sets out to overthrow the power of copulation, the assumption of male power upon the female subject. *Le plaisir* offers instead a utopian, masturbatory plural of sustained pleasure. To the traditional hero of romance, Barthes opposes his "contre-héros" in the form of the reader. (In the *scriptible* text, one recalls, it is the reader whose [re]reading *writes* the text.)

This reader achieves his new state, not by opposing contradiction but by ignoring it, by renouncing the cultural force of concepts of unity. Instead of man acting, seeking, finding, we now have man masturbating: "ce contre-héros existe: c'est le lecteur de texte dans le moment où il prend son plaisir" (10).[21] The site of bliss (*jouissance*) for Barthes is the clandestine, at its highest or lowest appropriately, in the darkness of the cinema, in the masturbating spectator (of both the film and the erotic scripts enacted around or with him). Such a program may, Barthes realizes, seem like an escape from politics. But this he attributes merely to a traditional association of pleasure with right-wing politics. The puritanism of the left has too often ignored the social and revolutionary potential of pleasure (one recalls Barthes's championing of Sade). To do so is to ignore the role of repression in social organization, to ignore Freud's explanation in *Civilization and Its Discontents* of society's need to control the erotic in the name of production. Pleasure is a subversive force for Barthes because, he claims, it cannot be collectivized: pleasure is "à la fois révolutionnaire et asocial et ne peut être pris en charge par aucune collectivité, aucune mentalité, aucune idiolecte" (39).[22] The individual with his or her text, en train de prendre son plaisir, is Barthes's figure of resistance to mass culture and political power. Sexual taste, despite the power of collective images, remains stubbornly personal and perverse, a site for the realization of desires that contradict the order outside the dark rooms.

Language thus becomes an important element in the transformation of society, for it is in the very structures of language that power is embodied and conveyed. Every time we speak or write we reflect a structure of unitary meaning and of enforced subordination: it must always come down to subject and verb, or subject and copulative. The sentence is the clearest form of power structure: each element assigned a clear role in a unified structure of meaning.[23] Its closure is absolute, for as Barthes asks, "comment une hiérarchie pourrait-elle rester ouverte?" (*PT* 80).[24] Thus the discovery of an experimental language, the development of a prose freed from traditional norms of grammar and structure, is political. It puts into question the patriarchal structure of language (which is not of course to say that all experimental writing is by women or gay men, but rather that such language may become part of a strategy for combating the structures of thought that make up patriarchy).

By restructuring the sentence and the text the phallus can be liberated from its teleology. The domination of the teleological phallus is expressed not only in the Grail quest, but also in every narrative that seeks its end, its conclusion, its climax, as we so pertinently put it in English. If the text is to become polymorphous, protean, and textured, reading for its part becomes almost impossible except as a (re)creation or rewriting. One can observe this same phenomenon in many postmodern texts (but not in modernist texts, where it is a question rather of ambiguity, of meaning that is simply double and not infinitely multiplied), but it corresponds particularly well to a gay aesthetic, for the homosexual is by his/her nature, or rather lack of nature, *contra naturam*, never simple, never fixed. The homosexual is the product of the discourse of others, as the Jew is the product of the anti-Semite, in Sartre's formulation.

To recall that there is never an absolute homosexual, but only a cultural homosexual, it is useful to think of Arab countries where the distinction is made only, as Barthes noted in *Roland Barthes par Roland Barthes*, between active and passive, as in Greece, and not between homo- and hetero- sexual, as in modern northern European cultures. In the same section of his novel/auto-biography, Barthes declares, on the basis of his own "situation minoritaire" (Protestant and homosexual), that "le naturel n'est nullement un attribut de la Nature physique; c'est l'alibi dont se pare une majorité sociale" (*RB* 134).[25] In his/her lack of an object that is absolutely other, the homosexual is free to develop as a subject, to see his/her own body as a site of pleasure, to refuse sublimation. The homosexual text, like the homosexual body, will not produce meaning; it will be it. Such a text calls attention to itself, performs itself, or camps. As Susan Sontag put it, "the essence of Camp is its love of the un-natural: of artifice and exaggeration."[26] This is of course not a description of dominant gay literary practice, so much as it is an indication of Barthes's own sexual textuality and a call for a gay textuality freed from representation (although not from figuration).[27]

The weakness of the traditional Marxist position has been its belief that it is the subject of literature that matters, rather than its form. This conception is not surprising, given our cultural insistence on reading as an act of interpretation, of uncovering a hidden meaning. Literary study in this manner is compared by Barthes to a striptease: "toute l'excitation se réfugie dans l'*espoir* de voir le sexe (rêve de collégien) ou de connaître la fin de l'histoire (satisfaction romanesque)" (*PT* 20).[28] This of course was the connection drawn in *S/Z* as well. We have identified "satisfaction" ("I can't get no") with completion and achievement. What Barthes proposes is an aesthetics of process, in which nothing is ever complete, but always suspended. This amounts to diverting sexuality from its appropriation to the end of production, an appropriation reflected in all of our structures, from the most ordinary to the most "civilized." The structure of Barthes's early works is still there, underlying all our mythologies, but now it is contested. For narrative form and family structure are one. The sentence is the father of us all, to whom Barthes proposes we show our backsides (84),[29] an act of course, at once insulting and inviting. By re-eroticizing life we prevent its being channeled into something else, we resist the sublimation we are always told is the basis of culture. If all our bodies are constantly alive and alert, if the sexual antennae are never down, how then work, how achieve the finality of climax, how end the story?

Sexuality separated from procreation is ec-centric, consigned to the margins. So too the asides, the footnotes, the prefaces of a text. By challenging the hierarchy of the signified, Barthes allows us to place in question all such relations of value. Barthes reclaims the marginal, not by moving what has been termed marginal to the center, but by questioning the notion of the margin itself. His own textual practice is marvelously marginal, particularly in *S/Z*, the entire text of which is in effect a footnote to Balzac's tale: that footnote in turn having subsections, quotations, and footnotes. It is a perfect example of the plural text and of the critical act as rereading. Barthes's text does not supplant Balzac's but supplements it. Balzac is as much the margin of Barthes as Barthes is the margin of Balzac.

This radical textual politics accompanies Barthes's shift in his last decade to the presentation of the self through the text. What is important for Barthes is, as Susan Sontag has pointed out, the conversion of "write" into an intransitive verb: one does not write *something*, one simply *writes*. Increasingly Barthes makes clear his own sexuality and its central place in his thinking. When he writes his own biography and a critique of his own work, admittedly speaking "comme dit par un personnage de roman" (*RB* 123),[30] he calls attention to the pleasure granted by a perversion—and he cites "en l'occurrence"[31] homosexuality and hashish (68). Comme par hasard, as he might say, Barthes's text reproduces, as one of three *fiches* illustrating his way of working, a text that begins: "Homosexualité: tout ce qu'elle permet de dire, de faire, de comprendre, de savoir, etc." (*RB* 79).[32] Thus, though the final, or at least the published, text pluralizes the subject by playing on H (the name of the letter is slang for Hash[ish] in French), in its initial form the reference is clearly to the ways in which homosexuality provides a surplus, a way out of the fundamental dualism of our discourse. If homosexuality itself has been cast in those terms (i.e., the homosexual is the nonheterosexual), homosexual practice, in its refusal of such models, illustrates their arbitrary nature. How often gay men are asked, do you fuck or get fucked? Are you a subject or an object? Knowing that such questions are unanswerable, because they belong to another discourse entirely, one begins to see a way out of patriarchy, a way that may be pointed by gay men as well as by feminists. It is the path of refusal, of responding to the claims of fatherhood by not becoming one. This is Barthes's most visionary moment: "le sens et le sexe deviennent l'objet d'un jeu libre, au sein duquel les formes (polysémique) et les pratiques (sensuelles), libérées de la prison binaire, vont se mettre en état d'expansion infinie. Ainsi peuvent naître un texte gongorien et une sexualité heureuse" (RB 137).[33]

The idea of a masturbatory and autoerotic text is well defined in the famous conclusion of Le plaisir du texte, "ça granule, ça grésille, ça caresse, ça rape, ça coupe, ça jouit" (105).[34] To give back the materiality of the body to the body in its expression, its verbal manifestation: that is Barthes's project. This project corresponds to the transformation of a sexuality of production into one of jouissance, and to the re-eroticization of the whole body. The polymorphous pleasures of the homosexual are no longer, as they were for Freud, signs of perversity, the swerving from a supposed goal, but rather the marks of a self-sufficient textuality. Thus if one is seeking the homosexual text, one should not start with the story, which is always banal, any more than one is likely to find the Marxist text in the art of social realism, as Barthes pointed out in Le degré zéro. A text is not homosexual because there are homosexual characters, even less because two boys get married at the end: such texts are only the transposition of traditional heterosexual narration. A text will be "homosexual" to the extent that it presents itself as both subject and object of desire, a text in the act of beholding itself, often through the mirror of the other, and loving itself. The text will be continually in motion, for it is able to escape the genital organization to which psychoanalysis is so devoted. Without end, it will perpetually turn back upon itself, thus rendering any dualistic distinction unnecessary. Like Zambinella, he will be and she will not: en est-il? Neither S nor Z, that false opposition, or rather both at once, it will be read in all directions, will have neither head nor tail.

Barthes's practice moves increasingly in this direction. He affirms his marginality, but not in a contestatory manner, to reclaim his right to centrality. On the contrary, he shows how marginality is the product of a point of view, that from the margin's perspective, it is the center that is marginal. Already in S/Z we are offered a book that is almost entirely marginalia, annotations of another text (Balzac's) which becomes only the (literal) pretext and appendix to Barthes's text. If one reads as one customarily does in the West, from left to right as we say, Balzac follows Barthes rather than coming before him as chronology would suggest. This principle of putting into question the order of signification is pursued in *Fragments d'un discours amoureux*. The French title should be noted, for the position of the adjective allows us to see that it is the discourse itself that is amorous and not the person who utters it. These fragments are arranged around cited texts (themselves, thus, already fragments). Every text becomes, as Barthes demonstrated so well in *Plaisir*, a weave of other texts. We read Nietzsche or Goethe *through* the text of Barthes, but we suppose ourselves to be (and we are) readers of Barthes. His "sources" are no longer the origins but the sequels, the margins to an amorous text uttered in a café for an absent other. That café will be the site of Barthes's last amorous fragments, the posthumously published *Incidents*.

Barthes's own writing practice reflects his search for a language of the body capable of resisting appropriation. His love of the strange, the exotic, the neologism is in part his search for a physical text, one that must be felt as well as read, an application to textuality of the transformation of what might be heterosexually defined as *fore*play into simply play. Making us stumble over a word is not a display of erudition but an obligation to recognize the physicality of language that proceeds its function as signification. A glittering prose that recalls the dandy's p(r)ose, that revels in the paradox, bears witness in its own body to a refusal of meaning as abstraction. Barthes's use of the rhetorical term *tmèse* (or tmesis), a trope of interruption, deliberately stops his sentence—no matter how often I reread the text, I still seem to need to look up the word—by calling attention to itself and hence subordinating meaning to sensation. Example: Oh, my dears, he languorously sighed, the troubles I've had! Self-consciousness is one of the marks of his *écriture*, a reclaimed narcissism of language.

If an emphasis on the signifier instead of, or along with, the signified can help to break the tyranny of the paternal sentence, so too the fragmentary can be the principle of a gay writing practice through its refusal of teleology. Renaud Camus's text, *Tricks*, which gave rise to Barthes's most sustained exploration of the possibility of an *écriture gaie* is a collection of stories, presented as the transcription of sexual encounters, that repeat themselves but never end. They are singular, and without final meaning. For Barthes, in his reading of these texts, the *trick*, the ephemeral one-night (or one-hour) stand, represents on the sexual level all that is scorned because it does not last: for Barthes it is the "rencontre d'un regard, d'une idée, d'une image" (*Tricks* 18). It is the world seen and experienced as cruising.

Here, as so often, Proust is Barthes's master. In his last book, *Incidents,* which in some ways continues the *Fragments,* it is the rather obsolete world of the baron de Charlus who dominates the final pages, "Les soirées de Paris," where we are obliged to leave Roland Barthes waiting, sitting next to Gustave von Aschenbach. I find these texts drenched with an almost unbearable sadness, but also full of renunciation, the "non-vouloir-saisir," the search for a love without possession, a love always renewed and never fulfilled, that dominated Barthes's final years. The epigraph is taken from Schopenhauer, probably his last words, "Well, we came out all right." As with the German philosopher, we sense here an enormous bodily fatigue: the text is full of refrain-words like "tedium" or "bland." The evenings are long and lonely, even if there is no lack of gigolos to fill them. Barthes's great achievement was to have written this text without any story, to have accepted discontinuity as a creative principle. He succeeded in letting things take their own course, without needing to impose any sort of structure. He waits, he wants, he grows weary. He rejects literary narrative as he rejects the totalizing narrative of the bourgeois dream. There will be no "happy ending," the grandfather surrounded by his wife and offspring. So it is, my life, he says: feel it, touch it, follow it, let it go. Never had his courage seemed so great, and so promising. He announces to us at the same time a jouissance and a passing beyond the will. He asks us to write as we live(d).

It is important to stress Barthes's work as a gay critic and an exponent of gay writing practice because the critical reception of his work has operated, in not very subtle ways, to obscure that side of the man and his work. The enormous resistance to *Incidents* is more than a scruple for the author's intentions: it is above all an embarrassment at the frank avowal of desire on the part of a cultural figure imagined as somehow disembodied. Barthes's Moroccan text in particular insists upon the physical, on the smudge of dirt or cum that marks the pure white of the imagined object of desire. At the same time a recognition of Barthes's sexuality cannot blind us to the essentialist assumptions behind some of his work. If he is fully aware of the differences between a European and a North African conceptualization of homosexuality (the very word unfortunately giving voice only to the European conception), and indeed devotes much of *Incidents* to an exploration of those cultural differences, he also seems to imagine a gay experience that is not merely the product of a particular place, time, class, or race. But just as we have learned to recognize in *écriture féminine* a program more than a description, a vision of a writing of the body that is bodily specific, Barthes too may suggest the possibility of reading the gay male body. The body in question is that of a Parisian intellectual of the 1970s, not of an American clone of the 1980s. Yet strikingly there remain some of the conventions of a double-voiced relation to the dominant culture that may still be recognizable, in techniques of parody and irony, in self-display and self-doubt, in playfulness and anguished desire, in an exaggerated loyalty to the past and its culture, and a fervent desire to transgress that culture. It is the voice of the insider's outsider.

Notes

I have brooded on this essay for a long time. A number of people have contributed to it, although they may not be happy with the form it has taken. Special thanks to Lillian Bulwa, Lee Edelman, Joseph Litvak, Kevin Kopelson, and to Jim Nielson, whose encouragement was crucial.

Quotations from the original French editions of Barthes's works are cited in the text using the following abbreviations:

S/Z   *S/Z* (Paris: Seuil, 1970)

PT   *Le plaisir du texte* (Paris: Seuil, 1973)

RB   *Roland Barthes par Roland Barthes* (Paris: Seuil, 1975)

Tricks   Renaud Camus, *Tricks, préface de Roland Barthes* (1978; Paris: P.O.L., 1988)

1. Jonathan Culler, *Roland Barthes* (New York: Oxford, 1983), 30. Further citations will be given within the text.

2. Lee Edelman, "Homographesis," *Yale Journal of Criticism* 3 (1989): 202.

3. Harold Brodkey, "A Totalitarianism of Pleasure," review of Roland Barthes's *The Rustle of Language, New York Times Book Review,* 20 April 1986, 13–14.

4. Steven Ungar, *Roland Barthes: The Professor of Desire* (Lincoln: University of Nebraska Press, 1983), 124.

5. Michel Foucault, *La volonté de savoir* (Paris: Gallimard, 1976), 59.

6. One example of this may be seen in the feminist adoption of Barthes's concept of *jouissance* from *Le plaisir du texte* (1973). It recurs most crucially in Hélène Cixous's "Sorties," from *La jeune née* (1975), and Julia Kristeva's "Oscillation du 'pouvoir' au 'refus,'" *Tel Quel* (1974). As used by Cixous in particular and as received in North America, the term is defined as exclusively feminine, and Barthes's semination is silenced. See Jane Gallop, "Beyond the *Jouissance* Principle," *Representations,* no. 7 (Summer 1984): 110–16.

7. Roland Barthes, *Roland Barthes by Roland Barthes,* trans. Richard Howard (New York: Farrar, Straus and Giroux/Hill and Wang/Noonday, 1986), 63–64.

8. In this view I take issue with Frank Lentricchia's assertion of a break in Barthes's career in 1966, with publication of *Critique et vérité,* and even more with his privileging of the "early" Barthes which still shows, according to him, "a profound commitment to the historical nature of discourse" (*After the New Criticism* [Chicago: University of Chicago Press, 1980], 130). Lentricchia's comment betrays the narrowness of his understanding of that "historical nature" and even more tellingly his refusal to take seriously the feminist—and gay—critique of critical and literary practice. The degree of his anger (and it is widely shared) at the Barthes of textual play may be gauged by the sputtering violence of his language when he describes poststructuralists like Barthes falling into "the stupor of a self-satisfied solipsism" (141).

9. "To restore each text, not to its individuality, but to its function" (Roland Barthes, *S/Z,*

trans. Richard Miller [New York: Farrar, Straus and Giroux/Hill and Wang/Noonday, 1974], 3), with "function" a poor translation of the French *jeu,* or play.

10. "what plural constitutes it" (ibid., 5).

11. "for the plural text, there cannot be a narrative structure, a grammar, or a logic; thus, . . ." (ibid., 6).

12. Marianne DeKoven, *A Different Language: Gertrude Stein's Experimental Writing* (Madison: University of Wisconsin Press, 1983), xxi, xix.

13. "the endeavour of this hierarchy is a serious one [correctly, the stakes of this hierarchy are serious]: it is to return to the closure of Western discourse (scientific, critical, or philosophical), to its centralized organization, to arrange all the meanings of a text in a circle around the hearth of denotation (the hearth: center, guardian, refuge, light of truth)" (*S/Z,* 7).

14. "discourse of knowledge" (ibid., 13).

15. "Only writing, by assuming the largest possible plural in its own task, can oppose without appeal to force the imperialism of each language" (ibid., 206).

16. "And the Marquise remained pensive" (ibid., 216).

17. As Stambolian and Marks wrote in 1979, the plural " 'homosexualities' invites us to rethink differences, as well as to think in terms of difference" (30). Tellingly, they then cite Barthes on "this process of differentiation and pluralization" (George Stambolian and Elaine Marks, eds., *Homosexualities and French Literature: Cultural Context/Critical Texts* (Ithaca: Cornell University Press, 1979).

18. "Who knows if this insistence on the plural is not a way of denying sexual duality? The opposition of the sexes must not be a law of Nature; therefore, the confrontations and paradigms must be dissolved, both the meanings and the sexes be pluralized: meaning will tend toward its multiplication, its dispersion (in the theory of the Text), and sex will be taken into no typology (there will be, for example, only *homosexualities,* whose plural will baffle any constituted, centered discourse, to the point where it seems to him virtually pointless to talk about it)" (*Roland Barthes by Roland Barthes* 69).

19. "although feminine, the Moon is active; although masculine, the boy is passive" (*S/Z,* 70).

20. "The Sarrasinean artist tries to undress appearance, tries always to get *beyond, behind,* according to the idealistic principle which identifies secrecy with truth: one must thus go *into* the model, *beneath* the statue, *behind* the canvas" (ibid., 122).

21. "this anti-hero exists: he is the reader of the text at the moment he takes his pleasure" (Roland Barthes, *The Pleasure of the Text,* trans. Richard Miller [New York: Farrar, Straus and Giroux/Hill and Wang, 1975], 3).

22. "both revolutionary and asocial, and it cannot be taken over by any collectivity, any mentality, any idiolect" (ibid., 23).

23. One might here recall Virginia Woolf's comment on the sentence, whose "very form . . . does not fit [the woman writer]. It is a sentence made by men; it is too loose, too heavy, too pompous for a woman's use . . . a woman must make for herself [a new sentence], altering and adapting the current sentence until she writes one that takes the natural shape of her thought without crushing or distorting it" ("Women and Fiction" [1919] in *Granite and Rainbow* [London: Hogarth Press, 1958], 81). Barthes would hardly share the organicism of these views.

24. "how can a hierarchy remain open?" (*The Pleasure of the Text,* 50).

25. "minority situation . . . the natural is never an attribute of physical Nature; it is the alibi paraded by a social majority" (*Roland Barthes by Roland Barthes,* 130–31).

26. Susan Sontag, "Notes on 'Camp,' " *Against Interpretation* (New York: Dell, 1966), 274.

27. Barthes makes this crucial distinction in *Plaisir* 88–90. Figuration, linked to *jouissance,* is

the manner in which the erotic body makes its appearance, while representation is an embarrassed, or encumbered, figuration. Representation, Barthes concludes wonderfully, never leaps out of its frame.

28. "the entire excitation takes refuge in the *hope* of seeing the sexual organ (schoolboy's dream) or in knowing the end of the story (novelistic satisfaction)" (*The Pleasure of the Text*, 10).

29. The English citation appears in *The Pleasure of the Text*, 53.

30. "as if spoken by a character in a novel" (*Roland Barthes by Roland Barthes*, 119).

31. "in this case" (ibid., 63).

32. "Homosexuality: everything that it allows saying, doing, understanding, knowing, etc." (my translation).

33. "meaning and sex become the object of a free play, at the heart of which the (polysemant) forms and the (sensual) practices, liberated from the binary prison, will achieve a state of infinite expansion. Thus may be born a Gongorian text and a happy sexuality" (*Roland Barthes by Roland Barthes*, 133).

34. "it granulates, it crackles, it caresses, it grates, it cuts, it comes" (*The Pleasure of the Text*, 67).

Contributors

Jack Babuscio is a lecturer in history at Kingsway-Princeton College in London. He died in 1990 from complications related to AIDS.

David Bergman is the author of *Gaiety Transfigured: Gay Self-Representation in American Literature* and of *Cracking the Code*, winner of the George Elliston Poetry Prize. He is now engaged in a study of the Violet Quill writers and gay culture between Stonewall and AIDS. He is professor of English at Towson State University.

William Lane Clark received his doctoral degree in English literature from the George Washington University. An independent scholar and student of camp, he works for the Johns Hopkins University School of Medicine as a biomedical writer.

Marcie Frank is assistant professor of English at Concordia University in Montreal. She writes on film and gender studies and is currently completing a book on seventeenth- and eighteenth-century literary criticism and the gendering of taste.

Karl Keller was the author of *American Fiction: Post 1945; The Example of Edward Taylor;* and *The Only Kangaroo among the Beauty: Emily Dickinson and America.* He taught at San Diego State University until his death in 1985.

Kevin Kopelson is assistant professor of English at the University of Iowa.

Scott Long holds a Ph.D. from Harvard University. He is professor of English at the Loránd Eötvös University in Budapest. He has worked with the Hungarian gay movement and organized the first academic program in lesbian and gay studies in Eastern Europe. In 1992–93 he was a Fulbright lecturer at the University of Cluj, Romania.

Robert K. Martin is a professor at the Université de Montréal and is the author of *The Homosexual Tradition in American Poetry; Hero, Captain and Stranger: Male Friendship,*

Social Critique and Literary Form in the Sea Novels of Herman Melville; and the editor most recently of *The Continuing Presence of Walt Whitman: The Life after the Life.*

Esther Newton is an associate professor of anthropology at the State University of New York at Purchase. She is the author of *Mother Camp* and *Cherry Grove, Fire Island: Sixty Years in America's First Gay and Lesbian Town.*

Pamela Robertson is a doctoral student at the University of Chicago. The present article is the first chapter of her dissertation, "Guilty Pleasures: Camp and the Female Spectator." She is the author of "Structural Irony in *Mildred Pierce* or How Mildred Lost Her Tongue" in *Cinema Journal.*

Andrew Ross teaches English and cultural studies at Princeton University. He is the author of *No Respect; The Failure of Modernism;* and *Strange Weather: Culture, Science and Technology in the Age of Limits.*

David Román is assistant professor of English at the University of Washington–Seattle. His book *Acts of Intervention: Contemporary Theatre and Performance, Gay Man and AIDS* is forthcoming from Indiana University Press.

Marty Roth is professor of American literature and film studies at the University of Minnesota. He has published books and articles on nineteenth-century American literature (mostly Poe and Melville) and Hollywood film and popular culture. He has recently completed a book on mystery and detective fiction and is currently working on theorizing addiction.

Patricia Juliana Smith is a doctoral candidate in English at the University of California, Los Angeles, where she completing a dissertation on lesbian panic in twentieth-century British women's fiction.

Matias Viegener teaches at UCLA and CalArts in Southern California. He is the editor and cotranslator of Georges Batailles's *The Trial of Gilles de Rais.* His criticism has appeared in such volumes as *Queer Looks: Lesbian and Gay Experimental Media; Copy Culture;* and *Narrating AIDS.* His fiction and critical work has appeared in *Art Issues, Afterimage, High Performance, Christopher Street, Fiction International,* and *Paragraph.*

Gregory Woods teaches at Nottingham Trent University in England. He is the author of *Articulate Flesh: Male Homo-eroticism and Modern Poetry* and of a collection of poems, *We Have the Melon.*